"I tell you on my divine authority:
I am the Ancient One,
I am the Lord of the Universe."

Avatar Meher Baba

Christ Come Again
Volume One

By Ed Flanagan

CHRIST COME AGAIN

CHRIST COME AGAIN

CHRIST COME AGAIN

Acknowledgements / copyright

Times New Roman 12 pt. *italics* **bold** <u>underline</u>

ISBN 978-0-578-61861-6

Copyright © 2019 The estate of Ed Flanagan
All rights reserved

Cover and interior design Karl Moeller

All quotations and referenced text remain
the property of the copyright owners

Christ Come Again
Volume I

Ed Flanagan

The Life and Teachings of Meher Baba [1894-1969] and The Avatar's revelations of his hidden life as Jesus, compiled from original sources: books, journals, letters, tape recordings, online and personal accounts of those who met or lived with the Avatar.

CHRIST COME AGAIN

CHRIST COME AGAIN
VOLUME ONE
By Ed Flanagan

I   About Ed Flanagan - Rob Findlay
V   Organization of this book - Karl Moeller
VI   Introduction by Ed Flanagan

1 Chapter 1 The Avatar's Last 7 Major Advents
Meher Baba explains Humanity's Utter Need of the Avatar's Help. From Jesus to Meher Baba. Challenging the Jesuits. The *Only* Son of God. Revelation of the Magi – The Star Child.

30 Chapter 2 Christ's Return to Earth in the 20th century
The Man Born Blind. Jesus Points at Past-Life Sanskaras. Real Death and Real Birth – Soul, Spirit, Mind and Body. Mind is the Disease. The Blazing Journey from the Atom to Adam – the First Avatar. Teilhard de Chardin. Adam's Happy Fault. When the Wick of Righteousness Burns Low. The Yugas. How the 5 Perfect Masters Bring the Avatar to Earth. The Avatar's Declaration. The Avatar's Features and Weaknesses. The Universal Message. Where Religion Ends, Love Begins.

67 Chapter 3 Beyond Religion
Against the Idea of "Church." The Illusion of Rituals. The Avatar – Always Born in Male Form in the East. A Young Hero in Search of God. The Beautiful White Horse.

95 Chapter 4 The Birth of Merwan – All Merciful Light
Pinching Coins. In Trouble over Baily. A Close Brush with Death. Almost Losing Jamshed. Ghosts in the Tower of Silence.

115 Chapter 5 Merwan's Friends and Early Life
Two Saints Seek out Merwan. One Father – Different Children. Attending a Jesuit High School. The End of an Old Friendship. Lord Buddha Returns. Unveiling of Merwan's Divine Consciousness.

133 Chapter 6 The Kiss of Infinite Radiant Light
Drowned in the Ocean of Bliss. The Kiss of Infinite Radiant Light. Confronting Babajan. The Agony of Coming Down. Narayan Maharaj. Tajuddin Baba. Sai Baba of Shirdi. Upasni Maharaj. The Triple Crown. The Secret Journeys. Managing a Theatre Company. The Agonizing Journey Back Down Through the Planes. Drowning in a Tsunami of Thought Waves. Servile Labor in Sheriar's Cafe.

174 Chapter 7 A Mother's Agony
Songs of Divine Intoxication. God Joins the Navy. Baily's Inauspicious Fate. Merwan's New Toddy Shop. The First 40-day Fast and Seclusion. Prohibition. The Agonizing Opening of the Divine Heart. Shireen's Turning Point. "Be as it may." Beginning His Public Life as the Avatar. "A Friend from the Past – alas . . . ."

212 Chapter 8 First Disciples – First Ashram
Ghosts in the Night. Handsome, but "Nervous." A Birthday Party with His Two Mothers. Manzil-e-Meem. God as Both Father and Mother. Babajan's Messenger. Murder Plots. Watched by the Secret Service. The Mystery of Huma. Helping the Poor. Upasni Maharaj's Bamboo Cage. The End of Manzil-e-Meem. Gilori Shah and Meherabad's Origin.

248 Chapter 9 Meherabad and Persia
Smoldering Resentment. The First Glimpse of Meherabad. Snakes and Scorpions. A Proposed First Trek to Persia. The Master Wanders Alone. Baba's Enigmatic Monologue. Failing Monsoons – Farmers beg for Rain. The Rainmaker.

271 Chapter 10 The Avatar's Circle
The Mandali. 700 Years. Preparing Circle Members. Suffering for Individual Circle-Members. Suffering Taken on for the Sake of the World. Realization within 100 Years. Baba Blames "Thinking." The Wonderful Kind Stranger.

307 Chapter 11 Meherabad Flourishing
The Arrival of Mehera. Nervous. Meherabad's Free Schools and Clinics. Meherabad's First School. Hazrat Babajan High School. Baba's first Christian Mandali. The Coming Silence.

330 Chapter 12 In the Kingdom of Silence
Garbo Talks – Baba Doesn't. Never Again to Sing or Laugh. The cotton Sadra becomes the Master's standard dress. The Beautiful Dumb Man. The Book. Infinite Intelligence. The Alphabet Board – A Precursor of Laptop Cyber Language. The Beginning of Many Broken Promises. A New Sign Language. The Breaking of His Silence – Releasing the Word of Words. The Coming Upheaval of a New War. The Word took flesh and dwelt among us in Silence. 50,000 Attend Baba's 32nd Birthday. Brother Jamshed Goes to Baba. Striking the Set.

376 Chapter 13 The 2nd Long Stay at Meherabad
A Train Stops in the Middle of Nowhere. More Frustrated Disciples Leave. Everything is Like the Coiled Rope-Snake – a Total Fake! Who Is Greater – God the Father or God the Son? Real Darkness – Real Light. You cannot invite Bliss. It is ever present –

everywhere. A Feared Criminal's Darshan and Repentance. A Catholic Priest is the Avatar's 1st American Contact. The Meher Ashram School. The Prem Ashram – Gustadji's Silence. Neither God nor Perfect, I Am an Ordinary Man. Only the Avatar Controls the Sun. Shakespeare Reincarnated in India. The Rag Doll Discourses.

410 Endnotes

414 Multivolume Table of Contents

418 Reference Codes and Copyrights

About Ed Flanagan

Ed was born in 1936 and raised in West Roxbury, Massachusetts. After attending Catholic University, he entered the Maryknoll Missionary order of Catholic priests in the 1950s. Disillusioned with the Church after Vatican II and seeking further truths, Ed left his parish in South Korea, and soon the Catholic priesthood altogether, and moved to New York City in the late 1960s. Flanagan first heard about Meher Baba in 1975 but dismissed him as "just another Indian guru". It wasn't until several years later that he came to accept Meher Baba as "The Avatar of The Age."

Ed was the youngest of four. He had three much older sisters whom he adored and who doted on him. Affectionally called "Champ" by his working-class father who was the owner of a small vending machine business and who worked closely with Ed's mother running that business, Ed often referred to himself as a "latch-key" kid who spent a lot of time as a child on his own, and he liked it that way. Ed had no desire or interest in sports or even school, and so at a time when most young boys' idols were baseball players, Ed's focus and passion was in film and music. At this time he was an award-winning child actor on radio performing theater on Boston's WMEX FM. From a very young age into adulthood Ed loved jazz and classical music and was a big fan of the early big band crooners and jazz singers. He once described his musical tastes as, "...anything out of The Great American Songbook." Fascinated by film and with a particular passion for the grand MGM musicals starring greats such as Gene Kelly, whom Ed would work with and befriend later in his life, Ed would go to the movies and then come home and re-create lighting, dreaming of one day working on a movie set.

Ed attended High School at the prestigious Boston Latin School, the oldest existing school in the USA and the first public school in America, but admittedly did not excel because he was so preoccupied with music and whatever the new MGM movie was that week. At the age of seventeen he wrote to the head of production at MGM Studios, Dore Schary, who eventually became president of the studio during the 1950s. Dory was so taken by Ed that he wrote him back and personally invited him to take a tour of the studio to "see how movies are really made". His father traveled with him on train from Boston as far as Chicago and then got off for business, and a young Ed traveled the rest of the way by himself to MGM.

While there he visited the Pasadena Playhouse, a legendary acting school he had heard about and longed to attend after High School to study Directing. Upon graduation Ed's father insisted he attend college on the East Coast and so Ed attended The Catholic University of America along with actor Jon Voight. Ed graduated from CUA and much to his father's chagrin became a Maryknoll Missionary priest and worked in several parishes throughout South Korea.

After leaving the priesthood Flanagan settled in New York City and in 1970 he became a television and film producer. He initially worked on several Network specials for General Electric Theater and then worked producing documentaries, including one on jazz piano legend Mary Lou Williams whom he was intimate friends with. Toward the late 1970s, with his lifelong, ever-increasing urge to seek the innermost truths about himself and the nature of God, Ed studied under Bolivian philosopher and teacher Óscar Ichazo and later became an instructor both in London and New York City for Ichazo's Arica Institute. Arica was dedicated to teaching a complete system of holistic mind-body techniques for consciousness-raising, as well as ideologies for one to relate to the world in an "awakened" way.

It was during this time in 1975 that Ed first saw a photo of Meher Baba at Pete Townshend's studio in London where his Arica school was invited to experience a lecture on Meher Baba. Ed reported being so moved by Baba's photo that he would re- enter the room on several occasions to catch another glance, although at that moment in time he did not accept him as anything more that a spiritual teacher or perhaps a mystic or "just another Indian guru," as he often would describe his first impressions of hearing of Meher Baba. It wasn't until a few years later in his Manhattan apartment on 22nd Street in the morning during a quiet moment while looking at the sun's rays shining into the room though a hanging asparagus plant that he said "...it hit me instantly." He stated that at that point he knew, simultaneously, in both his heart and his mind, that Meher Baba was exactly who he said he was: "The Avatar of the Age."

From that moment on Ed was passionately compelled to absorb like a sponge as much on Meher Baba as he could and devoted his life to loving Meher Baba and seeking "Baba" in ALL things. This spiritual awakening and psychic change that Ed says he underwent that morning in his apartment eventually culminated into devoting the last 5 years of his life exclusively to writing this very book.

After the priesthood, producing, and his Arica work, Flanagan moved to Boston in the early 1980s close to his roots. There he made a living from his private practice where he conducted "Bio-Energy" treatments to clients with various forms of addictions, applying special (and very secretive) techniques and philosophies he learned from the renowned Yefim G. Shubentsov, known to many as "The Mad Russian," whom Ed had worked under for a few years. While living and working in Boston Ed made several pilgrimages to Meherabad, Meher Baba's home in the East, where he came to know intimately Meher Baba's last living disciples and family members.

Ed moved to Calabasas, California, on September 10th, 2001. He was originally booked to travel out on American Airlines Flight 11, scheduled to leave Boston the morning of September 11th, the very flight that was hijacked and flown into the North Tower of

The World Trade Center. Two days before his trip, Ed had strong feelings that told him to "Leave Boston right away!" and so he rescheduled his flight to be a September 10th departure instead of the 11th.

In Los Angeles Ed continued his Bio-Energy treatment practice and also pursued his childhood dream of being an actor. He appeared in many independent films all the while treating clients at his home office with quit-smoking and weight loss treatments. In his down time he began writing a biography on Meher Baba which eventually became what he repeatedly told me was his "true life's purpose," writing this book, *Christ Come Again.* It must be noted that Ed Flanagan was also a member of the first Board of Directors of the Avatar Meher Baba Heartland Center in Oklahoma as well as one of its major benefactors. This was a project, like this book, that was ever close to his heart.

In 2010 Ed retired from acting and closed his business in order that he could devote all of his waking hours to completing *Christ Come Again.* Ed Flanagan passed away at his home in Calabasas, California, on September 25th, 2016 a few weeks after completing this book's final draft.

Rob Findlay November 2019

Organization of This Book

There are generally two methods of organizing a nonfiction book: by subject or chronology. The first three chapters of this book are subject driven, covering everything from how and when a Jesus, for example, comes to the Earth, down to a bit of Ed's own history with the Catholic Church - for Ed was indeed Father Flanagan for some years. Make no mistake, Ed sees Meher Baba through the eyes and training of a Catholic priest. As of Chapter Four, Ed moves into a more conventional chronological approach to Meher Baba's life.

There are 69 chapters in this manuscript, which took Ed much of a decade to write. This first volume takes us through to Chapter 13 and 1927, with Baba and the mandali just settling into Meherabad. Based on the word count, this project will span five to seven more volumes, totalling at least 3600 pages. When completely published, it will be the most thorough biography of Meher Baba, second only to Bhau Kalchuri's monumental *Lord Meher*.

> Quotations of any length are indented, 'ragged right' justification. Foot/end notes are kept to a minimum, and are found at the end of the book. Excepting Ed's own commentary and linking text, every paragraph or section is referenced.

The key to these references is also found at the very end of the book. If you see a quote or paragraph with LM, or just numbers after it, that is a pointer to a page or pages in the online Lord Meher, www.lordmeher.org.

Karl Moeller, layoutwalla, 2019

Introduction
by Ed Flanagan

"Avatar" is a popular term in film titles, graphics and weekend workshops. It is actually a Sanskrit word meaning the total, direct descent of Reality into illusion–Personal God coming into human form on earth as the eternal Savior, the Highest of the High–the one and only Ancient One.

> The Unity and Divinity of All Life
> –Meher Baba, Sept. 12, 1954

Age after age, amidst the clamor of disruptions, wars, fear and chaos rings the Avatar's Call: "Come all unto me!" Because of the veil of illusion, the Ancient One's call may appear as a voice in the wilderness. Its echo and re-echo nevertheless pervade time and space, to initially rouse a few and eventually millions from their deep slumber of ignorance. In the midst of illusion, as the true Voice behind all voices, it awakens mankind to God's newly manifested human presence on earth. [1]

The time has come for me to repeat the call and bid all to come unto me. Regardless of your doubts and convictions, and for the infinite love I bear for one and all, I continue to come as the Avatar to be judged time and again by humanity's ignorance to help man distinguish the Real from the false.

The greatest greatness and greatest humility go naturally hand in hand. When the Greatest of all says, "I am the Greatest," it is but a spontaneous expression of an infallible Truth. The strength of his greatness lies not in raising the dead, but in his great humiliation in allowing himself to be ridiculed, persecuted and crucified at the hands of those who are weak in flesh and spirit.

Throughout the ages, humanity has failed to fathom the true depth of humility of the Avatar's greatness, gauging his divinity by mere religious standards. Even real saints and sages having some knowledge of the Truth have failed to understand the Avatar's greatness when faced with his real humility. History repeats itself age after age when men and women in their ignorance, limitations and pride sit in judgment over the God-incarnated Man as he openly declares his Godhood.

They condemn him for uttering Truths they cannot understand. He is indifferent to abuse and persecution, for in his true compassion he understands, in his continual experience of Reality he knows, and in his infinite mercy he forgives. God is all. God knows all. God does all. When the Avatar proclaims he is the Ancient One, it is God proclaiming his manifestation on earth. When man utters for or against the Avatar, it is God speaking through him. God alone declares himself through the Avatar and mankind. I tell you with divine authority we are not "we" but *"One."* Unconsciously you feel my Avatarhood in you; I consciously feel in you what each of you feels. LM 3552–53

Thus, every one of us is an Avatar, meaning everyone and everything **is** everyone and everything at the same time and for all time. He is the only Reality, and we all are one in the indivisible Oneness of this absolute Reality. When the one who has realized God says, "I am God, you are God, and we all are One," and also awakens this feeling of Oneness in his illusion-bound selves, then there is no question of the lowly and the great, the poor and rich, the humble and exalted, the good and the bad.

CHRIST COME AGAIN

Pay heed. I say with my divine authority that the Oneness of Reality is so uncompromisingly unlimited and all-pervading that not only "We are One," but even this collective term of "we" has no place in the Infinite, Indivisible Oneness. Awaken from your ignorance and try at least to understand in the uncompromisingly Indivisible Oneness, not only is the Avatar **God**, but also the ant and the sparrow, just as one and all of you are nothing but **God**.

The only apparent difference is in the states of consciousness. The Avatar knows a sparrow is not a sparrow; whereas, the sparrow does not realize it, and being ignorant of its ignorance, remains a sparrow. Live not in ignorance wasting your precious life span differentiating and judging your fellow men, but learn to long for the love of God. Even in the midst of your worldly activities, live only to find and realize your true Identity with your Beloved God. 3554

When Religion goes, God comes

One taste of Reality relieves an eternal hunger
Zen saying of Hakuin

The God you are searching for is not up in the sky. He is here on this plane! "I am That." I am in you, so search for me within yourself. I am not in any mosque, temple or church. 1006

God is Eternal Freedom, Bliss and Knowledge. Trying to put him within walls of man-made churches only proves our ignorance. To try binding fathomless God in narrow and limited dogmas, creeds and *churchified* conventions lacks the true perception of God's Omniscience. GG VI: 75–76

Any religion, method, system or practice within the sphere of reason and intellect, if followed in the right spirit, can lead one to the real Path above reason and intellect, leading one to the Ultimate Goal of humanity – God-realization. The various ceremonies, liturgies and rituals which are part and parcel of every religion constitute merely their shadow.

Dogmas, creeds and conventional ideas of heaven/hell and sin are total perversions of Truth. They confuse and bewilder the mind. Rituals and ceremonies instituted by priest-ridden churches have concentrated on outward forms while ignoring the real essentials of spiritual life – love, obedience, humility and sincerity. Man seeks life and is given a heap of stones. The mass of humanity confuses mere liturgical/ritualistic worship with religion. AW vol.2, no.4, p.5

I bless you that the spark of my divine love implants in your hearts the deep longing for love of God. World religions proclaim there is but one God, the Father of all in creation. I am that Father.

– Meher Baba, addressing 5000 at his historic East-West Gathering in Pune, India November 2, 1962. 4863

Eighteen years earlier as WWII entered its final year in 1944, a crowd of over 30,000 in India came to be with Avatar Meher Baba from dawn till midnight, captivated by his divine personality, drowned in the Ocean of his light and lost to the world. He addressed them:

When religion goes, God comes!

The organized religions of the world often fail to express the real vision of all those [Christ/Avatars] who have been the fountainhead of inspiration for their very coming into existence. Dogmas and beliefs, rituals and ceremonies can never be the essence of true spiritual life. When religion becomes a mere matter of external rituals and liturgies, it has become a cage for the soul.

Nor does it help to change one religion for another, like going from one cage to another. If religion doesn't help man to free the soul from spiritual bondage and realize God, it is useless. It is time for religion to make room for God, for *when religion goes, God comes!*

And so I am not interested in founding a new religion. The world is already divided by numberless sects, based on dogmas and beliefs. I have not come to give another cage to man, but to impart to the world the illimitable Truth. The world does not need mere verbal instruction.

It needs true awakening; it needs the freedom and the amplitude of divine life, and not the superficiality of mechanically pompous liturgies; it needs love, and not the display of power. The world task ahead of me is very creative. Really speaking, none of you need receive divinity from me. But what I give is the *experiential* knowledge of the Oneness of us all.

At the end of this 1944 discourse, Meher Baba was requested at midnight to bless the 30,000 devotees who in their longing gathered there the entire day to be with him. The Lord of the Universe stood in his full glory and raised his hands, his face aglow. There was utter peace and stillness in a blessing that spoke secrets in everyone's heart – a scene reminiscent of times in Judea, revived anew by the living Christ come once again on earth. 2440-41

May this book from one who was a Catholic priest help not only Christians but all in other traditions to make the jump from entrenched dogmas to new ways of understanding, as I myself had to. It is my real prayer that this book may serve as a bridge for them all.

I also ask the reader's indulgence for what will seem a long Introduction, for it sets the stage for a new proclamation of the greatest story ever told–the birth, life and death of the God-Man, Christ come again in the 20th century. It took me 7 years after resigning from the priesthood to even hear of the Master Himself – the Messiah returned–then 37 more years to distill his message and the exalted secrets he revealed as contained in these pages.

My experience of Avatar Meher Baba over those decades since his passing in 1969 is that he is very much alive and incredibly accessible as Christ, Master, companion, guide and the most intimate friend. His Tomb-Shrine in India is a daily direct *inner-net* link to his living Presence beyond the limits of time, space and the illusory physical gross universe.

His statement on the unique position and function of the Avatar was unequivocal–that he was, is and always will be One and the Same–*Emmanuel*: *God with us.* *"Lo I am with you always, even unto the End."*(Matthew 28:20) This one fact crashes down once and for all the Jericho-walls of theological differences and religious intolerance so dividing mankind.

If all men have been worshipping one and the same Avatar under his different guises and names in impersonal and personal aspects, then truly all religions are *One*. Their seeming differences are only in the false minds of men, not in the Divine Essence poured out by the Eternal Messenger. This is the 'thread' on which to string those separative religious beads.

Needless to say, not just early on but over decades I met with serious opposition from family, friends and especially my fellow priests and other Christians over Meher Baba "as Christ come again." How could it have been otherwise? It also happened in Jesus' time.

Meher Baba's similar humiliation was being ridiculed by unbelievers for speaking the Truth. I also experienced that trying to share him with others who not only rejected him, but were embarrassed for me – the utter foolishness of one who should have known better.

In the tumultuous late 1960s, conditioned by years of rigorous theological training as a Catholic missionary priest in the Far East, I had just freshly emerged from religious life, courtesy of my petition to Rome for early retirement, only to then deal with the culture shock of being back in the "unreal" real world after 13 years of being "out of it" – an expression many comically and perhaps accurately used to describe me in those days.

I transitioned back to life as an ordinary layman with barely skipping a beat, landing a job in the Madison Ave. television and film world. We were in the middle of producing a 1-hour network General Electric Theatre TV special with folksinger John Denver.

Robert Riger, my boss and also a Catholic, walked into my office one morning and questioned me: "Ed, what do you think of Meher Baba?" He went on to ask if I thought it possible that Christ might have recently returned to earth in human form as promised.

It seemed his son had just returned from India, reborn and "buzzing" about a silent Master there called Meher Baba, believed by hundreds of thousands – Hindus, Muslims, Christians and even Jews – as the "return of the one and only Christ-Avatar" to earth.

"What?" I asked incredulously, then fired back facetiously, "Well, *I* certainly didn't catch it on the evening news!" I had to keep from laughing at his ludicrous question. For as a priest I knew far better from such nonsense; or so I thought. But when I began exploring, I witnessed the ecstatic charismatic movement, complete with tongue speaking and prophesy in the previously sober Catholic Church which was experiencing a massive exodus of religious – priests, brothers and nuns – including myself.

CHRIST COME AGAIN

It wasn't hard to make out the legend *TITANIC* on the hull of the quickly sinking barque of Peter, having sprung a fatal leak in colliding with the icebergs of irrelevancy and denial as it neared the 21st century. The Pentecostal movement had burst forth among American Protestants at Meher Baba's birth in the late 1800s.

It was now curiously reappearing in early 1969 as I was transitioning from the priesthood and Meher Baba was finishing the final touches of his work on earth for this age. It was happening once again after millennia. His was the most significant life lived in this age, though few on this side of the globe were yet aware of it.

Once again we now had Pentecostals – *Catholic* ones, no less. They had First appeared following the crucifixion and the outpouring of the Holy Spirit. I was actually seeing it recur now in modern times – Catholics and Protestants praying together in each others' homes – popularly referred to in the late 1960s as the "underground church."

It was a brotherhood of unprecedented friendship beyond the urgings any official ecumenical movement could have ever anticipated. It made me realize something spiritually new and exciting was going on. But what was it? It was *some* kind of ecumenism; certainly not of ideology, but of shared, heartfelt experience. People were now – God forbid – bypassing their churches, as heart was finally winning the battle over mind. In its heydays from 1920 to the mid 1960s, Maryknoll, the missionary order I joined, had 2000 members at any given time. Today in 2015 it has less than 300, as all denominations cease being the magnetic centers of human lives. Clergy are now being looked upon as fossilized growths stubbornly clinging to decayed and crumbling walls.

People were totally fed up with the various organized, racist religious "isms" and the wars they continually spawn, cataclysmically hurtling us uneasily toward a disastrous future. We are now becoming *the priests of our own consciousness*, thirsting for true spirituality and mysticism without lifeless, dried-up dogmas and the trappings of worn-out falsities.

Leaving the priesthood, I, too, was caught up in the outpouring of Spirit beyond religion. Swimming in it with countless thousands, I felt like those early astronauts in that same year of 1969. We were making a choice about the future of humanity.

We had to stop looking in the rearview mirror and trying to live by the tombstone-rules of past established religions with their rigid dogmas based on a kind of fear dividing humanity so as to control the masses. Without exception, all had lost the way.

The future was ominously coming toward us at light speed, challenging us before it was too late in the face of the birth of a New Humanity to understand who we are *now,* and not who we were back *then.* We had to unlearn, painfully at times, false "religious certainties" that we had always assumed were true but are not.

When the Lord came again into this world, people beseeched Him to *do something* about this mess religions have gotten us into. The unification of the world's major faiths, *"like beads on a string"*– Meher Baba's own term – is one of the single most real promises Christ gave for his work in this new millennium. Will it be accomplished before we destroy each other and the delicate fabric of the earth's mantle in the 21st century?

I had no clue about Meher Baba. He sounded like one of those Beatles' Maharishi fads I so disdained. How could I guess he was a manifestation of the living Christ come yet once again with his old/new outpouring of the Holy Spirit? Later on, I was especially intrigued to see so many Jews having a strong affinity for Meher Baba even from the 1930s.

This is when he first came West to Europe and America. And it continued following the holocaust with the evangelical messianic Jewish movement taking off in the early 1970s just after Meher Baba's passing. Groups like *"Jews for Jesus"* grew in major U.S.

cities as well as in Russia and South Africa. What was happening here?

Since the 1960s there has even been a Meher Baba Center in Israel that Baba directly communicated with. Only later did I recall early Church fathers proclaiming the Lord's return at the Second Coming would occur only when Jews *finally* accepted Jesus as their own Prophet, said to be a manifestation of the gathering of the lost tribes of the Diaspora.

This gathering was Jesus' final mandate to His Apostles: *"Go not to the gentiles, but to the lost tribes of Israel."* But that so *many* Jews would make the double leap to take and accept Meher Baba for exactly who and what he said he was – the Messiah, the God-Man, Christ on earth-returned, thereby also including and embracing Jesus – no, this was nothing I could have even remotely anticipated.

Whatever the religion, people had left God aside to worship instead their pet rituals – prayers, rosaries and dry scriptures which had supplanted true love for God. This caused a violent reaction of great unrest and deep social upheaval. Rituals once commanding respect had degenerated into routines no longer speaking to the true spiritual needs of God's people.

They created a foreboding spiritual vacuum. When God became less important than scriptures, the world cried out with Buddha: *"The oceans have dried, mountains crumble, the pole star is shaken, the earth founders, and gods perish like frogs in dry wells."* Meher Baba assured us he didn't come to establish anything new, but do away with the *rust* of dogmatic religious ceremonies and rituals so long encrusted over the kernel of Divine Truth.

He stressed that God *needs no worship* and only values honest love, hearing not the language of tongue or mind, but only the language of love coming directly from the human heart. Listen to the universe's secret and its goal as embodied in these words of Meher Baba:

> The soul's existence is everlasting, and its Eternal Existence is one with God. Do not mistake soul's Eternal Existence with the mind or intellect. The soul makes the intellect work, but nothing controls the absolutely independent Soul. Intellect is but an instrument of the totally independent Soul. It is a means to attain the Original, Eternal Existence and to experience it. Love, service, devotion and dedication can make a person know God. 1375
>
> To know Himself, God *became* each individual Soul. He embodied himself in them, thereby becoming bound by his actions. And thus, it is the responsibility of the Avatar [the God-Man] coming to earth age after age to unbind man's actions, which then leads to God-Realization. 689
>
> Consciously or unconsciously, every living creature fundamentally seeks one thing based on a memory – dim or clear – of its essential unity with God. For every living thing is a partial manifestation of God, conditioned only by lack of knowledge of its own true nature.
>
> In fact, evolution is the evolution from unconscious divinity to conscious divinity, in which God Himself, essentially eternal and unchangeable, assumes an infinite variety of forms, enjoys an infinite variety of experiences, and transcends an infinite variety of self-imposed limitations. From the standpoint of the Creator, evolution is **a divine sport** in which the Unconditioned tests the real infinitude of His absolute knowledge, power and bliss in the midst of all limited conditions.
>
> But from the creature's standpoint, evolution's limited knowledge, power and capacity for enjoying bliss is an epic of alternating rest and struggle, joy and sorrow, love and

hate – until in the perfected person, God balances these pairs of opposites, and duality is forever transcended.

Creature and Creator then experience themselves as One. Changelessness is established in the very midst of change; eternity is experienced in the midst of time. God knows Himself as God, unchanging in essence, infinite in manifestation, and ever experiencing the bliss of Self-Realization.

He continually experiences fresh awareness of Himself by Himself. This Realization can only take place in the midst of human life; for only in the midst of life can limitation be experienced and transcended, and subsequent freedom from limitation be enjoyed. Di 266–67

The above quotes pose that evolution must necessarily be based on the development of consciousness; thus, **consciousness drives evolution**, and not the random selection of the fittest as Darwin would have it. Meher Baba's explanations are grounded in ancient eastern traditions, but nothing in terms of traditional religious or spiritual practices surround him.

There are no rigid meditations, initiation, membership, rituals, diet, dress or prayers. He cautions "Do not observe prolonged silence nor meditate. Do not serve yourself by doing so. You who are dedicated in my Cause have no need for such discipline." Aw vol.19. no.2, p.1

Still, Meher Baba gave 3 extraordinary prayers to humanity in this Advent: the *Prayer of Repentance*, *You Alone Exist*, and *The Master's Prayer* [O Parvardigar], all of which we will encounter in this book's ongoing pages. Meanwhile, there's also no study course, or scripture to be read or mastered. False mind is now forever by-passed in favor of heart.

The Avatar was often celebrated in huge public gatherings of thousands. But he discouraged his followers from proselytizing on his behalf. He said: *"Let your life itself be my message of love and truth to others."* There's no eternal damnation, or any need to be saved, for everyone without exception by their very existence is already saved. This means *everyone* is *God in human form* – no exceptions here: *"There is no separation between you and God. Lover and Beloved are One. You yourself are the Way. You are God."* 3519

Failure in this game is no option, for any exception would be outside of God and therefore contradict His infinite state. But we are all temporarily veiled by a mind composed of false impressions from past-life forms not yet eliminated on our journey across creation's "7 days," meaning the 7 stages of evolution [stone, plant, worm, bird, fish, animal and our first human form] followed by a process of countless human reincarnations.

We do not yet experience that glorious final state, the goal of every creature under God's sun. But the knowledge of such a certainty should cause joyous waves of optimism, even in the face of whatever earthly suffering we might still be destined to pass through from past incarnational bloopers, whether good or bad, funny or sad . . . .

> "God alone is Real. There is nothing but God; everyone and everything is God. To awaken this Truth in humanity, Infinite God periodically assumes a precious human form, known as the Avatar. Wholeheartedly loving the Avatar – the God-Man – is a most natural way of realizing the goal of life – union with God the Eternal." GG VI: 10

> Each earthly advent of the Avatar is a matchless mystery, and owing to his boundless compassion it occurs time and again. Age after age in His compassionate omniscience Infinite God chooses to become man. To quicken the life pulsating in everyone and everything, the Creator re-involves Himself in his age old game of creation. GG IV: 1

He is the *God-Man Messiah*, also called the Buddha, the Christ, the Rasul or the *Saheb-e-Zaman* [Arabic: Supreme Commander and *Lord of the Universe*]. These terms refer to abstract God appearing on earth in solid, palpable 3-dimensional human form.

From the beginningless beginning, the Messiah-Avatar is the *only* Perfect Master to repeatedly take birth on earth again and again to awaken humanity to his sublime Truth which all organized religions have either forgotten or have carefully hidden.

And he comes to give the actual experience of it. The Infinite Consciousness of the Avatar is in no way affected by life or death. His awareness includes individual awareness of each being in creation. *"Always aware, always on the air,"* doing his universal work, God keeps coming down in human form again and again for the sake of his beloved children.

Except for the Avatar and Perfect Masters, all beings on dropping the human body reincarnate back in the gross world to continue perfecting themselves. After leaving his body, a Perfect Master disconnects from the illusory creation.

The Avatar alone is connected to one and all for all time and eternity, as he repeatedly takes new human forms.

Thus, Abraham, Zoroaster, Rama, Krishna, Buddha, Jesus, Mohammed and Meher Baba are all incarnations of that very same *Ancient One* – Adam – the Original Avatar from our endless past. As the eternally active source of God's limitless love and grace, the Avatar does not drop his body in the same way a Perfect Master does. Eruch Jessawala who became the Master's chosen apostle in 1938 – his *new St. Peter* in this advent – explains it:

> "When the Avatar sheds his man-form, he continues to be infinitely conscious of his creation and its creatures, and

mindful of his lovers who adore him in their hearts. Shedding his physical body, there is no lessening. He keeps exercising Infinite Love, Mercy, Compassion, Authority and Power. So, anyone seeking help at the Avatar's Tomb is not only assured of external benefits, but also derives spiritual benefits due to his direct and lucky approach to God for assistance."AO 201

The Avatar transcends the unimaginable gulf between Infinite Unconsciousness to Infinite Consciousness and God-realization. From eternity without beginning, he is the only God-Realized being who ever reincarnates, repeatedly coming into the world from time to time every 700-1400 years. RD 147 *"Among the Perfect Ones, it is only I who does not preach, teach or tolerate any particular religion or allow any sectarianism."* 1580

Our world has left the Age of the word and has now entered the post-modern age of the image. And so, unlike his advent as Mohammed, Meher Baba fittingly left us his image in photographs and films, as well as drawings, music and poetry to convey to us his presence and teachings. This is a far more aggressive and universal advent than ever before – far more than his 6 previous advents in this last 5000 year cycle.

With the viral disease of selfishness now global, Meher Baba travelled and worked all over the world as the only Avatar whose impact has been on *all* the nations, rather than on a small limited Eastern region as in the past. The universality of Meher Baba's Avataric work is also seen in the infinite degree of attention given to details in written accounts of his life, activities and teachings, besides the countless photo images he left behind.

He used 7 languages: English, Hindi, Marathi, Gujerati, Persian [both Farsi and Dari], Telegu, and being silent after 1925, his own extraordinary system of gestures, hand signs and facial expressions. Although birthless and deathless, the Avatar as Lord of the

Universe is eternally bound by His Father's business to come down age after age.

He returns in "swaddling clothes" – his bodily form to work for the sake of the entire universe. This means one thing only: *to suffer*. This duty not even the 5 Perfect Masters always on earth can accept for him. In November 1952, standing with 50 of his closest men prior to touring to meet hundreds of thousands of his lovers, Meher Baba stated: "I'm destined to take this body again and again. "And so I *have* to come into the world.

"But you at least should be free from this unbroken chain of being born again and again – growing, marrying, procreating and dying. God is as soft as He is hard, as compassionate as He is harsh. Invoking Him, if He is touched even *once*, the work is done. The impossible becomes possible." 3146–47 And so this book might equally be called "Abraham, Zoroaster, Rama, Krishna, Buddha, Jesus and Mohammed *Come Again*."

Now in Meher Baba they have *all* come again. All are One and were never two. In 1927, Meher Baba said: *"I am the Christ, and because of me the entire world exists! There is no time, space, cause, effect, duality, or anything besides me – only unity."* 686

And thus, the false illusion of "needing to be saved" is absolutely and irrevocably done away with once and for all. Guaranteed salvation is the absolute individual soul's Divine birthright, automatically emanating from its Divine Origin. This is *The Real Good News*, at which narrow and limited fundamentalism in any form can only gnash its teeth.

And so there is no religious hierarchy, priestly intercessions, communities of worship or organizations. Those are now done away with. As Baba himself said, *"Rome, go home!"* No one has exclusive rights or inside tracks to Truth, as all are equally One with it. 1800

CHRIST COME AGAIN

On January 9th 1941, with WWII escalating to brutal fullness, Meher Baba stated he gave no importance to creed, dogma, caste or performing religious ceremonies or rites, but to the *understanding* of the following:

The 7 Realities

1. The only **Real Existence** is that of the One and only God, the Self in every (finite) self.
2 The only **Real Love** is the love for this Infinity (God), which arouses an intense longing to see, know and become one with its Truth (God).
3. The only **Real Sacrifice** is that in which, in pursuing this love, all things – body, mind, position, welfare and even life itself – are sacrificed.
4. The only **Real Renunciation** abandons amidst worldly duties all selfish thought and desires.
5. The only **Real Knowledge** is that God is the in-dweller in good people and so-called bad, in saint and so-called sinner. This requires you to help all equally as needs demand, without expectation of reward, and when compelled to take part in a dispute, to act without the slightest trace of enmity or hatred; to try to make others happy with brotherly or sisterly feeling for each; to harm no one in thought, word or deed – even those who harm you.
6. The only **Real Control** is the discipline of the senses from indulgence in low desires which alone ensures absolute purity of character.
7. The only **Real Surrender** is when one's poise is undisturbed by any adverse conditions, and amidst every kind of hardship the individual, is resigned with perfect calm to the will of God.

Baba had thousands of copies of this message sent out to disciples in various cities in India, instructing it especially be given to priests and others in charge of *"churches, temples, mosques and ashrams."* Thousands were then sent to the West early in WWII, through which the Avatar directly guided human civilization behind the scenes lest it be destroyed. 2183

The Avatar's work is to uplift mankind's awareness to a new understanding of the nature of love and the very goal of existence, including the awareness that without exception every being in the creation is to be treated with great care and respect. For in reality *we are not we, but One*. Regarding this particular age and the Avatar's role in it, Meher Baba said:

> Avataric periods are the springtide of creation, bringing a new awakening of consciousness for all by means of a Divine Personality, an incarnation of God in a special sense – the Avatar who appears in different forms under different names at different times and in different parts of the world. His appearance always coincides with man's spiritual rebirth.
>
> And so, the period immediately preceding his manifestation is always one in which humanity suffers from the approaching birth pangs. Man seems more than ever enslaved by desire and greed, held by fear and swept by anger. The strong dominate the weak, the rich oppress the poor.
>
> The masses are exploited for the benefit of the few who are in power. The individual who finds no peace or rest seeks to forget himself in excitement. Immorality increases, crime flourishes, as corruption spreads throughout the social order. Class and national hatreds are aroused and fostered.

CHRIST COME AGAIN

Wars break out while humanity grows desperate. There seems no possibility of stemming the tide of destructions. At this moment, Christ as the Avatar appears. Being the total manifestation of God in human form, he is the gauge by which man can measure what he is and what he may become. He trues the standard of human values by interpreting them in terms of the divinely human life.   Di 269

Life after life, the principle of Illusion – *Maya* – beats man mercilessly. To save him from its clutches, the Compassionate One takes periodic human births. On New Year's Day 1951, prior to entering a 100-day fast and deep seclusion during his historic *New Life*, characterized by total renunciation and annihilation, Meher Baba vowed the following:

"My oath is so irrevocable that from today, January 1st, it's unlikely even one of you will remain with me as I expect something superhuman. I am in the soup with you. To be cheerful in all conditions is superhuman! So let's do our best to help each other. Baba then offered a prayer to God with his disciples and companions in Jesus' name: 2808–09
Oh God Most High! Grant guidance to Baba and lift up his heart with Your love. O Christ, everlasting Truth, that he may live the New Life with faithfulness to the end! May the work of these 100 days seclusion be fulfilled to Baba's entire satisfaction, and the desire of his heart come to pass with the aim of the New Life being achieved for all.
Grant his body be sound and healthy during this deep seclusion and give strength to him to bear whatever sufferings may befall him in the coming New Life! Grant, O Most Merciful God, these desires of Baba be fulfilled through the grace of Thy Son, Our Lord Jesus Christ! 2970

CHRIST COME AGAIN

My salutations to all – past, present and future Perfect Masters, real Saints – known or unknown – Lovers of God and all beings in whom I reside. 4193

It is I who loves you. Remember this in the future. When anyone hurts you, it is I who hurts you; when anyone loves you it is I who loves you. If someone laughs at you, it is I who am laughing; when you love anyone it is I whom you love. I am in everything and in everyone. How can you realize my Infinite Presence if you shrink from me in those who hurt you and welcome me only in those who please you? Aw vol.8, no.4, p.9

Start learning to love God by beginning to love those you cannot love. In serving others you are truly serving yourself. The more you remember others with kindness and generosity, the less you remember yourself; and the less you remember yourself the more you forget yourself. And when you completely forget yourself, you find me as the source of all love.

Give up parroting in all aspects and start practicing what you truly feel to be true and just. Don't make a show of your faith and beliefs. You need not to give up your religion but give up clinging to the outer crust of mere ritual and ceremonial observance – Shariat.

To get to the fundamental core Truth underlying all religions, reach beyond religion. Through endless time, God's greatest gift is continuously given in silence. But when mankind becomes completely deaf to the thunder of His Silence, God incarnates as man to give a spiritual push to the world by his physical presence on earth. Then, the Unlimited assumes the limited.

He shakes Maya-drugged humanity to a consciousness of its true destiny, and gives a spiritual push to the world by his physical presence on earth. He uses his Universal body for his Universal work, to be discarded as a final sacrifice as soon as it has served its purpose.

God has come again and again in various forms, and spoken again and again in different languages the very same one Truth – but how many live up to it? Instead of making Truth the vital breath of his life, over and over again man compromises it into a mechanical religion as a handy staff to lean on in times of adversity, as a soothing balm for his conscience, or as a tradition blindly following the footsteps of the dead past. Man's inability to live God's words makes them a mockery.

How many Christians really follow Jesus by "turning the other cheek" or by "loving thy neighbor as thyself?" How many Muslims follow Muhammad's precept to "hold God above everything else?" Do Hindus "bear the Torch of Righteousness at all cost?" How many Buddhists live the "life of pure compassion" expounded by Buddha? Do Zoroastrians "think truly, speak truly and act truly?"

God's Truth cannot be ignored. Mankind's ignorance and weakness produces a tremendously adverse reaction, while the world finds itself in a cauldron of suffering – wars, hatreds, conflicting ideologies and Nature's rebellion in the form of floods, famines, earthquakes [and militarily engineered "extreme weather events?"] When the apex is finally reached, God manifests anew in human form.

He guides mankind to destruct its self-created evil so it may be re-established in Divine Truth. My silence and its immanent breaking is to save mankind from the monumental forces of ignorance, and to fulfill the Divine Plan of universal unity. Only the breaking of my silence will reveal to mankind the universal oneness of God and bring about the universal brotherhood of man. My silence had to be; and the breaking of my silence has to be 4448–51

CHRIST COME AGAIN

The above, from Meher Baba's final 1958 discourse *God Alone Is*, reflects the deepest universal truths of the Hindu Vedas, Buddhic discourses, Christianity, Muhammad's Koran and all known authentic spiritual traditions. Witness Jesus' words in St. John's Gospel 10:34 – *"It is written in your law, 'You are Gods!' And the Scriptures do not lie."*

You cannot limit God saying, *"God is this or that."* God is just *God*. Illusion is God. God is not one or two, but just God. Nothing and everything are so merged in each other you cannot say, "This is nothing," or "This is everything." Nothing, too, exists – *but* as total illusion. 1827

God is absolutely independent, infinitely independent and absolutely perfect within Himself.

He is also beyond Perfect Independence, because when we call Him independent, then we have the contrary thought of *dependence*. When we say He is *without* attributes, we begin having thoughts of *attributes*. When we say He is *One*, we then have the thought of *two*. So, it's best to just say IS . . . .

You must empty "is" of meaning, while not taking "is not" as real.
–A Zen verse

> One should call on His mercy from the depths of one's heart. If you go on praying for 100 years without heart, you'll gain nothing; while a mere *second's* heartfelt prayer is instantly heard. So, with full inner devotion, just call on Him and you will experience the rays of His utter mercy. 3358

When we identify ourselves as "I'm an American;" "I'm an Indian;" "I'm a Russian" or "I'm a Christian, a Jew, a Muslim or Buddhist," or as "Catholic/Protestant," we regress into the abyss of delusion where we've floundered for thousands of years. This is the realm of *separation, strife, war and destruction* and very opposite of the expressed teachings of all religions. Meher Baba sums up these ideas in the following words:

> "My cure for a worried world answers the questions, *'Whither and Whence.'* The knowledge that all have the same beginning and end, with earthly life a happy interlude, will go a long way in making brotherhood of man a reality, and this in turn will strike at the root of narrow exploitation. I bless you all to realization this, the true aim of life." 1789

Over the years, Meher Baba's life was an open secret. He travelled extensively to the West, for which he claimed he especially came in this advent. On February 10th 1954, in an isolated part of north India, he finally and publicly revealed he was the Avatar of this age.

He revealed God, achieving manhood, descended as Him, the Ancient One. He who had been each of the past Christ/Avatars in man's endless history came again and again to bear full responsibility for the entire creation. In New York City 2 years later in July, 1956 on NBC-TV he historically repeated his truly unique Avataric claim. 4008

Writing this book over a period of 10 years, I was merely the pen in his hand. Perhaps not strangely, but clearly sensing my lowest worldly desires and previous acting them out on leaving the priesthood, I was surprised and grateful that they both virtually ceased when I began this writing. Then I came across this passage which made it so clear:

> "When one is absorbed in a subject concerning me directly, I can connect him with me by merely his thoughts on

me. An opportunity is created to work spiritually – to dislodge the seats of low desires in the mental body of the person, making them impotent without being put into action by the physical body. This one is also being given the chance to serve me, whether he knows it or not – an opportunity he'll not get again in this lifetime." 1645

Still, we must be aware that even an exalted biography of God in human form, providing food for mind and heart in revealing the deepest spiritual secrets never before experienced of oneself as *Infinite Truth*, is only a book. And so it is only that – *a book* – like the Zen koan on pointing at the moon, while actually *becoming* the moon is something else.

A week before passing, Meher Baba instructed his night-watchman-disciple, his new St. John, Bhau Kalchuri, to write his biography, adding, *"Make it interesting!"* I hope, though a generation removed from that mandate, I too have made his life most interesting for you, dear reader. Baba said, "Do your best and don't worry. Be happy, and I'll see to the rest."

Beloved Godman, just wait till they hear you came back again!
    –elf

CHRIST COME AGAIN

Chapter One

The Avatar's Last 7 Major Advents

"There have been Buddhas before me and there will be Buddhas after me," said Gautama Buddha, predicting the greatest one would bear the name "The Compassionate One." The name "Meher Baba" means "Compassionate Father." Before his advent as Buddha, Krishna said: "When virtue declines, evil and injustice resurge in the world. Then I, the Avatar, take human form again." Throughout history His message is always the same.

However, meeting a man who had complete Christ-consciousness, one might have difficulty seeing he was the same Christ; really, the exact same one? The personality – the hat and coat – would be different, as the message never clothes itself in the same body twice.

It always has a new "freckle or two." The message assumes a vehicle suitable for its time and place, expressing itself in terms only understood by people of that period. Returning in the 20th century, Christ as Meher Baba repeats his age-old message: GGV5:161

> I am that Ancient One – Zarathustra, Ram, Krishna, Buddha, Jesus and Muhammad. Now I am Meher Baba. In this form of flesh and blood I am the same Ancient One whose past is worshipped and remembered, whose present is ignored and forgotten, and whose future advent is anticipated with great fervor and longing. 3227 I intend to destroy the bindings of all superfluous religious rites and ceremonies. The times of Jesus and Krishna were different from the present.

CHRIST COME AGAIN

I must guide you in the needs of the time. Material progress in the present atomic age has reached a zenith, but is merely a shadow of internal progress in the realm of spirituality. Except your being infinite, everything is illusion. 1772 From the beginning, Maya is hanging around my neck with all of you, and for that reason I have to come again and again among you. 3869

Meher Baba explains Humanity's Utter Need of the Avatar's Help

The soul's consciousness is in bondage – caught up in a purely imaginary universe. And since there is no end to imagination, man is likely to wander indefinitely throughout the endless mazes of false consciousness. The Perfect Master or the Avatar [Christ incarnate] can help him cut short the different stages of false consciousness by revealing the Truth. Without *experiencing* the Truth, the mind is likely to go on imagining all kinds of weird things forever.

The soul can imagine it is a beggar or a king, a man or a woman, etc. The soul thus goes on gathering the experiences of the opposites. Wherever there is duality, there's a tendency to restore balance through the opposite impression. For example, say a person experienced being a murderer.

That is counter-balanced by the experience of *being murdered*; and if the soul experiences being a king, it has to be counter-balanced by *being a beggar*. Thus, the soul wanders endlessly, life after life from one opposite to the other without being able to put an end to its false consciousness.

The Master can help one to arrive at the goal by giving a perception of the Truth and **cutting short** the working of imagination which would otherwise be endless. He helps the soul in bondage by sowing in him the seed of God-Realization. Still, it always takes some time to attain God-realization. Every process of growth in the universe takes TIME. Aw vol.1, no.3, p.33–34

> To know the road up the mountain,
> ask the One who goes back and forth on it.
> -a Zen saying

Over time, the Avatar keeps returning to the earth for his destined work. In this most recent multi-millennial cycle, the same Avatar was known in several sequential major incarnations c.5000 BC as Abraham to the Israelites, c.4000 BC as Zoroaster to the Persians, between c.3000-2100 BC to the Hindu races of India, c.1400-1200 BC as King Ram and Lord Krishna, c.525 BC as Gautama Buddha to India, Ceylon, Burma, China and Japan.

Then He came as Yeshua to the Jews, known to the Romans and Greeks as Jesus, born in 4-6 BC, and again in c.570 AD as Mohammed the Prophet to the Arabian nations – the *identical* Ancient One whose ways and emphasis are different in each successive advent.

Meher Baba often repeated that the Avatar quietly does his Universal work in each advent. He is mostly unknown to the public during his earthly life when he cuts a *hole* in the door separating the gross world from the First subtle spiritual plane.

That piece hangs in the door by a thread and constitutes his "collecting phase" of humanity's false impressions. For 100 years after dropping his physical body, he is then in the "cleaning phase," after which his Universal Manifestation always occurs, as the entire world comes to know and follow him:

> "When the world is gripped by pain, misery, suffering, and chaos, I manifest. Materialism is at its lowest level and spirituality reaches its pinnacle. Then with the passing of time, spirituality diminishes and materialism increases.

From the beginning of time this game goes on for eternity. I have a law of my own in managing the affairs of the universe. But when I speak, that law will be put aside as the spiritual push will be universal.

"The law will be set aside. But again the law establishes itself; then the spiritual power gradually diminishes and materialism increases. Material unrest and chaos will have to reach a climax, then I'll manifest when spirituality is at its highest." 820–21

Jesus' mission was to the scattered lost tribes of Israel. Meher Baba's mission this time as the 7th and final Avataric incarnation in this latest 5000 year spiritual cycle, is the greatest. His message is to all global nations in one. In this age as the Compassionate Father of all humanity's East/West tribes, he is the universal Avatar.

Still, he said he came this time "especially for the West." It was not a question of choosing the West, but a question of where his work was most needed for spirituality and materialism go hand in hand according to God's plan. T 211

The sphere of influence of all previous Avatars in this cycle took place mostly in the immediate region or countries surrounding their life on earth. Meher Baba is the first Avatar in this last 5000 year cycle to encompass and travel the globe several times.

He dispensed divine love and compassion in total silence, laying worldwide cables for a *spiritual* New World order – *The New Humanity* – to be born from the rubble-remnant of the earth's false and distorted New World Order in the mid to latter 21st century.

Seekers in the counter-culture movement began finding Meher Baba as he ended his work on earth in 1969 – especially the flower children and the Jesus-freaks. Having shed their former skins, many of new ones heard of him through his hardball admonition against drugs, including, *"If God is found in a pill, He isn't worthy being God."*

His most famous saying is, *"Do your best, then don't worry. Be Happy in my love and I will help you."* This became the famous expression, *"Don't Worry, Be Happy."* Thought to be a mere "pop" phrase, it has deep spiritual basis behind it. It is also the basis of Krishna's *Bhagavad Gita* and Jesus' admonition: *"I tell you not to worry about your life."* [Luke 12: 22-34] – coming multiple times from the mouth of God.

Well, coming from the priesthood, all this was utterly new wine to me, and I had a decidedly old wineskin. New eyes are needed before one can even begin to see the enormous possibility of the God-Man coming once again on earth. I am attempting to provide that new way of seeing – that my eyes, mind and heart may become virtual vehicles to facilitate it.

The power of that Truth is in these pages. The reader has only to grasp the Light of that silent Word-Sword to slay all falseness, within or without and without a doubt! The following comments on love for Jesus will become in future ages a new book of "Epistles."

They are the early letters to the faithful from the "new apostles," in this case Eruch Jessawala, Meher Baba's chief male disciple whom he truly referred to as his *new "St. Peter."* Eruch Jessawala wrote to Christian disciples in the early 1970s shortly after Baba's passing:

> Our Beloved Lord Jesus was also accused of being one of the false prophets and crucified along with 2 others of disrepute. Did this in any way affect His Christhood? Now, 2,000 years later Jesus is worshipped as the Christ – the God-Man – despite being condemned, slandered, persecuted and crucified. Pay no need to believers, adversaries or even the so-called evangelists . . . .
>
> Whatever they say about the God-Man, most important is *your faith and love for Him*. If you have that you are

blessed indeed! And it's enough, even if you were the only one in the world to believe in Him at this time of His Advent. How blessed you are to love and adore Christ!
LFM 81

Love him with all your heart and soul without any reservations or confusion. Let not the demon of dual concept of Baba and Jesus ever stand in the way of your one-pointed devotion to Christ. Let there be no conflict in your heart. However your mind may try, let not your mental concept of Baba stand in the way of wholehearted devotion to Christ . . . .

Don't force your mind, but allow your heart to work it out by His Grace. Meanwhile, heed His ancient warning of which you are well aware – *"run not after false prophets, babas, and masters."* I salute your deep love for and firm faith in Christ. May your love for Him lead you to Him. He is compassion incarnate. He is love.

–Eruch LFM vol. 2, p. 15

The typical pilgrim season at Meher Baba's Tomb-Shrine in India has over 100,000 pilgrims with groups representing 45 countries, including Australia, El Salvador, Argentina, Mexico, Spain, Italy, France, Germany, Switzerland, Norway, Holland, Sweden, Yemen, Serbia, Russia, England, Ireland, Scotland, the United States, Canada, Iran, Israel, Egypt, India, China, Korea, Japan and others. This includes a group of Armenian Christians from Iran whose culture predates the dominant Islamic one by over 1000 years.

They are from all major and minor religions, including those who never subscribed to any particular religion and so-called atheists, all drawn by the magnet of the Avatar's Divine Personality. Many are perplexed coming upon Meher Baba. "In this total information age, how on earth had I not heard of him before?" It is a common question and has two answers.

Meher Baba said the Lord always comes veiled like a thief in the night, quietly does his Universal work of suffering for humanity and leaves. Only well after he has gone does the world begin to awaken to his new advent with the full outpouring of His Holy Spirit. This is termed his *Universal Manifestation*, always occurring about 100 years later.

But at the Avatar's public Manifestation +/− 2069 it will be a totally different story, when most will directly *feel, recognize, accept and welcome* his return, even if they missed it when he was physically present on earth silently dispensing his love to humanity.

I knew two of Meher Baba's brothers, but especially his sister, Mani [*Mah*-ni]. Raised in Catholic schools, she grew up loving Jesus and wanted to become his nun. In a letter to Western followers in the early 1970s Mani explained:

> While oblivious to it, the greatest event for the world is when God visits the earth as Man. Of all planets in the 100 billion galaxies of universes [more than all the grains of sand on earth], Earth alone is where this miracle happens again and again. But when it happens, poor Earth is unconscious, like a king who is crowned in his sleep and misses his own coronation. The God-Man as the Avatar visits Earth when it is *dark*. When it is in pain and sorrow, He comes in the dead of night.
>
> Only a few see Him by the light of His Love. The Dawn comes only after He leaves. And with it comes the growing awakening, remorse and agonized waiting for His next return – the resolve not to miss Him that next time. Many a 'next time' has slipped through many a worn out

resolution, until that time is here. *That time is here, now!* But this God-visit is to be different.

Our Earth-world will not be left asleep in darkness. The Compassionate One will shake it awake to witness His Love's rising in the dawn of His Word. The entire world . . . will know Him when He breaks open His silence and gives His Word to the world. FL 324

When asked how come he knew he was the Christ and others didn't, Meher Baba responded: "I knew it from *before the beginning-less beginning, before anything* was. How can others know I must take this particular human form? Jesus was unknown by his intimate companions, even by Judas who grew up with him, was always near and would kiss him.

"As Judas couldn't understand, you, too, don't understand me in my physical form. It is because as the real, infinite Christ I am within you as within everyone . . . . I knew it before everything. I came from my own *Self*. One cannot know Existence until one exists in that very *Existence*." A57; 1512 "Were people to ask, 'Have you seen God?' I'd reply, 'What else is there to see?' If they ask, 'Are you God?' I would reply, 'What else could I be?'

"Were they to ask, 'Are you the Avatar?' I would say, 'Why else have I taken this human form?' The only message I've ever given is: *Love God and find your own self is nothing but* God." One is reminded of the Gospel passage about Jesus: *"These were such hard sayings many turned and walked with him no more."*(John 6:66) 3518

To make sure people knew of his life, just 7 days before leaving his body, Baba ordered his disciple Bhau Kalchuri, author, poet, night watchman – his beloved "St. John," and my friend for over 34 years to write his biography – *Lord Meher.*

This twenty-volume study of the Avatar's advent also includes Bhau's personal experiences of being in Meher Baba's close contact day and night for 16 years, from 1953 until Baba's passing in 1969. In these pages I have freely drawn from his biography with online page numbers without any letter code prefix. They are from [*www.lordmeher.org*]. Bhau's poignant memory of that final day is from his diary after Baba had left his body:

> You completed your seclusion work on the afternoon of January 30th 1969. I was with you and remember how glorious you looked. Victory was yours, but I could not grasp what was happening. Each afternoon, completing your work, you gave me lines for ghazals [pronounced 'guzzals'] song-poems expressing the rapture, anguish and longing of a lover's heart for his divine Beloved.
>
> On that final day, you looked at me and gestured, "Here's one more line for a ghazal." But even a little movement of your finger caused such spasms as lifted your body off the bed, causing such pain that you told me your bones were breaking. You looked at me and shed tears.
>
> How it pained my heart seeing you suffer so. In sorrow I said, *"Oh, Baba, Please don't give me the line now; later when you're feeling better."* But there was no later. Your fingers moved, and from your silence came that one line: *"What will we do, living, when you have gone away?"*
> 5414

Bhau Kalchuri writing Lord Meher, 1971

Meher Baba's passing was a shock deeply distressing Bhau Kalchuri and the other disciples for long after. But remembering Baba's order to him, Bhau spent the next 2 years interviewing countless other disciples and collecting data from vast resources – documents, diaries, letters and messages carefully collected over the previous 50 years under Baba's orders. No other Avatar has left such a complete record of his life.

When Bhau actually sat down to write it by hand, he didn't even have enough money for paper to write it on nor for food. His young children chipped in and bought him a fountain pen and the best ink that wouldn't fade over time. While writing, it was as if Baba were directly guiding him, filling in the minutest details, such that Bhau often really didn't know in whose hand the pen was. Baba appeared to Bhau during the writing. GuG 765

He'd snap his fingers to hurry and finish the work he had been given. Bhau hand-wrote 18 hours a day without break, often in tears and developing carpal tunnel syndrome before it was ever known as that. He completed the 20 volume 7000 page English biography, *Lord Meher* in just 7 months. With its extraordinary details of Baba's earthly sojourn, it is the most documented record of any Avatar's life in human history. *Meher Darshan*, a 28,000 line rhyming poetic version of the Hindi biography was written in a 4 month period.

From Jesus to Meher Baba

Once a general initial understanding about the Avatar is assimilated, and specific information on Meher Baba's life is grasped by the reader, we will then examine the fascinating and previously unknown hidden aspects of Jesus' life and teachings. These astounding revelations will rock the world. But before validation of Meher Baba is fully established, what he said of his previous advent as Jesus might be considered as unsupported.

But once Baba's life is grasped in these pages, Jesus' life will open like a flower, revealing undreamed of historical and mystical insights. This information was revealed in minute detail in conversations Baba had with his disciples during a period of over 40 years.

These were statements made drawing parallels to his present life and teachings with specific incidents occurring in what he claims was just *one* of his previous Advents in which he was known as Jesus of Nazareth. Besides that advent and this present one, the Ancient One had an additional 5 advents, totaling 7 in just humanity's last 5000 years.

They will all be detailed as chapters unfold. And so, He whom we call Jesus lived on earth more than once. All previous 5000 year cycles saw 7 major advents of the same Christ going back into humanity's endless past, far beyond recorded history or imagination.

All Avataric cycles in illusory time begin and end after 700-1400 years. This Avataric advent has come at the end of a *cycle of cycles* which is 5000 years long, during which the same Avatar makes 7 major earthly appearances, once every 700-1400 years. The great Saint Ramakrishna once said: "God reveals Himself in the form the devotee loves most, whether as Hebrew, a Zoroastrian, Hindu, Buddhist, Christian, Muslim or non-believer."

I have chosen this particular path of exposition because it is how I myself, a Christian and former priest stumbled upon it, from the known to the unknown; from Jesus whom I loved, to one who despite the raging resistance of my theologically and dogmatically trained mind, drew me with a spiritual fragrance, troubling at the start, and then wondrously identical to Jesus Himself. I was drawn like a moth to the flame, or as Ramakrishna said:

"When the flower is in full bloom, bees will simply come on their own." So now like a worker bee I'm returning to the hive, wings buzzing with the urgent message. "Go – the rarest of blossoms for whom all other flowers bloom, is nectar-ripe, waiting for you."

This rare gift, freely given to me and hundreds of thousands in the 20th century, will be offered to incalculably more in the 21st century and for ages to come. What follows is a new piece of cloth – a quilt if you will – woven from many patches and threads gathered over decades from voluminous written records on the Avatar of this Age.

These include books, discourses, conversations with family members, recordings and casual talks with countless people in various countries who were blessed to meet and then fall instantly in love with the God-Man. I spent years hearing directly from Meher Baba's closest companions about his life and teachings and their intimate years of living with him.

This research filtered through the Catholic ideological/theological mindset in which I trained, but most importantly is distilled from my own heart which he has obviously and deeply touched. Entering the orbit of a true Master, no matter in what age he lives, the present or thousands of years ago – for the Infinite One is timeless – the chalice of one's heart must literally be turned upside down, emptied of old wine so it may be filled with the new.

Jesus himself said, *"New wine cannot be poured into old wineskins."* You yourself must *become* that new wineskin. Life coaches say, "To find your true life path, just follow your bliss." Probably my deepest hearing has come from listening to his *Silence*.

He was silent throughout the last 44 years of his life. When he passed in 1969, before I knew of him in this life, by a strange but perhaps divine coincidence one of the top songs on the charts was Paul Simon's *"The Sound of Silence."* Driving around New York in the early days of 1969 after returning from the Far East and resigning my priestly duties, I kept hearing this song on the radio, *"The words of the prophets are written on the subway walls and tenement halls,* **and whispered in the sound of silence.***"* Meher Baba said, *"Things real are given and received in silence."* **1654**

I made innumerable visits, tracing places he had been in America, Europe and Asia, always culminating in India. My first visit there was for several months to finally bow down at his Tomb-Shrine. Here his human form lies for all humanity over ages to come.

Quiet tears flowed from unmistakable feelings that I had truly and finally made it back home after wandering long through the desert of both my gross and spiritual past. The living presence of love incarnate and the void inside me felt within his Tomb was singular.

Though one could not see him, one who had supposedly died, his aliveness to the heart was touching and palpable. Before his passing, Baba told his disciples they'd soon see the result of his work – "How my children from all over the world will come."

Those disciples had no idea what he meant. As far as they were concerned he had left, and now the story was pretty much over –

time to close the shop. Little did they know! Then, countless thousands came and still come more and more every year from every corner of the globe. I consider myself lucky to have been in the initial first wave.

His resting place draws countless pilgrims yearly from over the world – Hindus, Muslims, Christians, Buddhists, Jews, even one-time atheists. They come to the treasure house where he said each and every human being has *their own* divine treasure waiting for them, un-claimable by any other, as during his physical lifetime Baba said he personally worked and suffered *to inscribe their very own name upon it*.

Knowingly or unknowingly, man is ever seeking the goal to realize his true Self. In his last years especially, Meher Baba shattered his body to revitalize his internal links with the world so that intimacy with his lovers' hearts could be fully established.

That link is vibrantly active to this day. Though his body is under a marble slab, that little domed-room holds the key to unlock any human heart sincerely calling on God as the Eternal Beloved, from whatever religious background or even lacking one.

I also had the good fortune over the years hearing accounts of the Master's life in my interactions with his family – 2 brothers, a sister, aunt, nephews, a niece, cousins and intimate disciples of his outer and inner circles – his *mandali* [from Sanskrit, *mandala* = circle] as he called them – archetypes through whom he would work to help all humanity. 3445

Some of his mandali, particularly his new "Peter" and "John" – Eruch Jessawala and Bhau Kalchuri – were the most ordinary, engaging, selflessly down-to-earth people I ever had the pleasure of meeting. He lived and died for them, as they did for him.

Their position was directly beneath the lantern, closest to the source of light, yet veiled in the shadow of its Truth. He seldom gave his disciples conscious experiences of the inner spiritual planes. Living with the Avatar was never a bed of roses; more often a bed of thorns, for spirituality entails grinding down one's egoistic, false self-assertions to utter dust:

> Dust under his feet –
> His challenge to become that –
> thousandsTo grind yourself out.   –elf

Baba's disciples had to let go of self-concerns completely. Their security, likes, dislikes and moods all had to be laid at the Master's feet in a painful and agonizing process. Life with Baba was a day-by-day experience of Jesus' call: *"Leave all and follow me."* Though each had a definite character, he taught them to live in harmony.

Each was to be the one to "give in." Never minimizing their differences, he brought them to the surface saying, "I don't want stones around me." Thank you, Eruch and Bhau, for your years of friendship and sharing such treasured memories of your life with the Avatar.

Besides my companionship with his intimate disciples and listening deeply over 20 years to stories of their lives with him, there were also letters, emails and online chats over those years. *Matchless*, is the only word to describe his intimate ones. They are truly the new Apostles, and written memoirs of their years with him will go down in history to be read by millions in future ages, just as we read epistles and New Testament accounts of Jesus.

By now it is obvious that this material is highly unconventional. To some it may be disturbing or even sacrilegious. Others will get it immediately, because their hearts have been yearning so long and so deeply for it. The Divine has been drawing them individually and inexorably more inward and away from traditional external religious forms and values.

The Divine draws us away from illusory Maya, that master showman who misdirects your attention, pointing toward the illusory world which doesn't exist, while what is actually happening is somewhere else where you're not looking and *what really does exist*.

Maya, the principle of illusion, can blend in with any background like an octopus. We all know how an octopus sends out a black, inky trail to fool predators or to catch prey for millions of years, and to us too. *Maya* is the master of smoke-screen illusion.

She lures us with her black smoke-and-mirrors to fall time after time. Moment after moment we fall for her delusion of false consciousness. But in His unbounded cleverness, God has staged this great play to extricate humanity from Maya through Maya.

I remember in 1982 in Goa, a Portuguese city on India's west coast, almost being thrown out of a luncheon I'd been invited to with several Jesuit priests and theologians for simply suggesting that the same Ancient One whom we love as Jesus was on earth officially as the Christ several times before he was known as Jesus, and 2 more times since then.

Challenging the Jesuits

I arrived in Goa from Bombay on the overnight ferry, the same steel-hulled boat Meher Baba took on 3 trips there decades earlier and still in service in 1982. Then I took a local bus to the town of Old Goa where I met a Jesuit priest on a street corner, asking him directions to St. Francis Xavier's tomb. After a short chat, he insisted I join him for lunch.

A heated discussion during lunch had the Jesuits defending the old dogma that Christ came only once, with me citing some unnerving possibilities that cutting-edge theology is rethinking that premise, and that the God-Man as the one Christ re-appears on earth in predictable cycles. Well, it's good everyone had finished eating when the subject came up, as there was nearly an uproar, fueled by my confident and certainly expressed convictions.

CHRIST COME AGAIN

After practically choking on his post-lunch biscotti as I spoke, the flushed Jesuit superior of the community offered his own adamant doctrinal ideas to contradict me. He then neatly folded his napkin and ended the meal on a reluctant note, *"Well, if that were the case, I would certainly have to change all my theological views."* He then abruptly got up and walked out, leaving an awkward silence around the table.

Well okay, maybe it was an upstart move on my part, but I had earlier warned my new Jesuit friend, "Please don't put me on the spot and ask me to talk about the research I'm doing here in India; let's just not go there today."

But he was so intrigued by what I'd shared with him earlier on the street corner about Meher Baba as the Avatar of this age he did *just* that. Well, as any 5 year-old could easily see, the result was worse than stirring a doctrinal hornet's nest.

The co-founder of the Jesuit Order, St. Francis Xavier, was one of my patron saints during my seminary training and missionary years in the Far East. His body has lain for 500 years in an uncorrupt state, simply as a vivid sign of his inner honesty before God. His burial crypt is the greatest Christian pilgrim center in India, and within the Basilica of Good Jesus in Goa, which Baba himself visited and beside which we were having lunch that day.

I didn't go there to argue with the Jesuits, but to bow down to Xavier as Baba himself had done decades earlier. The first time he came alone, climbing up to the bell tower through a dark spiral staircase. Years later he returned with his men. Then in the 1930s, he also brought some of his Western followers there.
556

Entering the Basilica 3 times during his life, Baba imparted the atmosphere of his Divine Presence for the benefit of those coming in later times, saying Xavier was spiritually advanced. I was simply retracing Baba's footsteps. And who knows but he wasn't looking over his shoulder, seeing one day I, too, would visit here and dare to speak openly about him to these Jesuits as an equal. I left there with a secret satisfaction.

Something happened that day beyond anything I'd ever attempt on my own. Clearly, I had just shaken loose some pretty old tiles on the venerable roof of the old Basilica of Jesus where we were gathered. Perhaps even St. Francis himself was calling and urging me on during that luncheon to speak the truth as I knew it – exactly what he had done centuries before when he preached Jesus to India's unbelieving Hindus.

Built in 1594, exactly 300 years before Meher Baba's birth, the Basilica of Good Jesus in Old Goa, India, where the incorrupt body of St. Francis Xavier lies. To the right is the Jesuit residence where the author was invited to lunch.

Another similar event, also unplanned, happened with a group of nuns from India interacting with me as they tended a religious goods shop high above the dome of St. Peter's Basilica in Rome. That amusing story is in my own biographical narrative *Book II:*

Empty Chalice – The Diary of an Ex-Priest, Chapter 7, under *Meeting God's brother* on my first pilgrimage to Rome, India and Meher Baba's tomb in early winter of 1981.

Well, theological times really haven't changed since then, and undoubtedly this will be a very difficult and dizzying jump for many traditional Christians, to say nothing of the clergy. The final irony is that several priests who had given young Meher Baba – Merwan Irani – his high school education 70 years earlier were assigned from this very Jesuit province in Goa to teach at St. Vincent's High School in Poona – such a paradox.

There are several priests now quietly loving and following Meher Baba as Jesus returned, including an American Catholic Bishop – the first of a huge wave coming in the future. Meher Baba's 2 younger brothers were also students at St. Vincent's high school.

The priests derided the younger brothers over claims others were making about their elder brother's *spiritual state*. "Isn't this the Merwan we taught in chemistry and English class?" Draw any parallels that seem to fit. Meher Baba's 2nd favorite Christian male saint after St. Francis of Assisi was St. Augustine who is most famous for this one sentence:

> "That which is now called the 'Christian Religion' existed among the ancients, and never did not exist from the very beginning of the human race until the Lord came in the flesh. Then, that true religion, already existing, now newly came to be called Christianity."

Prior to Meher Baba's birth by 25 years, and exactly 100 years before his death, Ralph Waldo Emerson in 1869 quoted this same passage from St. Augustine in his famous speech to the Free Religious Association of America, as did Theosophy's founder Rudolph Steiner in 1904 in his *Introduction to a Spiritual World-View*.

In this notion of religion we include Judaism, Zoroastrianism, Vedantism, Buddhism, Muhammadism and the countless other *"isms"* from times immemorial as a direct result of the Avatar's repeated human incarnations going far back beyond humanity's memory; in the sense of *"Emmanuel, God is with us,"* and in human form no less.

The *Only* Son of God

Someone once asked, "Was Christ God's only son?" Baba replied, "*Christ*, and not just *Jesus*, ***is*** *the only son of God*. Christ is He Who is one with the Infinite Father; and all who realize ultimate reality are *in* that identical Christ-state. When Jesus said, '*I and my Father are One,*' he proclaimed the attainment of his own Christ-state; Jesus means the God-Man of Nazareth who attained to Christ-consciousness and Perfection." QA 12–13

Most Christians believe the God-Man came only once, and on finishing His spiritual work, basically abandoned being here on earth *"among us and as one of us"* for all other times and eternity – belief in the Second Coming notwithstanding. So much for *Emmanuel – God always being with us!* They also minimally and erroneously believe the only legacy Jesus left behind is found in the totally altered and redacted New Testament.

And there is a further explicit belief that unless you grab hold of *that one* particular manifestation of the Savior, then you are damned to hell for eternity. This is not only an ugly picture, but it is hardly something that could ever come from the compassionate Jesus.

He who *"bruised not a reed,"* could never have uttered, intended or implied such a thing by the stretch of anyone's imagination. This humiliation was brought upon Jesus by the darkness of orthodoxy on one side, and blind fundamentalist extremism on the other.

Even Pope Francis early in 2016 completely abandoned the notion that a relationship with God is available only through Jesus.

The pontiff clearly expressed his belief that all major religions are different paths to the same God for all His children.

And so if such a being as a "God-man" exists, then he is unequivocally the prime actor, factor and moving force on the stage of human existence, and indeed across the entire creation. Would it not be strange if he came at least *once*, then he certainly might have appeared in other *sequels*, to say nothing of all those *prequels*?

As Adam, the first God-Realized soul in the universe – known in India as Shiva – he obviously owns the franchise, while humanity goes through stages where it needs periodic, fresh dispensations of divine love – *"fresh, live and in person."* If spirituality were food, you wouldn't give birth and present your child with a tractor trailer of canned-goods saying, "Well, here it is – all you'll need for the rest of your life." Humanity is no different.

The Lord said, *"I am the Way and the Life,"* and He manifests as that Way and Life in an event beyond imagination, incarnating in the Christ-state repeatedly over the course of human history according to its needs and in each new age every 700–1400 years.

No one comes to the Father except by Christ. But *Christ* exists long before the body of Jesus and well after it. Christian fundamentalists need finally to grasp that *Christ is a divine office* and not merely an individual personality occurring only once in time on earth.

Abraham, Zoroaster, Rama, Krishna, Buddha, Jesus, Mohammed and Meher Baba are all in a circle holding hands in the Beyond as One – manifestations in just this most recent 5000 year cycle as that same Ancient One – humanity's original and Beloved Adam.

This office has been filled by the same Ancient One, the first soul to become the Christ – Personal God – countless times in different bodies with different names, and never limited to a single historical time-event. To repeat: He came to earth in 7 major advents in just this last 5000 year cycle, while he appeared in countless other times over endless prior cycles.

Only understanding this from the source Itself can we be freed from our self-made cage of limited understanding. Something great comes in grasping this, as we do not lose Jesus or any of our other Avatars. Rather, we gain them and the rest of humanity across various world religions as *true* spiritual brothers and sisters, like all those clustered lights on the Christmas tree or the Hanukah menorah – beads on one string around the neck of God.

These are his children from his other incarnations, family you never even knew you had. And one day what a party there'll be! Meanwhile, is there a Christian child who has not sadly wondered why Jesus came only *once* and so very long ago?

Is there a devout Hindu, Buddhist, or Muslim who has not searched their hearts with the same burning question: where are Lords Rama and Krishna, the compassionate Buddha and the noble Prophet when we so sorely need their living presence on earth right now?

The shocking and exalted premise here is that one of the Lord's appearances occurred more recently than you'd have ever imagined, and it is drawing you closer to your own and all your brothers' and sisters' spiritual destiny throughout the world. This undeviating destiny is the same for all and completely transcends all notions of religion, heaven or hell.

While some might feel anguish because they "missed the show," not knowing the Lord was actually here in the 20th century, my reaction was joyful that even in the cloud of unknowing I had somehow sensed his presence. I was thrilled with even the mere thought I was a human being living on this planet at the same time he was.

Though our paths never directly crossed, they came close by 100 miles or so in July, 1956. I had just entered the seminary in Pennsylvania and on my 20th birthday Meher Baba was in New

York City proclaiming on NBC Television that he is the Avatar of this age.

He certainly must have been gazing on me that day, seeing I'd take up his Avataric call to produce this work through which he would one day reach out to millions. I hold myself doubly fortunate, since Baba said the "priests" would be the last ones to find him.

Well, I'm happy to be an exception. I know honestly discarding that persona put me on a path where he had a better chance to reveal himself to my heart as he gradually emptied me of old religious forms and false hierarchical "specialness."

Not having heard of him at the time, I made my fateful and difficult decision after 13 years to leave religious life in January 1969, the exact year and month Meher Baba dropped his physical form, his "garment of disguise," as he called it, to live eternally in the hearts of all his lovers. With ever-present gratitude, I undertake this excellent adventure of telling you his life story; and how anxious I am to get to it.

But these long introductory pages were necessary. The new mysticism of Meher Baba is ancient yet ever new, opening wide the spiritual gates to bring the mysteries of heaven down to earth, equally to kings and sweepers alike. From hints Jesus gave about the Avatar's reappearance, early Christian fathers definitely expected his return before 1000 years. This belief in the early church is easily researched and referred to as the *Millennium*.

Of course they weren't expecting him as early as 570 A.D. when Jesus returned as Muhammad, and certainly not expecting this time he'd be wearing an Arabian hat and coat. They were looking for the same old familiar Jesus they had known – just another classic misunderstanding of the Avatar's words and misinterpreting the periodic grace or *barakath* of history. Meher Baba explains his endless appearances as the one Avatar:

God is always One and the Same. From time to time in different cycles, He adopts different human forms and different names. He is born in different places to reveal Truth in different garbs and languages, to raise humanity from ignorance and free it from the bondage of delusions. HM 33

Whether there have been 26 Avatars since Adam or 124,000 as sometimes claimed, or whether Jesus was the last and only Messiah, or Muhammad the last Prophet, is all immaterial and insignificant when eternity and reality are considered. It matters little to dispute if there have been 10 or 26 or a million Avatars. The Avatar is always one and the same.

The 5 Perfect Masters bring about the advent of the Avatar-Christ-Prophet on earth each time. This goes on cycle after cycle. Millions of such cycles must have passed by and will continue to pass by without affecting eternity in the least. [2] GS 249–50

While on earth, 5 Perfect Masters share the same eternal state of God-Realization as the Avatar, wielding Infinite Knowledge, Power and Bliss for the spiritual benefit of the creation, moving and shaking it in its never ending journey toward its very own Godhood.

Each Perfect Master wills his own death when his Universal work on earth is completed. When he drops his body, another God-Realized soul then becomes a Perfect Master, completing the council of 5 Masters that must always be present on earth.

The Avatar uses Infinite Knowledge and not his Infinite Power and Bliss. Otherwise, how could he suffer helplessness for humanity's sake as Savior? He worships the creation.

In this last 5000 year cycle, appearing as Zoroaster, Rama, Krishna, Buddha, Jesus, Mohammed and now as Meher Baba, there were at least 2 exceptions to the 700-1400 year time-frames;

the advents of Jesus 625 years after Buddha, and Mohammed who came about 570 years after Jesus. It was exactly 1400 years from Mohammed to His new advent as Meher Baba – the exact timeframe the Prophet Himself had clearly foretold.

With countless Avataric cycles in humanity's endless past and relatively endless ones in the future, the God-Man's universal work in each age gradually lifts and trues humanity out of the thralldom of its enmeshed ignorance as lived in the gross world.

Previously, Baba rarely mentioned Abraham, confusing many at this. But let's review what Baba said in *The Highest of the High*: Of the most recognized and much worshiped manifestations of God as Avatar, Zoroaster is the earlier – having been before Rama, Krishna, Buddha, Jesus and Mohammed.

Abraham was not mentioned to avoid confusing him as "Zoroaster come once again." So Baba said, "Don't put that in,' explaining at the time of Abraham, the Zoroastrians were expecting Zoroaster to reappear. So Abraham was referred to as Zoroaster, causing confusion if there was one incarnation of Zoroaster or two. This led Baba to **not** emphasize Abraham as one of his Avataric advents, though he surely was.

We are chained in those 2 prisons to witness its own gross-physical, subtle-emotional and mental-thought worlds. The infinitely pure soul itself never participates in those life-illusions, though it lives in the midst of them blinded to its own divine origin and nature.

Creation then becomes a reincarnation production line to create the consciousness necessary for the Soul to know that *all souls were, are and will be eternally God as Over-Soul.* Then after ages, the soul arrives at the threshold of the real spiritual path where it begins traversing the 7 inner planes, finally ending in full God-Realization – Infinite Bliss, Knowledge and Power – experienced by each soul individually and eternally.

The golden age of an unprecedented spiritual creation with 7 major incarnations, each separated by 700-1400 years, is part of the push about to take place for life in all 7 kingdoms of creation during this entire most recent 5000 year cycle. Meher Baba proclaims the Good News in this way:

> "The happiness of God-Realization is the goal of all creation and worth all the physical and mental sufferings in the universe. Suffering is then as if it were not. The happiness of God-Realization is self-sustained, eternally fresh, unfailing, boundless and indescribable. And for this happiness has the world sprung into existence." GS 130

Meher Baba, his Master Upasni Maharaj and Buddha stated that without the Avatar's intervention the journey is endless, requiring 8,400,000 pre-human evolutionary forms from stone to animal kingdoms, and another 8,400,000 human births to finish the journey. LBE 185

At an animal preserve in 1929, Baba revealed:

> Tigers take hundreds of thousands of years to take their first human birth. Bears are the most lustful among animals; monkeys and gorillas are the most advanced. Their first human incarnations are as native savages. 1048–49 A fair question is why the gross human state at all? The reason is this:

Infinite Bliss – Brahma – being formless and one, i.e., being *Alone*, is not conscious of nor enjoys its own state of Bliss. When it desired to see and enjoy its own state, with the help of Maya [self-desire: *"Who Am I?"*], it began to evolve itself for that purpose, till it assumed a form capable of enjoying its own status. The last form it evolves to accomplish this is the human form.

The human form is the natural evolutionary outcome of Brahma – formless, infinite Bliss itself. The human form is the last of 8,400,000 stages in evolution. Just as numerous blocks are needed to build a house, 8,400,000 stages are needed to build the *first* human form; then an additional 8,400,000 human reincarnations needed to complete the goal to God-Realization. Gl Int May 1995

It is vital to cultivate self-forgetfulness. One of the best ways is to concentrate on a picture of the Master. And when the picture on which he concentrates becomes alive, this is called Illumination. Souls not destined for God-Realization receive *moksha*, eternal Liberation – Infinite Bliss and Knowledge without Infinite Power. But once it enters the first spiritual plane, a soul's destiny is full God-Realization and not simply *moksha* – Liberation without need of rebirth.

A filmmaker from my early teens, I wrote this book like filming and editing a movie – each scene carefully framed, photographed and edited as a major motion picture is conceived filmed and finished in final post-production. With the reader's patience, by the end of Chapter 3, things will begin to unfold in a lucidly cinematic way for your ultimate enjoyment and realization of Meher Baba's exalted life story.

Called by different names, Meher Baba says the Avatar is always one and the same, and all worship returns to him. The sigh within the prayer is the same in the Christian, the Muslim and the Jew who are all indivisibly longing for the same One God – one's one Self.

Humanity is now at the end of its most recent 5,000 year cycle. A new advent begins in 700 years when the God-Man returns as a new manifestation of the Avatar, in a new guise with a new hat, coat and name. This will mark the beginning of a new 5000 year cycle.

Revelation of the Magi – The Star Child

To finally set the scene for this thrilling divine romance, we look back to the ancient mathematician-astronomers. In their wisdom over the ages they perceived how to track the cosmos and predict periodic re-appearances of certain comets and heavenly signs said to appear when God incarnates in human form on earth and then leaves it.

There once was an ancient tradition that the 3 Wise Men bearing gifts at Jesus' birth were mystic Zoroastrian sages from Persia. But a newly re-discovered ancient Syriac text may change that. What we didn't know is revealed in *"Revelation of the Magi,"* found deep within the Vatican archives and reported on ABC news December 23rd 2010.

This ancient text tells a strikingly different version from the Gospel of St. Matthew, as the Magi come from the far eastern idyllic land of *"Shir"*– China. Like a divine mission control-central these far-eastern sages were astrologically tracking Lord Buddha as the God-Man re- appearing and monitoring his return from the Beyond in human form again on earth.

Harvard PhD translator of the rediscovered Vatican text, Dr. Brent Landau, reveals the Star of Bethlehem not only *led* the Wise Men, but *transforms* into the very Christ Child: "The star descends from heaven, filling the cave with light which eventually concentrates and reveals a small, luminous human being – *'a star child,'* who is the infant Christ. What the star child unveils to the Magi is startling: He tells them:

> This is but one of many occasions I have appeared to the peoples of the world. I am everywhere, as a ray of light shining in this world from the majesty of the Father. He has sent me to fulfill everything spoken of me in the entire world and in every land by unspeakable mysteries. And I

accomplish the commandment of my glorious Father, who by the prophets preached of me to the contentious house, in the same way as befits your faith, it was revealed to you about me. [3]

Statements by the Christ-child and the Magi reinforce the revelation that Christ is the hidden source behind all humanity's religions. If this startling text is authentic, traditional Christianity can then no longer reject the validity of all other religions.

Jesuit priest Karl Rahner [1904-84] was deeply insightful and one of the 20th century's most brilliant Catholic theologians. As a key architect of the Second Vatican Council his views on the God-Man as given in his *Theological Investigations* resonate deeply with what Meher Baba revealed by his life and teachings as the Ancient One come once again on earth.

Rahner puts forth the notion of *anonymous Christians* – meaning that non-Christians diligently pursuing their own paths from their own religions were recipients of God's grace from "previous or post advents" of the earthly Avatar, and not just from Jesus' advent. Thus, from the beginning-less beginning the original Messiah-Avatar-Prophet is the only Master who takes birth on earth age after age. He is One and the same.

Only His name changes. We have Jesus' own words in John 14:6, still frequently quoted by Christians against other religions: *"I am the way, and the truth, and the life. No one comes to the Father except through me."* That one Christ in *all* religions endlessly leads humanity to the Father, age after age after age . . . .

Chapter Two

Christ's Return to Earth in the 20th Century

He will enlighten the ignorant atom with
knowledge of its very Divinity
Making it one day drink the wine
of its own Immortality- elf

Christ's advents include Zoroaster/Abraham, Rama, Krishna, Buddha and Prophet Mohammed. That same Ancient One was now returning for his newest scheduled reappearance in a new incarnation and a new guise as Jesus of Nazareth. And so the first ones to track and find Jesus are from an earlier religion – His previous incarnation as Buddha.

This was not just a star or a comet they were tracking in the heavens. They were likely on a far more inside track, drawing on deeper inner perceptions of spiritual cosmology, based on their own wisdom of the universe and beyond. After the Avatar, the 5 Perfect Masters who bring him down age after age are the most powerful spiritual beings in creation.

Embodied on earth in every age, when one of these 5 Perfect Masters drops his or her physical body for all time, another is raised from the 6th plane to the 7th – the state of God-Realization – and becomes the 5th Perfect Master for that time. Thus, the spiritual hierarchy on earth is always 5 Masters; never less, never more. An additional one as the exception to the rule is when the Avatar himself takes human form.

And they are not so-called "ascended masters," channeling through some medium or other, but are the descended Realized Presence of God. They live on earth with the roadmap of inner divine awareness guiding and unfolding all events, spiritual and material on this planet and throughout the endless universe. Think of it as universal spiritual GPS.

They control all social and natural phenomena – wars, revolutions, epidemics, earthquakes and floods – all directed through the release of forces from the exalted planes on which Masters are consciously stationed. They also use agents and hidden forces. In this way they bring about cooperative, coordinated spiritual work.

They hold frequent meetings on the higher inner planes of consciousness to secure their only goal – humanity's advancement toward divinity. They act in each age as foundation key-stones of the entire creation. In Avataric times, they step into the background only after they have unveiled the Avatar, for it is then his stage for the next 100-200 years, fading until his next advent between 700 to 1400 years later.   Di 192

Were the wise men real persons or purely symbols of 3 of the 5 Perfect Masters present on earth at the time of Jesus' advent? The Gospels name John the Baptist as the first and primary Master of Jesus, the one who unveiled him at the Jordan River.

The remaining 4 Masters not clearly named in the Gospels had to summon the fullness of divine love incarnate and precipitate Christ's coming to earth again from the Beyond. They bring the Avatar down from the Beyond into human form under a veil, without which the balance between reality and illusion would be profoundly disturbed. Be 37

The specific roles of each of the 5 Masters in every Avataric age are to unveil him at the proper time and confer upon him their 3 *Infinite* crowns of *Knowledge, Bliss and Power*. More will be learned about Perfect Masters and how they acted in this age to bring about the Avatar's Advent and birth in 1894, and then unveil his divinity at age 19 in 1913.

The Man Born Blind

Nature moves in cycles of seasons, complete with birth, growth, fruition and death – spring, summer, fall and winter. Then there is the cycle of day and night. The planets themselves cycle about the sun, and the sun itself revolves around the center of our Milky Way galaxy. We also observe cycles in the process of our own daily lives.

As birth is common to all life on earth, so the whole of existence depends on the law of reincarnation. Buddha describes reincarnation as the inevitable consequence of ignorance:

> "Ignorance produces desire, causing rebirth, which causes sorrow. To be rid of sorrow, one must totally escape rebirth. For that, desire must be extinguished. That occurs only when ignorance is destroyed once and for all [in *Nirvan* – the state of false mind destroyed forever].LBE 3

> "Each individual taking birth brings along past mind *sanskaras* [Sanskrit: psychic impressions or *amal*, as termed by the Muslim tradition]. The physical body is nothing but the perfect mold of these past mind sanskaras. In the course of reincarnation, these sanskaras go on changing. As they are different for everyone, so each one's face and body will differ.

> "This is understood looking at the human face, each different from the other. In each birth, one spends only sanskaras from the *previous* life. But spending them one *unremittingly* collects new ones which must be spent in the next life with a new face and a new body." STP 7

Jesus Points at Past-Life Sanskaras

On and on it goes. Meher Baba's extraordinary revelations on sanskaras never before unveiled are fully dealt with in Chapters 34-37. In St. John's Gospel 9:1–2 we read of Jesus: *"And as he went along, he saw a man blind from birth. His disciples asked him, 'Rabbi, what happened here? Who sinned, this man or his parents that he's born blind?'"*

Jesus' disciples simply want to know the reason for the man's blindness. They suggest only 2 possibilities. Either he was born blind due to the sins of his parents, or he was reaping the fruit of his own past sins. Either case can only be understood as past-life sanskaric impressions. If we do not exist prior to this birth, and if the man was born blind, then when or where could he commit sins causing his blindness?

His soul must have existed prior to that birth in a corporeal setting with others to commit acts of ignorance with or against these people. So the blind man definitely must have had a previous life. This clearly indicates the soul's pre-existence as understood by Jesus' disciples, contemporary Israelites and early Christians, as historical records clearly show. Otherwise, why ask such an unusual and foolish question?

Jesus doesn't marvel where they got such a strange idea. As we see in the "blind man" and other scriptures stories, reincarnation was obviously understood not only by Jesus and his disciples, but undoubtedly by ancient world peoples far beyond Palestine. How on earth did we lose this stellar awareness? Who dumbed us down? We must look to Rome for the answer and the blame – the early church fathers of course.

The New Testament was founded on the reality of the pre-existent soul evolving to perfection over many lifetimes. But matters of faith are often based on temporal politics, such as the Nicean Council in 325 which literally *hijacked* Christianity away from Jesus.

Then the 2nd Council of Constantinople in 533 A.D outlawed and deleted from the early gospel manuscripts and Church doctrine Jesus' own teaching on reincarnation. Early references to it were burned, thus forever destroying as untraceable this vital aspect of Jesus' message. The doctrinally pure earlier church father, Origen (AD 185-254), wrote definitively:

> "Every soul exists from the very beginning and enters this world strengthened by the victories or weakened by the defeats of its previous life, determining its place in the coming world." MC 173

The Abrahamic religions – Zoroastrians, Jews, Christian and Muslims citing reincarnation, claim Avatars Zoroaster, Jesus and Mohammed said there is *"only one birth, one death."* Meher Baba sheds critical light on this in his seminal work, *God Speaks*:

> The discourses of some saints and Perfect Masters tend to confuse us with seemingly contrary statements. For example, it is "said" Muhammad and Jesus declared there is *no* reincarnation; while it is also "said" Krishna and Buddha declared there *is* reincarnation. Now, who to believe? Take my advice: accept *God Speaks* as the final authority. Nothing like this was ever recorded before. 4610–11

One birth and one death" is exactly what [Jesus and Muhammad] said, *but* referring not to our countless occurring bodily births, deaths and rebirths, but to the *one birth-one death* of the *false mind*; for as long as it is not annihilated it will keep on taking countless bodies, life after endless life.

The real goal of life isn't the death of the ego, but the death of *false mind* which is born from the very beginning – even before the stone form. This birth takes place only once, and once born, continues travelling across the evolution of all forms and countless human reincarnations to its final death [false mind's annihilation in *Manonash*] at the moment of God-Realization. [4]. PL 49

Real Death and Real Birth – Soul, Spirit, Mind and Body

I am never born, I never die. Yet, at each moment I take birth and undergo death. Countless illusory births and deaths are necessary landmarks in the progression of man's consciousness to Truth – a prelude to the Real Death and Real Birth. Real Death is when one dies to false self, and Real Birth is when dying to self, one is born in God to consciously live forever His eternal life. 3477

Soul: is beyond everything, is in the Infinite Self, and so is infinite in its individuality.
Spirit: The Soul, experiencing the [illusory] subtle and gross worlds through [false] mind and body, gets illusionary limits, apparently becomes "finite" and is termed "Spirit"
Mind: is the medium of the Spirit to accommodate the false impressions [residual scars] of its previous past life experiences and to work out expressing these impressions as thoughts and desires.
Body: There are 3 bodies: the mental, subtle [energy] and gross [physical]; these 3 vehicles are for the experiences of the Spirit through the mind. Totally false mind might be compared to a cup; intellect may be compared to milk in the cup. Intellect has nothing to do with desires, but

mind has everything to do with desires. Intellect is thought power experienced by the mind. LA 87

Meher Baba explained mind as the ego-self which is born once and dies once. But in between, one picks up and drops countless bodies; and herein is the truth of reincarnation. Thus, we say the first real birth of the soul is in its descent from the Beyond, and the last real death is of the false mind after its almost endless journey across evolution through pre-human forms, and then an equal number of reincarnations in human form.

This journey includes further involution on the 7 inner spiritual planes to reach God Realization at *Manonash*, the final annihilation of limited false mind. Not until the soul sheds its last vestige of false mind does it finally and forever experience its true Infinite state.

Manonash implies the breaking up of the mind's intellectual tendency which had been gaining momentum for ages and has reached it zenith, creating a separation at the expense of the mind's 2nd and more important function – *its heart quality*. Mind now must give way to heart for a unity of experience to be created. LA 336 --37

Mind is the Disease

The East discovered this basic truth and has always held it. Western psychology says mind can either be healthy or ill. But the East says *mind itself IS the disease*, because it is divided and can never be whole. At the most you can make it *normally ill*.

That means we all have the same illusion-illness as everyone else; or we are abnormally ill with neurosis or psychosis. But mind itself can never be healthy. *Manonash*, used repeatedly in these pages, signifies the blessed end of false mind which must go the moment before God-Realization. Even the higher inner planes are still in the realm of mind's illusion.

And so it is not the mind traversing planes which gets Realized. Mind itself never gets realized but must itself be finally annihilated. Meher Baba said this often and in many ways:

> Mind wants to know that which is beyond mind. To know what is beyond mind, mind must go – vanish in Manonash [Annihilation in Nirvan], leaving no vestige of itself behind. The humor of it is that false mind wants to retain itself and yet know Truth which is infinite. This is the position of those who seek Truth through intellect. Mind must go while consciousness remains. Few grasp this fact, and so most grope and grapple in vain. EN 47 Imagine your body is your shell and your body must be totally consumed by you in the course of the 6 stages of Gnosis [Knowledge]. LA 157
>
> You'll have to do this with your own mouth, piece by piece at each stage. Finally, your own mouth must eat itself! This is Manonash – the annihilation of false mind, and why I keep saying it's impossible to realize me without my help . . . . For the mind to stop in annihilation is as difficult as carrying the Himalayas on your head! 4202

> Sitting at table, a six-course meal was served.
> "Eat it all," God said.
> The true Hero chomped on maya, plates and all,
> thus losing false mind
> After the last bite, the plates had to eat themselves,
> then came Manonash! -elf

Meher Baba says, "When mind's affliction goes, complete renunciation comes. To be rid of this mental curse, long for divinity so much that you totally forget yourself. To gain renunciation is to totally lose your false self, and that occurs only when every thought, word and deed keeps Beloved God present and your lower self [false desires] absent."1041

Meanwhile, we must pass through millions of so called false "births and deaths" which are really neither births nor deaths at all, but simply the "falling asleep in one body only to wake up in another." Really speaking they are not reincarnations at all. Only the Ancient One – the Avatar – really and truly reincarnates in the strictest sense of the term. Baba continues:

> The many deaths over one whole life from the beginning of the evolution of consciousness to the end of the involution of consciousness are like so many sleeps during one false lifetime. 4382 As they perpetuate the false self, as long as sanskaras are there, mind is there and one remains bound.
>
> In a very real sense this is a virulent disease that needs treatment. But each needs a different treatment for the identically same disease of the false self. The Avatar, knowing each person's impressions, treats each as to their individual impressions. His treatment wipes out impressions obstructing God-Realization. STP 7
>
> Were I to say you are God, you wouldn't believe it, because your ridiculous idea of God is some old man with a white beard watching you from an easy chair in heaven! You ask yourselves, "How can I, a lowly human, be God Himself?" The very idea absolutely petrifies you!
>
> All dressed up in rags – the Great King in amnesia –
> knows not Who He Is   -*elf*

But it's a fact. Your ignorance of that knowledge and your mind's false impression that you're only man or woman prevents you from experiencing you are God. If you're a millionaire and don't carry it all around in your pocket, does it mean you're penniless and don't own it? Know that every one of you is God, but you just don't know it yet! You are God, but must *Realize* that. 649–50

Believing in God is one thing, but to know through actual experience that you individually are God is quite another. *Feeling* God is higher than knowing God. *Seeing* God is higher than feeling God; and *Realizing* God is the goal of spiritual life. So, don't go around calling yourself *"God"* simply because you're acquainted with the Avatar's terminology. MeM, vol. 1, no. 12

The extraordinary meaning and scope of Christ's purpose in coming to earth age after age remains unknown to the world at large until about 100 years after he drops his body. Then comes his Universal Manifestation when the world comes to know of him by the explosion of his divine grace in their hearts, as he pushes forward all kingdoms in creation, moving them closer to blessed human birth and humans closer to their final spiritual destiny.

Once Realization is attained, reincarnation stops. "The exception is the Avatar himself, who comes again and again to redeem humanity." He reincarnates repeatedly in his major advents to suffer on earth, or comes unofficially without duty in up to 3 minor advents between each major one. Minor advents will be seen later in Chapter 20, *Baba in Italy*. 3686

Reincarnation is like God giving Himself another chance to play the game of life – tossing the dice again in the Universe game. Each human is subject to this necessary law of rebirth for burning off unwanted, obstructive impressions gathered over our countless lives.

The Lord's cyclic, periodic rebirth is not out of necessity, but purely out of His compassionate love to take upon himself these obstructive impressions veiling us from experiencing our own Divinity. This constitutes his perennially ordained crucifixion.

The Blazing Journey from the Atom to Adam – the first Avatar

From the moment of the original *whim* in the Beyond-Beyond state, God began *wanting* by asking the original question, *"Who Am I?"* Then the very first "drop-soul in the ocean of consciousness, known as "Adam," made the solo journey of coming down as the original torchbearer: "Adam became Christ when as the firstfirst Soul He ended His journey from unconsciousness in the Garden of Eden to Infinite Consciousness in Paradise [7th plane]." NE 138

Thus, Adam travelled down through each of the 7 inner spiritual mental and subtle planes to the most rudimentary finite state of being an *atom* in the gross world. Then for eons, that atom evolved to gain more and more atomic and molecular weight/complexity.

It travelled across the 7 kingdoms of evolution as Gas/Stone/Metal, then as Plant, Insect, Fish, Bird and Animal – a maiden voyage through all 6 pre-human finite mind life –forms with the sole purpose of gaining more consciousness at each stage of the journey.

And while at each turn it gained more consciousness, it was still *false* consciousness, as the original want expanded into so many more different illusory wants. "I want to know myself; I want this and that," continuously getting more "apparently real," but really false answers to God's eternal and original question, *"Who am I?"* As consciousness first evolved minutely into stone, both energy and mind were present, but latent and still undeveloped.

We now grasp Jesus' true meaning in declaring, *"For I say unto you from these very   stones God is able to raise up children unto Abraham."* [Matthew 3:9] Then after stone form, energy starts developing in plants and mind as sensation starts to develop in worm/insect form. "With advancing consciousness, sexuality also increases; the more consciousness, the more the sexual longing, and the less the consciousness, the less the sexual longing." 508

Consciousness continues to evolve higher into fish, bird and animal, passing through all 6 lower forms until finally becoming complete in its glorious 7th and first human form – the Original Man, lovingly celebrated as *Adam* – the *Divine-Human Prototype*. Adam passed across the entire creation to evolve mind. And though now *infinite* in Adam, mind was still false, veiled and unaware of its infinity, while evolution of illusory wants went on and on.

Adam was making his journey longer with countless desires, twists and plot points in the Film of Creation, until finally he passed beyond mind to know himself as God. Genesis *symbolically* refers to these 7 forms as "7 days." That 7th day, arriving at the first human form, was the day of God's resting. Creation was finally complete, as only in human form can God truly *rest in knowing Himself as God.* EN 105–08

Adam now had to *re-enter* the inner planes through which his soul had descended in its first *unconscious* journey into gross form as gas/stone/mineral, plant, insect, bird, fish and animal. Ascending now with full human consciousness, Adam carries the Olympian torch of *individualized* infinite consciousness across the 7 inner spiritual planes to his final goal.

Passing the torch in a divine relay, he finally comes to the real, final answer to that original Olympic question: *Who Am I? I AM GOD. I AM WHO AM – An-al-Haq*! In this way Adam groped his way through all finite forms to man, and then on to Perfect Man/Godhood.

CHRIST COME AGAIN

Teilhard de Chardin

When the spiritual journey of the first man ending in God-Realization is seen in the way Meher Baba describes, one can appreciate the extraordinary insights of Pere Chardin SJ, the grandson of the French philosopher-writer, Voltaire. His full name was Abbé Pierre Teilhard de Chardin, a great early 20th century French geologist, paleontologist, philosopher, Jesuit priest and theologian whose work brought him to a great intuition.

He intuited Christ as the *"Alpha and Omega – A–Ω,"* the beginning and end of creation. Alpha is the soul's appearance in creation as the first *"atom"* evolving to become *"Adam."* Omega is the individual's state of Christ-consciousness in God-Realization. And so Adam's couplet might well be: *"I guessed the game from A to Z. The Alpha and Omega is truly Me!"* The Christ Omega state is the *only* Son of God and Lord of Creation.

The universe arises out of Him from its very first atom to the final Realization of its highest infinite and divine conscious-state experience. When God as the Son incarnates in human form, He is equally in everyone and in everything – One without a second. This is the extraordinary meaning of the Divine Incarnation and mystical body of Christ, never grasped even by the best Christians or most theologians.

Chardin's insight into the Alpha and Omega was a milestone expression of 20th Century Catholic theology, as was his classic definition of the human state: *"We are not human beings having a spiritual experience; we are eternal spiritual beings having a temporary human experience."* He lived during the time of the Avatar without being consciously aware of him or his teachings.

My own opinion is that Meher Baba was guiding him – inwardly and solidly. Admired in some quarters, Chardin was never fully appreciated by mainstream Catholic theology, much less by the ordinary faithful who today wouldn't even recognize his name.

His passionate views fired the hearts of poetic and truly mystical theologians, and his insights will be seen in the future as groundbreaking and inspired. This chapter began with my couplet: *"He will enlighten the ignorant atom with knowledge of its very Divinity, Making it one day drink the wine of its own Immortality."* Chardin would grasp this instantly.

Realization is the experience that God Alone Exists as Infinite Knowledge, Power and Bliss. Adam's journey, evolving across 7 forms – again, Genesis' proverbial 7 days – and then across the 7 inner spiritual planes, happened far more rapidly than in our own case.

Adam was blazing a path with fewer obstructions than in the countless souls following him in the eons down to our present time. For the gridlock obstruction of false impressions in gross, subtle and mental worlds is now beyond imagination and conception.

Adam's Happy Fault

The Catholic Easter vigil's ritual liturgy is full of references to the first soul, Adam and his *"happy fault"* of original sin – the making of two from the Oneness of Truth; buying into the game of duality and biting the apple of false, illusory dual-mind as the necessary vehicle to arrive at God-Realization. We have seen how Adam was the first soul to go through that process, emerging from evolution and involution as humanity's first Perfect Master and Avatar.

He is the only Avatar ever to have manifested. Through Him, God completed His first journey to conscious divinity; unconscious man became aware of Himself as conscious God-Man. Thus he shouldered the terrible duty/responsibility of governing the entire Creation that followed Him and the infinite suffering entailed each time He comes in human form to earth.

There is only one *God-Man*. Now, switch those words and you get the *Man-God* – a *post*-Adam God-Realized man. After Adam comes the God-Realized Perfect Master, the *Man - God*. After attaining God-Realization, he/she remains in that Infinite state while still in the same gross body, making the return journey back down into conscious awareness of the illusory gross world/universe. As stated, there are 5 Perfect Masters on earth at all times.

As Adam embarked on the original maiden voyage of this incredible journey he followed the divine plan and whim every step of the way. When Adam realized himself as God, he was the first human to achieve Realization without the aid of a Perfect Master.

But all souls after Adam need a Perfect Master to become God-Realized – to bridge the infinite chasm between the 6th and 7th spiritual planes. *That's* why we celebrate Adam. Becoming the first Perfect Master, Adam subsequently made 5 more humans God-Realized.

Then he brought those 5 back down again in a further journey in their same bodies, returning to *"perfect sobriety;"* meaning coming back into full gross-conscious awareness of their bodies *and* the false universe to fully function as Perfect Masters. They reassume gross consciousness while simultaneously retaining awareness of their Infinite state.

When a Perfect Master drops his body at the end of his life, another predestined soul on the 6th plane is then God-Realized and installed as a Perfect Master in his or her place. Later counterparts of those 5 were then able to call Adam back down, again and again in each age every 700-1400 years for His recurring role as the original Avataric *God-Man*.

God now directly becomes the *God-Man* without again having to pass through processes of evolution and involution. There are always 5 Perfect Masters, and one is often a woman. They bring the Avatar down to redirect creation back toward its divine source.

Thus we see the difference between a Perfect Master or *Man-God*, and the *God-Man* and Avatar – the Master of Masters – who goes beyond the former in effecting his boundless power, while taking human birth on earth in each advent to suffer for the sake of love.

To sum it all up: at the appropriate time, these 5 brought down into Creation the first re-occurring advent of the Avatar as the God-Man, in each age wearing a different "hat and coat" – whether as Zoroaster, Rama, Krishna, Buddha, Jesus, or Mohammed.

In his latest appearance he is Meher Baba and in 700 years will be in another recurring advent. A Persian couplet states, "*You were free, but on your own and for the sake of the world you got Yourself bound.*" Australian disciple, Francis Brabazon puts it this way: GS 249

> "Shortsighted men say Jesus was the first bringer of love, implying before this God was loveless. Then they'd have that love is now sealed with no further need of His descent, example and sacrifice. But God does not admit of a first or a last: God is never of more or less. All his bright Messengers were nothing but the same *One Love Incarnate.*" SG 19

Due to the gridlock of false impressions, Meher Baba says without the Avatar or a Perfect Master's help each individual soul requires the full 8,400,000 human reincarnations to complete the spiritual journey to reach eternal consciousness of its Divine Self. That final infinite jump still requires a Perfect Master or the help of the Avatar Himself.

He then steps to the front of the line to pay the debt, cutting the journey short for all who truly love and follow Him as the Divine Beloved in *any* of His past incarnations. But even without consciously following Him, the individual soul will still manage to eventually complete the journey; it just takes a seemingly endless time – countless eons – until the last, almost infinite jump between the 6th and 7th plane is bestowed.

From His first advent in the endless past, the Avatar eternally became responsible for each soul in the Creation to eventually realize Oneness with God. He comes down on earth in human form age after age to give every soul in each and every kingdom of Creation from stone to man the most needed spiritual push towards its own ultimate Truth. He can never be free of His responsibility and duty. And so this is His eternal suffering as the Ancient One.

When the Wick of Righteousness Burns Low

The *Bhagavad Gita* proclaims, *"When the flame of righteousness burns low, God descends as the Avatar."* Every 700-1400 years the gridlock of humanity's negative impressions on earth curtails the 5 Perfect Masters' abilities to keep humanity spiritually afloat. At that point, the ship is literally going down.

In their infinite compassion and unbounded love for humanity these 5 Perfect Ones –not always known or physically seen in the eyes of the world – act in a special way to precipitate the Advent of the original God-Man back down again into human form on earth.

This is not just for a single appearance, but for His countless re-appearances down through the ages. Only the garment He wears changes for each of His earthly sojourns –whether the garment of Krishna, Buddha, Jesus, this Avatar or that one.

Many people in different traditions cannot understand or accept this, as by their nature these traditions have crystallized in the past – frozen in a kind of time capsule that cannot admit the reality of the changing landscape of such periodic cycles. Just look at how the sun, a symbolic figure of the Avatar, repeatedly rises and sets. Francis Brabazon said:

"The last Avatar supersedes his previous advent, else it was idle for that One to come again; His first coming would have been sufficient to the end of time . . . . But just imagine anyone taking the trouble of making a world and then visiting it only once!" SG 22

The last is the same as the first; meaning if you worship one of His previous forms, you receive His grace *from His most recent form*. So if I pray with all my heart to Krishna, Buddha or Jesus, whatever I may receive accrues directly from his *latest*, most recent appearance on earth as the God-Man, whether I knew or was aware of Him in that form or not. The avatar returns every 700-1400 years as the needs of humanity change by yugas.

The Yugas

1) Satya Yuga is the golden age of Truth; the ages of Zoroaster and Rama;
2) The Dwapara Yuga – one of a little less Truth; the ages of Krishna and Buddha;
3) The Treta Yuga – where ignorance plays a main role in everyone's life, dominating and controlling them, though ultimately it cannot succeed – the ages of Jesus and Mohammed;
4) The Kali Yuga – [ours] is the worst and mercifully the shortest cycle in which there is no love, honesty or truth; where false intellect plays the main role in everyone and the devil of false mind has its day. In our current Kali Yuga, Meher Baba appears as the Avatar.

How the 5 Perfect Masters Bring the Avatar to Earth

The 20th and 21st centuries saw the climax of the Kali Yuga's outer progress of consciousness, but no inner. God is mostly forgotten, while Illusion and the mayavic dream-universe take on major importance and proportions. Chaotic misery abounds everywhere:

> "Ages have made the mind so dirty it is hard for it to be pure and honest. It is mind's nature to doubt, to reason, to be happy, to be sick, to be sore and so forth. Had it not been its nature, there would have been no need for our countless births after rebirths.
>
> "Imagination has created all this, and the world is so ensnared in it, it's as if bogged down in mire, and extrication from the morass becomes impossible. There's only one remedy for it: honest love for God and help from a Perfect Master." 3350

Divinity's launching pad – the jewel of earth floating in space –NASA

Then out of infinite love, God as the Avatar, Christ, Messiah, Buddha and Prophet comes from the Beyond to revisit his blue-green jewel planet. Once again he takes on humanity's suffering. The 5 Perfect Masters carefully arrange the circumstances of his birth as they make the formless Infinite One enformed and finite as Man.

Deciding where he is born, they carefully choose his parents, watching the embryo being molded in his mother's womb. In affecting his descent, they carefully safeguard his birth and growth under a veil of ordinary consciousness, so he *appears even to himself* to be an ordinary person acquiring normal life experiences. Only then do they suddenly remove the veil. Recall the dramatic scene of John the Baptist unveiling Jesus at the River Jordan.

The time is ripe when his humanity and instincts are mature at around the age of 18-19. He's then ready to shoulder and begin his divinely ordained work. The moment they lift the veil the Avatar experiences his eternal existence as God and loses earthly consciousness.

What happens next is the most critical period in his awakening. Working in concert, the 5 Perfect Masters now train the Avatar to balance his state of *unlimited* God-Realization with the *limited* consciousness of the material gross world, which having no substance of its own is but a dim 7th shadow of God's Infinite Existence.

They then hand over to him the reins so he may take charge of the world and the entire creation with all its kingdoms and universes. Thus, on first entering his Infinite state, he loses consciousness of the false illusory universe – the very medium in which he must do his Universal work for creation. And that's why the 5 Masters must then train the Avatar.

He must learn to maintain his state of total enlightenment, his God-Realization, *Nirvikalpa Samadhi*, while existing simultaneously in a dark world of shadows without dissolving them into light. Here he enters a spontaneous state of natural *Sahaj Samadhi.*

That means the delicate balance termed his "down-coming," agonizingly painful for the Avatar to achieve. In Meher Baba's case it took seven years to become fully re-established and grounded back in gross consciousness. But it was essential, for it afforded him the ability to effect changes in the structure and destiny of the world and in the entire fabric of creation. He achieves this in all he does, as his every act is grounded in his limitless existence as God.

The Avatar's Declaration

The entire creation comes out of Me. I am in everything and still separate from the Universe and from everything. I am the Producer of the whole creation; I direct and control the mental, subtle and gross planes, heavens and space. Infinite suns, moons and stars are My shadow imagination. NE 3

I experience infinite bliss and infinite suffering simultaneously, and once I drop the body, there is only bliss and bliss, as nothing exists but bliss. From ages past I have been coming, so how old I must be! And yourselves? You, too, are coming from ages past, and are the same despite it. No one really comes or goes, is born or dies. To experience that, we must free ourselves of bondage. 3739

The Avatar's Features and Weaknesses

Meher Baba said that each time the Avatar comes he has certain features in common – a characteristic long length and arch of the eyebrow, slim legs, a prominent nose, moderately short height. He always has the same face and long hair. *"Each time my Friend bears a different name, manifests different signs, and yet through all times the same Face assumes different forms of beauty and grandeur."* 630

"The Avatar is always perfect in all respects, spiritually, and especially physically [Buddha especially so, Baba said]. He always has a charming personality, a beautiful, symmetrical face and body; while Perfect Masters on the contrary are generally odd in size and shape, with certain defects sometimes so abhorrent one doesn't want to look at them.

"Zoroaster, Ram, Krishna, Buddha, Jesus and Muhammad were Avatars. Hence they had charming personalities. So is mine. Upasni Maharaj, Narayan Maharaj and such present Perfect Masters [1920s to early 1940s] have one personal defect or another.

"Upasni Maharaj's stature is too big – like a giant. Narayan Maharaj is too short – like a dwarf. But physical differences between the Avatar and Sadgurus make no difference in their spiritual status which is always Divine." 1225–26

Each time he comes, the Avatar makes one "big mistake" as part of being human. For example, Baba said his mistake as Buddha was not to reveal the state of Realization immediately after the black, empty void of *nirvana* – the passing away of false mind; of not mentioning the state of *Nirvikalpa Samadhi* – the Realized state of Infinite Radiant Light.

This omission was later misinterpreted in Buddhism as "there is no God – only consciousness." Buddha should have told of the *I Am God* state. He also said he was a mere man, not a god – perhaps foreseeing later attempts to worship him. He corrected this in His next incarnation as Jesus, truly claiming His divinity: *"I and the Father are One."* In 1953, Meher Baba detailed his other Avataric weaknesses in this last 5000 year cycle:3502

Left, Meher Baba in 1927 on Meherabad Hill.

All Avatars have one weakness, as Perfection includes imperfection. Avatar Zoroaster [Zarathustra] was stabbed in the back by his enemy while praying. Just before he died, he flung his rosary at his assassin, who it is said caught on fire and instantly burst into flames. This was weakness on the part of Zoroaster – the instinct for self-preservation is so strong.

Ram denounced his beloved. Even though his wife Sita had been pure in heart and mind and proved herself so after her return from captivity in Sri Lanka. Thus, Ram bowed to his subjects' opinions and thereby kept his throne. He should never have done this.

Arjuna was always an intimate friend of Krishna. In the battle of Mahabharata he declined to fight his relatives, despite Avatar Krishna's order. Krishna then unveiled to Arjuna his Virat Swaruup [Universal Body with all his forms containing Arjuna's relatives whom he hadn't wanted to kill] to make Arjuna obey. Krishna should never have done this. Buddha explained to his lovers the goal of life was

Nirvan, but he did not reveal and explain to his lovers the 3 states beyond Nirvan – [Majzoobiyat, Sulukiyat and Qutubiyat], which follow Nirvan. This was Buddha's weakness. He should have told the people of the "I Am God" state.

Jesus knew he'd be crucified and felt it. He was all bliss. His suffering was universal, but alongside it he was on all 7 planes! That's the state of Perfect Divine Consciousness. So, Jesus felt the crucifixion on a lower state of consciousness. He was waiting for it and had warned his disciples of it. And when he was finally crucified, suffering in his lowest state of conscious, Jesus cried out: "Father, even You have given me up! Why have You forsaken me?" With all power, knowledge and bliss at his command, he should not have cried out in pain when crucified.

Lastly, Muhammad never revealed He was God in human form, professing to be only a "Prophet Messenger of God," and received the Koran from the angel Gabriel. He thus made himself separate from God, when he knew undoubtedly he was God in human form. He should have declared he was the God-Man, at least just before his death.

Undoubtedly, I am the Avatar and have weaknesses – 2 of them. I'm innocent and guileless, allowing my lovers to say whatever they like. And the 2nd weakness I'll tell you when I come again after 700 years in my next advent. When we're all together once more, I'll again tell of the Avatars' various weaknesses and add, "Oh and by the way, Meher Baba had this weakness . . . ." 4943

That gave everyone a good laugh. But Baba was indicating that compared to unconscious Ahuramazda [formless God], Zoroaster is definitely greater, as He was not only God in human form, but the Avatar.

"Like Mohammed, had Zoroaster said to worship him, they'd have thought Him an enormous egotist and absolutely crazy. They'd have denounced, harassed and murdered Him. So He taught them to pray to formless God. But by worshiping formless God, they were really worshiping Him; and so they gained the Impression that formless Ahuramazda was greater than Zoroaster." [5] 662

The Signs of a New Advent and the Birth of a New Culture

Meanwhile, if you're not on an insider's track, you can perceive the outer sign of Christ's new advent in the sudden explosive birth of a new culture on earth, precipitating a great healing crisis as the dregs and dormant evils in the global collective unconscious boil over, worsening the pain and misery already present as part of that particular Yuga or Age.

I recall in the 1970s watching Manhattan's East river being dredged. Its waters were clear and flowing. But as the huge dredge-bucket dug deep into the riverbed, it came up dripping with all sorts of muck and forgotten buried garbage, totally fouling both the river and air. The mind retains similar bindings for millions of years.

God's compassion allows these age-old mind impressions in the mind's hard drive to be dredged up to the surface where they can be expressed, neutralized and skimmed off by His Universal work during his advent. LBE 27–28

In a healing crisis things may get worse before getting better. Then comes a polar shift – a dynamic spiritual push forward in all aspects of life as a new culture is born. Life is quickened as all kingdoms in creation get pushed up to the next level. The 20th century gave birth to the atomic bomb. There was also to a parallel explosion in civilization.

Just see the advances in technology, communications, travel, medicine and various forms of mass media – radio, landlines, cell phones, film, television, computers, satellites, space travel, the internet and robots – mimicking privileges only great past yogis enjoyed.

Anyone at any age can now enjoy learning without having to go back to school. You don't even have to take a correspondence course; you simply have to be savvy with internet search engines – truly a gift to mankind in the new millennium.

We can barely keep up with the advances granted to humanity whose purpose is to unify human consciousness across time and space, to increase the speed of consensus and unified agreement among humans. Just see how our knowledge of the universe is expanding daily. Here's how 5th grade kids from 1995 perfectly predicted how the Internet would be in 20 years by 2015. They said: "Hey, why should we be on the Internet?

"Because it will be our TV, phone, shopping center and workplace. In less than an hour we can visit Jupiter or the moon, tour of the Sistine Chapel in Rome. We can research the Brazilian rainforest. We'll get soccer scores for a team in Italy and download a recipe for cat food cupcakes. Are we going to raid the Internet? YES!" was their resounding reply. [6]

Well, they certainly knew their p's and q's and were right on the mark as history has clearly shown. The internet is in creating what some call "an intelligent planet." The planet's skin is becoming an intelligence network for people to communicate as just the first step.

The planet's personal, scientific, medical or geo-physical speed of consensus has increased exponentially in the last 100 years more than in the last 5000 years put together. Just think of that for a moment. The remarkable 20th century worldwide surge has resulted in an unprecedented global transformation of material life that has only just begun.

Economists estimate more goods and services were produced in the last century than in the entire prior history of man on this planet. Absorb this fact: until the mid-1800s, the primary sources of power were muscle and fire. In less than 2 centuries we've gone from the steam engine to splitting the atom to traveling into outer space. These are merely some of the outer visible signs of the Avatar's inner workings.

He brings with him advanced souls from other planets incarnating into earthly form. Their intellectual/scientific gifts help give a push to world culture – the Einsteins, Carl Jungs, the Teslas, Marconis and such scientific geniuses appearing in each Avataric age. GuG 176

At the same time there is an inward movement within global societies, a spiritual cleansing which breaks down entrenched, ancient prejudices, hatreds and caste systems. Powerful, non-religious spiritual forces are now working to remove such negative obstructions to finally cleanse the planet's auric field and unify the human spirit in what Meher Baba christened the New Humanity.

It will be oriented with new ears for music. To "love God and each other as oneself " will be the end of the illusory separateness of mind and the world. And thus will be the beginning of the New World. 4562

In the 1800s it took weeks to get a letter across country. Now we transmit voice, pictures and massive documents anywhere across the globe in milliseconds. A few months after Meher Baba finished his work on earth and dropped his physical body, mankind's giant leap in 1969 was not simply the technical know-how to put a walking-man on the moon. Undoubtedly more so was the unprecedented global unity of those who witnessed that event.

For the first time in history, billions of people all over the world stood in singular unity, suspended in awe at TVs and radios, or gathered together in town squares worldwide – in big cities and small villages.

CHRIST COME AGAIN

They watched in breathless anticipation, focusing their hearts and minds as one-heart, one-mind, sending waves of love, support and God-speed to our astronaut brothers who appeared to be breaking the bonds of earth's gravity to open up a New Age.

In that moment, there was no Muslim, Jew or Christian, but one heart, one mind focused in wonder on our mutual destiny as humanity. There was one voice crying out, "We did it!" meaning not the Americans, but humanity had physically transcended gravity to go beyond the earth. Each time it is shown you might say, "Oh, that tired old film-clip again."

But what it really signifies isn't what may have happened on the moon that day, but on earth – the unprecedented global unity of all hearts that beheld it. Surely it was a transient moment, but also a spiritual allegory for the deeper unity humanity or its remnants will share in the coming age. If the long predicted catastrophic events foretold by Meher Baba come down upon us, they will represent the planet's preparation for the coming New Humanity.

Clearly, an enormous evolutionary impulse was given to the planet, catalyzing entire processes of civilization. Who could have given this unprecedented push? The answer is in plain sight. Yet in the face of it humanity will remain totally unaware of it until the latter 3rd of the 21st century. By then, Meher Baba's Manifestation as the Avatar will be a fact.

Everyone will know not by TV, but direct inner experience that God had taken human form again. Meanwhile, humanity is being distracted with the sheer volume of utter and deliberately bogus news put daily on its plate by viciously controlled mass media outlets.

When astronauts turned cameras around to photograph earth from the moon, humanity forever changed the way it looked upon the blue-green jewel we call home. The Chinese proverb, "A picture is worth 10,000 words" was never truer than on that day.

That one photo was more instrumental in showing our place in the universe and how fragile life is than any other discovery made at any time in recent centuries. Still, here's how even this glorious but "bogus news" of the outer illusory world was spun by Meher Baba:

> "However far man may fling himself into outer space, even if he were to succeed in reaching the furthermost object in the universe, man will not change. Wherever he goes, he will remain what he is. When man travels within himself he experiences a transformation of his self. The universe has come out of me, and must come unto me. It is an inward journey.
>
> "For the infinite treasure, God, is within man and not found anywhere outside himself. When mind soars in pursuit of things conceived in space, it pursues emptiness. But when man dives deep within, he experiences the fullness of existence." 5042
>
> He further said, "We should know him truly rich who though owning nothing, possesses the priceless treasure of love for God. His poverty kings could envy, making even the King of kings his slave." - The Beloved, by Naosherwan Anzar, p.110-11

Despite quantum physics pointing us toward spiritual truths, we've not kept up with revelations of the inner world given to us by present spiritual Masters. Great discoveries in spiritual realities unknown before in humanity's past have now been unveiled – one Infinite Intelligence repeatedly manifests as Love Incarnate, the God-Man in human form, fully unveiled as the Messiah, while fully veiled in and as you.

How to grasp the meaning of "in and as you?" Meher Baba put it this way:

"Seeing me behaving as an ordinary man, I am an ordinary man. Finding me angry, I am angry. Expressing ignorance, I am ignorant. I am whatever I say I am, and whatever you see and feel I am. There's no need for me to keep up appearances. When I come here, I become everything in the material universe. You see me as a man; so an ant sees me as an ant."   LH 4

When God incarnates as the Avatar, He literally becomes each of these things while conscious of Himself as the Divine-human Prototype, experiencing Himself in and as everyone and everything. This is not poetry. Baba terms it his Universal Consciousness:

"The Avatar is God, and God becomes man for all mankind; and simultaneously God also becomes a sparrow for all sparrows in Creation, an ant for all ants, a pig for all pigs, dust for all particles of dust in Creation, a particle of air for all airs, etc., for each and every thing in Creation. The 5 Perfect Masters effect the presentation of Divinity into Illusion.

"Divinity pervades and presents Itself in innumerable forms – gross, subtle and mental. Thus, God mingles with mankind as man and with the world of ants as an ant, etc. But unable to perceive this, man simply says, 'God becomes man' remaining satisfied with this understanding in his own world of mankind." GS 252

But something far deeper and pervasive is going on. To make sure humanity grasped this, in the early 1960s Baba dictated the prayer *You Alone Exist* to his night watchman, Bhau Kalchuri. Its 56 couplets is the only prayer describing the all-pervading nature of God in creation. Baba said one day this prayer will be recited in households the world over. The very last entry in this book's end Supplement contains the full prayer; here are a few couplets:

> There is no one without You! You are manifest and unmanifest, as You alone exist. You are man. You are birds. You are fish and animals, for You alone exist. You are the moon and the stars, the dawn and the night, the sun and the light. For You alone exist.

It is time for humanity to understand the secret working of God's repeated incarnate presence on earth. For at the end of it all, this is your story and the only reason you as a single "drop" in the ocean of consciousness took birth in the first place; or perhaps we should say in first place, since the Avatar declared, "Everyone is first and no one is second." Di 121

The name "Meher Baba" means "Merciful Father." The remaining chapters of this book on his life and teachings comprise but a small record of his legacy of unbounded mercy and compassion for humanity during his most recent life on earth.

He was silent, not speaking after July 10th 1925 until his passing on January 31st, 1969. How could it have been otherwise? His message to humanity could never be in words, but only expressed in his Great Silence. Let us consider what Meher Baba revealed about God's "predicament" – 3 conditions of consciousness necessitating His taking repeated human forms and perhaps God's "original sin" in letting Himself to be so led astray:

> "When God achieved full consciousness in the state of man [Adam], He let Himself be led astray by the false awareness thus gained to identify Himself not with His unlimited, infinite 'Self,' but his most perfect image in the

shape of a human being continuing His false, vacant dream. It appears as the most fantastic imagination.

"Yet it is a fact the very life of man is the veil shrouding his ultimate reality as the eternal existence of God Himself. It is the irony of divine fate that God gets lost in man only to find Himself. And the instant man gets lost in God, God realizes His Reality as infinite and eternal Existence."

One day speaking about prayer Meher Baba asked: SS 61 "Why do people tend to look up when praying? There's nothing up there. God resides in your heart. So pray to Him with a clean heart. There's nothing in the sky!" He added people need a firm resolve to attain God, not by crying out with some selfish motive.

Once when Baba asked someone to pray, the devotee began: "O God, grant me health, give me long life that I may serve Thee . . . ." Baba interrupted him: "This isn't prayer. It's a list of your wants! Real prayer praises Him through love and nothing else! When you know you're in total illusion, why ask for more of it?" 4998
Oh God give me a wife, give me a son, give me wealth, let honors flow to me!" That kind of devotion is insipid – totally empty and dry. Devotion should be offered with intense desire to see and become one with God. This 1–pointed devotion should completely absorb the mind . . . no thought of one's surroundings, relatives or the world at all. And it doesn't consist of reading books all day or chanting God's name for hours on end. That's not devotion; it's a side-show of sheer deceit." 1040
God doesn't listen to the language of the tongue, with its repetitions, mantras and devotional songs; neither does he listen to the language of the mind, which constitutes meditation, concentration and thoughts about God. He lis-

tens only to the language of the heart, which constitutes love. So, love God and become free in this very lifetime. 3444-45

When the tongue is silent, the mind speaks; when the mind is silent, the heart sings; when the heart stops singing, Soul begins to experience its original Self. In deep sleep tongue, mind and heart are silent and one is unconscious. If one can go into deep sleep and remain awake One has it and becomes what one originally was and eternally is – GOD. 4597

As to God listening, Baba explains if one remembers God wholeheartedly and sincerely from however long a distance the connection is instantly made and one's cry is instantly heard. There's no question of distance, as he's the center not only of this gross-world universe, but of subtle and mental worlds with its various levels and inner planes.

How can the prayers and calls of millions be heard at one and the same time, bringing immediate connection with the Avatar or the Perfect Master? As the ruler of infinite and unlimited powers, to him there's no question of 1 or 21, a 1000 or 100,000 or even millions and billions. But the call must be from the innermost depths of one's heart.

Only this can reach his ears, regardless of distance or traffic on the line. "All prayers and sounds are a mere show if not originating from the heart. If not, then such prayers, however loud and long, are quite meaningless. But compared to this, offering hired prayers through priests is far worse – nothing short of sheer hypocrisy. 1043

Macbeth said ordinary life without spiritual awareness "is a tale told by an idiot, full of sound and fury, signifying nothing." Meher Baba's 1958 Universal Message, explains his coming to earth age after age.

The Universal Message

I have come not to teach but to awaken. Understand that I lay down no precepts. Throughout eternity I have laid down principles and precepts, but mankind has ignored them. Man's inability to live God's words makes the Avatar's teaching a mockery. Instead of practicing the compassion He taught, man wages crusades in His name. Instead of living the humility, purity and truth of His words, man has given way to hatred, greed and violence.

Because man has been deaf to the principles and precepts laid down by God in the past, in this present Avataric Form I am observing Silence. You have asked for and been given enough words. It is now time to live them. To get nearer and nearer to God you have to get further and further away from "I, my, me and mine." You have not to renounce anything but your own self.

It is as simple as that, though found almost impossible unless you renounce your limited self by my Grace. I have come to release that Grace. I repeat. I lay down no precepts. When I release the tide of Truth, which I have come to give, men's daily lives will be the living precept. I veil myself from man by his curtain of ignorance and manifest my Glory to a few. My present Avataric Form is the last Incarnation in this cycle of time. Hence my Manifestation will be the greatest.

When I break my Silence, the impact of my Love will be universal; all life in creation will know, feel and receive of it, helping every individual to break himself free of his own bondage in his own way. I am the Divine Beloved who loves you more than you can ever love yourself. Breaking my silence will help you to help yourself in knowing your real Self.

All this world confusion and chaos was inevitable and no one is to blame. What had to happen has happened; and what has to happen will happen. There was and is no way out except through my coming in your midst. I had to come and I have come. I am the Ancient One. 4447-48

One can never understand God "who surpasses all understanding." Lower mind's duality of knower/known, lover/beloved is but the charm of love generated between lover and the beloved. It is so great God cannot resist taking human form, rolling the dice with the individual human being's divine consciousness as His ultimate goal and grand prize.

Where Religion Ends, Love Begins

Beloved God in everyone and everything is deaf to formal rituals, ceremonies, prayers in mosques, churches and temples. 4008 When more and more rules are created, there's more efficiency, and soon religion becomes an organization. Free-flowing Love begins to disappear, and the dryness of the organization begins to creep in as religion is governed more and more by regulations [dogmas and rules of rituals], rather than the love which prevailed in the beginning. This is the beginning of religion, where do's and don'ts eventually govern the place where love once reigned. RT IV, 200

True love gives and never asks. What leads to this Grace is not cheaply bought but gained by being always ready to serve and reluctant to be served; wishing others well at the cost of one's self; never backbiting; tolerance supreme; trying not to worry. That's almost impossible – so try! Think more of others' good points. When Christ said, "Love your neighbor." He didn't mean fall in love. When you love, you give; falling in love, you want. Love me in any way you like, but love me.   1844

> As to spirituality most prefer menu-chewing
> to eating the food   –Zen saying

Happiest is he who expects no happiness from others. Love delights and glorifies in giving, not receiving. So, learn to love and give, and not expect anything from others. You should feel and consider yourself happiest and most fortunate among all that you've renounced illusion and surrendered to a Perfect Master . . . . But your mistake is to again place the burden on your own head. Place it on the head of One who accepts it with full responsibility.

But you keep it hanging over you, hesitating to give it up lest you lose something so valuable! You don't allow it to rest on the head of the One who wants it – Baba. You hang it between the two, putting both under suspense and aggravating your suffering. Either keep it or give it up entirely! 2037

In the 1920s, Meher Baba revealed himself only as a Perfect Master to his innermost circle of disciples, and then in 1931 to Mahatma Gandhi, guiding him spiritually from behind the scenes. He taught both Gandhi and Mother Teresa, and through them Albert Schweitzer and others by his own example how to love and serve the lepers in India with true compassion.

CHRIST COME AGAIN

Mother Teresa, a 20th century servant of India's poor, who met Meher Baba and deeply recognized his Christ likeness.

Mother Teresa instantly intuited his Christ-likeness. But knowing the Vatican could never understand, she asked a Meher Baba disciple V. Ramarao to whom she revealed her experiences of Baba that he not speak of this to anyone until after her death. He met with her several times while driving a truck to deliver goods donated by his company to her orphanage. The following is from his diary released after her passing:

"That Sunday alone in her room, after seeing a Baba photo button on my coat lapel, she asked me if I were a Meher Baba lover. She then said in a very reverent manner, 'Meher Baba is the most Christ-like . . .' and here she broke off and was silent a few seconds.

"Then she continued: 'I'm a Roman Catholic nun governed by Vatican dictates, but I know this: Meher Baba worked with lepers, and then we too became involved – myself, Baba Amte, Gandhiji [Mahatma Gandhi] and Albert Schweitzer. Following that, India is now pursuing leprosy eradication. The World Health Organization has a program to wipe out the disease by the end of the century!

"After further affirming her feelings about Meher Baba's divinity, she asked that while she was alive I never tell people of her acknowledging Meher Baba's Christ-like life."

She was very aware that Rome would consider her Meher Baba experience as heretical.

Chapter Three

Beyond Religion

Meher Baba came to the West to personally meet and uplift troubled Americans in the great depression era of the early 1930s. He revealed himself privately not only as a Perfect Master but as the Avatar – the return of Christ in this age – a revelation that would not take place openly and publicly in India until 1954 and then most openly in America during an NBC television interview on July 23rd 1956.

And now at the beginning of the 2nd millennium, only a short time since his reappearance, the conviction that he is the most recent incarnation of the Avatar for modern times has spread to 100s of 1000s worldwide and is growing daily. It will reach a global heightening around the 3rd quarter of the 21st century, the expected time of Meher Baba's Universal Manifestation. Commenting on his Avataric claim, Baba said:

> When I say I am the Avatar, there are a few who feel happy, while some feel shocked. Many hearing me claim this, would take me for a total hypocrite – a fraud, a supreme egoist or simply mad. If I were to say every one of you is an Avatar, a few would be tickled, but many would consider it blasphemy at best or maybe a joke. Being One, God is Indivisible and equally in us all. So, we can be naught else but One. But this is too much for duality-conscious mind to accept.
>
> Each of us is what the other is. I know I'm the Avatar in every sense of the word, and each and every one of you is an Avatar in one sense or the other. It is an unalterable, uni-

versally recognized fact since time immemorial that God knows everything, does everything.

Nothing happens but by His Will. So it is God making me say I am the Avatar and each of you is an Avatar. It is He Who is tickled in some; shocked in others. It is God Who acts and reacts, Who scoffs and responds. He is the Creator, Producer, Actor and Audience in His own Divine Play. 3553

Against the Idea of "Church"

Meher Baba never wanted, promoted nor allowed propaganda; nor was there even the slightest purpose to create creeds, dogmas or converts. On the contrary, his mission was to literally demolish such things, explaining the various religions are like patent medicines – over-the-counter remedies which may at best alleviate one's symptoms, but never cure them.

The Illusion of Rituals

In the early phases of awakening, the aspirant is often taken up by established religions with their rituals encouraging the spirit of love and worship. Only to a very limited extent these may help in wearing out the thick ego-shell in which human consciousness is trapped. And if followed unintelligently or mechanically without heart, the inner spirit of love and worship dries up.

They then harden the ego-shell, instead of wearing it out. Unintelligently followed, rituals and ceremonies cannot carry one very far towards the path, as they bind like any other unintelligent action. When deprived of all inner life they're far more dangerous than other unintelligent actions.

They're pursued, believing they help towards God-realization. And so, lifeless forms and ceremonies are a self-deluding sidetrack to the spiritual path. One can become so habitually attached to these external forms that intense suffering may be required to dispel their imaginary value.   LH 176

The Ancient One now repeats his advent and puts his seal on all rites, rituals and ceremonies – ending them. His very advent among man is the sacrifice of all sacrifices; His very being in human form surpasses all these existing rites; His very presence on earth is the very Seal, sealing all in the external world, and at the same time unlocking the gate leading to the very core of one's being. 4506

When they are informal and spontaneous, expressions of worshipful devotion praising the Highest of the High constitute true worship of God. It reaches and is acceptable to Him. But when the mind expresses itself in patterns of formal rites and rigid liturgies, it's no more than an empty echo of countless generations of habits, performed automatically without "heart." Such worship not only does not reach God, but holds the worshipper more firmly in the grip of his own ignorance.4917

Can one be a true Christian by not following Christianity's Dogmas? American author Anne Rice, raised Catholic, left it in her late teens only to re-unite with it in her 50s. She claimed:

> "Following Christ doesn't mean following His followers. Christ is infinitely more than Christianity and always will be, no matter what Christianity is, has been or might become. In the name of Christ, embracing Him, I quit Christianity; quit being Christian.
>
> "I need no middle-men or fundamentalist 'quarrelsome, hostile, disputatious, and deservedly infamous' baggage – whether Catholic or Protestant.' " Anne and countless others are not hereby divorcing God, but clearly skipping the false middlemen for a direct relationship with the radically

compassionate Jesus. Thus, one can be a true Christian by not following the dogmas of Christianity. [7]

To bring about the new era of spirituality it is clearly unnecessary to establish a new Church with inevitable dogmas, doctrines, rules and regulations, organizations and priesthoods who exercise a hierarchy of authority. These things cause division, disputes and conflict. And in the end, the Church exists for the sake of itself and its own survival.

In fact, Meher Baba was so expressly against the idea of "Church" that he gave an explicit mandate to his disciples in the ages following his 20th century appearance on earth that they never start or allow a "new religion" to grow as a result of his current advent.

Organized religions, he said, were mistakes made by well-meaning disciples in each of his previous advents; but after 100-200 years that particular religion had already become corrupt. Regardless from which advent it had sprung, it was soon spoiled by hierarchical priesthoods, dogmas and rituals covering him over rather than revealing him.

Zoroastrians, Hindus, Jews, Christians and Muslims – he spared none of their priesthoods. He said there was only one real religion: to love, find and experience God as one's own Real Self, and not merely as an article of faith. God's Truth cannot be argued, defended or limited by scriptures. Before one realizes God, scripture is misunderstood.

After Realization, scripture is totally unnecessary, for Truth is then experienced as one's very own eternal identity. Like it or not, we will get God-Realization as the inalienable birthright from our very Divine Origin. We have come from the Divine and must return to the Divine. There's no other place to go.

CHRIST COME AGAIN

The 16th century poet and Perfect Master Kabir said:

> "The sacred spas are fine for a bath. But take Kabir's advice and bathe at home. It's far cheaper. It's okay to visit shrines to see the idols, graven images and Shiva's phallus. Some are beautiful art, but they cannot speak to you or open the doorway to your heart.
>
> "The Koran and Upanishads [and the Gospels] are mere words; inspired words, but mere words. What do you seek: a clean body, a stone statue, a 100,000 words or the One? Listen! His hiding place is so much closer than you think."

The journey takes as long as we want and not a moment longer, based on our own individual choices. If you hitch your wagon to a star – like holding fast the Avatar – he takes you directly non-stop on the merciful path of love without detours. He clearly says:

> "If you lose hold of the mantle of this guide, there is only despair in store for you. The gateway to the highest state of being One with God is firmly closed to all who have not surrendered their false minds to the true guide."
> 2442

Or you can opt for various side-trips, layovers and "holiday packages" as listed in the brochures of life urging you with their incessant mantra to "obey your desires" – any variety of addictions – drugs, sex, cyber, name and fame, a few lifetimes of hedonistic promiscuity or hyper-materialistic abundance/prosperity venture-schemes as may be offered in such things as "The Secret," invariably misapplied for egoistic, self-serving ends.

These packages will endlessly mislead you about the true nature of your own consciousness, necessitating further countless reincarnations. Or simply pick a wrong new-age guru or false messiah who instead of smashing it will "deify" your false ego-mind.

The Avatar is not only in everyone and everything, but is everyone and everything. He is "It" from the very first moment of creation. This is the real meaning in the game of tag when kids say "You're it!" And being "It" he is totally and irrevocably responsible for the entire creation, arising continuously and ceaselessly proceeding out from him. Baba says:

> "Now listen to what I say. The Avatar comes after so many ages. Lawless God, unbound by law, comes down on earth to be bound in law. The law can never touch him, but he touches the law. He grasps the law of Nothing and acts like an ordinary human being.
>
> "He uses his power, knowledge and Infinite bliss for those bound by the law – to free them from that very law. That's why I say, 'When you go, I will come.' This means you should let go of this Nothing, so I, the Everything, may reside within you. There being no 'you' left, you become me! The Nothing is absolutely nothing, and to let go of it is for you to realize it is truly absolutely nothing and you can never be bound by it." 3379

When summoned in each age by the Five Perfect Masters for his scheduled periodic return, he is born again as the Christ-Avatar to suffer and put his very neck on the block for humanity's final liberation. This alone allows him to declare himself Lord of Creation.

The only reason for the very existence of the creation is so God can become conscious of himself in you, as you. And all the while this entire, seemingly endless amazing journey takes place solely and unbelievably in the realm of pure imagination.

"Just think," Meher Baba insisted, "this whole universe with all its vastness, grandeur and beauty is nothing but sheer imagination." He made a sign with his forefinger and thumb touching to make a circle, a sign which he always used for both "perfection" and also for "zero." Baba describes the universe as the playful whim of God's own game: 344

> "The universe is the outcome of the Lord's whim. When He realized His own whim and observed its outcome in the form of the creation, He took responsibility for the entire universe upon Himself, turning the creation into a playground for His own divine game, but at continuous great cost to Himself. As mankind cannot recognize or understand Him in His impersonal formless form, in His game He visits earth in human form.
> "Born as a child, He places His seal on humanity ONE, stamping it onto every aspect of life. Completing His work, He drops the body as an old man so creation may feel His universal push on all levels of consciousness . . . . The mischievous child eternally feeling the urge to play visits our earth and forms a circle of friends to play with in His self-created universal game."

In 1953, someone asked Baba how old Adam was: AA 111

> If I were to answer that the first man [Adam] came on this earth 84 million years ago, what would that mean to you? But that explanation would help you understand how the first man evolved, and how this first evolved man has repeatedly, millions of times, been appearing not only on this earth, but on millions of earths [that have burned out and been replaced]. And so he is ageless – timeless.

But this must be explained properly. The Book I personally wrote in one year [1925-26] when I'd just stopped speaking to enter Silence . . . so clearly explains this point. It's important for the world and all the scientists to know, and therefore I have explained about cycles.

The position of the earth for Realization, the earth dying, and the simultaneous evolution of another earth – not just any other planet, or when the first human being evolved, when was the first Realized Being, whether chicken or the egg came first – all is revealed in detail in that Book.3271

The big book I wrote will be the future Bible, Koran, Avesta, and Veda, and accepted universally by all castes and creeds. Never before have such spiritual secrets been revealed. 834

It is this same Ancient One, the very first Avatar who comes back age after age as all subsequent Avatars that we celebrate on Christmas, whether the Christmas of Abraham Zoroaster, Rama, Krishna, Buddha, Jesus, Mohammed or any in the endless line of Avatars before or after them. Children understand this instantly in the allegory of the Pied Piper, an excellent story for grasping this infinitely complex yet utterly simple divine reality.

The first soul – Adam in Genesis – is known as Shiva in Indian traditions. Meher Baba humorously refers to him – meaning himself – as "The Mischievous Chicken" and narrates an amazing allegorical story of this chicken's adventures in consciousness. Before the Beginningless Beginning there was nothing; absolutely nothing. But there was a hen![8] Its chick escapes from under mother hen's wings to experience the world in all its illusory glory. Baba drew a sketch of himself as the Mischievous Chicken. In future ages, every child will know this story, identify with his drawing and make its own versions of it.

CHRIST COME AGAIN

Left: Drawing done by Meher Baba, July 30, 1953, of Himself as the Mischievous Chicken – the Ancient One. Right: Could this little one be the mischievous chicken peeping out from its mother's wings?

If believing the Ancient one came only once is based on scripture or any other tradition, then it is clearly a misinterpretation of that scripture and its tradition. We keep referring to Jesus' warning that old wineskins of entrenched religious belief or traditions simply will not do here. This is utterly "new wine" for traditionalists, regardless of their creed. Ancient religious rituals are impotent to advance the human spirit into the New Age.

It is this new wine and its periodic new dispensation that inevitably came into conflict with the exclusive, traditional, fundamentalist religious establishment. And it was attachment to their own misunderstanding, derived from a misinterpretation of scriptures that became the stumbling block for the Jewish leaders in Jesus' time, thus attracting His crucifixion – what He actually desired beyond desire, as will be made clear in Chapter 40.

Faced with the enigmatic reality of Meher Baba, traditional religionists now run the danger of falling into the exact same mindset as the scribes and Pharisees 2000 years ago. Meher Baba may prove to be a similar stumbling block for some. He certainly was for me.

As Jesus was face to face with them, so that same Avatar faces them again today. They neither see nor hear Him. All they can see and hear is their past traditions and a limited understanding of Old Testament scriptures, already utterly and totally compromised.

The New Testament is no different. It was originally intended as an inspirational text for converts, not a forensic historical document. Up to 800 AD there were literally 100s of 1000s of erasures, additions, corrections and substitutions made to the original texts.

Many have great theological significance, ranging from alterations of single letters to insertion of whole sentences, at times doing away with or giving rise to entirely new doctrines in the early church. The New Testament at best reveals a "Bible-in-process" and a very long distorted process, because the true Word of God is never a written word.

For as soon as something is written it becomes subject to endless scribbling and mutational distortions; so it must be false. The living Word is a Person whose Truth cannot be contained in any book, however exalted. Is there a lesson here for us in these times?

And to say God is, was and will be is also wrong. For in saying so, we depict not God, but time. God simply IS. So we say nothing has ever happened or will ever happen. All happenings in eternity happen now. Illusion says everything happens. God says nothing at all happens, as there is no time. This is a secret we cannot express with words.

Books of inspiration like the Gospels, imbued with Hellenistic overtones, were at best a bare-bones outline for new Christians coming from classical pagan Greek and Roman traditions. Their aim was also to suppress all Eastern concepts – especially reincarnation.

This is why the precious and most cherished Library of Alexandria was deliberately destroyed by catastrophic fire, while the priceless lore of Israel's reincarnation manuscripts and secret cabalistic teachings from Egypt and India perished along with Gnostic Christian traditions. The early Church foolishly destroyed traces of her own root beginnings.

What was left were dry bones without flesh – bones highlighting only certain time-line/events during extremely limited periods of Jesus' life. And thus the Church finally managed to discipline her flock by means of craft, cruelty and credulity, all styled in the name of "orthodoxy." Meher Baba said as he was the one who lived them, many of these so-called facts are wildly inaccurate. Who could bear a better witness to this truth?

In 1960 he stated:

> "Although truth can never be expressed in words, scriptures have their own very limited importance. The effect of reading depends upon the kind of books and the value you attach to them. We find people quarreling in the name of religion over their holy books like dogs fighting over bare bones without a trace of marrow in them."

Baba then asked his disciple, Aloba, to repeat the lines of the Realized Perfect Master Hafiz (1325-1389) on orthodox believer/fanatics. Hafiz [9] says:

> "O God, forgive the orthodox and fanatics, for they see not the Truth." Baba continued, "Real men, lovers of God, pay no heed to ritualistic books, but instill in their lives truths revealed by the Perfect Masters." 4804

As reported in the Gospels, all that Jesus said and did could be compressed into a very short time-frame. In fact, 3 of the canonical

Gospels – Matthew, Mark and Luke – employ narrative accounts covering only the final year of Jesus' public ministry in Judea, with only Luke's narrative adding an account of His birth.

The 4th Gospel of John deals only with the last 3 years of Jesus' Judean ministry. So where are accounts of the other 30 years before the crucifixion, or the 50 years following it – over 80 years all together? New historical revelations will begin to boldly assert themselves on the length Jesus' life on earth, not in His euphemistic "resurrected" body, but outside Judea in His physical body for 5 decades after and beyond the crucifixion.

We will finally come to a shocking and wondrous grasp of that in 2 later chapters. And as a result, humanity will have to totally revise its understanding of Jesus as given only loosely in the New Testament and canons of traditional Christianity. Still, He remains the Christ/God-Man/Avatar of His age, and a Being whose all-encompassing glory even the most sublimely faithful Christians have not grasped, but have rather fully underestimated.

Additionally, the Gospels do not contain the secret Gnostic teachings revealed by Jesus to His inner-circle of 14–12 male apostles and 2 female inner-circle members [Mother Mary and Mary of Magdala]. He initiated them in a very different way from the masses. Don't think for a minute that Jesus gave the same inner wine to all.

Each was given what they individually were able to absorb and not a drop more. Those in His inner circle had definite contact with him in His previous advent as Buddha. The rest He veiled, for they had not yet the capacity to contain His Truth. It is clearly said:

> "When he was alone, the 12 and others around him asked him about parables. He told them, 'The secret of the kingdom of God has been given to you directly. But to those on the outside everything is said in parables.'" (Mark 4:10-11)

As the Gnostic teachings of Christianity are hidden, so are they in the Sufism of Islam, as in the Cabala of Hebrew tradition; not because they're in any way forbidden, but they require great spiritual maturity and insight to even grasp, and so they are reserved.

The Avatar – Always Born in Male Form in the East

As the home of Avatars, Prophets and Masters over the ages, India has played a most prominent role in shaping humanity's spiritual history. Its contribution to humanity's evolution is unparalleled. Someone asked Baba if the West would ever produce an Avatar.

He clearly stated, "The Avatar has always been and will always be born in the East. This is due to the peculiar situation in the evolution of the universe and gross plane existence which necessitates the manifestation of the Avatar only in that particular region."

When asked, "Will the Avatar ever be a woman?" He replied, "Never has there been a female Avatar, nor can there ever be one. The Avatar has been and always will be in a male form." Yet he comprises within himself both male and female aspects. 1619–20

And so it is the glory and exalted role of woman to unveil the Avatar's human form as her ultimate gift to the creation, as from her loins he takes his priceless human birth. She is the tree of life producing the fruit of divinity. An incarnation as of Jesus, although conceived without lust, is always the result of the natural union between woman and man.

The Avatar's nativity is never what has been termed a "virgin birth." The Avatar's birth is human in every sense of the word – fully God becoming fully man. This is the glory of human birth, as each mother gives birth to the Divine, however veiled. HM 457

Only a Perfect Master who himself is the embodiment of that wine and Truth can shed real light on these matters. While we presume to limit Christ's consciousness to one historical persona/event, He has inhabited countless Divine-human personas in His endless past advents, as different wardrobes of a divinely versatile actor and not simply as Jesus – however much Jesus is loved and worshipped as the God-man and Avatar of His age.

Without intending to offend anyone, it will be clearly seen and felt by the end of this book how misunderstood the notion of "the one true Christ" has been in traditional Christian circles and doctrines; how limiting and demeaning to God's infinite love and wisdom, and how disastrous to humanity such misinterpretations of that sublime truth have become.

Baba said:

> "I don't want to be called Redeemer, Savior or Divine Majesty. Disciples, through love and enthusiasm, bestow such titles; while also many misunderstand me, calling me Satan, Devil, Anti-Christ. It's all the same . . . I know who I am."

God saw the real fix religion got itself into and provided the only remedy – Himself come anew. Never has an Avatar – especially one who claimed, "I've come this time not to teach, but to awaken" – left such a legacy of teachings and information on spiritual realities previously and totally unknown by human beings; a veritable treasure house from A–Z, yet to be even discovered by humanity, let alone mined. GLI Spring 2009, p.11

Those secrets are contained in the work you are now reading, defining the record of God's continuous periodic appearances on earth time and again for all. In 1922, 3 years before undertaking his lifelong silence, Meher Baba made clear he wanted to set the record straight so no mistakes are made again as to his Reality.

"In time to come, I will give you such writings to convince you without doubt of the validity of my Reality."

Pining for this knowledge for ages, the world is still ignorant of its existence. And such "book knowledge," however illuminating, cannot be compared to the inner-knowledge coming directly from the Master himself; for only He can initiate and impart that knowledge individually.

"God is not to be learned, studied, discussed or argued about. He must be contemplated, felt, loved, lived and fully experienced as one's Real Self."3047

Meher Baba enjoined his disciples: "It's your job to place my name in humanity's ear. It's my job to bring it from there to here," pointing to his heart. The awakening journey is a very long one, while the awakening itself happens in a flash. The breathtaking fragrance of his life is just beginning to waft across the planet. With my dogmatic theological background how I was able to track his scent and sidestep my former shadow is a minor miracle itself.

The reason this could even happen was because I loved Jesus in my own way as a priest and even after my disillusionment with that life. And however much I stumbled over my own ignorant shadow it was his mystical "Christ-scent" that brought me to Meher Baba.

His followers are an eclectic spiritual movement of mixed messianic communities – Zoroastrians, Hindus, Jews, Buddhists, Christians and Muslims. As Christ, He is at the center of creation and Lord of the Universe – God working for the sake of God, the world, all mankind and all universal beings. He said, "Being blind and not knowing the way out of Illusion, seek the One Who knows the way." Baba then told this story illustrating blindness.

There were 4 blind men sitting one day talking about elephants. "I've heard the elephant is a huge animal," said the one. Another added, "So big he needs tons of food." The 3rd said, "I'd really love to 'see' this big animal." The 4th added, "Providing he's not too hungry!"

As they were talking, along came an elephant and his keeper who overheard the blind men and decided to give them the experience of 'seeing' the elephant. "Not to worry, friends, I've brought you an elephant! Now you can find out for yourselves how big an animal he really is."

And as the 4 blind men went to the elephant, one touched his legs; another, his tail; the 3rd one felt the trunk, while the 4th ran his hands over the elephant's ear. They we so happy and thankful they were given this experience. The keeper then led the elephant away.

As the men sat down to share their experiences, the one who touched the tail said, "The elephant is like a rope." The one who had touched his legs said, "No. The elephant is a tree. The one who had touched the ear said, "You're both wrong. The elephant is like a carpet." The one who had touched the trunk said, "Believe me; the elephant is just like a huge serpent. In this way the blind men fought about their individual experiences, each thinking the others were wrong.

So each thinks his own religious idea of God is best. And people fight like hell to prove they are right, like the blind men who couldn't even see the elephant. Illusion has made us all blind, and only the Master can restore true sight. Meher Baba's sister Mani whom I knew and loved recounts the Avatar's multiple appearances down the ages: AW 261–62

CHRIST COME AGAIN

In India it's common to refer to God as "the One Upstairs" – as if God stays way up there in enjoying permanent retirement after creating the world, and only now and then answering a prayer here or there. Lucky for us this isn't the way it is. Luckily, God loves His creation so much that now and then He dresses up in drag as man and comes "downstairs" to be among His children on earth.

To be seen by us He puts on the cloak of Perfect Man and stays and plays with us, laughs and suffers with us. But He keeps it all a secret. Only a few share this great divine secret. While downstairs as man, He's called the Avatar, because being God + Man = Avatar [the Christ].

After some time with us, God drops His human cloak and leaves it behind for the world to worship. Yes, God leaves His cloak with us [buried in the earth], but He doesn't leave us. Though we no longer see Him, His Love and grace flow more powerfully than ever – available to everyone.

God is One, the One and Only One. But God's cloaks are many. Each time God decides to come "downstairs," He chooses a different cloak from His beautiful wardrobe. Through endless time God has worn so many cloaks for the sake of his children on earth. As we know, the cloaks of God have different names, like Zoroaster, Rama, Krishna, Buddha, Jesus, Mohammed. And now as we know, it is Meher Baba. Not long ago I had a dream illustrating this.

In my dream I was driving with a friend in a small red convertible, a sports car with a back seat just big enough for one. When the car stopped at a traffic light, I felt a presence behind me in the dusky light. Turning, I saw a figure in Arabian clothes, and instantly I knew without a doubt it was Prophet Mohammed! He silently indicated He wanted to hitch a ride.

As I nodded, He got into the small back seat and we drove on. After a while, He signaled us to stop, got out and walked away. Curious about where He was going and why, I got out and quietly followed. Keeping a distance, I followed Him through a maze of tents of different sizes and shapes, like on the grounds of a big circus. At last He stopped before a big tent, and as He pushed open the entrance flap, I saw a long row of costumes hanging along its wall.

As the Prophet walked by the row of costumes, fingering them lightly before picking one for His next Act, I woke up from my dream. My heart cried out: "Dearest God, I didn't have to see the garb You picked. I know You picked the most beautiful One named Meher Baba. I know because I have seen You in that garb, love You as naturally as a fish loves water, lived my life with You – all I've ever wanted to do! Now there are so many countless ones who haven't seen You in Person.

But they have received you in their hearts and follow You implicitly. Among them are those walking the long path of surrender, daring to climb the mountain of obedience to reach You some day by Your grace. O Beloved Avatar, Your lovers await You. No matter what costume you wear for Your next Act they will know You. Their hearts will recognize and be ready to receive You. They wait, sustained by their longing for You and You promising them: 'I will come again!' " GB 143–46

Putting his advent as the Avatar in the context of time, Meher Baba said:

The Avatar appears in different forms with different names at different times in different parts of the world. His appearance always coincides with spiritual regeneration, and so the period immediately preceding his manifestation is always one in which humanity suffers from the pangs of the approaching rebirth. Man seems more than ever enslaved by desire, driven by greed, held by fear and swept by anger. The strong dominate the weak; the rich oppress the poor.

Large masses of people are exploited for the benefit of the few who are in power, as the individual forgets himself in excitement. Immorality and crime flourish, and religion is ridiculed. Corruption spreads throughout the social order. Class and national hatreds are aroused.

Wars break out as humanity grows utterly desperate. There seems no possibility of stemming the tide of destruction. Then suddenly, the Avatar re-appears as the total manifestation of God in human form – a gauge against which man can measure what he is and what he may become.   Di 268

I can't expect you to understand all at once what I want you to know. It's for me to awaken you from time to time down through the ages, sowing the seed in your limited minds. It must in due course and with proper heed and care on your part, germinate, flourish and bear the fruit of True Knowledge which is inherently yours to gain . . . . On the other hand, you may be led by ignorance. You may persist in your own way . . . that too is progress, however slow and painful.

After innumerable incarnations, it is eventually bound to make you realize what I want you to know now. Save yourself further entanglement in the maze of delusion and self-created suffering owing to the magnitude to your ignorance of the true Goal – AWAKEN NOW. MBC 20

I am merged in God the way Buddha, Christ and
Krishna were merged in and had become one with God. In
the same way, I live in God. As they knew God, so do I
know Him! You yourself and others can know God in the
same way and become one with Him! 1373

A Young Hero in Search of God

God acts in His own precisely timed moment. The one destined to be Meher Baba's father – our age's new "St. Joseph" – was Named Shahr-yar Irani. He was born in the town of Khorramsha, Persia [Iran] to a poor Zoroastrian family on Persian New Year's day, March 21st 1853. Shahr-yar means "emperor." Later he would simplify it to "Sheriar."

Avatar Zoroaster appeared in ancient Persia c.6000 years ago. His Master was a God-Realized Hebrew, but the world knows little about the religion descended from Him, as it was falsified by priests with rites and rituals long after his passing. 1066

He prescribed a life of "good thoughts, words and deeds," and was the first in our last 5000 year cycle of 7 Avatars. While prospectors clamored in their search for gold throughout the American West in 1865, Sheriar as a mere boy of 12 mined the inner gold of union with God, wandering as a spiritual seeker in the remote deserts of Iran in search of the Divine.

Although uneducated, as a child he one day suddenly gained full reading and writing knowledge of Persian, Arabic and Hebrew. A veil was suddenly torn from his mind revealing this past-life knowledge. In later life, scholars would seek him out to clarify subtle points in all of these languages. Every human mind contains all knowledge, but the curtain of impressions in our lower minds prevents access to knowledge from our ageless past.

A precondition of this gift is a state of desirelessness. And as he'd not misuse it, God gave back to him this rare knowledge. The stillness emanating from him was precisely a reflection of his utter desirelessness. He spent the next 18 years of his youth wandering with deep spiritual thirst through the deserts from Iran to India. RT III, p. 69

With no mystic traditions in Zoroastrianism, Sheriar chose to practice the Islamic mystical Sufi path. He was also the devout follower of a Muslim saint, while never leaving his Zoroastrian birth religion. As a wandering mendicant, he was chaste, lived on alms and was totally honest. But alas, it all seemed in vain.

Dervishes in Iran at the end of the 19th century.

He walked hundredss of miles each year, years on end begging his food. Cut by rocks and thorns, his wounds were nothing compared to his heart wounds. Burning love urged him on with the name of God, "Yezdan, Yezdan, Yezdan" ever on his lips, without even a glimpse of his Beloved God. Desperate at age 31, he reached the point of either Realization or death. 95

He undertook a 40-day fast in a remote Indian jungle.[10] It was a dangerous, heroic penance called *chilla-nashini*, where one sits in a hand-drawn circle for the entire time without food, water or sleep, facing whatever enters one's consciousness. If persevered to the end, it was said the angel Gabriel appeared to grant the devotee's sincerest wish.

During the time of Gautama Buddha, with the world in a different state of natural peacefulness, a yogi or hermit could meditate at these highest levels. In the 1950s, Meher Baba indicated there are three such ancient yogis still living today in blissful peace in remote Indian caves of Himalaya and Tibet where not even sound penetrates.

They have lived in the same body for the past 600 years by holding ether-vibrations from the subtle world. This requires fasting for 14-40 days together with certain specific secret penances. But with today's digital machine-age noise, it is next to impossible to achieve these highest states. LBE 169;

As time passed slowly in the state of chilla-nashini, Sheriar lost track and could no longer differentiate between the days. As he entered deeper into his 40-day fast, suddenly a ferocious lion appeared, ready to devour him with deafening roars vibrating the ground. They were replaced by a ferocious tiger, stalking the circle for hours on end. Sheriar did not move.

When the tiger disappeared, flames suddenly arose on all sides around the circle, moving closer and closer, convincing him to feel he was burning alive. Still, he did not move. Hideous gases and screaming giants appeared with spears pointed at his heart, their eyes and faces ominously dripping blood. He did not move.

Soon they too disappeared. These dreadful serial nightmares all possessed alarming faces of horror to torture him. It was nothing but his own false mind projecting itself outward onto the screen of his consciousness – hellish inner-plane hallucinations and nightmares.

But alas, he dozed and fell out of the circle, having remained within it only 30 days. He wept inconsolably at his 10-day shortfall and apparent defeat. Disheartened, bewildered and half-dead, he dragged himself away and collapsed on a river bank, falling unconscious into deeply needed sleep. He awoke to a divine voice clearly speaking to him.

> "He whom you seek and wish to see – His attainment is
> not yet destined for you. Your son will attain it, and through
> him – you!"

Was it the voice of Gabriel? Sheriar awoke with those words echoing in his mind, "Your son – through your son." A wife, a son? What could it mean? Exhausted with these thoughts, he fell sound asleep for three more days.

Then, pale and totally haggard, some power guided him to follow its force as he walked more than four hundred miles south toward Poona, India, without feeling any pain. It would be over 10 years before that Blessed son would appear. 98

The son foretold by the angel would retrace his father's steps 70 years later in dangerous Indian mountain wildernesses and scorching deserts, travelling in 1940 with his men and women disciples. Suddenly turning to his young sister Mani, that son, Meher Baba, gestured to the surrounding countryside, "Look around. You see all these mountain ranges?

"Here we're travelling by bus, but Father walked it all looking for me . . . ." Mani recalls: "I'll never forget Baba's expression when he said this, remembering our father, Sheriar. Even in a bus it was horrible. 'Father walked this barefooted, searching for me.' "

Disheartened, Sheriar completed the 400 mile trek to Poona, finally visiting his older sister Piroja whom he'd not seen since childhood. Alarmed at his still restless spiritual wandering, she begged him, "For god sakes, settle down! Get a job and get married!"

Incidentally, walking to Poona Sheriar passed through the small village of Arangaon, on whose outskirts his future Divine son would establish the greatest spiritual community of the modern age, including his and his family's final resting places. In 100 years it would become the world's foremost site for spiritual pilgrimage, and I myself would bow down there with loving gratitude many times before Sheriar's tomb.MM 2: 148

In 1883, still pleading with tears, his sister Peroja begged him to marry, promising to find him a good wife. Just as a little 5 year old girl clutching a writing-slate passed their house going to school Sheriar chuckled, "All right, if I marry, I marry her. No one else!"

Of course, he realized the absurdity of his offer with at least 25 years between them. But Peroja thought, "Why not? Who can say it's not in their destiny to come together?" So she rushed to her good friend and neighbor Golendoon, the child Shireen's mother.

She begged on her knees to save her dear brother and her happiness by consenting to give her daughter Shireen to Sheriar in marriage. In those days it was an unwritten code, always adhered to that one could never go back on one's word or break a promise once given, either in jest or in earnest. Knowing Sheriar's most pure spirit, Golendoon agreed. He was stunned when taken up on his word, knowing he could never go back on it.

And so began a chaste 9-year engagement. Shireen's father Dorabji was so violently set against it that even 9 years later in 1892 he boycotted the wedding when Sheriar was 39 and Shireen 14. They actually married due to their past life connections and sanskaras.

Sheriar always said, "Whatever happens is all God's will. What happened was to happen. And what is to happen, happens. It is God alone who does everything." It's all well planned and charted out, though we have no idea who we were in the past. Nor do we know how we have this great privilege to be associated with him now. But that's how it is.

Sheriar finally settled down, saving his money for some years as a door-to-door cloth merchant. Then he opened a Persian tea shop in Poona's famous Chaar Bowdi area, where his son's Master Babajan would later settle under a neem tree a short distance from Sheriar's tea shop. She, too, was destined from eternity to be there to unveil his Divine son.

Then he opened a 2nd shop, selling cold drinks, sandalwood and incense used in Zoroastrian religious rites. He eventually owned 10 shops, but was uninterested in worldly business for money's sake. God's name, Yezdan, was silently and constantly on his lips. He kept all family duties, carrying out the necessary tasks to provide for his household.

Apart in age by 25 years, they were also poles apart in temperament and outlook. Still, they made a perfect pair with Shireen's practical-no-nonsense personality, a sharply needed contrast in their roles of raising the extraordinary Divine child soon to come.

But that child would not be their first. On January 2nd 1893 at age 15, Shireen gave birth to a son named after the ancient Persian king, Jamshed. Suffering from post-partum depression, she was too young and unprepared to accept the responsibility of motherhood.

Living close to Poona in Lonavla and running a restaurant there, Shireen's older sister Dowla and her husband Faredoon were childless and more than happy to care for the new baby. And so they began raising Jamshed as their own son.

Shireen again conceived 6 months after Jamshed's birth but from the outset this pregnancy was very different., Shireen felt the natural joy of an expectant young mother. She had wonderful dreams which her mother Golandoon would interpret.

At the birth of the 2nd son on Shireen's 16th birthday, Sheriar felt the deepest meaning beneath it, as finally the one long foretold by the angel was now arriving. The child's amazing story unfolds with a prophetic dream hours before his birth, though Shireen was blissfully unaware she was giving birth to the Christ child and Avatar of our age. 104–06

As the midnight gong rang from Sassoon Hospital's clocktower 5 hours before his birth, Shireen awoke in alarm, confiding to her mother keeping bedside vigil in room 14 that she'd had a clear vision of an open space and a sea of people looking expectantly toward her:

> "And I saw a glorious person like the sun sitting in a chariot, his brilliance filling the entire atmosphere. A few people were pulling his chariot, while 1000s lead him in procession. The multitudes gazed on him, drawn by his divine radiance. I marveled at the luster on his face. His light fell on the whole procession." Tears of joy came to Golandoon.
>
> "Oh Shireen, a very auspicious son is being born to you? His name will spread the world over. He will be honored among thousands one day, carried in grand processions as you dreamed."

Comforted by her mother's words, Shireen fell peacefully back to sleep.

Entering at dawn with his first breath at 5:15 AM Sunday, February 25th 1894, the long-awaited one signaled his return as the Awakener of the world. Jesus said, "I lay down my life that I may take it up again. No man takes it from me, but I lay it down myself. I have the power to lay it down and the power to take it up again. (John 10:17–18) And so it was.

CHRIST COME AGAIN

He was taking up his life again as in Job's Old Testament refrain: "While night was in the midst of her course and singing stars transit the heavens, thy Almighty Word leapt down with joy from his heavenly throne to enter the womb of the world, while the sons of God shouted for joy." (Job 38:7) It was as if he proclaimed, "Arise now, I am the Awakener."

And so began a glorious new chapter in mankind's history. He inaugurated his new Advent by touching all its major religious bases – born into a dying Zoroastrian religion in the Iranian wing of a Jewish hospital and delivered by a Catholic nun, a Sister of Mercy, summoned during early morning chapel prayers to assist at his delivery.

Thus, the Lord of the Universe signaled the world from the outset that he belongs to none of these religions, but they in fact all belong to him. On being told, "You have another son!" Sheriar was filled with joy and immediately rushed into the room to see his

Sassoon Hospital, the birthplace of the Avatar, Poona India, 1894

long-awaited promised child from God. 107–08

One day a great cathedral-like memorial will rise here at Poona's Sassoon Hospital, enshrining the new Bethlehem of the 20th century messiah, including the message he gave them on its 100th anniversary: "I give my blessings to the administrative, medical and worker staff of this hospital in which I, the Deliverer of the world, was delivered to the world."   5374

He would later be educated at a Jesuit High School and graduate with honors at 17. In his 2nd year of college, his divinity would be unveiled by the 5 Hindu and Muslim Perfect Masters of the Age. He was born by the Zoroastrian calendar in the month of Meher – Light of the Sun, and so he was named Merwan. His parents affectionately called him "Merog."

To even begin to understand what would happen to him in later years, we will follow the broad strokes of his childhood, simply to get a flavor of the kind of boy he was and how even his early life gave clear hints of what he would later become.

Though he was her 2nd child, Shireen loved Merog deeply, and felt so bonded to him she thought of him as her firstfirst born. She was unable to understand her intense love for him in contrast to feeling rejection for Jamshed for whom she was unprepared.

Life was happy for Sheriar and Shireen with infant Merwan. But within a few months, Shireen had another dream that she related to Sheriar. It was a frightening, foreboding premonition . . . .

Chapter Four

The Birth of Merwan, the All-Merciful Light

Whether he is called the Highest of the High, Master of Masters, the Supreme Lover or the Matchless Beloved. Whether he is known as Redeemer, Messiah, the Prophet or the Avatar, he is always the same Infinite One. Nameless and formless, even when he comes in human form in certain ages. At first only a few know him and eventually the whole world comes to realize that something beyond imagination has happened in the world. -Sheriar Books

An older and younger Mother Shireen, affectionately called "Queen of Beauty."

Sheriar Irani in Merwan's childhood, early 1900s

> "I am never born, I never die.
> Yet every moment I take birth
> and undergo death."

With all the happiness for Sheriar and Shireen with infant Merwan, within a few months, Shireen had a disquieting dream that she related to Sheriar: "From out of our well arose the figure of a small, but striking woman – a splendorous Deva, like a Hindu goddess. As she rose, I admired her lavish green sari and the green bangles adorning her arms. On her forehead were painted bright multicolored jasmines.

"In her hands she held a tray with flowers, burning camphor, incense and oils. I stood in quiet fascination until she implored me to hand over Merog. "Give me your son; give him to me." Frightened, I held Merog tightly then awoke seeing him sleeping by my side." 108

After such dreams, Shireen increasingly thought of her son as having an exceptional calling, but as this dream foretold, one she would find agonizingly painful in later life. When the Avatar incarnates on earth, he is born under a veil – totally unaware of his divinity.

Only in this way can he acquire normal human knowledge and experience.

It takes 18 years for human instincts to mature and before the 5 Perfect Masters who bring Christ down from the Beyond can unveil him to awareness of his Real Infinite State; just as John the Baptist at the Jordan unveiled the same Ancient One as Yeshua – Jesus.

Meanwhile, Shireen's father Dorabji had been so furious with his wife and unyieldingly opposed to the marriage, he even forbade Sheriar to visit his house. They hadn't spoken for 11 years. But at Merwan's birth, Dorabji underwent a profound change of heart.

He was so attracted to his grandson that he visited Sheriar and Shireen in their home every day just to see the infant. So happy to gaze at Merwan's adorable face, he bowed to his grandson's sweet splendor. And the baby responded with great affection. Over time, Dorabji began looking upon his son-in-law Sheriar with deep respect and love.

Though he was veiled from early childhood, Merwan exhibited remarkable qualities, including being a mischief maker. Just before his first birthday, Shireen put him in a cradle outside under a tree and went in to finish some cooking. Coming out minutes later, she saw a deadly black cobra wrapped around Merog's little body as he happily played with it, swaying his head in rhythm with the cobra's movements.

As Shireen screamed out in terror, the cobra quickly slipped away from its innocent play with the child. Almost swooning, she clasped little Merog in her arms. He pouted at her interrupting his fun. As neighbors came running, the cobra left and was never seen again. But they assured Shireen it was an auspicious sign of her son's exceptional future. Shortly after this, Merog stood up and started walking on his own without even stumbling.

But Shireen found his new skill exasperating. No matter what she did, she couldn't keep him in the house, as he'd constantly escape outside making her feel desperate. One day, after repeatedly carrying him back in under her arm, she tied him like a puppy to the bedpost with an old sari, put down a plateful of puffed rice, some water, and went back to her kitchen chores. Upset at his loss of freedom, he started crying.

She ignored him, and eventually he fell asleep. When she went back in to check on him a few minutes later, there were tears on his sleeping cheeks that sparkled like pearls. He looked so helpless lashed to that bedpost. Overcome with tenderness, she gently untied him. And within moments of awakening, seeing he was free again, he ran back out into the lane. She had to regularly lash him to the bed until he got older and more manageable.

Sheriar would come home from work only to find his Merog tied up, and out of pity he'd free him. Then playing with his father awhile, again he'd escape outside till a passing neighbor tucked him under his arm and brought him back in the house, proving he truly was a Mischievous One. As Merwan began talking, he called his father Bobo and mother Memo.

He had golden hair falling to his shoulders and heart-melting brown eyes. And though healthy, he had one affliction – a sensitive stomach and weak bowels. Thinking he'd eaten the wrong things, Shireen sometimes spanked him. But Sheriar never laid a hand on him, knowing Merog was his promised son from God. Merwan's only superstition was cats, instilled early on by his grandmother Golandoon. 109–12, 128

He began school at age 5, and one day found a baby sparrow fallen from its nest in his yard. He picked it up and nursed it for some days, but the sparrow died. Merwan was very sad and cried over its passing. With his friends he carried the sparrow to a hole dug under a rose bush and buried it. Placing flowers on the grave, he solemnly recited a little prayer while his friends stood around with bowed heads. LOL 294

Pinching Coins

Wanting to buy candy, Merwan might take a coin from Sheriar's pocket. But one day, the candy store clerk gave the coin back, saying, "This money's no good. You have to give back the candy." Disappointed, he walked home and reproached his father.

"Bobo, this money's no good. Give me some good money!" So Sheriar handed him another coin. "What does this man want; money that can walk? All right, this one will walk." Merwan examined the coin. "How can it walk? Where are its legs? Is it a magic coin, Bobo?" Sheriar laughed and explained the expression to his innocent son.

Besides sneaking coins from his father's pocket to buy candy, Merwan might pinch a few extra for beggars coming down the lane. Soon they were boldly coming up to the door expecting handouts. Shireen complained to Sheriar not to keep pocket-change where Merwan could get at it. So he started hanging his coat high on a hook.

But when no one was around, Merwan would climb on a stool, grab more coins, and like a young Robin Hood give them to poor men waiting outside. One day as this routine was unfolding, Sheriar and Shireen watched from behind the lattice-work of their front porch.

She was rebuking Sheriar about it as Merwan came back in the house. She began scolding, "You're always stealing money. You're a thief!" At the reproach, he turned to his father, "Am I a thief, Bobo?" Sheriar laughed, "No, Merog, you're not a thief. Thieves don't give money to the poor!" Another incident happened when he was a bit older.

He was walking down the street on his way to meet up with his playmates in a nearby field when suddenly a large herd of water buffalo came stampeding down the street directly in his path. From their upper back porch Shireen screamed down a warning, thinking her Merog was about to be crushed to death as the buffalos charged straight toward him.

Then something almost miraculous happened. Onlookers said he was about to be trampled when they saw him sitting in the street with buffalos running to either side, barely avoiding him. Others claimed one buffalo stopped and hovered over the child, protecting him from the rest of the stampeding herd. Still others saw yet another scene.

At one moment they saw him actually trampled to death by the buffalos, but in the next moment saw him standing safely on the other side of the street as the herd charged on.

Whatever the true account, all were astounded at the child's seemingly miraculous escape. Yes, the 5 Perfect Masters had their

Left: the lane at the rear of the family house in Poona's Quarter Gate neighborhood where young Merwan was almost trampled by a herd of stampeding buffalos, circa 1900. The front of this house was Sheriar's tea shop. Right: the same lane as it looked in 1982.

protective gaze on him. 114

Dari was spoken at home. It was a common dialect in Iranian villages and also the court language of ancient Persia. Their neighborhood was like a little UN where the children also picked up other languages. Merwan's school teachers took special notice of him. One liked him so much she'd invite him home to dinner with her family.

On his last day at that school when he was 9, she embraced him warmly with words of advice. He listened with downcast, tearful eyes, knowing he'd miss her. But he soon made friends at the new school. Older students were especially attracted to him, wanting to play with him in the schoolyard and eat with him at lunch breaks.

He seemed loved by all, except for a few boys who were envious of his popularity. They formed a gang against Merwan and his friends. He tried to ignore their hostility and not react, believing as Sheriar taught him early on that today's enemies were tomorrow's friends.

The gang was led by Homi, a desperate kid with a mean streak and the older brother of Merwan's closest chum, Baily Irani. One day at a field-hockey game, Merwan's team beat Homi's. The angry boy whacked Merwan hard on the shin with a hockey stick. It hurt, but he took the blow without complaint. Outwardly, Homi acted like an enemy, but from that day on he felt a respect for Merwan. In later years that would transform into a deep love.

Merwan excelled in sports and cleverly balanced homework, reading and games. He'd rise early to sing his prayers aloud in an exquisite, melodious voice. Neighbors got up early just to listen to him, describing it as "rippling waters in a river of poetry." 119

He affected the hearts of all who heard him. Walking down the narrow lanes close to home, strangers would gaze into Merwan's soft brown eyes, entranced by the inner light shining from them long before anyone knew of his divine origin.

Merwan did have one nemesis – arithmetic – a great headache and maybe his first source of unhappiness; something I appreciate, as I, too, was a constant math failure. At times he'd sneak a peek at someone else's answers during a math quiz. Remembering it decades later, he once commented in a talk given at a school, "As a school boy I always had to cheat in arithmetic to get through my tests." 5005

Then one day he had an overwhelming experience in math class. He described it later in life. "I saw a great glitter of circles with tiny points in them as if suns, moons and stars were being projected from those points." He lost consciousness and fell off his chair. The teacher rushed over and laid him out on a bench, sprinkling water to revive him. When he came to, she asked, "Merwan, are you alright? What happened?"

He muttered, "A halo. . . I saw a halo!" The teacher didn't understand. "How do you feel? Do you want to go home?" "No, I'm OK." But as class resumed, he sighed in regret. Having glimpsed the true light of God – the Noor of divine effulgence – here was this awful arithmetic again. He reflected wistfully, "Maybe I should have gone home." 111–20

He loved to prod Sheriar for stories of his adventurous days as a wandering dervish in the mountains and deserts of Iran. And so from his beloved Merog's earliest years, Sheriar carefully taught him the inner secrets, as well as the mystical poetry of the Perfect Masters Hafiz and Rumi, remembering the divine voice that spoke to him of his most destined child.

Sheriar and Shireen were blessed with 9 children – 7 sons and 2 daughters. 3 would die in early childhood – 2 boys, Shirmund at 7 months, Jehangir at 2, and daughter Freiny at age 4 in the influenza epidemic of 1902 when my own father lost everyone in his family. 156

CHRIST COME AGAIN

The Beautiful White Horse

Freiny's last words, "I'm going now. The beautiful white horse is here!" echo Hindu Scriptures that the Avatar in the Kali Yuga Machine Age will be known as Kalki, the White Horse Avatar, a figure to play great prominence in Merwan's later life as the Avatar.

Meher Baba as Kalki Avatar. Painting © Cherie Plumlee.

The surviving brothers were Jamshed, Beheram, Jal and Adi. I would know the latter 2 and especially the very treasured last-born sister Mani. She outlived them all till 1996, becoming a dear friend and like my own sister for 15 years. 114

From age 16 before sleep Merwan respectfully bowed down to touch the feet of his mother and father. Then in the morning arising early, he'd approach their bedside and again gently touch their feet while they still slept. He considered this act of respect a sacred duty and continued it until the time of his Realization at age 19.

He was very loving and obedient to his "Bobo and Memo," as he always called them from his infancy, and they in return reciprocated the love of their dearest Merog more than their other children. And they did nothing to hide it. He was doted upon and adored even by neighbors who also referred to him with affection as "Merog." 120–21

Their home was on Butler Mohalla, a quiet, middle-class residential enclave hedged between busy commercial streets. It was made up of quaint lanes [mohallas], and neighbors were like joint families, caring and watching out for each other. If one received good news, everyone celebrated, and if a husband beat his wife, everybody was up in arms.

Pushcart vendors would pass by hawking treats, samosas and coconut candy. Sister Mani recalls, "Oh, those frozen ices! Mr. Hussein had a big mustache and a bright painted cart with a brass bell. Hearing it, we neighborhood children rushed out for his crushed-ice treats, made in whatever shape we wanted, generously flavored with syrup toppings." GB 22

Meanwhile, Shireen had to manage the household and family with care. She had to be practical having a husband who was apt to be too generous with his worldly goods – money, blankets and all sorts of things given to anyone whom he felt was in need.

This upset her, as she'd then have to penny-pinch the family's budget. She once quipped, "If we collected the amount of blankets

Sherog has given away we could have opened our own blanket shop!" That generosity would rub off onto Merwan as the Avatar. 193

In later life as the Avatar, he generously gave to the poor. His own pockets were empty and his disciples had to do with just the bare necessities of life – scant food, worn out clothes and a tiny bar of soap for both bathing and washing their few worn out clothes. TH 94

His temperament was mild – brave, loyal, funny, smart, strong and honest. He didn't like deceiving or lying and would keep silent rather than hurt someone's feelings. He endured whatever suffering he had and was even reluctant to share it with his parents. Strangers thought he was European, as golden-haired children are uncommon among Persians.

He loved playing cricket, but whatever sport or activity, he totally gave his heart to it. His gait was swift and graceful like a deer, his heels barely touching the ground even when walking. Merwan's cheerful companionship spread joy and delight every moment, dispelling any sadness others felt with laughter and joy always visible on his handsome face.

The magical charm in his intoxicating eyes stole the hearts and minds of everyone when first meeting with his strong, short-statured body, broad shoulders and loving melodious voice. 121 He held track records in school and in later life disciples had a hard time matching his agile stride, often riding bicycles to keep up with him. Merwan had a genius for friendship.

Baily Irani was his closest friend from childhood. But at times there were problems. In defense of his friendship with Merwan, Baily sometimes said or did things that hurt others' feelings. But he'd be furious if they complained to Merwan, as he couldn't bear a reprimand from his best friend. When criticized for his own shortcomings, Baily usually paid no heed and let it slide. Yet it bothered him that he was so submissive to Merwan. Several times he decided to confront the situation. Then as soon as he stood before Merwan, he'd completely chicken out. Merwan was also clever in studies, while Baily failed, was kept back twice in the same grade, and was about to be thrown out of school.

In Trouble over Baily

Baily easily fell in with bad company and habits that later in life would include drinking and gambling. There were no 2 ways about it; Shireen totally disliked the boy as a terrible influence on her favorite son. She'd scold him, "Merog, that boy's no good. Give up his company! Stop seeing him! I don't want him in the house."

Not caring, Merwan patiently bore her harsh words while seeing Baily on the sly. He tried to improve his friend's conduct and help him with his studies. It escalated to a daily exchange between mother and son as Merwan and Baily maintained their closeness – a closeness which was actually pre-destined from their past.

As the arguments went on, Merwan was usually in trouble with Shireen. Baily was totally unaware of this, until one day Jamshed pulled him aside and filled him in on what was going on at home. While Merwan tolerated Shireen's constant scolding, Baily now felt depressed seeing his best buddy always in trouble with his mom because of him.

So one day Baily cavalierly announced his intention to end their friendship. Merwan was stunned. "Well . . . if it's what you want, I can't stop you. But we part as friends. I was and will always be your best friend." Baily retorted, "But you know why."

"Yeah, I understand why, but how do you think it makes make me feel? I know you're trying to spare me my mother's tongue-lashings, but to break our friendship over it?" The boys just looked at each other for a moment and then made amends. But to keep peace at home, they continued meeting even more secretly than before so as not draw the attention of Shireen or her tattletale "spy," little brother Jal.

A Close Brush with Death

One day at play, Merwan fell off a wall and sustained a 2-inch forehead gash. He started crying and was rushed to the doctor. Bleeding continued while different doctors attended him for 3 days and nights. Finally as one last remedy was applied, a doctor warned Sheriar, "Your son is in critical condition, and if bleeding continues . . . ."

That night, Sheriar went into deep prayer. Miraculously, Merwan's bleeding suddenly stopped. The physician told Sheriar the next morning, "Your son has a new lease on life. I didn't want to tell you, but I was convinced he'd not survive."

Still, Merwan suffered headaches and weak eyesight for months. Afraid he'd lose his sight, Shireen wouldn't let him to read or write. But after 3 months, the headaches abated and Merwan's vision became normal, likely due to more of Sheriar's prayers. 122–25

Then came the inevitable brotherly quarrels. Jamshed was a year older and raised by his aunt Dowla. She pampered and spoiled him with her many indulgences, such that he developed an attitude and a sharp tongue. Then while the boys were still young, Jamshed at age 6 moved in to live with his real family. From then on the boys were raised like twins.

That's when the sibling rivalry and fighting began. Though doting on Merwan, Shireen disciplined him so he never became spoiled. Merwan was unaggressive, but Jamshed in contrast was hot-tempered and rash. Yes, they liked each other, but they had quarrels as brothers might. Merwan usually played the peacemaker, even accepting punishment for his brother's mischief to preserve their friendship.

If Jamshed lost control and got angry, Merwan would simply ignore him – like water putting out fire – enraging his brother all the more. Dreading Shireen's wrath, Jamshed would never pick on Merwan if she were around. One day, Merwan's close friend Khodu was arguing with Jamshed and wrestling on the ground. Merwan tried to break it up, but Khodu being tall and muscular had the better of Jamshed and punched him really hard.

As Khodu got up and started running, Merwan threw a rock and hit him. He fell down crying. Both brothers became alarmed. Jamshed ran home to tell Shireen, leaving Merwan to deal with Khodu. Luckily, it wasn't a serious injury, and after sharing their views, they shook hands and remained friends.

Later after years of separation, Khodu would rediscover that old friendship. He'd also discover a "new" Merwan and become one of his first disciples. This, too, was due to past-life karma with Merwan. Later on, Khodu would be the sole witness of another rock-throwing incident – one hurled at his dear friend's forehead, forever and blessedly changing Merwan's life for the good of all Creation.

On another day when Jamshed and Merwan were riding their bikes to the store on an errand for Shireen, Jamshed collided with a Muslim boy. Arguing who was at fault, the other boy swore at Jamshed and got punched in the face. Jamshed was about to hit him again, when Merwan quickly pushed the boy aside, taking Jamshed's punch himself.

By now a small crowd had gathered and saw Merwan take the blow for the other boy. This instantly defused the situation and the three got back on their bikes to continue on their separate ways. But it didn't end there. When Merwan and Jamshed got back home, the Muslim boy sporting a black eye was with his mother looking for Shireen and demanding an apology. When asked who punched him, the boy pointed at Merwan!

He took it calmly and offered an apology in front of all the neighbors. Satisfied, the boy and his mother left. Well, Shireen didn't believe it for a minute. Knowing Merwan again played the scapegoat, she scolded Jamshed to stop fighting. But the false accusation didn't bother Merwan. He seemed to enjoy it, and was smiling as he apologized to the boy.

Besides cricket, Merwan was also a champ at marbles and competitive kite flying. In fact, Merwan was a bit "kite-crazy." The tops of kite strings were glue-coated with glass powder, laboriously made by grinding bits of glass picked up off the street. The object was to cut the opponent's string. Battling in the sky, the winner could retrieve the downed kite.

If Merwan's string were cut, he'd watch it sway and sail into the beyond. Then he'd pick up more broken bits of street-glass, grind to it powder and glue on a new string. It was a laborious process taking a full day, but Merwan enjoyed it. 116

Almost Losing Jamshed

One day during a big kite-flying competition, one of the strings was cut and the kite quickly spiraled down. Running to retrieve it with his friends, Merwan suddenly stopped, asking, "Where's my brother?" The other boys said, "Oh, he's somewhere behind. Come on, Merwan, let's go or we'll lose that kite!" Merwan implored, "But where is he?" Jamshed was suddenly nowhere to be seen. Merwan pleaded, "We have to go back for him."

Reluctantly, the others abandoned the downed kite and began retracing their steps. While running, Jamshed had stumbled into an open sewer and was barely clinging to its edge. He couldn't even yell for help. They pulled him out just before the municipal water district released a torrent through the sewer that would have instantly drowned him.

CHRIST COME AGAIN

Still, his clothes were ruined. He got home soaking wet and reeking with sewerage. Blasted by Shireen, he started crying and was kept outside during dinner "in that filthy condition." Feeling sorry for him, Merwan snuck back out with buckets of water to wash Jamshed and his soiled clothes and then on the sly brought him out some dinner.

When Merwan was 14, sweet-natured Beheram was born. Of all the brothers he loved him the most. Young Jal was closer to Jamshed's temperament, and even in later years continued to be "mother's little spy," as we will see. MM 3: 140; 134–36

During Merwan's adolescence, the family lived behind Sheriar's teashop. While everyone else in the house was still asleep, Sheriar was opening the house-front tea shop as Merwan chanted his morning prayers. Baily had to get up early to get milk for his mother, so he'd secretly meet Merwan before going on his milk errand. At the crack of dawn he'd ride to Merwan's and softly ring his bike bell just once. Hearing it, Merwan came out.

They'd sit on the steps, whispering quietly. Even Baily was captivated by Merwan's voice, and would get there early enough to hear him sing his prayers. Unlike Shireen, with Sheriar's "be as it may" understanding, he tolerated Baily's friendship with Merog, and never commented on the boys' friendship and meetings. 122–24

With the auspicious signs surrounding Merwan's birth added to her own later dreams, Shireen had her favorite son's future pretty well planned out. She saw him becoming a doctor, lawyer or maybe an engineer. With a brilliant career ahead he would then marry, have a big family and one day be very wealthy. MM 1: 107

Chapter Five

Merwan's Friends and Early Life

Ghosts in the Tower of Silence

When he was 12, Merwan began stealing away at night to the Parsi Tower of Silence. It was a Zoroastrian custom for the dead to be left here to be devoured by gathering vultures. Fascinated by the dead, he'd stay well past midnight following in his father's footsteps. When he was a boy, Sheriar's father was keeper of the Tower of Silence in Iran, and young Sheriar would accompany him. Merwan had some unusual experiences here.

Baily was fascinated hearing about these good and pious spirit sightings. It sounded like great fun. So Merwan suggested maybe they'd go together, warning, "But none of your recklessness." With Baily's promise to behave, one dark moonless night they set off on their bikes. The Tower of Silence was on a desolate hill 2 miles outside Poona.

Even in daylight it was a haunting forest wilderness surrounded by foreboding dark stone walls. When they got to the tower at 11 in pitch darkness, Merwan whispered, "Baily, promise whatever happens we stick together and keep silent climbing the tower steps.

"And don't turn back home before bowing to the tower." Baily promised. "And whatever spirits we see, just keep silent and make sure you pray the whole way going up the steps." Baily agreed to the complicated conditions.

But knowing only a couple of very short prayers and feeling uneasy, he was having 2nd thoughts about this nighttime adventure. The moment the tower was in sight, Merwan silently dropped to his knees, placed his head on the ground and offered his silent

CHRIST COME AGAIN

prayer. He stayed like that for some moments as Baily mindlessly imitated him.

As all the caretakers had gone, no one was around. No voices or sounds were heard except the distant barking of dogs and foxes and the eerie fluttering of hungry vultures' wings nearby. Slowly but surely the dreadful atmosphere took effect on Baily. Icy shivers ran up and down his spine as he quietly implored, "Maybe we should just go back home."

"What's the matter?" Merwan whispered. "We're not going back. We've come this far." Baily wavered, "Well, maybe it wasn't such a good idea after all." Merwan was annoyed. "C'mon, be a man! I'll lead the way – just stay near me. I'm telling you there's nothing to be afraid of." Walking a bit further they came to a door where the corpses were taken inside. No one but the priests were allowed to enter As they approached the Tower, Merwan bent low offering obeisance. Baily did the same, but on rising, was scared out of his wits seeing a tall, aged spirit in white with a flowing white beard. The spirit ominously stretched out his hands, warning the boys to stop!

Terror-stricken, Baily shut his eyes tightly and started perspiring. His knees went weak. As Merwan started advancing toward the door, Baily couldn't contain his fear and cried out, "Merwan!" But as if led by some unseen force, Merwan kept walking. Baily was too frightened to turn back alone, so he grabbed Merwan's sleeve, pulling and pleading that they leave. Merwan obstinately shook him off.

"No! We're going on. Why are you trying to stop me?" Baily's tongue stuck to the roof of his mouth. "I-I saw something – his . . . ." "So what? That's what we came here for. If you're afraid of seeing things, stop now. I'll go on alone."

Baily burst out, "But if something happens to you . . . ." "Don't worry, just go! Even if I die, fend for yourself." Baily pleaded, "For God's sakes, Merwan, please! Let's get the hell out of here.

CHRIST COME AGAIN

Don't be so stubborn. For my sake come back alone some other time!"

Merwan sighed, shrugging his shoulders. What could he do? Again he knelt to the dead in salutation, with Baily, knock-kneed, doing the same. Creeping out, Baily stole a glance at that spot, glad the spirit had disappeared. As they descended the steps, Baily sighed in relief. They got on their bikes to ride back toward the city.

Then regaining some of his composure, Baily made a bold, out of place macho remark. Well, this was too much for Merwan, so he started teasing Baily. "Say what you like," Baily retorted, "but if you'd been alone and saw what I saw, I doubt you'd have been able to stand it." "What are you talking about? What else could I have seen except a bearded old man in white, guarding the door with outstretched hands?" "Uhh!! You saw him, too?"

"Well, I think so . . . but now I'm not so sure," Merwan teased. "Stop kidding! Honestly, did you see that spirit or not?" "Baily, don't be so thick-headed. I saw exactly what you saw." "And still you wanted to go on?" "Why be afraid?" "Were there more spirits?"

"Baily, did you lose your common sense with your courage? If I were in the least bit frightened, would I've agreed to go there in complete darkness? I'd have turned back like you, believe me. I didn't go there to die. My father told me it's good to meet such spirits and gain their favor." Baily was now convinced of his friend's courageousness.

After they rode their bikes in silence a while, Baily sheepishly said, "Merwan, just don't tell the guys I got scared." Merwan chuckled, "Don't worry." A nearby clock struck 2 AM as the boys parted. They had spent about 3 hours wandering in the night. This was Baily's first and last visit to the Tower of Silence, but surely not Merwan's. 129–32

CHRIST COME AGAIN

Sometimes for hours late into the night Merwan avidly gazed up at the stars. Friends often joined in, but he'd become so absorbed he'd be lost and not reply to questions or share in conversation. These late nights and very early mornings were the best times for him and Baily to meet so as to avoid Shireen, for by now it had escalated into her strictly forbidding Merwan to hang out with him, with "all spies on the lookout."

So they'd sneak out at night to stargaze. Merwan ravished the stars with eyes like fathomless pools of love to be drowned in. When Baily would ask what he saw in the sky, Merwan might say, "Oh, I saw the court of Emperor Jamshed, and oh, a peacock's throne." Once he said, "I saw the formlessness of God in form!" Then he'd laugh just to annoy Baily.

On summer vacations in their early teens, Merwan and Jamshed would spend a week in the countryside outside Poona. Merwan loved hiking the woods and hills, so they'd stay where Jamshed was raised till age 5 at their uncle and aunt's who ran a restaurant in Lonavla.

Two Saints Seek out Merwan

It was noticed each time Merwan visited, 2 spiritually advanced men suddenly appeared at the restaurant. One was a God-intoxicated soul known as 'Mast-Allah.' The other was a more advanced saint known as 'Wali-Allah.' The ragged-looking mast [pronounced must, meaning God-intoxicated] would sit outside, while the neatly-dressed wali [saint] would enter. [11]

These advanced souls living outside town were venerated by the local residents. Seldom venturing from their places, as soon as Merwan arrived, both would suddenly appear at the restaurant and remain there morning till night.

People would offer them tea or food, but they'd accept nothing – only from Merwan. So he usually gave the wali tea and the mast a loaf of bread. On the day Merwan would leave to go back home, both these spiritual personalities would just as suddenly stop coming to the restaurant, much to the puzzlement of the local townsfolk. 133–34

One Father – Different Children

As a youth, Merwan never favored any particular religion, caste or creed; something characterizing his future life as the Avatar of our age. He advised his friends, "All are from one God. Never criticize other religions. We should respect them as our own – one soul, one father with different children, different natures different bodies. Others' religions – why   speak ill of them? All religions are good; only we are bad." 197

These lines from an early poem of Merwan's show his understanding and purity of religious thought even as a teenager, something he surely imbibed from his father, Sheriar. In later life he'd say:

> "God is at the center of a circle whose circumference is the universe. The radii to the center are the various religions. The points near the circumference are distinctly and widely apart from each other; but as they approach the center, they come closer to each other. In the same way, as a person becomes spiritually minded and advances towards God, the more tolerant he becomes and the less differences he sees." ST 91

Here we jump decades ahead to 1962 when over 5000 people came from around the globe to be with the Avatar at his historic East-West Gathering in India. Meher Baba spoke to them, referencing the religious wars rampant in the world:

CHRIST COME AGAIN

I have come to remind all people they should live on earth as children of the one Father, until my Grace awakens them to the actual realization that they are all one without a second, and all divisions and conflicts and hatreds are but a shadow-play of their own ignorance.

Although all are my children, they ignore the simplicity and beauty of this Truth by indulging in hatreds, conflicts and wars dividing them in enmity, instead of living as one family in their Father's house. Even amongst you, who love me and accept me for what I am, there is sometimes a total lack of understanding of one another's hearts.

Patiently I've suffered these things in silence for all my children. But it's now time they become aware of their Father's presence in their midst and their responsibility towards him and themselves. I'll break my Silence and with my Word of words arouse my children to realize in their lives the indivisible Existence which is GOD. Over years I've given many messages and discourses.

Today I simply want to tell you gathered here in my love to shut the ears of your minds and open the ears of your hearts to hear my Word when I utter it. Seek not my Blessing; it is always with you. But long for the day when my Grace will descend on all who love me. Most blessed are they who long not for my Grace, but simply seek my will . . . . The great Persian poet and Perfect Master, Hafiz, said: "For ages, lovers of God longingly wait for What but one in 100,000 achieves." 4863–64

Attending a Jesuit High School

Merwan now began attending a Catholic high school – St. Vincent's, named after the French St. Vincent DePaul, known for his love and dedication to the poor. It was considered the best school

CHRIST COME AGAIN

in Poona and was run by Jesuit missionary priests, a few foreigners and some from the local province of Goa with whom I'd interact in 1982.

Merwan was never keen on science or geography, and of course his old nemesis, math. But good poetry always charmed him. By 16, he had read most of Shakespeare and the major English, Indian and Persian poets. He was top of his class in Persian, and especially loved its poetry and literature. Sir Walter Scott, Shakespeare, Wordsworth and Shelley were among his favorite English poets. Hafiz was hands-down his favorite Muslim poet.

This God-Realized Perfect Master's Sufi poetry made the boy's heart dance with joy, detaching him from everyday worldliness. St. Vincent's admitted all creeds and mostly boys from the wealthier Poona families. Where before Merwan's playmates had been Persians, his circle expanded to now include Catholics, Hindus, Muslims, Jews and Buddhists.

Religious study wasn't required, but discipline was strict, and getting the rattan was punishment for mischief – raps on the hand with a thin bamboo cane. Merwan took an instant liking to this school and was a favorite with both classmates and teachers. The principal was a German priest, Fr. Wilhelm Windhausen. He couldn't help noticing something extraordinary about Merwan's personality. This stirred some envy in some other students.

The gym coach also gave him special help, building on his already lithe body, natural grace and pure sportsmanship. He wasn't tall or muscular, even slight at 5'6," but extremely agile, excelling in long-distance running and high jumping.

He was playing first string on several school teams with older seniors, and was co-captain of the cricket team. He won several trophies and set many school records which remain unbeaten to this day at St. Vincent's. Besides literature, he had a keen interest in history, which is actually the extended record of all his past Avataric advents.

Of course he was blithely unaware of that. He had a remarkably sharp memory, and never forgot any particular fact about a subject he either heard or read about. Building upon the inner language of the soul his father taught him from childhood, Merwan received an excellent Jesuit education in a multi-religious setting.[12]

In fact, he was considered so intelligent for his age that a couple of teachers wondered if he cheated during exams; well, maybe occasionally in math. But no one grasped that his photographic memory stored every fact and was easy for him to recall during exams.

Convinced he was cheating, a priest once caned him, then later admitted, "There's something different about you, Merwan, something special. Forgive me." "It's all right," the boy replied, "forgiven and forgotten." While at St. Vincent's, Merwan read books on various religions and spirituality. He'd ask Sheriar to read him the works of the mystical poets.

Rumi and Hafiz in their original Persian were his favorites By now he was composing poetry in 4 languages – Urdu, Guajarati, Hindi and Persian. They were invariably on Sufi mystical themes, such as the tavern and wine shop, describing divine madness, intoxication and the soul's endless spiritual longing.

He had a deep passion for the poetry of God-Realized Perfect Masters, and though never reading their works, from Sheriar he could recite them by heart, quoting Hafiz even to the end of his life, as well as the entire Bhagavad Gita and Ramayana, even though again he had only "heard" and not read them. He also knew songs of the Hindu Perfect Masters Tukaram and Ramdas by heart. He never liked shallow novels or romantic love stories.

But good detective stories always held his interest, like Sherlock Holmes and especially Sexton Blake, published in a monthly British magazine. He even wrote a long fan letter to Blake. Later in life, Nero Wolfe would become his favorite, read to him by his sister Mani on lazy summer afternoons as a relief from his intense inner spiritual work.

During his freshman high school year, one of his short stories was published in the British monthly, The Union Jack. Although only a teenager, he possessed an uncanny deep wisdom. By now he was also composing ghazals – Persian love poems to God. Baily mailed one to Bombay's popular Gujerati newspaper, *The Evening News*.

It was instantly published under Merwan's penname, Huma. Thereafter, without fail every Saturday's issue contained one of Huma's compositions, in Gujerati, Urdu or Persian, "Huma" refers to the mythological Persian bird of paradise, similar to the Egyptian phoenix, a bird with incredible feats of flight – consuming itself in fire every few 100 years, only to rise anew from the ashes – exactly like the Avatar.

The Persians teach great blessings come to a person on whom Huma's shadow falls. It joins male and female natures together in one body, each sharing a wing and a leg. Another Gujerati newspaper, *The Bombay Samachar*, started syndicating his poems as well. When both these papers eventually folded, readers were still clamoring for more of Huma's writings. They'd have been shocked to know he was but a teenager.

One day visiting Bombay and walking by a music store, Baily was surprised hearing some Parsi lads singing one of Merwan's ghazals, Money, Ah, Money! The boys were singing and dancing to the lyrics with such zest that pedestrians were blocking the sidewalk just to take in the show. Merwan was also very drawn to acting and directing, often getting standing ovations for school plays at St. Vincent's and in local YMCA productions. 136–39

When Merwan was 15, Mr. Browne, a famous European astrologer who knew Sheriar, asked if he could predict the boy's future. He'd been very impressed with him for a long time, and now wanted to take a closer look at the boy's astrological chart. Merwan wasn't exactly keen on the idea, but consented on Sheriar's prodding.

Browne was also an adept palmist and wanted to do a palm reading on him before drawing up his chart. Looking at the boy's hand and minutely scanning the palm lines, Browne suddenly appeared very confused. He could usually do this in 10 minutes, but he was so astounded by what he saw he ended up spending an hour consulting various books.

Then he solemnly declared to Sheriar, "In the future, this boy will become the greatest philosopher of our age!" – a prediction having very little effect on either of them. Well, Merwan disliked fortune telling as well as philosophy, and so with passing time, the family forgot all about Browne's predictions. But years later, someone else gave Merwan's details to another noted Indian astrologer. Here are some excerpts from that reading:

> "The Person born under the planetary effect of this chart will be the doer of great and good deeds. He will be industrious and attain fame and glory all over the world . . . . His devotion is profoundly deep and intense, and there will come a day when total renunciation of worldly things will manifest. He will be acclaimed and worshipped as a Great Being.
> "All falling under his gaze will be captivated. The power of his attractive personality is utterly marvelous. This soul will do great work for humanity . . . . He is born to carry out the will and work of God on earth and be the salvation for all who come into his contact." 142

During his last year in high school, Merwan's family moved temporarily to a new neighborhood in Poona. With that change, Merwan wasn't seeing his old friends as often as he liked, so he founded The Cosmopolitan Club with the enthusiasm of a few wealthier St. Vincent's classmates helping to finance things. It had no fixed membership fee, but each contributed what he could from 1-50 rupees a month.

Though some of the club's rules were strict, all were followed willingly. The first was no one should enter after drinking liquor or other intoxicants, and no gambling was allowed. Discussing private family matters, gossiping or making fun of others, talking ill to form low opinions of others, using "swear words" etc. were unacceptable.

Brotherliness with each other and extending all kinds of help to others were encouraged. Card games, dice and chess were also played. Not only philosophical books, but also detective magazines like Sexton Blake and Gujarati or English newspapers like *The Times* were read. On Thursdays there was public speaking. These talks were lots of fun, and Merwan being President also had to speak. His talk was always judged the best.

There was singing on Sundays, and people passing by often stood outside the club listening and appreciating the music. Thus, the Cosmopolitan Club became renowned until Merwan had to drop out to attend Deccan College. Baily Irani's diary, Vol.1, pp. 8-9

The End of an Old Friendship

During their last year together in high school, Baily and Merwan, such close pals all through childhood, had a painful falling-out and finally parted ways. Baily was now over 6' tall and could be very prideful. His arrogant nature sometimes caused serious differences between them. As a result, in chagrin Baily ended up moving out of town.

He went to work at a grocery store in Lonavla where Merwan and brother Jamshed often spent summer vacations an hour away from home. Such close buddies from childhood, it would be over a year and a half before they set eyes on each other again.

Lord Buddha Returns

With Baily gone, another teen named Ramnath who lived close to Merwan, became very attracted to him. He wouldn't go even a day without seeing his new friend. He was an orphan from north India and a happy, good-natured lad, cared for by his older brother. Just to see him daily, Ramnath joined the Cosmopolitan Club, and a close friendship formed between them. Ramnath was a devout Buddhist and well read in other religions.

He always repeated Buddha's name and tried to follow Lord Buddha's precepts. Becoming loyal companions, the boys most likely had past-life connections. At night they liked going off to secluded spots, like the Hindu cremation grounds.

Here they'd sit, repeating different names of God, sometimes as late as 10 o'clock, exchanging views on God and spirituality. Ramnath disliked worldly subjects which he found difficult to deal with and lived only for these times with Merwan.

One day, he showed Merwan a new book he'd just gotten on the life the Buddha. Going through the pages, Merwan came to a passage where Buddha says: "When I return to earth, I will be called Maitreya – the Compassionate One." Merwan was thunderstruck.

He felt he was that very same Compassionate One referred to in this passage! Looking at Buddha's picture, he felt deeply within, "I am Buddha!" Again he asked, "Am I really the Buddha?" An inner voice again assured him, "Yes, Merwan, you are!" 3479

Then one night while they were watching burning corpses at the cremation grounds, Merwan suggested, "Ramnath, you're so interested in Buddha, why not go to that great Buddhist center in Rangoon where you can learn so much more." Taking his friend's advice to heart, the boy soon bravely traveled alone all the way to Rangoon, Burma, though he was only 16. But while there, he fell critically ill and barely made it back to Poona.

He was admitted to Sassoon Hospital where Merwan had been born and where he now visited Ramnath daily. The boy said, "I only came back to Poona to see you, Merwan." A few days later, the lad left this world with his head in his dearest friend's lap. 142–46

After graduating with honors from St. Vincent's at age 17 in 1911, Merwan began freshman year at Deccan College across the river from home. He biked across the river to class each day and also rowed on it many an evening with classmates from the rowing club. He continued playing cricket and even formed a college drama group. MM 1: 56

They gave a few performances at a local theater with proceeds going to charity. At this time Merwan was well-dressed and particular that his clothes be spotless and ironed. How that would soon change.

Then one fine morning during Merwan's freshman year at Deccan College, some classmates had come to Lonavla on an outing. Needing picnic supplies, they stopped by the store where Baily was working. Their teacher at St. Vincent's, Mr. David, recognized Baily and urged him to join them for the picnic. Having to work, Baily declined, but his ears picked up when someone mentioned Merwan's name. He asked how Merwan was doing.

They said fine and in fact he was right there in town visiting his brother Jamshed who was working in their aunt and uncle's restaurant. Still having karma with Baily and not wanting to deal with their painful parting, Merwan hadn't sought him out.

When someone mentioned his old friend would be joining the party, Baily quickly changed his mind, saying after the store closed he'd definitely try to join them. Just at that moment Merwan appeared with the rest of the party outside the store. Baily wanted to go out and ask Merwan's forgiveness, but hesitated, feeling embarrassed in front of the others.

Through the store window, they both caught sight of each other, and with raised eyebrows smiled nodding glances. Now, there was one in the group who knew them both and of their painful parting. So later that evening the lad addressed the group.

He asked their respected teacher to use his influence. "Let's bring together old friends who have parted company." Everyone, including Mr. David, was in the dark as to who these fellows were, and asked for their names. Baily felt embarrassed and confused.

But then after a close look at both boys, Mr. David sized up the situation and said, "Well now, I don't think Merwan needs to be swayed by my influence . . . but I suggest both might exchange a glass of beer to renew their friendship and add to our happiness!" Merwan stood, and with a beaming smile offered his old friend a glass of beer.

Deeply feeling Merwan's gesture, Baily accepted. All cheered as the reunited friends embraced. Baily then quickly moved back to Poona to resume their close friendship, as the only reason he left was the unbearable pain of strained relations with Merwan.

Then one day in 1912 while sitting in the lane by his house, suddenly Merwan's inner sight opened. He clearly saw the divine effulgence of God. Immediately losing all bodily consciousness, he had a far deeper experience of what he'd received only a glimpse of back in primary school. His eyelids remained open, but he was utterly merged in divine bliss.

Aunt Dowla, visiting Shireen from Lonavla that day, walked by and noticed Merwan sitting in an awkward position. When she called out to him and there was no reply, she went and told Shireen. Running out and shaking him, she called out, "Merog! Merog!" His eyes just flickered as he mumbled, "Oh Memo, please . . . don't bother me just now."

CHRIST COME AGAIN

He was stunned for a minute before getting to his feet. Shireen thought he must have had a dizzy spell. After this experience of the Noor – the light of God – Merwan increasingly felt he really was different from other men; a feeling that persisted, though he still had no awareness of his true spiritual identity. 149–51

CHRIST COME AGAIN

Unveiling of Merwan's Divine Consciousness

Meanwhile, time was fast approaching for the 5 Perfect Masters to take over the reins in Merwan's life and precipitate his unveiling. As John the Baptist unveiled Jesus at the Jordan, so would Merwan be, later saying John was not only a wondrous God-Realized being and the Master of Jesus, but also put his neck on the block and gave his life for him. 3596

The world has no idea of the 5 Masters' infinite love for Merwan. Veiling him for 19 years, they had watched over and protected him until the exact moment for his unveiling. These 5 divine ones, whoever they are in each Avataric Age, are the instruments bringing God to earth while gloriously unveiling His Infinite Consciousness.

The narrative interrupts here to explain more about the Perfect Masters, five of whom are always present and embodied on earth, and all of whom we will soon meet:

> The Five Perfect Masters made me take this human form to bear the Cross and undergo humiliation . . . . They are the five "greatest thieves in the world," stealing people's hearts. Periodically, they steal me from my highest state, for of my own accord I'd never come. 4168
>
> The Perfect Master becomes the center of the universe as the only absolute, changeless point around which the illusory universe constantly turns like a grinding mill with the Truth-realized Master its central pin. None can escape the repetitious, eternal crushing of this grinding mill, except those blessed grains which adhere to the central pin. A Perfect Master's redeeming act is a flash of the Eternal in what otherwise is nothing but rigidly determined causation. LB 21–22

The key to the world is only one, but it is in the hands of the 5 Perfect Masters. A safe has only one key and no other key can unlock it. The 5 Perfect Masters control the safe – the world. One Master is keeper of the key, without which the safe cannot be opened. The 2nd guards the safe, which cannot be opened without his prior consent. The 3rd is the one who alone has authority to insert the key to unlock the safe. The 4th has the right to distribute the riches of the safe.

Only the 5th Master has power to authorize that distribution. Thus, one key is equally shared by the 5 Masters. They, plus 51 other participating God-Realized souls share control of the key. These 51 are members of the 5 Perfect Masters' parliament. 51+ 5 equal 56 – a number that never changes [56 God-Realized Beings on earth at all times, and 57 when the Avatar incarnates LBE 217]. And so the game of the universe goes on and on. All this I'm telling you up until now has been kept a secret.673

The number 56 denotes perfection. The universe must be maintained, and to carry out its affairs in an orderly manner 56 God-Realized persons are required, as the view of one eye is limited. This infinity of illusion requires the 56 people for the universe's orderly management.

The 56 God-Realized human beings always on earth are completely unknown to the world at large. Only those who come back down [to regain awareness of gross illusion] for duty to the universe after God-Realization and become Perfect Masters fully understand and realize the workings of the world and the mind [the entire past record of all creation]. 780

It is these 5 duty-bound ones who constitute the earth's true spiritual hierarchy. They can interfere in the natural laws of creation's workings, but rarely do so, while the Avatar can change the divine plan by merely the breath of a wish.

What is God-Realization? It is becoming one with God. Union is possible only after the death of thoughts and imagination – false mind must die – literally and absolutely. How does one know he's realized God? It's automatic. You're human. Do you ever think to ask yourself, "Am I a human?" You don't, because you are a human being. In the same way, once realizing God, a man has full spontaneous awareness he is God by direct personal experience. 1061

I'll tell you another important thing you must each remember well. It's a fact that I am Lord of the Universe . . . . The universe has come out of me and has to come unto me. This is not idle talk. I say it with the authority of the experience of my being the Ancient One . . . . And as such, I am Omni-Present. Only the Avatar, living amidst mankind has to undergo such humiliation.

When there are 5 Perfect Masters, God Personified who control and look after the affairs of the universe, what need is there for them to precipitate the incarnation of God on earth? They bring Him down specifically to shoulder the sufferings of humanity. 4168

The Avatar's action on the gross plane is like throwing the main switch of a powerhouse simultaneously releasing great electrical forces into many channels, propelling countless factories, trains and trolleys and instantly lighting up millions of light bulbs in towns and villages. 4513

From beginning to end the whole universe is a materialization of the Original Divine Whim,   working irrevocably without default, deflection or defeat, unfolding on the screen of consciousness as each sequence of the film of creation and in the pattern of the very first Original Whim.

However, when God as the God-Man plays the role of the Audience, He can alter or erase at whim any happening destined from that Original Whim. For even the very arising of the Avataric whim was inherent in the Original Whim.

The Avatar or Perfect Master's actions are impulsive and arise from their infinite compassion. The functioning of this whim relieves and gives beauty and charm to what would otherwise be totally rigid determinism. A Perfect Master's action can only modify a previously determined Divine Plan in a limited way. But the Avatar can cause modifications on a universal scale.

Suppose it's divinely ordained war will occur in 1950. It must take place, and the train of events will punctually meet at that precise time. But the Avatar can ward off the catastrophe by some gross-plane action. And so, in the relentless working out of Natural laws there can enter an unseen divine caprice, spelling out peace instead of war in man's diary. Do you get it? EN 106 –07

It is said that only after cycles and cycles does one become God-Realized. Then very few regain normal consciousness. But One who does regain it has Sahaj Samadhi – natural, spontaneous, simultaneous full consciousness of one's Divinity, and at the same time of the false universe, but only as an actor. Being one with God, he is even on an ant's level, functioning simultaneously in the gross, subtle and mental worlds. He is also above everything. Sahaj samadhi is effortless oneness – as simple as moving the hands or blinking the eyes. 3582

There are 5 such Perfect Actor-Masters on earth at all times. One among the 5 has the responsibility of being the Qutub – a Persian term for the center or pivot-hub connecting all the spokes of a wheel. The Qutub is the head of the Perfect Masters who act together directing all the affairs of the universe, including natural and un-natural disasters.

They are the spiritual surgeons attending humanity's critical illness of "divine amnesia." When one of the 5 dies, a saint of the 6th plane is raised to the 7th plane of God-Realization, thus completing the circle of the permanent 5.

In the sweep of time, as the gridlock of impressions threatens to bring spiritual development to a standstill, the cry of mankind reaches God. This "divine love call" of the 5 Perfect Masters operating especially in messianic times precipitates the Avatar's descent. They bring down the Ancient One as the Son descends from the heaven of the Father.

His Perfection is later unveiled at the time of his maturity to take up his mission in the world. That unveiling was fast approaching for Merwan. As givers of light, Perfect Masters also give thoughts. They not only predict things, but can tell what will happen years into the future before it is even created in the mind of an individual.

They are one with the universal mind which gives everything. They not only predict, but predestine by the Perfect Masters' will wish or will. With a burning desire to know and see God, after countless lives that final experience descends upon them. 1124–25

As the nature of Light is to transform darkness unto Itself, the Perfect Masters have incomprehensible power to bring God as the Christ/Avatar to earth in human form. One among the 5 God-Realized Masters on earth is almost always female. For the needs of his Universal work, and particularly in this age for raising the role of women in society, a female Master was chosen as the first to unveil Meher Baba in this advent.

Her name was Babajan, meaning one with God. "Father Jan" was an aged Muslim woman whose sole purpose in coming to India from Baluchistan in north-west India between present-day Pakistan and Afghanistan was to unveil and awaken Meher Baba to his original Divine Consciousness. In a former incarnation Babajan had been the 8th century Muslim Saint, Rabia of Basra [Iraq], a woman saint of exceptional beauty and grace. 5043

Chapter Six

The Kiss of Infinite Radiant Light

In her younger years, Babajan's beauty was likened to the face of a rose. Her parents tried to arrange her marriage. "You want me to marry a man of your choice according to the ancient way? Rather run away and be buried alive is what I say" And that's exactly what she did, finally attaining God-Realization as well as the state of a Perfect Master at the age of 65 and a senior member in the spiritual hierarchy.

Following the inner star of the Avatar's birth from her native Afghanistan, in 1905 when Merwan was 11 years old, she settled 4 blocks from his neighborhood, taking her "seat" under a neem tree on Malcolm Tank Road. It was a slum area of Poona that could only be described as dirty, desolate and ugly – full of pestilence, vagabonds and thieves who deemed it an honor that she chose to associate with them.

Marvelous changes took place some years later when buildings were constructed. Teashops and restaurants appeared and electricity was provided. Due to Babajan's seat under the neem tree, Char Bawdi was transformed to a charming area to live and raise a family. 8–10

Here she devised a primitive shelter with a few sticks and burlap bags, remaining there conscious God in all seasons – monsoon rains and scorching Indian summers. Her presence was so magnetic no passerby could resist turning his head for a 2nd glance. She was short, wiry and had the agile gait of a youth.

Her skin was fair and sunburned against white, unkempt hair hanging loosely to her shoulders. Her voice was deep and sonorous and her eyes fathomless pools of liquid-blue light emanating her divine state. The love coming from her was so great people could hardly bear to leave her presence. "The earth was her bed, the sky and a tree her roof and her food whatever the earth through loving householders' hands gave her." SG 20

She slept little, and even that was merely a withdrawal to the inner plane of super-consciousness. Babajan addressed everyone, young, old, man or woman, as "child" or "baba." If anyone called her "Mai"– Mother – she would flare and rebuke them:

"I am a man, not a woman." As women are considered the weaker sex, she'd state God-realization is not for weaklings. There's a curious passage from the gnostic Gospel of St. Thomas, verse 114, which baffles most readers. It purports to shed light on the middle-eastern and early church's disparaging position regarding women:

> "Simon Peter said to them: Let Mary [Magdalene] go forth from among us, for women are not worthy of the life. Jesus then said: Behold, I shall lead her that I may make her male, so she also may become a living spirit like you males. For every woman who makes herself male shall enter the kingdom of heaven."

Now what exactly is Jesus pointing to here? Peter understands male biologically, while Jesus refers to maleness in the spiritual sense as so often used in the East. Besides reflecting Jesus' meaning, this strange declaration of Babajan was also faithful to the words of Prophet Muhammad describing a real man: "A lover of the world is a woman, a lover of Paradise is a eunuch, and a lover of God is a man."

The Beloved of the Father is the Son, as the Father is the Son's Beloved. All Sons of God are equal to the Father. People got around it by affectionately calling Babajan "Amma Saheb," – Mother/Sir. And thus she transcended traditional notions of "female" and had become a Man-God. Meher Baba referred to her as the Emperor.

She hardly ever ate, subsisting on frequent servings of strong, black Indian tea. Countless miracles and healings were attributed to Babajan. Her life is full of stories of great love and compassion for countless human derelicts crossing her path in that sultry area. Even people in distant places felt her miraculous powers in their lives.

Once as she lay sleeping, someone tried to steal a costly shawl, part of which was caught under her body. The thief had trouble removing it without waking her. Not opening her eyes, Babajan raised herself just a little to help the man achieve his purpose.

Another time, a wealthy devotee placed 2 solid gold bangles on her wrists. A thief, awaiting his opportunity, roughly snatched them off, deeply lacerating her wrists. Seeing this happen, nearby followers cried out and prevented the thief's escape.

When local police brought the culprit, much to everyone's dismay, Babajan ignored the thief and called upon the police to arrest his accusers. They were the ones disturbing her! For with such seemingly unorthodox ruses she was drawing these thieves and derelicts to herself and the spiritual path without their ever realizing it. Av 40–41; 12–13

She waited here 7 years for her beloved Son to pass by, not moving from that spot in all seasons to fulfill her spiritual duty to him on the day of destiny. Through this ancient woman and God-Realized Perfect Master Merwan Irani would come to experience himself as the very incarnation of God, who's promised return the world had been longing for over 14 centuries since the time of Avatar Muhammad.

Drowned in the Ocean of Bliss

Hazrat Babajan, Meher Baba's first Master, leaning against her neem tree under which she gave Merwan God Realization in 1913.

That day finally arrived when Babajan was 108 and Merwan was 19. Walking or bike riding, he'd pass the old woman's seat without paying her any attention, though he was aware she was regarded as a saint by local Muslims.

The Pathan soldiers guarding her were fiercely forbidding, and idle beggars living off money given her by devotees were a sorry lot. Passing strangers might consider Babajan totally mad or worse – a sorceress-witch. No, Merwan would hardly tarry there.

Then one May morning in 1913 as he rode past her on his accustomed short-cut to college through this rough neighborhood their eyes strangely locked as she pointed at him to approach. Gazing at her, he paused for an uncertain moment. Then he got off his bike and started walking toward her, drawn like steel to a magnet.

As she stood with arms spread wide and a glorious smile borne of years of anticipation, she embraced him with the fervor of a mother finding a beloved lost son. Tears streamed down her wrinkled, sunburned cheeks as she repeated all the while, "Mera piarra beta. Mera piarra beta! Oh my beloved son! My beloved son!"

He stood speechless and dazzled. As electric currents passed through his body, his individual consciousness was merging ecstatically in the Ocean of bliss. Though thoroughly dazed by the experience, he maintained enough awareness of his gross world environment to turn around and go home; no classes that day

With his previous year's experience of the Noor – the effulgence of God – and now this far deeper experience, his body was gradually being re-wired to withstand the ultimate shock to come some months later. For the most part he appeared outwardly normal, but inwardly he was deeply and profoundly affected and pretty much lost interest in everything else around him except for Babajan.

With this inner absorption he began neglecting family, friends, sports and college studies. He would spent evenings for the next 7 months in Babajan's company, seldom speaking and mostly sitting in silence with her until late night.

Life seemed empty except for her. He ignored people's slanderous remarks and head-wagging. "That Merwan was such a nice boy, the son of respectable religious parents. What a sin visiting the haunt of that old witch!" Still, he'd not miss a night's visit.

The Kiss of Infinite Radiant Light

Then on the final night in January 1914, 8 months after meeting her and a month shy of his 20th birthday, Merwan was about to take his leave at about 4 AM. As he kissed Babajan's hands, she held his face between them for a moment. Looking deeply into his eyes, with all the love in her Sacred Heart she placed a single kiss between his eyebrows.

As she initiated the unveiling of his eternal state, in a flash he began losing consciousness of the illusory gross universe. The old Merwan was passing away. Addressing her followers, she pointed her little finger at the dazed youth and declared:

"This is my beloved son. One day he will shake the world, and all of humanity will be benefited by him." Merwan just stood there, for as soon as Babajan kissed him, he became totally insensible, losing grip on a mind that was literally dissolving. It all happened beneath that same neem tree where Babajan had sat waiting for him for 8 years, so reminiscent of Buddha's Realization by an old woman beneath a similar neem tree.

No one knows how Merwan managed to get home, but he went up to his cramped attic room and lay on his bed. Within minutes the lifting of the veil accelerated. He re-experienced the same feelings after Babajan's embrace in May, but intensified a 1000-fold.

His breath suddenly became stifled as if countless hands were strangling him by the throat. Unable to breathe, he panicked, overwhelmed by the forces of some tremendous power. It was as if his heart had finally stopped as he entered the first part of the 7th plane, the vacuum state of nirvan, a state blacker than any black one could ever imagine.

His false mind was undergoing the process of total disintegration and annihilation in Manonash. In this vacuum state, Merwan knew not where he was, nor could he feel his body as his individual false drop-soul identity was being torn away.

Maintaining his individuality, he was passing beyond it and becoming Universal. One cannot imagine the utter terror of crossing this state beyond individuality and becoming that which exists eternally since time immemorial. He had entered the Beyond. His mind now became soundless – pure heart without thinking. 151–54

"To understand Merwan's frightened state, take the fear of a man who doesn't know how to swim forcibly held under water. He starts to suffocate and drown, experiencing fear; or consider the terror of one being violently murdered by strangulation.

"Even compared to this fear there was a vast difference in the terror Merwan experienced that night beyond mere human intellect. It had to do with the vacuum state of Nirvan, the Fana-Fillah state of self-annihilation, and the rising of spiritual consciousness latent in each soul's Infinite Unconsciousness." He later described this vacuum state a moment prior to his Realization: Printed Lord Meher p.199 Footnote: www.lordmeher.org/v1/index.jsp

In Sufism, 'fana' means "passing away." [ED: or 'absorbtion'] Before fana, you have consciousness of yourself, of mind, energy and body. Fana has 2 states. The first is absolute vacuum, where the mind, body, energy, universes, even "I" vanish – nothing is there except pure Consciousness. But the very next moment, the vacuum state is followed by the 2nd state of fana, where mind and body do not come back, even if they seem to be there, but the "I" of the I-Am-God state remains. This is the goal.

Few come back down from this state to normal human consciousness – the state of baqa; that is, abiding in God. In that state the Life of God is lived. In baqa, mind comes back as Universal mind, energy comes back as Infinite Power, and body comes back as the Universal Body which remains as it has to be on the level of every human consciousness – gross, subtle and mental. 3501

To gain God, we must lose Him. Suppose I am God; then I must first lose myself to be able to find Myself. Complete loss of God means wants and desires are not there, likes nor dislikes; you are not there, God is not there; in short, nothing is there [only pure consciousness].

This is Real "fana," following the Divine Vacuum state of Manonash. At that very moment, God comes into His own full glory of everlasting "baqa" [abiding]. This is not by the Western concept of Realization of "this inside" or "that outside," but is discovery of God, for God and by God PL 45

Immediately after passing through the black vacuum state, suddenly like a lightning bolt came the light of the 2nd and final part of the 7th plane – fana. Here Merwan felt as if millions of watts of electric current were speeding through his body, dissolving his flesh and bones. With body and mind vanishing, he was now made of electricity, his veins and arteries transformed into surging currents.

His body became the Divine Effulgence of Infinite Radiant Light, before which the sun is but a mere shadow in an infinite dazzling ocean. Babajan's kiss gave him the final answer to the original question, "Who am I?" The Infinite Consciousness of God alone was his only experience. With that one kiss from Babajan, the veil the 5 Perfect Masters had drawn over him at birth was now torn away.

With the "old Merwan" gone, he found himself to be the Infinite Self. He had gone beyond the creation point, drowned and absorbed in the Oceanic Infinitude of God, beyond all creation. He was no longer humanly-conscious; he had lost his awareness of time, space, his body, mind and the false illusory universe. 154

Restoring his normal consciousness would be an agonizing 7-year journey. But for now, Merwan had only the conscious experience of I Am God – An-al-Haq. Nothing else existed. All his divine experiences of unspeakable ecstasy and bliss were totally internal.

As unearthly silence pervaded his low-ceiling attic room, not a sound was heard from him. No one in the family had an inkling of what happened to him during the final hours of that night. He continues to describe the experience of God-Realization:

Man realizing God is like a drop of water swallowing the Ocean – no less! This is beyond your intellect. After the kiss from Babajan, I experienced I was the Ocean. I didn't want to come back to the ordinary "drop" consciousness from that blissful state where I alone was. But despite my resistance, the 5 Perfect Masters kept "pulling me down" to ordinary consciousness for my destined manifestation as the Avatar. 4909

That Bliss is something quite distinct from happiness and misery which are gained through experiences of the mind. Bliss is something totally different. After the death of the mind, what the soul gains through God is Bliss, while happiness and misery are due to the [false] mind.

While Bliss exists on account of the soul, it cannot be described nor grasped. It must be experienced. 1060 It is continuous, changeless, eternal and divine, having in it power, love, knowledge and infinite wisdom. When attained, it gives one everlasting existence in and as God. 3114

Meanwhile, thinking it odd he wasn't up before everyone else as usual or maybe he had gone out early, Shireen asked, "Where's Merog? Did he go out already?" No one knew. "Maybe he went back up to his room." She called, "Merog, come on, get up. Breakfast is ready; time to get going." Silence. She climbed the narrow ladder to his tiny attic room and stood by his bed, stunned to find him lying there staring outward.

His lips and eyes were motionless. He appeared alive, but his expression startled her – staring somewhere into a distance far, far beyond. "Merog! Can you see me? My darling what happened to you?" He was gone, gone, gone. Climbing back down the ladder, Shireen confided to Sheriar, "He must be terribly upset over something. He's so withdrawn he won't even talk to me. Well, maybe staying in bed all day he'll be okay by evening." What to say?

Sheriar just nodded in agreement. No matter what they did, he remained in this coma-like state for 3 days. All in the family were alarmed. A brother later found his bike down by Babajan's tree. On the 4th day, Merwan began moving about, just slightly conscious of his environment. Going downstairs, without a word he'd pace back and forth, back and forth.

His eyes hadn't closed over those days; his handsome face was vacant and hollow. It didn't seem like he was even there – no appetite or thirst, no food, drink or sleep. In the beginning, his actions were automatic without premeditation.

By the end of the 4th day he was pacing back and forth robotically. Once begun, actions continued until someone intervened, finally unable to stand it any longer and forcibly sat him down. Their beautiful household had not only lost their favorite son and brother, but now in his stead was a madman – or so they grimly thought. Only bit by bit would his gross consciousness return. He later tried to describe those days: 154–56

"With open eyes I'd just lie there gazing around. My parents felt so distressed. My mother at the beginning took me to be totally mad. Then doctor Bharucha was called to give me morphine injections. But no amount of drugging or injections could put me to sleep." Sleep is required by the limited mind, something Merwan no longer needed nor possessed.

Other physicians were called in as Shireen thought his brain had somehow been disturbed. She prayed the doctors could re-establish his "peace of mind." As nothing worked, she became more frantic, superstitiously concluding some "evil eye or witch's spell" was responsible for her son's condition. Well, wasn't his bike found down by that witch's tree?

Shireen prepared good meals for him, but they were far too heavy to process in his exalted state. So he hid the food in his drawer and later at night went out and fed hungry street dogs. Incredibly, for the next 9 months he neither slept nor ate even a morsel, subsisting occasionally on weak tea. Then one day, Shireen hatched a plan. 1244-45

The small "Bhopla" or Pumpkin House, named after the pumpkin-shaped stone at its entryway. While regaining normal consciousness Merwan often secluded himself upstairs in a totally dark, tiny attic cubicle called "The Thief's Den." This photo is taken directly across the lane from the present home where the family would begin living in 1919, four years after Merwan's Realization, and where he would begin banging his head on a stone in his L-shaped bedroom.

Confronting Babajan

With her mother Golendoon she'd go and confront Babajan – two against one. They walked the few blocks, but crowds were always milling around the old woman's seat, and one was subject to lots of pushing and jostling just trying to approach her. This hardly deterred Shireen. Forcefully pushing through the crowd, she confronted Babajan.

"I know Merwan visits you frequently. What have you to do with my son? What have you done to him? Why does he visit you? He never acted like this before." The ancient woman closed her eyes and simply murmured, "Oh my son, my beloved son."

Shireen flew at her, "The nerve of you! He's not your son, he's my son!" Then Babajan accusingly raised her voice, "Oh? And from where did you bring him? From where did he come? He belongs to the whole world, not to you! One day with his finger he'll move the whole world!" Again she quietly repeated, "Oh, my beloved son."

Then Golendoon and Babajan started reminiscing and swapping stories of the old days back in Persia, laughing and crying together like old friends and singing all the old songs. Seeing the hopelessness of getting a straight answer, Shireen went home feeling even more frustrated. Why was God doing this to her? 156–57,248

Remaining in a super-conscious state for 9 months, mostly oblivious to normal earthly life, Merwan's awareness of the illusory gross world only slowly began increasing, while he maintained absolute, effortless awareness of his infinite, eternal divine state.

The Agony of Coming Down

It is startling to realize this "down-coming process," never before documented or revealed in the slightest detail, is the same for all Avatars and Prefect Masters. Though the Gospels never refer to it, this was the exact path Jesus had to pass through in coming-down before taking up his public life as the Christ/Avatar of His age.

After Realization, it took 7 years for Merwan to become Perfect, meaning divine and normal gross consciousness fully integrated after what is termed "coming back down" to normalcy. Only from that period on is he able to begin fulfilling his divine mission on earth.

Coming back down is a process of slowly becoming fully conscious of immediate surroundings and being able to effect changes in the entire fabric of creation. In Merwan's case, this meant assuming his role as the Avatar of the Age in the effortless state of Sahaj Samadhi – Divine awareness with simultaneous awareness of the illusory false universe.

A year or so following Babajan's unveiling, as he gradually became more able to function in the ordinary world, Merwan began taking a series of foot and train journeys. Without having known of them beforehand, he instinctively began seeking out the other 4 Perfect Masters in India who aided in precipitating his advent. By divine law he now had to come into direct physical contact to receive their further help and gifts.

Even with the love and personal contact of the other Perfect Masters it would take the full 7 years for the divinely dazed Merwan to come back down through the 7 inner planes to normal gross consciousness, all the while maintaining infinite awareness of his divinity.

Narayan Maharaj

In April 1915, 15 months after his Realization, Merwan planned on leading the life of a wandering ascetic for several months. And so he bought a ticket for the town of Raichur, 300 miles south of Poona. But after a few stops, a sudden whim took him off the train at the remote country village of Kedgaon. Instinctively inquiring of the Perfect Master Narayan Maharaj, he was told, "He's at his palace giving darshan. Hurry now and get his blessings!"

There was a large crowd in the palace. Narayan was handsome and majestic though very short at 4'6," and though older, he looked like a cute teen-ager and spoke in a high-pitched voice. Children adored him as he frolicked with them, laughing and jumping about.

While most Perfect Masters live a simple poor life, owning nothing but the clothes on their back, Narayan was a Raja-yoga Master representing the material aspect of the world's abundance. Though totally poor at heart, he was living in the midst of enormous wealth. Surrounded by opulence while being utterly detached from it, he was seated on a solid silver throne in a palace built for him by the king of Nepal.

As Narayan was holding darshan, suddenly a stream of light shone through the crowd. A dazed, ragged young man appeared, divinity pouring from his eyes. Narayan held up his hand stopping the darshan and quietly asked everyone to leave. Placing a flower garland around Merwan's neck, he called for some mango juice which he sipped, giving the rest to Merwan to drink. They talked quietly for awhile but what was spoken no one knows.

Merwan then bowed to Narayan and disappeared out the door. The Master gazed at the youth till he was out of sight. Narayan was so pleased that there was no more darshan that day. His devotees could only shake their heads in wonder, "Who on earth was that strange, ragged youth?" Merwan went home experiencing the

Glory of his Godhood, as with this gift of Narayan's Grace, his light and bliss now began to dazzle others. 24–25, 164–65

The young Hindu Sadguru Narayan Maharaj, Merwan's second Master in 1915 at the time he conferred upon Merwan the glory of his Godhood.

Narayan Maharaj in the early 1940s seated on a silver throne, a gift from the King of Nepal and on which he seated Merwan, conferring on him the glory of his Godhood.

Tajuddin Baba

Merwan's 3rd Master, Tajuddin Baba, was a great Muslim Perfect Master who became God-Realized while serving in the British military. He gave up army life at this point, but was hounded by people wanting purely material windfall-benefits from him for stock market investing and horserace gambling. And so, despairing of a public life, he took matters into his own hands one day at a public British tennis match.

He deliberately paraded naked before players and spectators. Of course, he was immediately arrested and placed in an insane asylum where he was able to live peacefully for 17 years free of greedy people assailing him. Finally, the region's wise governor recognized that far from being crazy, Tajuddin was most spiritually advanced, and took him to live in his protected compound away from public harassment. 29

It is said he performed many miracles, even raising the dead. He was worshipped by Hindus, Muslims, Parsis and Christians, and would breathe his last in 1924 with over 30,000 attending his funeral. A few days after contacting Narayan Maharaj, Merwan was now to approach Tajuddin Baba. He boarded a train north to Nagpur to meet the most renowned living saint in central India.

Mentioning different Masters, Babajan had once remarked about Tajuddin, whom she referred to with great respect as Taj – a Persian word meaning crown of the Kingdom. "Taj is my Khalifa [successor]," she would say. "What Taj gives, he gets from me." 15

The large crowds of devotees were very concerned, as that day Tajuddin was in a particularly fiery, foul-tempered mood, venting his fury on all around him and abusing all who even dared approach.

Qutub and Perfect Master Tajuddin Baba,
Merwan's third Master who gave him his Divine Crown

Merwan was warned: "Look, it's really not a good day to see Tajuddin. The Master is in a very bad mood; so prepare to be severely abused – even a thrashing." Merwan chuckled, "Ah, he's waiting for me! Tajuddin is waiting for me to arrive!"

He quickly cut through the crowd to where the Master was seated. Suddenly, the air was perfumed with the fragrance of roses. To everyone's shock, Tajuddin silenced his abusiveness, stood and started walking forward, limping as if crippled and staggering toward Merwan with roses in his hand. No one knows what silent divine messages they exchanged.

With joy, Tajuddin brushed the roses across Merwan's cheeks and forehead. Not a word was spoken. Then waving the roses in farewell, with profound happiness Tajuddin gazed upon Merwan. As the perfume filled the air he murmured, "My rose . . . my heavenly rose." Before silently slipping away, Merwan murmured, "Taj! Taj! Oh, my Taj! No one knew what this meant, but Merwan had just received his Divine Crown.

Now lately Babajan had been repeating to Merwan: "My son, the treasure you seek and the key to it are not with me! I'm not the one to give it to you. The treasure is for you alone, no doubt about it, the treasure is yours! But you must have the key, my son.

"You must take the key . . . . The treasure is yours to have now. The key is there. Go to Shirdi, my son. There is a Sai, a holy one there . . . Go and see the Sai. See now if he'll give you the key. Take the key from the Sai, for it is yours alone!" 165–67

Sai Baba of Shirdi

In December 1915, soon after Babajan had said this, Merwan complained to his friend Khodu of terrible stomach cramps that just wouldn't go away. Recalling what Babajan had said, Khodu suggested, "If you come with me to Sai Baba maybe your pain will disappear. I've heard he cures all sorts of afflictions. Miracles oc-

CHRIST COME AGAIN

cur every day at Shirdi . . . . C'mon Merwan, what do you say we go see this old holy man!"

Well, neither of them knew where Shirdi was, and at 115 miles it wasn't an easy trip. When they arrived, villagers were lined up with clubs blocking the road. "No, you can't see Sai Baba. No one can see him! He's given strict instructions. No darshan today! Go back home!" Khodu pleaded, "But we've come all the way from Poona. We must see Sai Baba. Please understand." The villagers refused. "We have to obey Baba's order. No one passes."

Now Khodu was tall, muscular and very strong, but no match for all these villagers, sensing they were about to club him. Pointing to a tree, Merwan said, "Let's wait over there. If you're afraid, you can go back, but I will see the Sai!" The next morning after a freezing night under the tree, again they were blocked with the villagers refusing to let them pass.

Then later that afternoon word came: "Baba is calling just you. Go, but be careful; he's still in a very bad mood," they were warned. Sai Baba was 77 with snow-white hair, white beard and dressed in a white gown. Seated in his mosque, he totally ignored Merwan and pointed directly at Khodu, saying sharply, "I want to see that fellow only."

Khodu nervously approached and bowed at Sai Baba's feet, and while he was bowed down, the old fakir suddenly whacked him on the back, knocking the wind out of him. Khodu was stunned. "Who's your friend – what's he want?" "His name is Merwan Irani. He's very devout, Sai, and seeks your darshan. Babajan in Poona told us of you, and ~"

The old fakir's eyes suddenly went aflame. "Oh, no! No, No!" Sai Baba cried, "I won't allow him to see me! He's not to approach!" Then, stretching out his hand and glaring at Khodu, he barked, "Give me all your money – all of it!" Khodu emptied his pockets.

Sai Baba then shouted, "Now get out of here, and tell your friend I won't see him. He's not to come to me!" Shaken, Khodu withdrew and reported to Merwan standing off at a distance. Merwan just smiled. "Let's just wait. I have to see him and I will." 169

Now it's known that Sai Baba was fond of smoking opium, a practice making one notoriously constipated. So later that day feeling a rare urge to move his bowels, Sai Baba was led in a joyful procession to a field in a ceremony called lendi, complete with a brass band playing to celebrate the rare occasion. Everybody was happy.

It is said a Perfect Master or the Avatar when moving his bowels is doing specific work on the gross level for the whole universe. Sai Baba once explained that he contacted his spiritual agents on the inner planes during his lendi ceremony. On the way back, a large crowd followed the Master who was now finally in an excellent mood. 399 Footnote

As the Master passed, Merwan prostrated on the dirt path, stretching full length on the ground in front of his feet. At that moment, in a deep, deep voice, as if rising from the very depths of the ocean, Sai Baba uttered one majestic word; the Muslim name for Lord Vishnu, "PARVARDIGAR!" – meaning "GOD-THE-ALMIGHTY- SUSTAINER!" [13]

Transmitting this holy word, Sai Baba's eyes became lustrous with universes shining from them. He had just conferred upon Merwan the Infinite Power of his Divine State – another major gift of the Perfect Masters. Those around Sai Baba were astonished.

There was a sudden, palpable change in the very atmosphere, as if the sun had smiled on Merwan. Those 2 alone knew the reason. Even decades later, Merwan would remember, "Sai Baba's eyes were matchless. No one had such eyes in the entire world." GG V: 142

Merwan arose from the ground as the old fakir gazed at him. The message he delivered with his eyes Merwan alone could read.

They steadily gazed at each other, and the great word again came out of the old fakir's mouth, "O, PARVARDIGAR!" The holy word sounded from the depths of the old master's Godhood as he then proclaimed a third time, "PARVARDIGAR!" and prostrated himself before the young man. Onlookers were stunned.

Why in God's name was their Master bowing to this straggly, unkempt youth? With the final cry he rose, beckoning Merwan to walk on ahead. He and Khodu slowly backed off. The Age itself had now bowed down to Merwan. O Sai! How can we repay you for what you've done for us? You brought formless Parvardigar into form! 167–70

A rare original photograph of Sai Baba of Shirdi, Merwan's fourth Master.

Sai Baba in his last years when he proclaimed, "O Parvardigar, Almighty-God-Sustainer," conferring upon Merwan the Infinite Power of his Divine State.

CHRIST COME AGAIN

Upasni Maharaj

Instinctively following an inner directive from Sai Baba, Merwan picked up the pace and swiftly walked 3 miles beyond Shirdi to a small temple at Khandoba. Khodu had to run to keep up. Here Merwan's final Master awaited him – Upasni Maharaj – Sai Baba's chief disciple and the 5th God-Realized Perfect Master of the spiritual hierarchy.

Upasni [14] was sitting naked on the temple steps. Tall and wiry thin, he lived for 3 years only on water. As Merwan approached, the Sadguru stood, picked up a stone and threw it with force, striking Merwan's forehead where Babajan had kissed him, bringing him down to gross consciousness and establishing a new Divine Song in everyone and everything – in stones, trees, animals and the very dust of the earth – illumined with divinity.   SG 22

The holy force of throwing that stone drew Merwan's first blood shed for the world as the Ancient One, giving him Infinite Knowledge and the awareness he was the Avatar of the Age – the final gift of the Masters. The stone's impact would leave a lifelong forehead scar to remind the world when the Avatar began regaining consciousness of it.

With this blow Merwan literally began "seeing stars," again seeing more and more of the false gross universe's realm of illusion for the first time in nearly 2 years. Before this, he was divinely absorbed in his Godhood with little awareness of the world around him after Babajan's kiss. Upasni's stone restored ½ of his worldly-awareness.

CHRIST COME AGAIN

Sadguru Upasni Maharaj, never clothed in more than a burlap sack, after seven years would proclaim Merwan "Perfect" – Adi Shakti, the Primal Force, the Ancient One and the Avatar of the Age. Center: Infested with snakes and scorpions, Khandoba Temple 3 miles from Shirdi where Merwan first met his third Master,

CHRIST COME AGAIN

Merwan later recalled, "That was the beginning of my present infinite suffering in illusion which I experience simultaneously with my infinite bliss in reality." Normal false consciousness would increase daily to eventually return completely. But it would take the full 7 years for him to come fully back down to normal human gross-consciousness. Upasni Maharaj would guide his re-entry every step of the treacherous way. LH 247

Immediately on being struck by the stone, Merwan approached Upasni and they embraced. With tears in his eyes, Upasni kissed the bleeding wound on Merwan's forehead. They then disappeared into the dusty, dilapidated temple infested with snakes and scorpions.

Khodu just stood there a distance away, stunned and mystified at what he'd just witnessed. What a bewildering day with Sai Baba's beatings and cries, and now this naked yogi bashing Merwan on the head with a stone. But all Khodu could do now was wait. He dared not interrupt or even go near that forbiddingly strange temple.

Hour after hour passed as he paced up and down outside wondering and fretting. If Merwan were seriously hurt, what the hell would he tell Shireen? He'd faced her wrath before, and knew it could be formidable. As evening fell, Khodu became even more alarmed. Shivering in the cold, he only longed to know what was happening to his friend.

"Is he seriously hurt? Is he still bleeding? What's going on in there?" The atmosphere became more forbidding by the hour. Still, he dared not interfere. The same obsessive thoughts kept plaguing Khodu's tormented mind.

Then after 2 days and nights, Merwan finally emerged from the temple with Upasni at his side. Well, he seemed alright. But that wound was really deep. Now what was he going to tell Shireen? Upasni pointed at Khodu. "Take care of your friend here and make sure he gets back to Poona OK." With all his money gone, Khodu somehow managed to get them back to his house where he and his wife cleaned and bandaged Merwan's wound.

Arriving back at Merwan's home, Khodu made some excuse about his falling and injuring his head. Shireen accepted it, but later banned him from the house, blaming him for what would now become her son's terrible ongoing involvement with Maharaj. 170–71

The Triple Crown

By now, each of the 5 Perfect Masters, Babajan, Narayan Maharaj, Tajuddin Baba, Sai Baba and Upasni Maharaj had provided Merwan with a different piece of the divine puzzle, wrapped in the veil of his humanity – each a different aspect of the "key."

Thus was bestowed his Triple Crown. Bringing him down, Babajan unveiled him with a kiss, and in less than a millionth of a second conferred on Merwan the Crown of Infinite Bliss – the realization He was God. Sai Baba conferred upon him the Crown of Infinite Power, while Upasni Maharaj bestowed the Crown of Infinite Knowledge that he was the Ancient One and the Avatar of the age. Such were the Masters' Infinite gifts.

With this final one, Merwan began his return to full awareness of the illusory gross world. This would enable him to stably function as the Avatar. In Jesus' time "the Magi's 3 gifts" signified these 3 aspects of Divine Consciousness. Years later, Meher Baba would say, "Bliss is God's original state. Power is God's existence, and Knowledge is God's duty." GM 362

CHRIST COME AGAIN

Such was the power and importance of Avatar Meher Baba's Advent that He literally had five Satgurus. From the top, going clockwise: Shirdi Sai Baba, Babajan, Tajuddin Baba, Narayan Maharaj, and Upasani Maharaj.

Babajan's merging Merwan's consciousness in Infinite Bliss began a long journey. His spiritual duty was now to regain full natural consciousness of the illusory gross world – an agonizing sojourn from the bliss of the super-conscious state of Reality back down to full consciousness of the illusory world, while still retaining full awareness of his Infinite state.

This dual-consciousness, fully divine and fully human in Perfect, effortless balance constitutes the state of Perfection – Sahaj Samadhi – of being a Perfect Master, and in Merwan's case the direct Avataric descent of God into illusion. After contacting

Upasni Maharaj, Merwan was repeatedly urged by Babajan on different occasions to "Go back now, my son, and get your full share from that Hindu."

Meanwhile, Upasni had moved from Khandoba's Temple and was now staying in the village of Sakori. Merwan became a regular visitor to Upasni's new abode beside the local cremation grounds, always stopping at Shirdi to spend a few moments with Sai Baba. 188

An Irani family photo, Poona 1914. Left to right standing, brothers Beheram and Jal; seated is Merwan, Uncle Khodadad, Adi, Shireen and Jamshed.

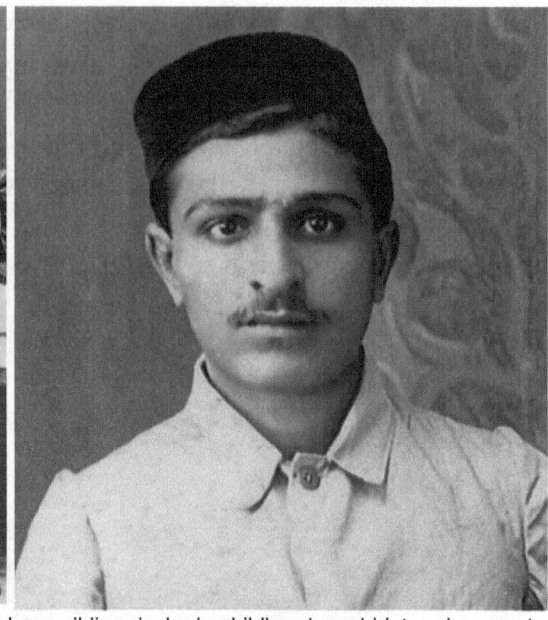

Merwan and Brother Jamshed, whose sibling rivalry in childhood would later give way to intense love and worship of his God-Brother, circa 1916. Right: Detail of previous photo, Merwan at age 22, still dazed three years after his Realization.

The Secret Journeys

While growing up, Merwan was very devoted to his aunt Piroja, Sheriar's kind older sister living just a block away. She enjoyed having Merwan's friends over after school, whereas Shireen didn't. Piroja worried if he skipped even a day stopping by. Going back to Sakori, Merwan couldn't announce his plans at home or there'd be trouble. So he'd quietly inform aunt Piroja. Once, he told his mother he was going to Bombay.

Now he actually did go a couple of times to visit brother Jamshed who was now working there. But Shireen became suspicious and pestered her sister-in-law to tell her where Merwan had really gone. Piroja feigned ignorance. But little brother Jal, the "spy," had followed Merwan to the bus station and saw that he didn't buy a ticket to Bombay but took a bus to some other place. From Jal, Shireen knew full well Merwan wasn't with Jamshed.

She got very upset with Piroja for not telling her where he had really gone. On his return she scolded Merwan bitterly: "Merog, I'm telling you for the umpteenth time – get a job and keep it. Start thinking of your future and earning a living! Start thinking about getting married! Stop wasting your life going here and there to these saints and holy men! Stop it! Do you understand what I'm trying to tell you?"

Unsparing in words, Shireen's constant pestering became a source of affliction for Merwan, as if he didn't have enough to bear. Fed up with her badgering, one day he blithely announced, "Well, guess what? I'm joining the army – off to fight in the war!" Shireen was stunned and panicked, "Oh no you don't! Not you! You're staying right here in Poona."

Well, the ploy worked for a while, and he was left in relative peace to continue his journeys to Maharaj. When not together, Merwan and Upasni wrote letters back and forth. None survived, but they were said to be completely unintelligible to others.

Managing a Theatre Company

Meanwhile, Shireen kept pressing him about getting that job. "Get into some kind of business, Merog, for God sakes!" Now a rich Parsi relative and businessman in Calcutta, well-known in theatrical circles, met Merwan and felt deeply attracted to him. He invited him to stay at his estate, promising to treat him as his own son. Though Merwan refused, the relative kept pestering him to become manager of his theatrical company.

Finally with Shireen's forceful urging, at age 22 he reluctantly accepted work for this travelling theatre company. On tour in Lahore, he wrote his friend Behramji: "I'm forced to do what I don't like, eat what I dislike, and wear clothes – suit, shirt, tie and a fez – which I also dislike. Oh God, what entanglements!"

It was here he began stealing off to solitary places to bang his head on stones just to relieve the agony of re-entry. When the theatre owner died some months later, the company was dissolved. Relieved of this burden, Merwan returned to Poona to resume his visits to Upasni Maharaj in the dicey process of "down-coming. 174–77

Then on December 15th 1918, close to his 25th birthday, a baby sister Manija was born. They called her "Mani" [Mah-ni]. He visited her in Sassoon Hospital, where he too had been born, and was the first to see Mani and bring her gifts. Against protocol, he picked her up and kissed her even before the nurses had bathed her. At home, he'd rock her cradle and sing to her, beaming, "She's so fortunate to be mine." What great past life connections they had. Baba revealed that when he was Krishna, Mani had been his sister Subhadra. RT I: p.7

Merwan, the theatrical manager, 1916

Meanwhile at Sakori, Maharaj gave Merwan his first lifetime disciples, Yeshwant Rao and Gustadji Hansotia. Their sole duty

CHRIST COME AGAIN

was to provide for Merwan's comforts and needs. In winter, seeing Merwan had only light cotton clothes, Yeshwant made him a warm coat of coarse woolen "kamli" blankets. Worn continuously for 8 years from 1921-1928, this coat would become Merwan's most spiritually charged possession in this advent. 3570

Gustadji would work in Merwan's soon to be opened toddy shop. Back and forth from his home to Upasni's, Merwan also stayed for longer periods, still not closing his eyes but pacing up and down and seldom even laying down to rest. Upasni would go to his room calling out, "Come, Merwan, come." They'd sit alone in Maharaj's thatched hut near the village cremation grounds where often till 2 AM Merwan noted down the Master's dictation.

He kept these notes in a wooden box in his room. No one knew what was written. However in reading Maharaj's discourses from time to time published online on the Meher Baba Israel site, I'm struck by how many of Maharaj's themes are echoed in Meher Baba's later teachings and discourses – from Master to disciple. Late one night in 1921 they took a break to sit outside and gaze up into the heavens. 255

They tried counting all the universes, but it was so impossible they both practically fell over! At another time Merwan got into serious trouble attempting this. Were it not for Upasni saving his life, he'd have dropped his body. Years later, Baba explained it:

> In what's called space, numberless universes are constantly created, sustained and destroyed. This procession of creation continues so long as God goes on "Imagining." When God's Imagination is suspended, as it is in Eternity when God withdraws Himself into His Sound Sleep State – as a man's imagination ceases when he is in deepest sleep state – the Creation is withdrawn and dissolves in Mahapralaya [total collapse]. Creation–Preservation–Dissolution are based on Ignorance.

In fact, there's no such thing as "creation," so "preservation" or "dissolution" never actually occur. The very cosmos is founded in the Ignorance it is a reality; that birth, death, old age, wealth and honor are real. Knowledge knows the cosmos is a dream and that God alone is Real. EN 87

One night at Sakori, Upasni and I were sitting in his hut when the topic of counting the universes arose. In trying to count as many universes as possible, Maharaj had to stop the continuous flow of emerging sanskaric chains. To do this, both his mind and the whole force of creation had to be concentrated on stopping the universes. This is difficult and extremely dangerous.

From the Oneness of God, duality is born, and this duality may prove humanly fatal at times. The tension created by such concentration could cause one to drop the body. So when I tried, Maharaj prevented me from stopping the chain-flow. It truly threatened my life. I could have easily died.

Maharaj told me, "No Perfect Master was ever successful in this counting, as the flow of direct knowledge is from the Master himself. If it is stopped to count the universes, there's a reaction in duality and the Master's life is in danger." How was the universe created? It was automatic.

There are so many innumerable universes interlaced with one another; one universe creates another in a chain reaction. These universes are so numerous Sadgurus can't count them, though we both tried. Though the chains [cf. quantum physics string theories] of these universes come out of the Sadguru then merge back into him after eons, they are still uncountable through his physical eyes. 247

This is called Mahapralaya, the total collapse of the universes. When they disappear, they are no longer in gross form, but remain within the Universal Mind. Each individual gross mind then rests in the Universal Mind. Although it's all a magnificent illusion, the individual souls of all beings inhabiting the universes remain within the Universal Mind. Then after eons, evolution reboots.

At this point, each incarnate soul gradually takes form as to the level of consciousness it had before the cosmic event of Mahapralaya. For example, in deepest sleep you're unconscious of both your body and the world. For you, this is individual dissolution or mere pralaya. When you awaken each morning, creation again begins for you. You come back, and the world again exists for you.

But Mahapralaya happens on a universal cosmic scale. It is the same as individual dissolution, except that here all universes dissolve; so it is called Mahapralaya – Maha meaning great. And so this happens every day in an individual's deepest sound sleep state. Then after ages and ages, it happens universally. This is what is meant when it is said in the Koran [and New Testament] "On doomsday, everyone will rise up from his grave." 866–67

In descending back down to creation consciousness, Merwan passed through 5 major stages: (1) God alone exists, (2) the universe functions for him alone, and (3) everything exists because of him; (4) he is everyone and everything, (5) he is responsible to help everyone and everything in the creation. He'd later state: "There is nothing beyond me, nothing without me; yet, I am and can always be captured with love." 2591

As the first God-Realized soul, this is the duty of Adam who inherited responsibility for the entire creation for all time and eternity as the original Avatar – a journey he would make countless times down through the ages as the incarnate Christ/Avatar on earth. Merwan was now descending back down, returning on that ancient journey through consciousness of the 7 inner planes to bring him back to more and more awareness of the false gross world.

This is the purpose of his being and identity – his Avatarhood. In God-consciousness there is nothing pertaining to the universe or consciousness of anything else existing outside of Infinite Self. After recovering normal gross consciousness, the universe which the Avatar or a Perfect Master sees and is in charge of is a mere 7th shadow of God's consciousness.

The Agonizing Journey Back Down Through the Planes

The Five Perfect Masters must train the Avatar to consciously maintain his infinite state while coming back down into awareness of the false gross universe, the world of shadows, without rupturing and dissolving those shadows into Infinite Radiant Light.

Like divine tightrope-walking, it is a harrowingly difficult balancing act to achieve. But it is essential, for it enables him to effect change in the structure and destiny of the world and entire universe, while remaining grounded in his limitless existence as God. Years later, Meher Baba recalled this period: "That was the beginning of my present infinite suffering in illusion, which I experience simultaneously with infinite bliss in reality." LH 249

During each stage in the process of re-entry while coming back down to regain worldly consciousness, Baba began descending through the 7 planes; the fire and light of the 6th plane – seeing and experiencing God outside oneself in everything and everyone, just as Moses experienced in the "burning bush," but not yet able to enter "the Promised Land" of the 7th plane – God Realization. From the 6th plane, Merwan descended to the 5th plane.

Here he simultaneously experienced the individual thoughts of all human beings in the universe pouring into his Universal Mind the instant they were thought. Their devastating effect could only be withstood because his mind had become stably Universal.

Drowning in a Tsunami of Thought Waves

Thought waves vibrate faster than any speed known to man; thus, all thought waves of all humanity on earth would stream into and permeate Merwan's universal mind. At the onset of this stage, he happened to be sitting alone by a water canal near Maharaj's hut.

Within minutes, the force of countless millions of people's thoughts on earth and beyond entered his universal mind. This experience was so agonizing that Merwan felt his mind pulled apart by billions of contradictory thoughts. It was so staggering he had to plunge his head underwater for several minutes just short of drowning to break the shock. 246

> In God-Realization infinite power sustains the physical body. With their Universal Mind and body, the Perfect Ones can approach and contact anyone at anytime, anywhere. Time and space do not exist for them. The infinitely complicated universe is so infinitely simple. 2091
>
> But to know and understand this is infinitely difficult. When you know what Universal Mind, Energy and Body are, and their relation to individual mind, energy and body, you'll understand how the Perfect Master knows everything. Compare the individual mind to a radio station where one hears all stations' broadcasts if tuned to the right frequency.
>
> In this instance, the Perfect Master is the radio connected to every individual broadcasting station, and consequently he hears everything that is broadcast. In my Universal Body are contained the bodies of all the innumerable

beings and things in the entire universal creation. In the same way, the subtle energy body and the mental thought body of each and every individual is also a part of my Universal Energy and Universal Mind, respectively.

The infinite distance between a drop here and a drop there in the same ocean makes absolutely no difference to the drop's relationship with the ocean. Any drop anywhere within the ocean is within the entirety and homogeneity of the ocean. What one individual mind thinks in the ocean of Universal Mind is not known to another individual mind, but the Universal Mind knows it instantly, as all minds are in the Universal Mind and are inseparably one with it.

This all-comprehensive Knowledge comes in a flash, but takes an eternity in illusory time to acquire as you gradually die to your false self. This dying means completely losing your false self in God, and finding your Real Self as God – no easy task. Raising a corpse is far easier. 4643–44

The speed of the revolving universe is so tremendous it's impossible to tell it's even spinning in motion. Look how many people, creatures and inanimate things there are in this world. Every person and thing has a pulse; everyone has 100s of thoughts per minute . . . . Such tremendous speed is incalculable. It looks as if it's at a standstill. The pulse of the whole universe is so infinite. But this pulse I measure, observe and feel. Just think of what that must be like!

It takes not a micro-second to know what the U.S. President thinks or will think tomorrow – or the Prime Minister of England, because the universe has stuck to me – is part and parcel of my being. I know and understand the thoughts of every living being and thing in the universe.

CHRIST COME AGAIN

I've clasped the universe to my bosom so tightly that I feel each heartbeat in creation – even the breathing of a stone. My universal mind is the central station linked to each individual mind. Wherever one may be, I know what he is thinking and doing at every moment. 1003   I also know what you will think tomorrow or after 1000 years, and also know what you thought 1000s of years before. This is real knowledge – infinite, indivisible and totally beyond your imagination. 1354

Then 15 years later on May 31st 1935, Baba indicated: "I can see the creation and dissolution of universes very clearly. I can count them, and even though they are numberless, they are quite clear to me. Only the Avatar and Perfect Masters can see them with their gross eyes; no one else can. People would think it a wondrous sight. But for one who has realized God and experiences eternal bliss every moment, it is nothing." 1678

In 1919, Merwan's family moved from the "Pumpkin" house, so called for the large pumpkin-shaped stone outside its entrance, to a larger home directly across the lane which is still visited by pilgrims today. Coming back down into illusion was such a devastating experience that just to seek some relief Merwan daily banged his forehead against a stone sticking up from the floor of his bedroom in the new house, sometimes for 4 hours at a time.

He did this quietly if others were home. Shireen was puzzled one day to hear a strange, dull thudding. As Merog's door was always closed, she had no idea what went on in there. But on this particular day, she quietly pushed the door ajar just a bit. Peering through the crack, she gasped at what met her eyes and screamed. The family came running.

Merwan's face was covered in blood. "My God, have you gone mad! Are you totally mad?" He cleaned his face off with a towel. "No, I'm not mad. I've become something else."   Sickened,

Shireen turned on Sheriar, "Just look at him! Look at your son! Only a total madman would bang his head on a stone floor? You're all crazy! You men of God are all madmen!" she cried helplessly.

She was devastated over what had happened over the past couple of years, convinced now her Merog was permanently insane – ruined and never to be cured. But Sheriar alone understood. It was the other way around; his son was the only sane one – Divinely sane.

Heartbroken, she cursed Babajan and Maharaj from the depths of her heart for taking her son away and shattering his beautiful life. From then on if Shireen were home, Merwan would steal off alone to some other secluded spot to continue this gruesome practice; if not on stone, then against walls and window frames, often shattering them. 196

The relief this dizzying pain gave him from the mental agony of descent was necessary to keep him grounded in his body, matching his emotional agony with a physical component. He did this regularly until as it were "the shuttle had safely landed."

Merwan with a forehead bandana during his agonizing re-entry into the illusory gross universe, Poona 1919.

He'd wear a bandana to hide his wounds, while relatives casually thought, "Oh, it must be some kind of new fashion trend." Merwan's close friends saw what was going on, but they were a total loss to understand it. He later conveyed: "Much blood flowed onto that stone. It will be worshipped universally in times to come." I reverently touched my head to it in the 1980s before it was later covered with a small glass dome.LJ 34

Shireen now began coaxing her

mother Golandoon to go alone to Babajan. But when Golendoon asked about her grandson, Babajan simply replied, "He's my son, not hers! My Beloved son belongs to the whole world! One day he'll shake it to its very foundations! Why worry about him? He's out of your hands now." Her remarks touched Golendoon heart.

But Shireen was in no way consoled, and finally out of frustration started going to Sakori to boldly confront Upasni Maharaj directly. If she suspected Merwan was on his way there, she'd desperately try to head him off and talk him into coming back home.

Each time Upasni greeted her lovingly, and then with finesse he'd casually shift the conversation until she forgot all about Merwan, only remembering on the train heading back home. "Damn! she'd say, "That old yogi fooled me again!" 248

Servile Labor in Sheriar's Cafe

Returning to Poona from Sakori, Merwan would undertake physical labor to supplement his grounding work with Upasni and prepare for his public life. Regaining normal human consciousness required fulfilling works of pure virtue with deep humility. This helped tremendously to stabilize him on the perilous down-coming journey.

The old teashop, transformed into Sheriar's Café, was now serving inexpensive toddy, a whitish, low alcoholic drink from the sap of toddy palm trees. So now the God-man had a part-time job as a bartender. Besides serving customers, he cleaned toilets, scrubbed floors, washed dirty dishes, cups and glasses – tasks he would do for the next 3 years.

Chapter Seven

A Mother's Agony

Most of Sheriar's Café patrons were poor and crude, the usual unsavory characters in such places. They were illiterate and dressed in shabby clothes. It was a far cry from Sheriar's old tea shop. Though the work was squalid, Merwan showed genuine interest and fully gave his heart to it. 247

Sheriar's Café, early 1920s where Merwan did 3 years of servile labor in the process of coming back down into the illusory gross universe.
Right: Sheriar's Café in 1990.

Despite working each day, he still was not yet fully gross conscious, and this was the goal. He couldn't always keep his mind on the business end of things and was easily cheated by customers. His movements came solely from the divine will acting through him, without him being fully aware of his actions or surroundings.

For example, riding his bike to work one day he overshot the toddy shop and kept going 8 miles further outside town, not realizing it till he was pedaling out of breath up steep foothills heading into the mountains outside Poona. He got to work very late that morning.

CHRIST COME AGAIN

If a customer had too much drink and became intoxicated, Merwan would sit with him and happily chant from the mystical poet Tukaram's Book of Songs. The drunkard would merrily join in, clapping his hands and singing along. In this way the toddy shop became a mystical tavern for Beloved God, while Merwan as its Divine tavern keeper distributed the wine of love and the intoxicating joy his heart embodied for all who came.

If customers became rude or disorderly, swearing or starting brawls, Merwan would handle them kindly, influencing them to change their ways. At other times he might refuse to serve someone, advising him not to overindulge or even abstain. Hearing of this, Shireen railed, "Merog, are you trying to share in your father's business or ruin it! What's wrong with you? If people stop drinking toddy how will the business survive?"

Meanwhile, they came – beggars and wandering sadhus, lining up outside the shop if "Merwanji" was minding the bar alone. For then he'd reach into the till, grab a handful of coins and throw them out on the sidewalk where beggars scrambled for them.

Now this sidewalk was also the home of an old opium addict who slept there all day and woke up about sunset. At night, he served as an alert watchman for all the local shops. Then in the early morning he'd wake the shopkeepers for their morning prayers.

They'd give him tea and a few coins, and this how he earned his livelihood and paid for his nighttime habit. Despite his severe addiction, the old man had a good heart and had such faith in Merwan that he gave him his small life savings to put aside and see to his funeral expenses when that time came. Merwan had a soft spot in his heart for the old man.

He agreed to take care of things at the end. That day soon came, and Merwan saw to the funeral on a wonderful scale by inviting everyone – entertainers, brass bands and dancers. It was more like an upscale wedding party instead of a funeral, and for days was the talk of the town. Such was Merwan's compassion as we will witness throughout his life. TH 301–02

Songs of Divine Intoxication

Merwan's generosity spread quickly among the beggars who made a habit to stop by daily. He'd recite Hafiz's mystical poetry for them and sing ghazals in his extraordinary voice, songs of divine love which he'd instantly compose, leading them on gently toward another kind of divine intoxication. Here's a ghazal he composed and sang to them:194

> How wondrous is the murderous mercy of God. His mercy has graced the rose with thorns. Justice manifests in the glory of God! Cruelty is hidden in his kindness. It matters not whether, Oh God! What bliss lies in love's intoxication! The wine of man can never bestow bliss. One cannot experience love by reading books – love can never be described in words.
>
> I have never read about real love – for it cannot be written. Love is portrayed with the blood of one's heart – Oh God, only then will it be Yours! Oh God! Grant me the gift of Your union – I have died in your separation. But in Your ledger You need not count the pains I have felt away from You. Blood is pouring from my heart which has become like minced meat!
>
> Only missing is the salt which You sprinkle on the wounds of the heart. Why should one question the lovers of God about Him? One should ask God directly! Oh God! You are found in the very question as well as in the answer. I have seen God; He is the same God everywhere!
>
> His abode is every heart. God is the wine seller in the house rich in purity though he lives in the house of ruina-

tion. Why should one feel restless experiencing misery, cruelty and the difficulties of the world? Oh Huma, if God showers his mercy on you, then your bliss is felt in its pain. 179–80

Jumping ahead a couple of decades to 1931 and his first visit to new York, it is said Meher Baba had a man named Bill Wilson as an elevator companion at the Hotel Astor in Times Square. Silent glances were exchanged before the man got off at his floor.

It took 2 more years, but Bill's obituary recounts that he finally checked himself into a detox unit at Towns Hospital about a block away from the Astor Hotel in 1933, and again in 1934. There he proceeded to fall into a bottomless depression, crying out with all his heart, "If there's a God let him show himself! I'm ready to do anything! Anything!" Then it is said that the room suddenly lit up with a great light.

It seemed Bill was on a mountaintop and a wind, not of air, but of spirit was blowing and lifting him. "And then it burst upon me - I was a free man." He shared his experience with another alcoholic doctor friend and they recovered together.

Realizing alcoholics could truly help each other, they adopted the 12 Step Program already existing in Europe, but not at all popular or well known. Once they started promoting it in 1935, the program quickly spread, becoming the worldwide movement it is today.[15]

God Joins the Navy

With World War I raging on, Merwan's old friend Baily Irani had joined the British-Indian Navy and traveled to England, France, Greece, Egypt and Arabia. Faithfully writing back and forth, Baily would read Merwan's letters over and over.

Then he got a temporary transfer to Poona and a month furlough prior to reassignment. He headed right for Merwan's toddy shop. Baily had greatly missed him, and every moment of his leave tried talking his best buddy into joining the navy with him.

Merwan finally gave in. "Okay, I'll join on one condition. You arrange it so I'm stationed wherever you are." Baily promised to arrange it. Since the military needed all the recruits it could muster at that time, they could almost name their own terms.

So early next morning Baily took Merwan down to the induction center and had him enlisted. Papers were duly signed with a date for Merwan to report for duty. Baily was elated his best friend had officially joined the navy to serve the British Empire and India. Of course, Merwan never mentioned a word of this at home, but continued his day-job filling in at the toddy shop, while Sheriar worked the night shift.

A navy recruiting officer stopped by after work that evening as he often did for a drink on his way home. He mentioned to Sheriar, "You know, your son's really to be complimented. You must be so proud of him. It's a big sacrifice for him volunteer service to his country in this bloody war." Sheriar looked at the officer blankly, presuming him tipsy.

"M'friend, I think you've had one too many tonight. My Merog a recruit? Nonsense! He's not the type." The orderly was surprised that Sheriar was in the dark. "I'm telling you, I saw the papers Merwan signed." Alarmed, Sheriar waited till Merwan got home from his usual night-visit with Babajan and confronted him.

"I heard some shocking news today. Did you enlist in the navy?" Merwan admitted, "Yes, I'm joining up to be near Baily. We're going to travel the world together." "No, no. Listen, son, you have to stay away from such things! Tomorrow morning go down and have your name withdrawn!" But Merwan refused. "Once my name's registered it can't be stricken. I want to join. Give me your permission, Father. I want to see the world!"

Sheriar refused to hear another word of it. "Nonsense, Merog, you're not meant for such a life! How can you go away like that? It's hard enough to let you out of my sight for even a few days at Sakori, much less years at a time? Tomorrow I'll go down to the navy office and make sure your name is stricken from the roster."

Sheriar's remarks had no effect, and Merwan disregarded them. But the next morning Sheriar did go down to the recruiting office, and using his influence had his son's name removed. Merwan was crestfallen, to say nothing of Baily's letdown. 183–84

Baily's Inauspicious Fate

Soon after this, Baily ended up getting transferred to Aden, a navy port on the Arabian Sea. From there on in things got very bad for him. Before he left, Merwan begged him to visit Babajan and take her darshan. Baily was irritated at even the suggestion, as he had nothing but contempt for her. Like Shireen, he considered her a sorceress-witch who lived under a tree and had totally impaired the life of his best friend.

He especially resented Merwan even calling himself her "disciple." But not wishing to displease his friend, with great reluctance Baily finally agreed to go and at least see her before he left on his new assignment. He would note years later in his diary:

"In my arrogance I told Merwan I absolutely refused to bow down to her, saying, 'I bow only to Him, wherever He may be. Except for Him, neither my body nor my mind will I lower to anyone else.'" Merwan just smiled and shrugged, "Whatever . . . ."

But the instant Babajan's eyes met Baily's, he was dumbstruck. He raised his right hand:" Salaam, Babajan." "Oh, welcome, my son, welcome," she mumbled sweetly in an almost inaudible voice. "Come and sit near me . . . who are you, dear? From where do you come?" Anticipating this question, Merwan had told Baily exactly what to say.

"I come from your son," to which she replied: "Except for God, who else could my son be? So if you've come from God Himself, I'll inform Him you have met me! Is there anything else?" Baily then explained he was in the navy and about to leave on new assignment to Aden, and would she permit him to do so? She listened with great interest.

Then closing her eyes, she repeated softly, "Aden, Aden!" Then suddenly in a loud voice, quite startling from her previous sweet tone, she spoke in a hoarse, sorrowful whisper:

"Aden is my land! . . . It has come out of me, I created it, and today it wants to mock me!"

Then her sweet voice returned. "Well, son, you may go. God be with you! But when will we meet again?" "Whenever it pleases you," Baily replied. She went into deep thought. "You'll have to wait . . . 5 years? . . . No, tells me 2 years . . . . No! No, I won't allow 2 years! So, come exactly after a year and a half. I will be with you and I will also keep my child with me. I am with the world and God is with me!" Then she extended her left hand.

Baily held it for a moment, then submitting to some secret feeling, kissed it with deep reverence. When Baily recounted meeting Babajan, Merwan remarked cryptically: "You know, maybe it's better not to understand the rigmarole of all these great saints. But whatever she signified I believe refers to some calamity for you. The future doesn't bode well. You'll have to face some terrible difficulties and suffer a lot! May God protect you!"

Baily gave little credence to his friend's warnings, and left that very night for his new assignment. He hadn't the faintest idea of what lay in store for him. As they parted, Merwan emphasized, "I'm telling you, I wouldn't like going to a place like Aden. By all means, try to get the order cancelled." Baily tried but failed.

The sanskaric die was cast. Meanwhile, Shireen never gave up the idea her beloved Merog would be "cured of his mental affliction," settle down, raise a family and finally make something of his life. 185–87

Merwan's New Toddy Shop

Now we meet a young man named Behramji, who though only 22 and illiterate, was a very shrewd businessman, and like Sheriar had several tea and toddy shops by the time he befriended Merwan and became one of his first followers.

After Merwan taught him to read and write, Shireen quietly took Behramji aside and offered to advance half the money necessary to start another toddy shop if he'd make Merwan his partner. Of course, Behramji was delighted and immediately took up the offer.

And so on August 1st 1918, Behramji got a license in partnership with Merwan and opened a new toddy shop at 723 Kasba Peth Road, down by the river in a neighborhood of fishermen not far from Sheriar's Cafe where Merwan had already been working.

The new toddy shop was really just a "front" for Merwan to continue his lowly physical labor while Maharaj grounded him more securely on the physical gross plane. But Merwan had conditions: "Let's run this shop not just for business, but as a place to do public social service and where we can meditate in solitude." 247

Behramji was well known to be rough with rowdy drunkards and daily beat at least one and threw him out. No sooner was its purpose served, widespread protests and riots against liquor and toddy shops began at Mahatma Gandhi's urging for prohibition. It was also the year of the devastating world-wide Spanish flu pandemic which took Merwan's young sister Freiny and 50 million lives – more than were killed in WWI. 193-94

Over the next year Merwan received no letters from Baily deployed in Aden. Finally the reason became clear. He'd taken up a raucous lifestyle, frequenting brothels, living way beyond his means and incurring pressing debts. He'd also developed an alcohol problem that shadowed him in later life – even to his death in the early spring of 1969. Embezzlement charges were filed and he was arrested due to his horrific lifestyle.

A significant plot point enters here. At that time in Aden, the highest ranking non-British military officer was a Colonel M.S. Irani, with the same family name of Baily and Merwan, even to Merwan's initials, M.S.I. But they weren't related – yet. That puzzling yet will become surprisingly clear in Chapter 61, "The Final Decade." [no peeking!]

Colonel Irani's sister Daulat and her daughter Mehera were soon to be Merwan's close followers. Mehera, age 17, was to be his chief woman inner-circle disciple and the only human being who'd love him more than any other on earth. Described as the moon to Meher Baba's Sun, she reflected his love and beauty as no other could.

The Colonel, stationed as an army doctor in Aden, came to know of Baily's troubles. As he was a fellow Zoroastrian and shared the Irani name, he felt sorry for the young man and arranged bail until formal charges were filed. But then he learned Baily was the disciple of a certain "bogus Parsi saint," the leader of a "gang of thugs" who would come to be known as Meher Baba – a very bad first impression indeed. But then it gets worse.

A few years later in 1924, Daulat and Mehera went to live at Meher Baba's ashram. Previously, the Colonel had been kind and solicitous after the sudden passing of Daulat's husband and Mehera's father, and he began looking after them.

Now returning from Aden, the Colonel stormed into Baba's ashram to demand his relatives give up living there. He was convinced Baba was a spiritual charlatan out to get his sister's fortune. But Daulat and Mehera refused to leave, despite the Colonel's insistence. He ended up warning them, "All right then don't listen, but you'll regret it." MM 1: 110

CHRIST COME AGAIN

This became the occasion for him entering into a long and vicious public writing campaign to bring this "false-master-gang-leader" down, and served for decades to create great opposition in the press and the public's mind against Meher Baba.

Surprisingly, Baba couldn't have been happier, for Colonel Irani was helping his cause. "This is all according to my will. No one would be interested if he wrote favorably about me, but by writing against me, my name is being plastered all over." But this was just the beginning. Colonel Irani will later enter the narrative several more times, both in this lifetime, and as hinted, related to Baba in his next life as a very young boy. M 35–36, 707–10

Meanwhile back in Aden, a military tribunal found Baily guilty on all charges. He was stripped of his rank, court-martialed and jailed. His 2 year conviction was then reduced by the judge to "a year and a half," thus fulfilling Babajan's prophecy.

After serving his sentence, Baily was dishonorably discharged from the navy and returned to Poona where he was treated like a pariah by his family and former friends. They certainly didn't want to associate with a criminal and would have nothing to do with him.

He looked for job after job, but no one gave him an even chance, outright refusing to hire him. Well, his hot temper likely helped make things worse. For months he really made an effort to atone for his previous bad behavior, but the community was unbending.

He was not only unforgiven, he was completely ostracized. He quarreled with his parents when they called him a total disgrace. After reaching bottom, he felt there was nothing left but suicide. Strangely enough, on that very day Baily's older brother Homi stopped by Merwan's Café for a drink. Merwan casually inquired about his old friend.

"Where's Baily these days? We used to write, but I haven't heard from him for over a year now." "Oh, didn't you hear? Baily's been back in Poona for months now, kicked out of the navy for embezzlement after serving jail time." Merwan gazed at Homi. "No, I didn't hear. Go get him now. I'll give you a round of drinks, but bring him here immediately."

Merwan gave him horse-cab fare and Homi raced to where Baily was staying and rushed up the stairs. The door was locked. He called out, but there was no reply. He kept pounding on the door. Finally, Baily yelled back, "Whoever it is, go away!"

Homi said, "It's me!" Baily repeated, "Just go away . . . I don't want to see anyone!" "But your old buddy Merwan wants to see you . . . Open up! Come on with me now and we'll have a nice little drink with him." "I don't want a drink. I don't want to see you or anyone else! Just leave me the hell alone!" By now, Homi's blood began to boil.

He shouted back, "Open the door or I'll break it down! He feels terrible you haven't come to see him even once since you've been back! I'm telling you, Merwan feels so bad and wants to see you now! He's still your friend, you damn fool! He insists I bring you at once. Now open the door or I'm breaking it down!"

Baily had been about to drink poison but quickly hid the bottle as Homi began kicking the door in. Only then did he reluctantly open it – just a crack. But before he could protest, Homi pushed it wide open, grabbed him by the arm and dragged him tumbling downstairs to the waiting horse cab, telling the driver, "Back to Sheriar's café – fast!"

But on their arrival Merwan wasn't there. He'd left a note saying he was out on "a quick, urgent errand," asking Baily to wait. Here Baily's diary takes over: "I didn't have to wait long. Within a few minutes I saw him coming. I was pacing up and down the sidewalk, and no sooner seeing me he came running and swept me into his arms – embracing me warmly, kissing me all over my face and neck. Tears flowed."

Merwan embraced Baily lovingly as if no one else was as dear to him as his beloved friend. Baily broke down. He'd forgotten what love was. Although family and friends had turned their backs on him, Merwan still cared. Overcome and speechless, Baily stood silently looking at Merwan's glorious face. Oh, how he'd changed. He looked much more normal than when Baily had seen him last, though his eyes were still a bit dazed.

Merwan led him into the toddy shop, sat in a quiet corner and poured him a drink. Baily in turn poured out his heart and all that had happened to him in the last couple of years. Hearing the full story, Merwan said, "Let the past be gone. Why worry about past wrongs? Everyone's done something wrong . . . God is there to forgive." Baily was so overcome by what Merwan said that his suicidal depression immediately vanished.

Merwan around the time he reunited with Baily at Sheriar's Café

"Why didn't you write me about this?" "I did! Do you know how many letters I wrote? You never answered even once!" Baily said in tears. "Then I heard you were some kind of . . . well . . . spiritual figure, a guru or something, and maybe you'd even left Poona." "Okay," Merwan said, "I think I know what happened. Now, I want you to come and see me here every day – every day, and I promise everything will be ok if you do." Baily agreed.

Merwan made Baily understand he'd never be left helpless again. Realizing his old friend just saved his life, he no longer thought of suicide and began hanging out at the toddy shop every

CHRIST COME AGAIN

day. Merwan became Baily's pillar of strength and the source of his deepest love.

So what happened to all of Baily's letters? It was discovered they'd been hidden away by Shireen, so afraid Merwan might go to Aden to see Baily. She couldn't bear him going so far away, especially to a foreign country during the war.

And who knew? Maybe he'd sign up again. When confronted, Shireen honestly admitted her fault, and of course Merog forgave her. After this, Baily remembered Babajan's and Merwan's cryptic words and clearly understood now what they signified.

Only gradually did Baily learn of his beloved friend's spiritual attainment, at first erroneously attributing it to Merwan's "deep religious beliefs and prayers from childhood." Shortly after this, he joined Merwan's new band of intimate disciples and discovered how wrong all his earlier misconceptions had been. 208–11

Baily would outlive his beloved boyhood friend and Master by just 2 months. He had been born 25 days after Merwan, in the same ward and in the very same bed at Sassoon Hospital – even delivered by the same doctor and nuns who had attended Merwan's birth. They were obviously destined to be together from the very beginning. If Merwan was said to be the Light, Baily described himself as the Dark! In his final words:

> "I was so fortunate to live in Baba's constant companionship day and night, but unable to realize, value or appreciate his Divine Power. Careless, ignorant and inattentive in my private life, I've experienced no change. All those who know me can surely say that. Only Baba can say whether or what I have gained . . . ." Baily Irani's unpublished diary, Vol.3. p. 39

Though together on and off for a few years of Merwan's public life as "Meher Baba" and into the late 1920s, they were physically apart in later years due to Baily's radically unstable life and experiences. By the 1960s, Baily had separated from his wife and began living a hand-to-mouth existence in a Poona shed owned by his sister-in-law, Dolly Bastani. Then one afternoon he showed up on a bicycle at Baba's door.

After a private meeting in the hall, Baily said, "Forgive me." Baba handed him a rose which Baily ate. He never saw his friend again. After moving to Hyderabad, he ended up in a home for destitutes where he died in March 1969, 2 months after Baba's own passing.

In his final days he met a nurse, also a Baba-lover, and gave her a manuscript he was working on running to 6 handwritten volumes. The 2nd volume of his memoirs with Baba is unfortunately missing and likely forever lost, leaving 5 remaining volumes detailing Baily's time spent with Baba from early childhood to when he joined the disciples. 4702

Baily's detailed and comprehensive memoirs of Baba will one day be published in full. And thus, their amazingly close brotherly journeys would end, with Baily loving Baba with all his heart and soul to the very lonely end of his hard and convoluted life.

Meanwhile, one evening after closing their toddy shop, Behramji went to stay over at Merwan's with Gustadji, another new follower now working at the toddy shop and hanging out with him on the advice of Upasni Maharaj. That night, Shireen had a very disquieting dream similar to the one she had shortly after Merwan was born. Startled, she awakened, calling out to Sheriar and recounting her dream:

> "I was sitting on our doorstep. Merog was under a tree across the lane. Suddenly, I saw the delicate figure of a beautiful Hindu girl with her hair tied in plaits with golden flowers. She wore jeweled necklaces and bracelets and had a small boy at her side.

"They emerged from our courtyard well and approached Merog with outstretched arms. Merog rose and stood before the girl. I came forward and asked her, 'Who are you? Why are you here?' She answered, 'I am Paramatma [Almighty God], and I'm taking your son.'

"I held Merog, saying, 'I won't let him leave.' Then Merog spoke, 'Let me go, don't hold me back, Memo!' I held him tightly, ordering the girl to leave! Suddenly the figures jumped back into our well and disappeared."

Resting in his room, Merwan overheard his mother narrate the dream to Sheriar. He called Behramji and Gustadji, laughing as he told them, "Memo just had this dream . . . bad, bad – very bad!" Shireen overheard him joking about her fears and became all the more upset, shouting down the hall, "Merog, why are you laughing? Tell me what it means!"

This just made him laugh all the more. "Oh, I know what it means," he taunted, mischievously. "It's bad, Memo – really very bad!" Shireen was furious at his refusal to reveal the dream's meaning. Of course, Paramatma – the Infinite Consciousness of God Himself had indeed united with her Merog. But for her, it was bad indeed, as it foreshadowed what we will soon see in the next very difficult period of Shireen's life. 236

Merwan and Gustadji, sent to him from his Masters, Sai Baba and Upasni Maharaj – a most blessed and beloved disciple who would achieve God-Realization at Meher Baba's hand upon this early disciple's passing in 1957.

The First 40-day Fast and Seclusion

One day, Merwan told his new disciple Sayyed Saheb, "I've decided to stay in a secluded place without the slightest disturbance at the Bhorgad cave near Nasik where Upasni Maharaj fasted for almost a year. Will you go there with me?" With Sayyed agreeing, they took a train to Nasik and climbed up Bhorgad Hill to Maharaj's old cave.

Sayyed stayed on the mountain cliffs, while Merwan remained in the cave alone for 40 days and nights, similar to when he was Jesus. He fasted only on milk, which though he never particularly liked, Sayyed would bring daily from the village below.

After this, Merwan left the remote mountain area to stay for some days at Sayyed's house in Nasik were he called his close

Poona disciples. Witnessing Merwan's great spiritual strength, Sayyed was impressed such that he no longer liked the name 'Merwan.' It was too ordinary. With the Poona friends gathered, Sayyed suggested changing Merwan's title.

The Compassionate Father

Various names were suggested, until in the end Sayyed himself proposed the name "Meher Baba" – Meher: "Merciful or "Compassionate" and Baba: "Father." It was endorsed by all, and from that day on in 1920 anyone becoming intimately associated with Merwan Sheriar Irani referred to him as Meher Baba. 227

Although they were true apostles, Meher Baba did not refer to his intimate disciples by that term, but as his "mandali," meaning "circle members" (Sanskrit: mandala = circle, connection, community). They play identical apostolic roles circle members must always play in any Avataric advent, such as there's always a "Peter," a "John," a "Judas," etc.

During this time, disciple Sadashiv Patel's wife Geeta passed away. With Baba attending her funeral, bystanders were impressed finding Muslims, Iranis and Parsis taking part in a Hindu funeral procession. It demonstrated to the Poona people that Meher Baba was different – far above caste, creed or religion, and people of every community were included among this universal spiritual leader's followers. 236

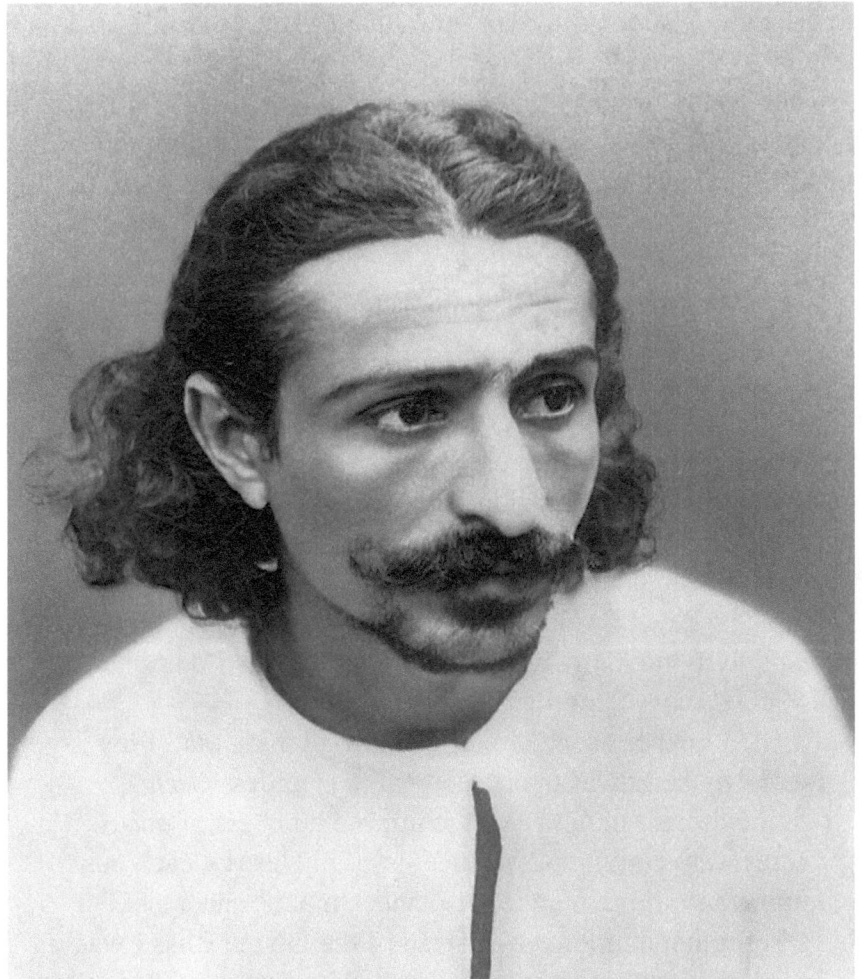

Merwan in 1923 after his early disciples re-named him Meher Baba, the Compassionate Father.

Prohibition

With Mahatma Gandhi's followers continually picketing toddy shops, by July 1921 business had dropped drastically, and the shop would soon close due to prohibition. Using this unrest as a pretext, Merwan announced at home he was going to Sakori to "consult on this business matter" with Upasni Maharaj, and would be back in a week or so . . . .

That "week or so" turned into 6 months before he'd return to Poona, as Upasni worked day and night on the finishing touches of Merwan's exhaustingly painful process of down-coming to normal awareness. He later described passing through various stages: 241

The Agonizing Opening of the Divine Heart

For [those first] 9 months, God knows, I was in that state to which very, very few go – even in cycles of time – with no consciousness of my body or anything else. I roamed about, not eating . . . I didn't sleep, because I was unconscious; and then what happened is very rare. It is only for Avatars, who take on themselves the suffering of the world . . . . One day, I suddenly I felt nature's call and sat there wanting to move my bowels – impossible, for I'd not had any food those 9 months.

Then I experienced circles of lights coming out of my heart. My heart was open; there were countless circles within circles bursting. All the infinite numbers of universes were coming out of me, out of my heart – each containing an infinite number of planets, moons and suns! 246

From that moment on, instead of the Divine Bliss I was in for the first 9 months, I was in such tortures no one in the world can ever understand. I'd bang my head to relieve my pain, scarring my head on floors and walls. I couldn't contain myself. It was as if the whole universe was on my head. I'd break windows with my forehead. Muhammad had a similar experience during his Realization and subsequent down-coming when an angel appeared, cut his heart out and cleansed it. 3979–80

CHRIST COME AGAIN

With Merog's prolonged stay at Upasni's, not wanting to return home and ignoring her letters, Shireen was still in motherly panic and resumed her protest visits to Sakori. But unlike past visits, this time she was determined not to fall for Upasni's tricks.

As she entered his compound, he saluted her, "Oh, mother! Welcome, welcome!" Irritated by his oily greeting, she asked, "How could I be your mother when you're so old!" "Oh! But you're the mother of the entire universe, dear woman," Upasni replied. Sensing he was up to his old tricks again, Shireen warded off, "Look, I won't be deceived by your compliments. I'm not here to be flattered. Just tell me where my son is; I've come for him!"

Upasni gently said, "Mother, please . . . just sit here a while with me." He then sent word to his chief woman disciple, Durgabai, who loved Merwan deeply, that she should cook up something very special for Merwan's mother.

Meanwhile, Shireen forgot to garland Upasani with flowers she'd brought. As she unwrapped them, he exclaimed cynically, "Oh, what a lovely garland of old shoes you've brought me!" "What are you talking about? I brought these lovely flowers all the way from Poona just for you . . ." "Yes, yes," Upasni interjected, "and I know what you were thinking – how you'd fight with me when you got here, abusing me in your mind the entire way!"

Shireen lowered her eyes silently acknowledging the truth of his remark. But also sensing he was again maneuvering to outwit her, she quickly countered, "Now Maharaj, please don't get me sidetracked again. I've come to speak with my Merog. Where is he?" Looking around, Upasni gently replied, "Oh . . . I guess . . . he's around here somewhere."

Then, lowering his voice, he leaned toward her, confiding more intimately, "You know, Mother, I don't even know why he even stays here. Your son seems . . . well, mentally unbalanced. I really don't know what to do about him. I don't force him to stay. I even beat him with a stick to try to chase him away. Still, he won't go.

PAGE 193

What am I to do with him, Mother? What do you propose when you take him back? Do you really think it will help?"

"It certainly will," Shireen insisted, "I'll arrange his marriage as soon as we get back to Poona!" "Now that's a grand idea!" Upasni replied enthusiastically, slyly adding, "But Mother, do just one more thing. Before you take Merwan, when you find a nice girl for him, see if you can also find one for me. Then we can both come with you to be married."

Incensed at his outrageous proposal, Shireen countered, "Who'd ever give his daughter to a dirty old man like you?" "But as your son, how can I be unsuitable?" Upasni gently asked. Irritated all the more, she insisted, "Stop teasing me and please call Merwan!"

Sighing, Upasni turned to another visitor, Gulmai Irani sitting nearby. This was a truly pivotal moment, as Gulmai would play a major role in the Avatar's future life and also give him the Meherabad property outside Ahmednagar where his ashram and Tomb would be located and where she, Shireen and Sheriar would one day all be buried together in the shadow of his bliss. So Upasni now introduces them:

"Mother, this is Gulmai Irani from Ahmednagar. She's also Zoroastrian. Why not make friends with her now, and later when you see Merwan, don't pester the boy with all these questions. Talk with him cheerfully so you can leave for home with a happy heart.

"Dear lady you're so fortunate to have him as your son. It's all because of your good past lives. What can I do about him? You have to encourage him to follow the spiritual path. Don't throw him into the hell of worldly life. He will get married one day."

Hearing this and talking with Gulmai, Shireen felt somewhat pacified, but only somewhat. Meanwhile, Upasni kept shifting the conversation to distract Shireen, until Durgabai brought them a delicious lunch. Then when she and Gulmai had finished eating, Upasni suddenly exclaimed, "Oh dear, it's late now! Hurry mother!

You're going to miss that last train for Poona!" Falling for the ploy, she quickly grabbed her things.

Returning to the train station by horse cab, she again ended up leaving her son at Sakori, and only when on the train heading home would she remember she'd missed even seeing Merog. It was too late now to get off the train. She looked at her young son, Beheram, who'd accompanied her. "Damn! That yogi deceived me again!"

Unable to control her distress, Shireen then went to Kedgaon to plead with another of Merwan's Masters, Sadguru Narayan Maharaj. He received her with great kindness: "You're so very fortunate. Your son is Jagat –Lord of the universe! You'll be worshipped in times to come as mother of the entire universe. Be patient. Everything is all right, and one day you'll know who your son truly is." Memo was comforted by Narayan's gentle manner.

But she wasn't fully consoled, nor did she remotely understand the Sadguru's wondrous remarks. She just couldn't bear the separation any longer. On top of Merwan's refusal to come home from Sakori for a visit, or even write her, she now had to bear the increasingly bitter ridicule of the local community. Many of the spiritually backward Parsi/Zoroastrian community mocked her son's spiritual tendencies.

They warned, "Merwan will run off to the Himalayas as a naked sadhu like that Upasni Maharaj. You'd better put a stop to his seeing that yogi." Then they'd start abusing Babajan. "And why does your Merwan bow to that old sorceress? She's bewitched him!" Well, Shireen knew that, but hearing it from others disturbed her even more and only increased her already hand-wringing anxiety over her Merog's future as a normal person.

Of course she'd convey all her fears to Sheriar, but he was totally resigned that his son belonged only to God. Be as it may, God's will would prevail here. His resignation just added to

Shireen's painful frustration. She wanted Merog near her; even if he refused to marry and settle down to raise a family.

Then one day during Merwan's absence at Sakori, his younger brother Beheram began lighting a prayer candle in Merwan's room which he kept spotlessly clean. Both he and younger brother Jal had by now accepted Merwan as someone spiritually great.

Brother Jamshed, the first born who fought with Merwan in childhood, was the one among all the brothers to have full conviction of his divinity. He was also the first brother to worship Merwan's photograph, a practice he'd observed father Sheriar doing. 247-51

Decades later, Meher Baba, would comment to his American followers, "Isn't it amazing? My own father used to worship me – even my photograph!" Still agonized by the separation, a week after her previous encounter with Maharaj, Shireen boldly went back to Sakori, this time more determined than ever and armed to the teeth with resolve. 4000

She confronted him, railing, "Why don't you just give him back? You've taken my son away; now bring him back for God's sake!" "What the hell are you talking about?" Maharaj countered, now fed up and raising his voice. "I never held him prisoner here. Take him! I haven't held him captive! I haven't chained him up somewhere!"

Shireen was infuriated. "You know full well Merwan won't come home unless you order him!" Upasni replied, "I'm not going to order him! It's totally up to him to decide." Then glancing an ominous smile at Shireen's youngest son Adi who accompanied her that day, Upasni slyly continued. "Tell you what, Mother. Do this for me. I'll order Merwan to go back, but you must leave young Adi here with me." Well, this was just too much.

"What? How dare you! Swallowing up one son, now you want to swallow up another? Call Merwan this instant!" Upasni tried appeasing her, "Please, please, calm yourself, dear lady." With true respect he bowed to her feet and then called the boy. Merwan arrived looking dazed and bedraggled. Shireen eyed him closely.

A steadfast mother Shireen during her trips to Sakori, and Merwan as he appeared in those days.

Oh my God. He looked so pitiful – unshaven, his clothes dirty and torn. She had brought him some nice clean ones, but why was he refusing to put them on? Then Upasni spoke up plainly: "Your mother's back again. She wants you to go home and get married. Every time she comes here she's angry and fights with me. I'm fed up with her abuses. Now go back with her!" Then he added, smiling, "Become a thief, tell lies and end up in hell!"

"Don't joke about it," cried Shireen. "I'm serious! I want my son back!" Merwan had been smiling, but now he sat down beside Maharaj and appeared truly sad. Just then, lunch was brought. Shireen and young Adi went outside to eat with Durgabai who deeply felt Shireen's pain. "What can we do?" Merwan doesn't want to leave Maharaj.

"He's only given him a tiny room. It's empty and dark with no windows. He gives him no comforts. Still, your son loves him and wants to stay here. I can't explain it." Shireen started weeping, pleading with Durgabai, "I don't understand why he won't give him back to me? Does he wish me so much grief? Why doesn't Merwan want to come home?"

At this, Durgabai also began weeping. Then Shireen went back inside. This time Upasni was very strong, saying definitively, "Your son doesn't want to go home, doesn't want to get married, and doesn't want children. Forget your ideas and go home. He wants to stay here with me." Upasni embraced Shireen, whispering softly in her ear with tears in his voice, "I bow down to your love." Unconsoled, Shireen left in anguish.

She spoke to no one at home, but went to her room and wept bitterly. She just couldn't be reconciled to losing Merog. However much Sheriar tried – and he truly tried – he failed in his attempts to console her, and she wept bitterly for days, her heart utterly broken.

Still distraught, after a week she again gathered up strength from her inexhaustible motherly resources to return to Sakori, and dug in with even clearer battle lines. Standing her ground, she confronted Upasni and Merwan for three days straight. But the amazing mother's attempts were tragically doomed, and in the end she lost the bitter, heartbreaking battle. She returned to Poona that final time, totally defeated and in complete disarray.

With this last Sakori visit Shireen suffered a serious breakdown. Her health rapidly spiraled down. She'd lie in bed, weeping insensibly. Unable to cook, the house and children had to be looked after by servants. Concerned about her state Sheriar called a doctor.

Both her mother Golandoon and Sheriar did their best to nurse her, but she was utterly disconsolate – her heart in despair. With weeks passing and no sign of recovery, Sheriar sensed Shireen was on the verge of death.

Shireen's Turning Point

One evening as he kept vigil at her bedside, he saw the door open and two figures approach her – spirits. One resembled Merwan and the other wore a white turban and robe, resembling Sai Baba. The figures stayed for a few moments gazing intently at Shireen and then vanished as suddenly as they had appeared.

She immediately awoke and speaking clearly for the first time in weeks asked, "Sherog, would you get me some water?" Amazingly, Shireen's condition rapidly improved, as she became well and normal again to the great relief of all in the family. 251–53

She had to undergo these terrible trials for the sake of the world and her beloved son. It was like Mother Mary's agony at the foot of the cross, though far more prolonged. Then one has to wonder if Mary didn't go through similar experiences after Jesus' unveiling and down-coming. The Gospels weren't meant to give such intimate details of Jesus' life as this account, but just a few events of his public life for teaching new converts.

Still, the images of Mother Mary coming to us from the Gospels and devotion to her for over 2000 years contrast so sharply with the feistiness of mother Shireen. The poignancy of suffering in witnessing her son's sacrifice for the sake of the world outweighs anything we know about mother Mary. Yet, who can say Mary herself didn't pass through such trials during Jesus' own down-coming. Both unknowingly were the mothers of God.

We will witness Shireen having many such moments. Although eventually she accepted her son's divinity, she always remained "Shireen," and even many years later was a source of great exasperation to her Merog. Still, he loved her deeply and said one day the entire world would worship her. Only in later years did she achieve understanding, finally seeing what the Five Perfect Masters had given to her beloved Merog.

CHRIST COME AGAIN

She returned with great honor to garland Babajan with flowers. But Babajan had Shireen put the garland around her own neck. She hesitated, but did as requested, then took it off and put it around Babajan's neck. Babajan then put the flowers on Merwan's photo, hung on a rusty nail. Touching it, she began to weep, "My son will shake the whole world!"

How often had she repeated this; but was the world listening? When she was 9, Baba's young sister Mani recalls visiting Babajan. "She took my hand and then turned and put her forehead on Baba's photo hanging on that rusty nail and began to cry. MM1: 90-91

Babajan continued living on Poona's streets, and over those 40 years thousands of hearts were wounded by the dagger of her glance. Around her was an unseen fire where all kinds of impressions hovered and burned. Shireen and Sheriar now have tombs on Meherabad Hill next to their son's, where countless pilgrims come to bow down to them. 15, 703

Over the decades, Baba himself would often lead devotees up the hill to visit his parents' tombs. In 1958 he predicted, "70 years after I drop my body [2028], this will be a place of world pilgrimage. Lovers of God, philosophers and celebrities will come to pay homage. How fortunate you are to be in my living presence up the hill today with me." 4269

With Sheriar's death in 1931, Baba said, "Because of his untold sufferings to gain spiritual knowledge, a true pilgrim on the path, I was born as his son." He added Sheriar was the only man in the world at that time worthy to be the father of the One who will shake the world to its foundations, ushering in a new age of spiritual awakening. 798; MM 3: 437

By 1914, Merwan gradually returned to normal consciousness while retaining full God-consciousness. After 7 years of these frequent visits to Sakori and intense seclusion with Maharaj, 1921 began a signal year in that process. He was now over 75% normal.

He could do ordinary acts, speak normally and respond immediately, fully grasping everything said to him. That July began his final 6 months with Upasni in the small room at Sakori. He had just a sheet, 2 quilts and small wooden box filled with his notes, laboriously taken down from talks late into the night, such as follows from one of Upasni's discourses:

> "Be as it may"
>
> Animals like dogs are always in the state of "Be as it may." The God-Realized are also always in the same state. What is meant by this expression? One should quietly suffer without any feeling from all bad things, dirty things, heat, cold, rain, fasting, beatings, and so on. If one receives the opposite to all this, then one should not feel pleased in any way; one is not to try to cause change in one's surrounding or environment or any affairs of the world.
> So one should continue to face all things as they come without any attempt at interference. And while in the midst of all such things, one doesn't have to try to make any change in himself to ward them off or protect himself. Just face things as they come. This is the meaning of "Be as it may."
> Remaining in that state, one always experiences the state of God's Infinite Bliss. Instead, you try to have things as you need them right from your birth. The behavior of a God-Realized one is exactly opposed to that of yours. As they behave opposite, you take them as insane; but he, poor man, always remains in the state of "Be as it may," and doesn't worry what you think of him.

http://avatarmeherbaba-israel.com/Talks of Upasni Maharaj, Vol. 2A, p.229

During the last 6 months of his 7 year journey, Merwan wore the same tattered cotton pants, shirt and precious sandals Babajan had given him, preserved today at Meherabad's Museum. In this last critical phase, Upasni gave the final touches integrating Merwan's God-consciousness with lower gross consciousness of the mundane world – the final preparation to assume his public life and role as the Avatar of the Age.

Merwan would spontaneously start singing at any time of the day or night. Those listening were enraptured as his melodious voice filled the rural solitude of Sakori. The sound emanating from him was so magnetic it seemed their lives had no other purpose than to hear him sing. His was the voice of God incarnate, song after song pouring from his heart.

Echoes from the divine ocean filled the air, and even Upasni shed tears of joy in the bliss of Merwan's songs. He never slept during this final 6 month period not closing his eyes for even a few moments, but continuously paced back and forth or sat upright.

At first Merwan ate very little every few days, never bathing or changing clothes. Even when he hadn't yet gained full awareness of his thin, lice-ridden body with dirt-caked skin, he smelled fresh as a rose. After spiritual songs at night, he'd sit in Upasni's hut until 4 AM taking notes. It's said they wept together with rapture echoing in their cries. 253

But there was also murderous jealousy at Sakori. How on earth could a Zoroastrian become the favored chief disciple of a Hindu Perfect Master? Decades later, Meher Baba recalled when Maharaj confided to his two closest disciples, "Merwan is now 'Malik – Owner of the Universe.' Hearing me called Malik, these Brahmins wanted to kill me.

"When my disciples increased, they got all the more annoyed, just like the disciples of John the Baptist." But the local villagers adored Merwan. Overcome with his loving nature, they now began bringing him delicious home-cooked meals. For unlike the earlier years, toward the end of his down-coming he became ravenously hungry. TIW 72, 318–28

He was reconnecting with the "eating world" aspect of the illusory universe, "dressed again in the triple garment of the world – his gross, subtle and mental bodies, though loosely – his God-brightness undiminished." SG 21 Upasni now gave Merwan the final push allowing him to function as the Avatar with perfect finite and Infinite consciousness in wedded balance.

The triune state of Infinite Bliss, Power and Knowledge were thus conferred by Babajan, Sai Baba and Upasni Maharaj. Only then could God be said to have again performed his periodic miracle of down-coming.

We conclude that with Babajan unveiling him on the 7th plane, Masters Narayan Maharaj and Tajuddin Baba took Merwan down from the 6th and 5th mental planes; Sai Baba brought him across the dangerous 4th plane of Infinite Power and down the 3 planes of the subtle world. Upasni's final touch fully established Merwan's consciousness in the gross world with his Perfection and readiness to assume his supreme role as Avatar of the age. 242

Beginning His Public Life as the Avatar

After completing the long and difficult journey with its agony, wonder and glory, one day in late December 1921 Upasni announced to Merwan that he was Perfect – he had achieved the knowledge and authority to control the activity of the universes and to function on earth as the living Christ come once again.

Days later in January 1922, Upasni called him to his hut and with folded hands solemnly proclaimed, "Merwan, you are Adi Shakti. You are the Primal Force, the Avatar and direct descent of God!" As Babajan made Merwan feel what he was, now he experienced himself grounded in the false world as the Ancient One and Lord of the Universe. Merwan bowed at his Master's feet.

CHRIST COME AGAIN

Upasni held and rocked him in his arms for a long time, weeping, "Ah, Merwan! Ah, my dearest Merwan!" There were no more words left to express his love. Merwan then left Upasni's hut for the last time. As he swiftly climbed into a waiting horse cab and galloped away toward the station to catch the train to Poona, Upasni gazed down the dust-stirred road with silent tears streaming down his cheeks till the cab was out of sight. 257

The scene of Merwan riding away from Sakori that final day was also witnessed by young teen-aged Mehera Irani. Visiting Upasni with her mother Daulat, she caught brief sight of Merwan 4 times that day. Watching him now ride away, little did Mehera know she was destined in the coming year to become his chief beloved woman disciple.

Now almost 28, Merwan was gloriously young, handsome and strong and ready to begin his public life in Poona. He had 47 more years of impassioned work and intense suffering for the universe looming ahead. Over the next few years, Maharaj spent hours with Merwan's early disciples, remarking about Merwan's spiritual stature: M 17

> "All of you heed what I now tell you. Merwan is the Avatar. I've handed over the key of whatever I possess to him. He is the sole heir of my spiritual treasures. I'm totally naked now, so don't bother me; best follow my advice and hold to his feet with both hands! Merwan will make the whole world dance on his little finger! Even people from the west will come for his darshan and blessing, and by God's grace you will reach the goal." 289

After leaving Upasni at Sakori, Meher Baba settled on the outskirts of Poona. By a roadside field near Fergusson College, a 6'x4' tent-shaped bamboo and straw-thatched hut was built at his request by a devotee. He'd rest in the hut at night rather than bear the strain at this parent's home. During the day, he'd sit outside the hut under a shady tree..

In this beautiful setting he'd soon begin the process of wiping off his disciples' faces and stripping their false minds to prepare them to become the absolute Truth. One notion he corrected in his new band of disciples was: Where is God? This is how he addressed it: 263

> To say "God is everywhere" is a general term and nothing new. But you must find, feel and experience it. To say "God is in the heart" is again only part truth. If God is everywhere, as you all know and say, why then should you limit His being only in the heart and not in the head or your thumb or toe? Why try to see Him in one particular spot and not in the other?
>
> It's a common mistake and human weakness to spot the highest and most beloved or revered up above, somewhere in the skies or heavens; or when sought in the body, to find Him only in the cardio-vascular system – parts men like best, i.e., in the heart or the eye, as if He did not exist equally elsewhere in other parts, in the back or the bones, in the nails or in the flesh.
>
> Is God in the rose and not in the thorn; or in flowers and not in filth? This weakness of seeking God in things you like and shuddering at the idea of His existence in things you do not like or abhor, must be overcome. Only when you rise above all these ideas of good and bad, and recognize, see and feel flowers and filth alike, and find God equally in all, can you be said to have learned and known something real. Otherwise it is all parrot-talk, false conception and illusion.
>
> It's taken for granted the best, most ideal abode for God to dwell in the human body is the heart. But even in this

best abode dedicated by human beings for God to dwell, He who is the purest of the pure would not come in unless that abode, however lovingly offered, is absolutely clean, empty and void of any foreign element. A slight hindrance of an alien thought prevents His coming. For God to dwell in the heart, it must clean and empty of selfish desires, i.e. lust, anger, greed, etc. 2030–31

Baba also told them of an unprecedented future-coming tsunami of divine love to flood the spiritually dry river beds of organized religions with a whole new life, connecting them to the Ocean of God's Infinite consciousness. Finally, he used a clear analogy to describe the impersonal or impassive aspect of Divinity.

"God does everything, and in a sense does nothing. Although God does nothing, those approaching Him with love and surrender derive everything spiritually, even though he does nothing in particular towards them. God is like sandalwood, emitting a sweet scent in all directions, though only those who go near it have the benefit of its charming fragrance.

"We can't say the sandalwood did anything in particular towards those who approach it, because emanating its sweet scent goes on all the time and is not specifically directed towards any person. It is available to each and all who care to come within its range.

"The sandalwood gives in one sense, and in another it doesn't. Another example; the river gives water, so if thirsty people approach to drink its waters their thirst is quenched. But the river does nothing to invite them to itself or to fill them with its waters." Be 39–40

CHRIST COME AGAIN

And so, under a simple tree his local devotees would gather for discourses, games, and devotional singing as Meher Baba began his 20th century public life as the Avatar. On Sundays the crowd resembled a festive carnival. One of the first duties of a Perfect Master on coming back down into awareness of the gross universe is to gather his circle members. 264

In Jesus' case this was gathering His apostles, simple Galilean fishermen. This gathering process began while working before the final 6 months with Maharaj. Then one day, he stopped by a local Poona office on work related to his and Behramji's toddy shop. A Muslim clerk, Munshi Rahim at least 15 years older, was so struck and taken by his appearance that he neither greeted him nor asked how he could help.

He just stood there gazing in wonder. "Who on earth is this striking young man?" Baba introduced himself and went on with the business at hand. But recognizing something extraordinary and wanting to see him again Munshi invited the young man to his home.

Now although a good Muslim, Munshi wasn't exactly orthodox. He was very fun-loving, had an open heart, and secretly enjoyed a little gambling and card playing. But he never mentioned this to his new friend. Then one day Baba said, "Hey Munshi, what do you say we play a little game of cards?" He was delighted, so they started playing. And in this way Munshi gradually came to know his new friend could read his thoughts.

One evening while home alone, Munshi – usually a big meat-eater – was thinking it had been ages since he'd had a good piece of fish. "Tomorrow I'll go out and get some." But the kind of fish he wanted was out of season that time of year and not found in the market.

Leaving the house next morning, Munshi was amazed to see Merwan on his bike peddling toward him with a big fish in his hand – the exact kind Munshi had been longing for. With a grin as big as the fish, he handed it to him and pedaled off without a word, proving to Munshi that Merwan really did know everything.

Munshi's home in the Kasba Peth fishermen's neighborhood gradually became like a small spiritual center. After work in the toddy shop close by, Baba would stop by Munshi's whose friends were Muslim. They'd read Hafiz's mystical poetry as Baba explained the poems' spiritual meaning; or they might play cards and have some light entertainment. Munshi was also a great cook, so he'd gladly rustle up food for everyone. 197–98

"A Friend from the Past – alas . . . ."

Another Muslim intimately close was his childhood friend, Abdul Ghani, Merwan's neighbor for almost 20 years. Born in the same hospital in the same year, they were close playmates growing up and also went to high school and college together.

But as Merwan had quit college in sophomore year after his contact with Babajan, Ghani lost track of him over those next 7 years. Meanwhile, Ghani went on to finish college, and though failing in medical school, he became a homeopathic doctor in Bombay.

Then one evening he was visiting Poona and casually stopped by to see his old friend Munshi Rahim. After all these years, he was shocked to also find his old boyhood chum there. Ghani cried out, "Merwan! What the hell are you doing here? I thought you must be dead all these years! Whatever happened to you, ol' buddy?" Merwan gave him a big smile.

But Ghani's Muslims friends didn't at all like his flippant familiarity addressing their Guru. Sensing their reproach, Ghani defended himself. "Merwan here is my old friend. We grew up on the same street, played on the same teams and were classmates at St. Vincent's and Deccan College." But Ghani's remarks fell on deaf ears and received only eyes of scorn.

CHRIST COME AGAIN

Munshi remarked: "A friend of the past is an awkward customer, alas!" Ghani was taken aback, thinking "Did I do something wrong? Why are my fellow Muslims mistaking my intentions? And why are they paying such respect to Merwan?" Baba intervened and had his old friend sit near. Talking affectionately, they recalled their boyhood pranks together.

This relieved the tension and gave the others a few good laughs. Baba ended advising Ghani, "Definitely visit me when you're in Poona. I'll always be happy to see you." Baba then left for his nightly visit to Babajan. Just waiting till he was out the door, they pounced on Ghani. "Don't you know who he is? How dare you talk that way in front of him!

"He's no ordinary man! He is a Qutub! A Hazrat close to the Perfect Masters Babajan and Tajuddin Baba!" They then explained Meher Baba's spiritual status, with each one describing his experiences when in the Master's contact. Ghani apologized, clueless to what they were driving at, as he knew Merwan far better and longer than they did. 227–29

When Ghani visited Poona later on to see Baba, they'd go to an Irani restaurant opposite Babajan's seat. Over cups of tea Ghani would discuss various topics, usually long-winded political diatribes, while Baba listened patiently. And though by this time Ghani was deeply influenced by Baba and spent many more evenings at Munshi's house, he'd not yet remotely acknowledged his boyhood pal as a spiritual Master.

Ghani was considered so intelligent that he was nicknamed "Socrates," and also for size of his large head. But even this giant intellect would one day bow at Meher Baba's feet. In fact, so much Meher Baba revealed about spirituality we owe to Dr. Ghani. If he were eager to hear a discourse from Baba, he'd say something in jest somewhat sarcastically, and in this way was able to goad out so many spiritual gems from the Master. 229

CHRIST COME AGAIN

He was sometimes called "His Master's Voice" after the 1915 RCA Victrola logo with his ability to explain Baba's spiritual concepts, messages, discourses and statements with illustrations from daily life. He acquired this capacity trying to measure Baba's knowledge in the years before accepting discipleship of one who was his childhood friend.

He was very well read on Sufi, Vedantic and Christian mystic schools of thought and would put difficult questions to his childhood friend, knowing well he had never read such books. Baba surprisingly answered all his questions with ease. TY 8–9

But there were no two ways about it; Ghani was disappointed seeing his old friend wearing a white robe – his cotton sadra – and commented, "For God sakes, Merwan, you were the cleverest one in the class, and is this the only way you can find to make a living?"

A fanatic Muslim, Ghani later admitted it took Baba 8 years to break him down, saying, "I was the chronic disciple of the incorrigible Master!" Ghani will prove the most uniquely colorful, witty and daring of Baba's circle members, and a source of endless entertainment for the Master and his close disciples. RD 380-82; 2279, 2617

Babajan usually wouldn't let anyone touch her, but when Baba left Munshi's late at night to sit under her neem tree, she'd have him scratch and rub her back for hours at a time. His fingers would be so stiff he couldn't even uncurl them and had to massage them to straighten them out. But he never refused. During 1919-1920, two things he never missed were sitting nightly with Babajan to scratch her back and banging his head on stone or walls.

The Kasba Peth area of Poona was Baba's base of operations where from 1917-1921 he opened his "spiritual wine-shop" to start his public life. It was a place of simple neighborhood fishermen – hearty, virile, uneducated men earning their living fishing on the nearby Moola River, just as Jesus gathered his Apostles along the Jordan River.

Here Baba's disciples sensed his spiritual light in their hearts and became totally devoted to him. Like a new Galilee with the toddy shop as his net, these simple fishermen became the new Apostles. "Drawing more closely his net of love, he pulled them from the terrible ocean of conditioned existence to swim with other fish, bright-hued or dull." SG 23

Babajan's and Maharaj's devotees were told, "The child is now capable of moving the whole world with just a sign of his finger." With Narayan Maharaj they were now openly revealing Baba as the Avatar. MM 1:446 This fact he revealed to his Western disciples in 1931, publicly in India in 1954, and most publically in New York on NBC television on July 23, 1956, my 20th birthday and 100 miles from where I was beginning my priesthood studies.

Chapter Eight

First Disciples – First Ashram

About the time at the thatched grass hut on Ferguson College Road Baba said: "For 4 months I began living independently, surrounded by men forming the nucleus of the first mandali [inner-circle] members. Some were drawn intuitively before having any idea of my inner state. Others came through Babajan or Maharaj's hints. Others I drew directly." LH 250

He would read their thoughts with astonishing detail, winning their hearts with jokes and games, music and singing together with his deep empathy and unabashed affection for 100s of people, rich or poor, men, women and children, as well as scholars and the illiterate.

Not just the good or those on the spiritual path, but the bad who's whose lives were caught up in the illusion of Maya now came to his hut in groups. Morning till night, grateful to pour out their hearts to him, they returned peaceful to follow his advice and orders. 276

Ghosts in the Night

He explained that a Sadguru can be in 10 different places at once, while the Avatar has the power to be seen in physical form in 1000 places. There's no necessity for him to take his physical body to go to different places; however, in certain cases it must be done with his body. So on some nights he might suddenly vanish from his hut. 5020

One evening, when childhood chum Baily was on night-watch inside the hut, he suddenly found the Master had disappeared bodily from inside, though the doors remained locked from outside.

CHRIST COME AGAIN

He was shocked and frightened to see weird, giant figures approaching.

Later, Baily's brother Homi heard of his night-watch scare. With still lingering feelings from schoolboy years, he came to confront the Master, unable to understand why Merwan accepted his rascal brother as a disciple.

But he also found Merwan's appearance profoundly changed since he last saw him at the toddy shop when he'd dragged Baily there. Now gazing at him, Homi's heart began to mysteriously ache. After Baba embraced him warmly, they reminisced about old times. From this moment Homi's devotion to the Master was born.

Another disciple, Arjun, was on night watch outside with strict orders never to enter Baba's hut while on duty. But one evening he was startled by hearing rustling leaves. Peering into the darkness, he saw two gigantic figures suddenly getting larger and more ominous, reaching almost 20' in height. Petrified, Arjun rushed into Baba's hut against strict orders never to enter at night. Startled, Merwan glared at him. "What's the matter with you?"

Tongue-tied, Arjun pointed into the darkness. Of course, nothing was visible. Baba scolded, "Didn't I tell you never be afraid when I'm here and never ever enter no matter what happens? These ghosts are coming to me for rebirth. Such dead spirits have committed suicide and can't take another birth for several centuries. They come to me every night."

He explained Ghosts are suspended in the lower astral sphere, seeking a body to possess to spend their remaining gross sanskaric impressions. One aspect of a Sadguru's and the Avatar's work is to liberate such spirits down from the astral sphere and allow them to reincarnate again and normally process their previous life impressions of consciousness.

As Baba retired at night, these spirits of suicides came into his vicinity, materializing in their astral bodies when they got near enough to touch his resting body, pleading for reincarnation. But as seen, during the night he was often out of his body doing Universal work. So having his body disturbed at such a critical time by a disincarnate spirit was extremely dangerous. The incident with these 2 ghosts would later prove fatal for Arjun.

Although a strongly built fisherman, from that time his health began to steadily deteriorate. He kept losing weight and would literally waste away 4 years later. There will be many such ghost stories in later chapters, as well as hard lessons about obedience. 282–83

Some time after this incident, Baba told the men he hadn't rested the previous night due to a peculiar noise outside as if someone were leveling the ground with a heavy roller. "This ghost spirit is always with me, wherever I go. He's one of the ghosts Arjun saw outside the Poona hut. Maharaj has put him in my charge. If you see this spirit, don't be afraid."

One night while Ghani was massaging his legs, Baba further explained about ghosts and having his body massaged: "My body's physical contact with another human keeps the spirit world temporarily away from me and enables me to snatch a little rest. 333–34

He distinguished these spirits from typical so-called "ghosts" who linger around cemeteries, saying the latter are simply discarded astral shells and less than nothing – a mere wiggle – like when you chop a worm or a snake into pieces it wiggles for a while.

The presence of a waking person kept these spirits away. So when Baba retired, there was always someone sitting awake by him throughout the night with strict orders to never move away. This practice was continued throughout his entire life. HM 265

Handsome, but "Nervous"

Around this time on a chance visit to Bombay, Baba came across a young Persian lad named Khodadad Irani. He had strikingly handsome matinee-idol looks and a burning ambition to become a movie actor. Obsessed with the idea, he had spent months making rounds from one movie studio to another. But casting directors never chose him for a role. The young lad became so depressed he'd never make it he was close to despair. During his deep inner turmoil Baba was walking through the city and came across the dejected young man sitting by the roadside. He stopped to gaze at him. "Who are you, m'friend, and why so sad? You look like you haven't a hope in the world!"

Khodadad glared back, "What business is that of yours? Who are you, anyway?" "Oh," Baba smiled, "I runown a film company in Poona and I'm here in Bombay auditioning actors. You wouldn't happen to know anyone looking to work with a bright, upcoming production company would you?" Khodadad couldn't believe his ears. He stood up excitedly, "Yes, sir! I've been looking for that job for 3 months now!"

Baba said, "Fine, then you're hired. Can you come with me now to Poona?" He immediately agreed and was taken to Poona then and there. But on arrival, Baba said, "Well, to begin with I want you to work in my toddy shop. Ah, but that's just temporary. My film company's in its final stages of formation, and as soon as it starts up you'll be working there full time." Khodadad was more than happy to agree.

But in Baba's spiritually intoxicating atmosphere the young man soon forgot all about his acting ambitions and became totally dedicated to his new boss's spiritual activities. Khodadad would appear uneasy at the slightest mishap, and even more so in the Master's presence. So Baba nicknamed him "Nervous." 211–12

Nervous then won a lottery held after someone gave Baba a brand new bicycle. Baba told Nervous to give up his old bike in exchange for the new, and then ordered the mandali to break up the old one and throw the pieces into a nearby well. It was done immediately, although the men felt it was strange, as the old bike was in perfect working condition.

This occurred while some of the mandali were away with Baba. When he returned to the Poona hut, Baily told him he had accidentally fallen into the well near the hut and had been rescued from drowning in the nick of time by a passing stranger.

When asked when this happened, the other mandali realized Baily's near drowning and subsequent rescue took place at the exact moment when the pieces of Nervous' old bicycle were being thrown down the well. Baba later explained, "Instead of allowing Baily to drown, I sank the bicycle in the well. It was simply an exchange of gross mediums." 272

A Birthday Party with His Two Mothers

In February 1922, Baba's 28th birthday was celebrated at disciple Sadashiv Patel's home. He lavishly decorated the top floor of his Poona house and invited all the Master's followers. Baba arrived early in the evening, and after a wonderful meal, a master musician from Bombay played the sitar and sang beautifully. Mother Shireen also attended.

With the music lasting late into the night, Baba suggested that Gulmai, whom Shireen met at Upasni Maharaj's ashram and was now very devoted to Baba, should spend the night at his family's Poona house rather than have her travel 80 miles late at night back to her home in Ahmednagar. Shireen took Gulmai by the hand, and as they were leaving. Baba significantly said, "These ladies are my mothers – one worldly, the other spiritual."

During later decades these "mothers" would spend much time together having their differences which will soon become apparent. Baba often let them play out for his own work purposes. He had previously revealed to Gulmai, "You are truly my mother, and I am your son. I've taken birth by you in past lives. We are connected from the beginning." 266

Although Baba had moved out of his parents' house, he'd still often stop by for lunch. One such day in the lane near his parents' home, he suddenly crouched down, staring at the ground in silence, puzzling his men. Then he stood up and made an astounding revelation. "Do any of you know what I'm doing? Every minute, bodies are dying and then coming back again; every second it occurs. I was watching and orchestrating it all! 279

Manzil-e-Meem

By now Baba had gathered 40 men of various faiths – Zoroastrians, Hindus and Muslims, reminding me of my favorite childhood tale, Ali Baba and the Forty Thieves, read to me by my mom as a bedtime story. Baba often called himself a "thief" – a stealer of hearts. With these men as his core group he'd now start up his first ashram in Bombay.

To raise money for their new venture, Behramji began frantically selling off his tea shops and liquor stores, including the one partnered with Baba. Each had to unknot personal and business ties to be totally free for a new life of total dedication to the Master. AO 126

Then on May 22nd 1922, at 2 AM under the cover of darkness, Baba abandoned his roadside Poona hut and walked all day in blazing heat with his 40 men. That was the start of a 5-day, foot-blistering 100 mile trek to their new Bombay ashram. Baba would name it Manzil-e-Meem, "The Abode of M," for Meher the "Compassionate One." 298

The men were exhausted tramping in the blazing hot sun, and some fell asleep, stumbling while walking. Ramjoo recalls: "Walking beside me, Behramji would actually nap, lurching against me with half-closed, bleary eyes and bumping me on the head with his

CHRIST COME AGAIN

sitar. The rest of us dragged and shuffled our legs only by sheer will-power." RD 47; 290–93

The inside of their thighs were rubbed raw, forcing them to walk bowlegged. After 5 days and half-dead from the exhausting march, search for a suitable bungalow in Bombay was begun. One was found, but as it needed renovations, they stayed at the home of Munshi Rahim in a local neighborhood where he'd recently been transferred from Poona.

It was here that Munshi expressed his heartfelt wish to have the first "official photo" taken of the Master since his Realization. Baba said OK if it were a spontaneous as-is candid shot without fuss. A local photographer was quickly summoned.

Baba asked the photo be taken without delay as he sat chatting in a happy mood with his companions. The camera, tripod and customary background drape were hastily set up, while Baba gave very precise instructions about the focus prior to the photo's taking. The following is a paraphrase of Baily Irani's eyewitness account of that photo shoot:.

This photograph is special, as Baba put his whole being into it. He was sitting with his right arm supporting him on the floor as was his folded right leg. He was wearing a dirty old, tight-fitting, small size coat and trousers. His left leg was upright, bent at the knee with his left elbow resting on it.

His head was supported at the temple by his left hand. His hair was short and moustache neatly trimmed. Though it's not an especially attractive photo, Baba said it has its own importance. The moment it was taken he paid full attention to the focus, and that was important. This is the first photo taken of Baba after his achieving God Realization, and the first photo exposing Baba's pure lotus feet – very useful and suitable for worship. Baily Irani's unpublished diary, Vol.5, p. 14

CHRIST COME AGAIN

Meher Baba, barefooted and still looking somewhat dazed in ragged clothes in his first official photograph after Realization and taken at Munshi Rahim's Bombay home in 1922.

God as Both Father and Mother

When the Manzil was ready, Baba and the companions moved in. By now they'd grown to 50 from different religious and social-caste backgrounds, and would have to learn how to get along. While before they lived with him as a friend, here they were turned totally upside-down, living under iron-strict, prison-like rules with visitors discouraged.

In those days Baba could suddenly become very fiery. Yet, he showed no trace of malice in his actions. He was simply a mirror, reflecting what was in his disciples' minds when they weren't dancing to his tune. Then a new thing was introduced as he began micromanaging every aspect of their lives. This was toward their inner unfolding and possible only through their willingness to obey and serve him with all their minds and hearts.

Though the narrative seems to gloss over it, surely there were times of great joy living in such intimate proximity with Baba. Otherwise, how could they bear the difficult rigors and times of suffering the Master passed them through as he ground and pulverized their false minds to dust? He later commented, "My mood was constantly changing.

"I'd beat up everyone in temper fits, and then in a good mood I'd lovingly embrace them. In His pity, God makes mincemeat of you!" One day, he told them all to line up and push against him in a tug-of-war. All 50 robust young men, some of them wrestlers and seasoned athletes, collapsed in sweat, unable to budge him an inch. 3868, 315

Their daily routine reminded me of the exacting routine I followed during my 8 years of seminary training, obediently living under what was called The Rule, but with a huge difference. Baba was their live-in divine mother and father.

"As their mother, he served their every need; as a father teaching and chastising them to remove their hindrances to pure self."

CHRIST COME AGAIN

SG 25 The Manzil was a venue of intense practical spirituality. On being Divine Father and Divine Mother, Baba said in 1956:

> God is One – both Father and Mother in one. Of course He's in everything and every one, and everyone knows it. But God is beyond this, too. I'll tell you about God in His Divine Beyond state, where he is both Father and Mother in one. When God descends as the Avatar on this gross material earth plane, he always takes a male form. He is never born as a woman.

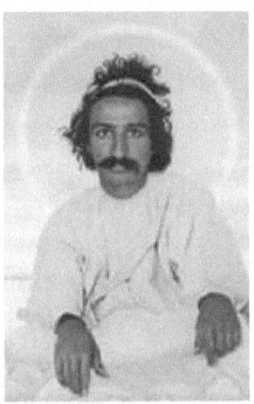

Detail from painting by Cherie Plumlee of Meher Baba from 1922 Manzil-e-Meem period.

> Avatars are the Sons of the Father in the Beyond state. All past Avataric periods witnessed the presence of the Avatar as the healthy, bright, intellectual Son of the Beyond-God. This means in my previous advents, I always remained the Beloved Son of my Father . . . .
>
> But in the past, the Beyond-God did not have the occasion of playing the part of God the Mother. In this Advent, God the Father is very pleased with my being infinitely bright, infinitely intelligent, infinitely brilliant, masterful, etc., always giving promises but never fulfilling them. I am bright and shrewd, as my Father wants me to be – the Beloved Son of my Father.
>
> At the same time, in this form I'm physically disabled. In 1952 in America, I broke the left side of my physical frame from head to foot. Now [1956] in India, the right side has been completely shattered in this 2nd most recent auto accident. Besides being physically disabled, I am infinitely innocent, guileless and easily duped. So I listen to all you say and then yield to your wishes.

CHRIST COME AGAIN

> I haven't the strength to say no to any of you, nor refuse any of your requests, despite my plans, instructions and circulars. Thus, I am the well-beloved Son of God as the Mother also. In this Avataric incarnation, God has the chance, as it were, to play both parts – Father and Mother. 4282–83

Decades later, Hilloo Kotwal recalled her childhood with Baba:

> All of us children look back on our time at the Retreat on Meherabad Hill as one of the happiest of our lives. Baba was the glorious sun in whose warm, divine love we all basked. Mehera was the beautiful moon, whose calm radiance pierced our hearts as she shared love for her Beloved. Mani was the greatest of the sparkling stars, twinkling in everyone's heart, spreading joy everywhere.
>
> In that heaven Baba loved and cared for us children in all aspects of our lives. Sometimes He was like a mother to us, giving tender, loving care to the few children privileged to live with Him in Meherabad and experience the human side of the God-Man. And in playing the role of our Big Daddy, Beloved Baba put any worldly father to shame. *He Gives the Ocean*, Meherwan Kotwal, p.67

But back at Manzil-e-Meem, what alarmed his men most was Baba's new propensity for suddenly out of the blue-nowhere asking them what they were thinking. Under obedience they had to admit their thoughts, which at times were pretty dreadful. Only once a week could outsiders visit, and pretty girls would often appear in the darshan line.

One Sunday as a girl bowed down to Baba, Adi Irani's mind instantly went where it shouldn't have. Baba asked him, "What are you thinking?" "Nothing," Adi said. Well, the probing went on for days, as Adi kept protesting, "Nothing!"

Baba's childhood friend Dr. Ghani was also not free of such thoughts. So one day, Baba took them aside. "Do you think I'm a fool and I don't know what you're thinking? I know everything – about yesterday, today and tomorrow. Past, future and present are open books to me." Then he really startled both by citing some very intimate incidents from their past before they'd even met him – dates, persons and acts only they could know.

Dumbfounded, they began weeping. Baba fired back, "Then don't lie to me. You've lied to me for days." Adi burst out, "Then don't ask such embarrassing questions in front of others." "Nothing of the sort! I'll ask whatever and whenever the hell I like. Just obey me!"

He continued probing them to admit all their thoughts, good or bad. A dozen years after Baba's passing, when I began visiting India from 1981 on, I saw that his men often had that same ability to perceive things which others might not. Surely Baba continues his work through them, just as though he were still amongst us in human form.

Most of them now had outside day-jobs, except Adi who was attending college. So he was ordered to write down all his thoughts on the 3 mile bus-ride to and from school. Later reading the notes, Baba would shake his head. "Don't you have anything better to think of than this?" So Adi began trying to keep his thoughts on God when out of Baba's presence!

The Master was grinding down and cleaning out the latrines of their false minds. When he displayed fiery moods, his terrified men would flee and run to their rooms or hide in bathrooms to avoid his firing line. He might pick up and throw anything at anyone nearby. But always, his fiery moods would subside as quickly as they'd arisen.

Then he'd embrace them lovingly, as if nothing happened. Again, he was simply a mirror reflecting the subjectivity of their own distorted minds, or using them as foils to accomplish work needed in that moment perhaps somewhere else in the world. 314–16

Like any great director, Baba had an excessive eye for detail. His primary duty was to prepare his mandali for God-Realization and make them fit vessels of his grace for others. It was more daunting than taming teams of wild horses. As he constantly worked with great unseen forces, his orders could not be violated.

Eating food at the wrong time or place or from an unauthorized source could be a serious violation of spiritual protocols that Baba just didn't have time to discuss. An order was an order, simply to be obeyed. Failure to do that could be very dangerous to him.

Babajan's Messenger

On September 10th 1922, an exceptionally beautiful white dove suddenly flew into the Manzil looking ill and exhausted. Baba lovingly held and caressed it, but it was so sick it couldn't even walk. He looked after it and was up three times during the night nursing it. The next day he told his men despite his care, the dove had died.

He told them to see how the bird had passed in such a peculiar position – on its legs, its head bent as if offering a salutation. He then posed a question: "How did this dove suddenly appear and then just as suddenly die? Do you remember I recently told you I'd be receiving an important message from Babajan? This dove came with that very message.

"Its importance can be gauged, for as soon after delivering its heavy burden the blessed dove died." He then dug a hole in the backyard of the Manzil and buried the bird in a grave covered with a green sheet as to Muslim burial rites for Babajan. Flowers were strewn, and he wrote the following ghazal, dedicated to this beautiful bird:

> O blessed Dove! I accepted you as my honored guest, for you came from the Emperor! And what a guest you were! By obeying the Emperor's orders, you became the dust at His feet. No one knew from where you came or why, but your coming portends our departure. You came to annihilate your life of duality in illusion, and now you won't be born again, as if you had never, ever suffered.
>
> What a message you brought from the Emperor! Its importance cost you your life! O God! What a wondrous game You play behind the veil! Though You are ever-manifest, your game is a riddle to those who have eyes, but are blind. Oh, Royal Dove, You have become a Saint! You now are buried at Manzil-e-Meem and Merwan kisses your feet in reverence. 322 –23

Each morning at 5 AM Baba had the mandali retire to their respective rooms on the ground floor for 45 minutes, repeating silently any one name of God as to their own choice, while Baba retired by himself in his own room on the upper story.

The pin-drop silence of their silent prayers vibrated with repeated sharp, loud head-knocks on the wood floor and windows above them, as was Baba's practice a few years earlier in the agony of coming back down into the full awareness of Illusion.

One day after splintering a window ventilator in the Manzil, he again took to wearing a bandana around his head to hide the bruises, showing clearly he was still suffering from every point of view in one way or the other. Still, at the end of the prayers he'd greet them in the breakfast room with a smile and lovingly serve breakfast with his own hands, not making even the slightest reference to his terrible head poundings. RD 90

CHRIST COME AGAIN

Then on October 14th he gathered the men to discuss his next journey to Sakori:

> "My sufferings are now becoming unbearable. By going to Sakori, Upasni Maharaj will take some of the load off my shoulders; but in doing so, he'll have to suffer so much internally. If he suffers, he may even beat, abuse me and disgrace me in the presence of you all, precisely at the time of Diwali [the Hindu New Year]. I've been telling you this all along.
>
> "Advanced saints and mahatmas will disgrace and beat me, as at this moment the spiritual world is against me. So it's possible Maharaj may take matters into his own hands, insulting and beating me. But if I don't go there, you've no idea what I'll have to suffer."

It was agreed Baba should definitely go to Sakori. In fact they decided to leave that very night. As it turned out, Maharaj greeted Baba lovingly. But the real reason for this trip was only an excuse to afford Baba the chance of being introduced to Mehera Irani, visiting Maharaj that day and destined to become his closest and most beloved disciple. It was also the last time Baba set foot in Sakori during Maharaj's lifetime.

He'd not see his Master again for 19 years, until October 1941 for their very last meeting. But just as predicted, Maharaj would soon abuse Baba and his mandali. He'd even strike mother Shireen taking on a share of the Avatar's almost unbearable cross. Then early in 1923, Baba ordered Upasni Maharaj's biography to be written in 3 languages – Gujarati, Urdu and Marathi. Baily recalls being assigned to write the Gujarati version. 353–57

> One evening when Baba and I were alone, he suggested there'd be much activity in the coming 2 days.

CHRIST COME AGAIN

"Tomorrow will go down in history as a very important day. On this day 29 years ago I was born. No one yet knows who or what I really am. But gradually the world will not only start to know me, but will be prepared and eager to lay down their very lives for me. People of all classes, castes and religions will know me as God-personified.

They will have love, faith and devotion towards me and will obey my every word. They will reach the path of Liberation and I will set many free from the bondage of births and death. If you also desire and wish for the same, give me your love. Day and night think of me, keeping my name on your tongue at all times and leave all the rest to me. I'll only see to your betterment. Your relationship with me extends from several past lifetimes.

Because of the give and take of sanskaras from past lives, you are with me in this life. You'll play an important role in my work. Maharaj's life story must first come out in Gujarati only, and should be written in your hand and completed by you alone, Baily.

From this you can see how deep and strong our relationship should be that my Guru's life sketch will be published through your hands and made available to readers in Gujarati, then published in various other languages – English, Urdu, Marathi, Hindi, Bengali, Tamil, Telugu, etc. Baily Irani's unpublished diary, Vol. 3, p. 40, 264

But then after its release, critics rose in uproar against certain spiritual figures. Articles began appearing in various Bombay papers, mercilessly slandering Meher Baba. Amazingly, the more opposition among Parsis and Iranis spread around Bombay, Poona and Ahmednagar the more prominent his name became. Baba commented on this:

CHRIST COME AGAIN

Looking at these Parsis, I feel when I was Jesus they were the Jews seeking my crucifixion. Now I'm a Zoroastrian and they remind me of those old days. No doubt there's a group among them who truly love me, and that love compensates for the other group's indifference. 3744

After Realization, those who come down to ordinary normal consciousness must suffer some sort of opposition from people. But for the Avatar – God Incarnate – there's always the headache of a very severe opposition during every Avataric age – Zarathustra, Ram, Krishna, Buddha, Jesus and Muhammad – all had to face this opposition. The very same picture is before my eyes today. 3746

While the Parsis take no pride in my being a Zoroastrian, it is true a prophet is never recognized and revered in his own time and by his own people. This has been true since ages past. It happens in every Avataric period. But I wish Parsis would try to think of me and get to know me.

I like their jovial nature and "who-knows-what-will-happen-tomorrow-be-as-it-may" attitude. How really splendid if a few out of love boldly come out to do my work. Let them work, enjoy and do their family duty; their good luck might help them think about me once in a while. 3763

Murder Plots

The Gujarati newspaper, *Insaf*, went so far to print an appeal to public leaders to "take drastic steps to rip to pieces the net of the corrupt and depraved trio of Meher Baba, Babajan and Upasni Maharaj!" Baba repeated his prediction that saints and other Masters would also abuse and "beat up on him." That was soon coming. 401

As we've seen, such opposition was actually the medium for Baba's work. He'd not let the mandali defend him or his Masters, and writing newspaper rebuffs was forbidden. When Ramjoo was reading from a book about the Sufi saint, Mansoor, who was horribly martyred, Baba cryptically said, "I'll live for 54 more years, then undergo a tragic death! The Parsis will bring about my end in a pitiless way."

He meant not physical death, but abusing his reputation by character assassination. The result of his inner work was now manifesting in such opposition from Parsis and Iranis in Poona, Bombay and Ahmednagar. Although it was a medium for his work, the virulent opposition actually did become a threat to his life. Amidst rumors of plots to harm and even assassinate him, after Baba made the above statement, the Zoroastrian community's opposition curiously and slowly began subsiding, as many Parsis and Iranis became his disciples, taking him as a true Master. But among many others the bitter opposition would last for many more years. 507–08

Iranis and Parsis are Zoroastrian groups from Persia/Iran. "Iranis" speak Persian/Farsi, and "Parsis" are Zoroastrians who migrated to India from Persia from the 7th century to escape religious persecution from Muslims. Both Iranis and Parsis speak Gujerati and live in Bombay [Mumbai].

Watched by the Secret Service

All the men were expected to go out and try to sell Maharaj's recently published biography. Ramjoo approached a family friend to sell him a book. The man, also a secret service official, seemed interested in spiritual matters. But in conversation he openly admitted he was really assigned to secure information about what was going on inside the Manzil – a seemingly suspect operation. He candidly told the startled Ramjoo that the premises were under surveillance for weeks by government agents, and some of the men had even been followed.

All telegrams and letters were being scrutinized as the Manzil was suspected of harboring a secret society with either criminal or anti-British political terrorist motives. As the agent detailed the police suspicions, Ramjoo clarified certain critical matters, explaining about Meher Baba and the different men living with the Master. To Ramjoo's surprise, the agent then ended up buying five copies of the biography. 367–68

The Mystery of Huma

When Baily finished the Gujerati translation of Upasni's life, Baba sent him and Gulmai's son Rustom Irani to the renowned Parsi author/poet Sohrabji Desai in Navsari, to say Desai is being asked by Meher Baba to edit the book. Greatly irritated, Sohrabji demanded, "Who is this man ordering me to edit his work? I'm no one's slave. I've no time for such foolishness. Tell him I simply can't." Though they tried their best, he was obstinate.

Rustom and Baily went back and told Baba about their cold reception. Then after a few days, Rustom was sent again with this message: "Sohrabji, only you can do this work; it is Meher Baba's wish." At this, Sohrabji got even more annoyed.

"Who the hell does this Meher Baba think he is? Tell him to stop being so damned arrogant!" He slammed the door. Again Rustom returned to Baba narrating what happened. But now when Baba sent him and Baily back a 3rd time with the manuscript, they were told to simply leave it there with a final cryptic message and not to say another word. When Sohrabji saw them again on his doorstep, he became truly livid and shouted at them, "Why on God's earth are you back here pestering me? What the hell's the matter with you?" They simply thrust the manuscript into his hands while delivering Baba's cryptic message: "These manuscripts of

CHRIST COME AGAIN

Upasni Maharaj's biography are presented to you by Huma –Meher Baba's pen name. This work must be done by you."

Sohrabji was thunderstruck. They had no idea that for over a decade he had longed with all his heart to meet the poet, Huma. Many years earlier as a teen-ager writing under that pen-name, Merwan had sent a divine-love poem to this renowned Gujarati poet, scholar and author, Sohrabji Desai. He was deeply moved by a particular poem and tearfully read it over and over, ardently wishing one day to meet its composer.

He had no idea who Huma was, let alone a mere teenager. But now hearing the name profoundly affected him. He immediately calmed and read the poem by Huma again. As he touched his forehead to Maharaj's manuscript in reverence, tears again came to his eyes. This is the note he sent back with the emissaries to his beloved Huma:

"Sir, excuse me. I bow to your order. You totally stole my heart long ago. Only today is the secret of your identity revealed! Your game is unique. I'm yours!" – Sohrabji.From this moment, Sohrabji Desai became a life-long and beloved disciple. 309–11

Helping the Poor

On Sunday October 29th 1922, Baba sent a couple of men out to buy 100 cotton shirts to be given to the poor. Others were sent to bring lepers, the blind and destitute to the Manzil. Normally, 1000 beggars needing food and clothing were easily found in Bombay. But strangely that Sunday it was hard to find even 100 truly needy, helpless or poor.

Rustom luckily found a crippled man and pulled him through the streets in a cart all the way to the Manzil. Onlookers glared at this well-dressed man doing coolie's work. How were they to know he hadn't a cent and the cart was borrowed? Ghani hunted miles with disappointing results, finding only one truly destitute person.

Vajifdar had better luck, for besides being a famous professional cricket player, he was very persuasive and convinced one of the destitute to loan him streetcar fare to take them all, promising the man he'd be repaid as well for the return journey. But how could these poor men be sure of the mandali's intentions?

How could a person who hadn't even streetcar or taxi fare possibly give them free food and clothing? It was hard not to suspect a trap – a scheme to lock them up in a homeless shelter or asylum. Well, imagine their surprise at Baba's lovingly warm reception.

All doubts vanished as he personally bathed many of the 200 poor and served them food. He gave each man and woman clothes, garlanding several with fragrant flowers. With smiling compassion he waved his hand in blessing and lovingly sent them on their way. Rustom took the crippled man back in the same cart, but what a marvelous change.

Fresh-scrubbed, he was beaming in new clothes and wearing a bright flower garland. After the destitute departed, Baba fed the mandali with the leftover food, breaking their fast. That morning he'd instructed they not eat a morsel till the poor program was completed. Shortly after this, two larger poor programs were held similar to this one. 363–64

Meanwhile, a Muslim priest, Moulvi Abdul Wahid of Hyderabad, arrived in Bombay with very little funds. He had searched in vain for an old friend and ended up having to crash at a local mosque across from the Manzil. While meditating he saw a bright light issuing from the Manzil, and immediately sensed there must be a "holy one" in that building.

The next day again during meditation, he saw a still brighter light, and in its brilliance the words MANZIL-E-MEEM. No longer able ignore his vision, Wahid stood on the sidewalk outside the Manzil in a dazed state all night long without speaking to anyone. Noticing the stranger the next morning, the Master sent Gustadji out to inquire of the silent sentry at their gate. Wahid told of the light he'd experienced across from the mosque, adding he felt profound inner peace just standing near the Manzil. By Baba's order, he was directed to Munshi Rahim's where he was given food and shelter and informed in detail who Meher Baba really was.

After dinner the men asked Baba: "Why is it we always hear of outsiders like this Muslim priest today having great experiences of your divinity and seeing "brilliant lights," while why we members of your intimate circle are left in the dark?" Baba gave them a brief but convincing explanation:

> "What happens when you place a lantern on the floor? It sheds light all around, but the area closest to its base, is always dark. So it is with you who are closest to me. What use are all these experiences of seeing lights? One day I'll give you the Real Light to take you out of the darkness forever! Now, wouldn't you rather have that?" 387–88

Upasni Maharaj's Bamboo Cage

Just after Upasni Maharaj's biography came out in December 1922, Baba's aunt Dowla visited Sakori and returned narrating: "Maharaj has become very weak after imprisoning himself in a small bamboo cage. He hasn't left it once in 3 months. He repeats Merwan's name, longing to see him."

Gulmai had also been to Sakori, and Maharaj complained, "Why the hell did Merwan publish my life? That book is no good and will drag me into tons of trouble! I don't want people to know about me! And tell them to stop performing arti before me. I don't want to be worshipped! I'm planning to die in this cage for you and the whole world!

"What does the world expect from me? It's God's will I confine myself like a criminal for your sake. This is no ordinary cage but the very ocean of bliss, a place for casting off all your sins! And whoever dies thinking of it will without doubt attain the state of Liberation and Eternal Bliss." Hearing these stories, Baba was silent. 393

Then more news came from mother Shireen. On his birthday, February 25th, he sent her to Sakori to "inquire of Maharaj on her son's behalf." Well, she returned pretty shaken. "When I went near Maharaj's cage, he put his hands out from behind the bars and catching hold of me with one hand, severely slapped me with the other. All my bangles were broken. I'm not used to such treatment. I was very upset and wanted to leave Sakori.

Upasni Maharaj self-imprisoned in a bamboo cage for a year to share the burden of Meher Baba's work, Sakori 1923

"But due to train schedules, I was detained for a day. Maharaj called me to him several times, not only abusing me each time, but shouted against Merwan and you men. He warned me, 'Why is your Merwan going around impersonating a Guru? He pretends he's a God-Realized Sadguru!' " Gulmai narrated Maharaj also warning her:

"For god sakes don't go to Merwan! He'll misguide you! You'll wither like a disease-afflicted tree and in the end you'll have to come back to me. For your sake, just stay away from him!"

At this Baba addressed his men: "So, what do you make of it all? Just a few days back, Maharaj spoke so lovingly of me to aunt

Dowla." They replied, "Well, you've hinted all along about being abused by saints and masters, and here it is!" Baba smiled,

> "Yes, I started this game. I wrote to Maharaj that I had no connection at all with him or anyone else at Sakori. Then I deliberately sent my mother to him. With this letter he's now taken the step he should've taken long ago. I started this game, but it won't end with me. It's in Maharaj's hands. Yes, I've been telling you this all along. You, Maharaj and the whole world will turn against me. And this is just the beginning, so be prepared; everything will turn against me."

Baba then directed Adi Irani to write the following to Maharaj: "Meher Baba did not at all like your remarks to his mother, made in the presence of others at Sakori. He's now fed up with his duty, the burden of the work, and wants to totally abandon it."

The letter was read out to the mandali while Baba again warned them not to be deceived even a minute by all this word-bluffing. "Be careful not to misunderstand the goings on between Maharaj and me, or be taken in by our exchanging harsh words."

Adi mailed the letter, but with the secret game being played here only the Masters knew the meaning veiled behind the bars of Maharaj's cage – a prison of penance for God to help take upon the burden of the Avatar. Baba seriously asked the mandali, "So? You still want to stay with me? You heard what Maharaj said. Even he's opposing me now." All vowed to keep their given promise never to leave him under any circumstances. 393–95

Meanwhile at the end of December 1922, weeks before the Maharaj brouhaha, Baba had further tightened the noose around his mandali's necks by having all 28 of the ashram's stiflingly-detailed rules and regulations written up, to which the men had to put their notarized signature under pain of death, etc., if not followed to the letter.

CHRIST COME AGAIN

A couple of months later, using some mistake of Khodu's as a boldface excuse, Baba raised a storm and told him to leave the Manzil. The mandali were then served a new notice posted on the board: "All should tear up their previously signed obedience forms." The men complied at once and tore up all their forms. Well, that made Baba all the more hot and bothered. He ordered all to the leave the Manzil and for the first time they refused his order.

Nobody budged, causing Baba to get even more heated. For a while nothing but great excitement reigned in the bungalow. Baba threatened, "I'm sick and tired of it! Either you or I must go!" After a half-hour of swearing and abuse, he calmed down.

"Alright . . . I'm willing to remain on one condition; hereafter no one should follow my orders." The mandali replied, "Be as you wish, but just stay with us." Then after a half hour, the atmosphere became quite normal, as the following notice appeared on the board: "All orders should be followed as usual." A great sigh of relief went through the Manzil, as yet another chapter in grinding down his men's minds subsided; well at least for now. RD 164

The End of Manzil-e-Meem

Meanwhile, it seemed the preliminary work of forming his circle and laboring intensely under dizzying obedience was finally over. As Baba put it, "When the money ran out, I closed the Manzil." Then in April 1923, he took his men on a maddening year-long series of wanderings all over India, supposedly heading for his first trip to Persia [Iran] and the home of his ancestors. LH 250–52

They travelled mostly on foot, zigzagging up and down, settling in one place then within hours or the next day he'd change plans, pull up camp and move on to another, and then yet another place. Or maybe they'd just stop overnight and stay under a tree. Wherever Baba travelled, he always did so for his inner work for the universe, never staying anywhere even a moment longer than necessary. Well, the men were dizzy trying to figure it all out. As soon as his work was accomplished, he had to leave immediately on one pretext or another. Defying appearances, none of his movements was purposeless. The men knew he was going somewhere, but none could fathom the inner work he wasbeing accomplishinged. He'd tell them,

> "The purpose I came here for is accomplished, and now I must leave immediately to start my work again elsewhere without delay to maintain the link. We must leave here at once and go somewhere else."

Though they saw him breathing, how could they know his every breath touched all animate and inanimate things in creation. 1685

Baba's work was done to have a saving impact on the whole world, to benefit all beings and things. People worship God, and God worships everything in his entire creation. And so it went; a rag-tag, disheveled group of shabbily-dressed men of mixed castes and religions, half of them bare-foot and dirty led by a striking, golden-haired leader. Local people didn't know if they were being invaded by a band of robbers or child abductors. 476

In the town of Navsari, a police detail was quickly dispatched to interrogate these suspected gang members. Recording their statements and taking down names and addresses, the police acted with total impertinence and intimidation. Then suddenly who should arrive on the scene but Sohrabji Desai, instantly recognized as Navsari's most respected author.

He spoke sharply to the police, "These men are Meher Baba's disciples. I've come for his darshan. Why are you harassing them?" The chief detective then fully apologized. Seeing the famous Sohrabji coming for Meher Baba's darshan convinced him

Baba must be a truly great personality. Asking forgiveness, the chief requested darshan. When the Master refused, tails between their legs, they quietly left. But how happy Baba was finally meeting Sohrabji. It was clear to the mandali this scholar was already a very close one in Baba's circle. Seeing Baba for the first time, Sohrabji wept with joy. How long he had waited for this moment. When invited, Baba agreed to visit his house.

Now humorously on the previous day Baba happened to pass by this house while Sohrabji's two young nieces were outside playing. Catching sight of him they became afraid, taking him to be one of those "Arab kidnappers." Baba smiled at the girls, but this just escalated their alarm. The older one bravely told her little sister not to fear.

"If we take Meher Baba's name, nothing will happen, and this evil man will go away!" Though Sohrabji's family was totally devoted to Baba inwardly, no one had actually met him. So the nieces couldn't recognize him. When he came to their house, how shocked they were to see "the evil and fearsome Arab kidnapper" was none other than Baba himself!

Sohrabji brought his widowed sister, Baimai, to Baba. Bedridden for years with a severe leg fracture, she was never to be able to walk again. But seeing Baba, she suddenly rose to meet him. Her tears erased years of suffering as she stood unaided for the first time and regained her ability to walk. Pointing at a painting of Zarathustra in their house, Baba declared, "This is exactly how Zarathustra looked. I am your Prophet returned." 443–44

Sohrabji would walk behind Baba, collecting the dust from under his feet. Baba once remarked, "The significance of the dust under a Master's feet is beyond imagination. Like dust trampled upon without complaint, so the one remaining under my feet will rise to the zenith. Your arrogance, conceit and pride are to be turned into dust, and then alone will your dust be seen in its full brilliance." Baba's words made Sohrabji ecstatic. 790

CHRIST COME AGAIN

After some discussion in October 1923, it was decided to make a walking pilgrimage to Sakori to pay respects to Upasni Maharaj. A week into the trek, Baba called for a timeout to play a game with the men in a field. But during it they were playing only half-heartedly. He was likely doing some deep universal work under the guise of this game-play, and became upset at their disinterest. So now came a new order.

No one should speak to him, and he in turn wouldn't speak to them. They thought, "Oh, just another one of his bluffs." But Baba immediately kept silence, speaking with no one except Behramji. How could they know what The Master's first silence foreshadowed? Next morning after their first good night's rest on this forced march, Baba was still silent, conveying his messages to Behramji who felt special that Baba was talking only to him.

A village cobbler was summoned, and after all their broken sandals were repaired, they resumed their trek. At the 5 mile mark, they waited for Baba to catch up as he was walking with Behramji far behind. Then they all stopped for a little rest at their favorite makeshift hotel – a simple, dirty railway station platform.

Baba told Behramji to ask the men if they wanted to go directly to Sakori, or might prefer a little side-trip to see beautiful Lake Bhandardara. A few wanted to visit the lake, but the majority decided to boycott it and go straight to Sakori. Baba's calm, undramatic silent treatment had totally unnerved them. They really wanted to see the lake, especially on Rustom's enthusiastic recommendation, but refused out of protest.

So Baba explained to Behramji, "I'm not talking to the other men so as not to hurt their feelings, since they obviously don't like the way I talk in my open direct manner." But compared to his constant goading censures, not speaking to them was far more disconcerting.

Hearing this, Baba told Behramji, "Oh, if that's so and they feel it so much, then I'll speak with them." Thus, the problem was resolved. They decided, "Okay! Let's go see beautiful Lake Bhandardara and then continue on to Sakori."

If God-Realization is through love, then the heart must be pierced and eventually broken. That pain draws the Beloved's attention arrow by arrow. The arrow of that silence was soon to become permanent and actually not so bad after all. 458–59; RD 111

After an enjoyable visit to the lake, they finished sightseeing and continued their exhausting 200 mile hike to pay respects to Upasni Maharaj. But in the last town just before Sakori, Baba craftily told them to just go on without him; that he'd wait there for their return in the evening after seeing Maharaj alone.

In the past whenever they visited Sakori, Maharaj would lovingly talk with them and discourse about spirituality for hours, always seeing to their comfort during their stay with him. But on this occasion, they were in for the Master's topsy-turvy ways. Approaching Maharaj's cage, the men were met with screaming abuse and feigned anger.

Maharaj lashed out at them, "Get out! Get the hell out of my hut! You good-for-nothing sons-of-bitches! Have you no shame going from place to place, keeping me imprisoned in this cage? You think you oblige me by walking 200 miles?"

He cryptically added, "Go on doing as you're told by whoever is your somebody! And return to wherever you've been told to return!" The men were totally unhinged by Maharaj fiery antics. They returned to where Baba was waiting in the next town, keeping a dinner of fresh-baked bread and hot vegetables ready for them. While eating, they told him of their strange encounter with Maharaj.

Baba spent the next 2 hours explaining how through his mandali Maharaj was taking some of the load off Baba's shoulders. Maharaj would later end his self-imprisonment to celebrate Baba's 30th birthday in mid-February 1924. 461–62

Before that, from April 1923, Baba and the men would make 4 train trips through northern and central India, then 2 major foot-journeys with their belongings on their heads, sleeping under the stars, and 2 stays in Bombay plus a whirlwind steamship trip to Persia.

That visit was aborted after staying there only a day. A more extensive 2nd tour from one end of Persia to the other would occur 6 years later in 1929, then a secret 3rd visit in 1931 when Baba would do very deep spiritual work related to his future Manifestation. There would also be a series of stays at a new place named Meherabad.

The Master explained to the men about the current melancholic mood in their minds:

> "One usually passes through three stages on this path. The first is keen interest and intense longing to know and experience God, resulting in bright hopes and pleasant expectations. The second is full of disgust with disappointment, apathy and consequent suffering. The third and last stage is Realizing God. All in my circle are in the 2nd stage which lasts a long time. So put up with it cheerfully and don't leave me for any reason." 377

The promised sugar-coated-quick-results were gradually wearing off the bitter pill of spiritual questing. Baba's guarantees of advancement were now seen as a mere ploy – a pure pretext to induce his men during the rawness of their discipleship to simply stick to him. All that changed now on January 20th 1923 with this startling announcement:

> "Whatever hopes or promises I held out to you to be fulfilled by February 28th, you must now consider unfulfilled. If you think your last two years with me were in vain

and a total waste of time, and you now no longer take me what you believed me to be for so long, then I can only say I'm sorry and ask your forgiveness. Still, if you wish, you may remain with me, but only for an indefinite period without any previous conditions or expectations.

"If you think I've beguiled or deceived you, you're free to express and rebuke or beat me as you wish . . . . However, if you trust me, believing I'm the One for whom you have love and faith, then as day follows night I can definitely say in this life and in this body you can be certain of spiritual awakening, whether you remain with me, away from me or even go against me!" How could they leave just because the carrot was removed? 482; RD 17, 23

It wasn't a question of faith, but rather that love had begun growing in them – promises or not. Meanwhile, in all these back and forth journeys Baba was fasting and suffering greatly. His natural physical weakness was for the sake of his inner work for the circle. The men were also fasting and restricted to liquids. It was a dizzying year for all as he helped them to tolerate absolute, unequivocal uncertainty. PM 58–69; LH 251

Why go on in hope – living yet deceiving self – die now the real death -elf

In March 1924, after a few short on and off stays, Baba settled down at his permanent ashram 170 miles south of Bombay and 80 miles from Poona. It was an abandoned, ramshackle World War I British military camp which he named Meherabad – Meher flourishing – and here the Master's compassion would forever flourish.

It would become the site of his final resting place with his inner-circle men and women. Baba later stated,

"The major portion of my universal work was done here on this Hill, and Meherabad will one day become the greatest place of spiritual pilgrimage on earth."

Gilori Shah and Meherabad's Origin

We now recall Gulmai Irani who met Baba at Upasni's ashram years before with his mother Shireen. Gulmai later became deeply devoted to Baba, who named her as his spiritual mother. Her sons Adi and Rustom joined the mandali who were very fond of them.

When Gulmai visited Manzil-e-Meem in Bombay for Baba's 29th birthday party, he casually remarked to her, "You know, I'm thinking of moving to some village for a while." She said, "Well, why don't you come visit our property near Arangaon village outside Ahmednagar?" "Oh? Why there?" Baba coyly asked. Gulmai said, "Well, your visit was foretold by a local saint, Gilori Shah." Pretending not to follow, Baba asked what she meant.

But before relating the story Gulmai told Baba about this saint, we backtrack to the saint's most unusual earlier life. Gilori Shah had managed to become Queen Victoria's head cook at Buckingham Palace in London at the time of Baba's birth in the late 19th century.

She liked impressing visiting dignitaries and lunch guests with the saint's wonderful Indian curries. He was a master chef of English and Indian cuisine and had deep knowledge of Ayurvedic medicine. God only knows what else spiritually he was doing there, as Baba later related, Gilori Shah was stationed on the 6th plane. 409–10 andFootnote

But at the end of 20 years, he informed the Queen he wished to return home to India. She was astonished! Who would willingly leave her majesty's royal service? She begged him to stay. He refused. It is said at his regretted departure she bestowed upon him a bag of gold.

He left with little else. Crossing over the Thames, it is said he threw the gold into the river, returning to India as poor as he had left it. In his last years, Gilori Shah attracted many devotees in Ahmednagar, including Gulmai Irani, her husband Kaikhushru and sons Rustom and Adi. Gulmai related the fascinating history of Arangaon to Baba:

> A few years back, my husband Kaikhushru got a contract to supply electric lights to the military barracks near the village of Arangaon, 6 miles from Ahmednagar where he'd visit on business. At the end of the war it was up for sale. But it was arid and impossible to cultivate.
>
> No one was interested in buying such "jungle land." So the owner approached Kaikhushru. When he asked my opinion, I wondered what we'd do with it. We'd certainly never move there so far out of the city. Still, he bought it, thinking it might prove useful in the future.
>
> The few unattended buildings became dilapidated, while any useful material was taken by local villagers. A Muslim saint who lived in Ahmednagar, Gilori Shah, came over occasionally for a meal. When your [Baba's] uncle Masaji was in Ahmednagar, he'd take bread and butter to the saint and even bathed him.
>
> Gilori Shah often mentioned he wanted to go to Arangaon to live out his "last days there." I thought it a totally unsuitable place and tried to dissuade him. "But Hazrat, who will bring your meals out there and look after you out in that jungle?" He'd frown, "All these people are useless to me. I don't need their help." There were some wealthy butchers who'd pay him respect and even offered him some land. But he really wanted our place.
>
> He'd only settle at Arangaon. One day he told me, "Give me a small portion of your land and build a room for

CHRIST COME AGAIN

me." On another occasion he said, "Take me there and also bring Upasni Maharaj and Meher Baba. Turn the place into an ashram for wandering mendicants and pilgrims."

I said the saint had been insisting on the land for some years now. So Kaikhushru promised to fulfill his request. That very day we brought Gilori Shah to Arangaon with some of his devotees. And there he selected a small plot of land by the road and told them, "Prepare my tomb right here . . . ."

His followers were totally surprised. Why would he want to be buried all the way out at Arangaon? They pleaded with him: "But Hazrat, who'll come out here so far to pay homage? This place is uninhabitable!" The saint reprimanded them: "You're like children. You know nothing at all! In a short time, this place will turn into a garden of pilgrimage. A Great One will come here. This land will one day belong to the people of the world! Only then will you understand."

Gilori Shah's small dargah by the walk to lower Meherabad.

So when I went with the saint to look at the site, he turned to me and said, "When I die, please bring me here escorted by a brass band and bury me here!" I pleaded with him. "Your Muslim followers will never permit a band!" He replied, "Yes, I know. So you'll have to drive them away. Tell them I had no caste or creed! "Meher Baba will

soon come here, and before he does, you should have my tomb ready. All will happen just as I'm telling you. . . ."
390–92

After relating Arangaon's history to Baba, Gulmai beaming with confidence asked, "So! When are you coming to Arangaon?" He grinned, "I may or may not; we'll see . . . . Meanwhile, construct Gilori Shah's tomb just as he wishes."

This is how Meher Baba worked by manifesting things outwardly in a natural sequence of events. While residing at Manzil-e-Meem, no one knew he was preparing the ground for his lifelong abode. It only came to light in this conversation with Gulmai. Who can guess the Avatar's impact on world affairs? Not a thing happens without his will. 392

At Rustom's Bombay engagement party, Gulmai again asked Baba to visit the land. "Your presence will sanctify the whole Ahmednagar area." So Baba accepted her invitation, but only for a visit, never promising to stay. Then came his Bombay birthday party when he broached the topic of sending some of his men back home, confiding to them:

> "In a few days, I'm disbanding Manzil-e-Meem. Then after Rustom's marriage at Ahmednagar in May, I'll remain at Arangaon, but in a very different way with only a few men who'll have to face great hardships. Arangaon life will be the reverse of here. Those who remain with me will work like common laborers – slaves!"

Dr. Ghani quipped "Maybe instead of Arangaon, you should call it "Hyrangaon" – "Hardship village." Baba then disbanded the Manzil, explaining his connection with those sent away remains as it was. He'd call them back later if they remained faithful to him. 402–03

CHRIST COME AGAIN

Meanwhile, still staying with Baba were his younger brother Jal, uncle Masaji and cousin Pendu, Gulmai's sons, Adi and Rustom Irani, Babu Cyclewalla, Baidul, Barsoap, Behramji, Padri, Nervous, Gustadji and Slamson – a baker's dozen.

These mandali were identical to Jesus' apostles witnessing the Lord's return. He would make them laugh and weep; feed them well and then make them fast; keep them in comfort and then make them suffer; keep them in palatial houses and then make them stay in huts or live under a tree. He would dress them well, then making them live like ascetics.

By playing with them and making them labor with tears; by joking with them and having them offer heartfelt devotions – through these different ways, the Lord revealed his wine shop, transforming their hearts to cups into which he poured his very Divinity 451

Chapter Nine

Meherabad and Persia

Manzil-e-Meem was Meher Baba's first experiment in forming his core apostolic group. Before this 10 month stay in Bombay, his relationship with them had been like one between good friends. In the Manzil, that relationship radically changed as the mandali were made aware that Baba was their Lord and Master, establishing the bond existing between any spiritually perfect God-Conscious Master and his disciples.

In countless and sometimes painful ways they learned the paramount importance of obeying instructions, no matter how insignificant they appeared. They had already accepted being away from homes and detached from their families; that was a done deal.

They were given the opportunity to live with men of different religions and castes – something none of them could ever have done before, but made possible in Baba's camaraderie. They were being trained to shed their individual differences, prejudices, likes and dislikes for the benefit of all – impossible without having spent these preliminary 10 very strict months living with Baba at Manzil-e-Meem. Now it all began coming together. 408

Smoldering Resentment

Just 2 days before Rustom's wedding, several Zoroastrian guests started arriving at Khushru Quarters, his family's compound in the mostly Muslim town of Ahmednagar, founded in the 15th century. While they gathered, deep hostility was brewing against Baba, as none of these Parsis or Iranis believed he had the slightest spiritual status, let alone being a Realized Perfect Master.

Real knowledge of spirituality was very limited in this dying Zoroastrian community. It was so dried up that for thousands of years, not even a single Perfect Master could be counted from among them. And unlike Hindus and Muslims, the Parsis had no real mystical tradition for even acknowledging saints or advanced souls.

So it was no surprise that nothing but sarcasm was aimed at Baba's so-called "spiritual state." They looked on him and his followers as deluded at best if not outright mad, and considered their relatives as nitwits to get themselves mixed up in this kind of "spiritual tomfoolery." The arrival of more Parsis and Iranis from Bombay and Poona only fueled the tension and criticism smoldering among Gulmai's relatives.

She would be harassed for years by her family for taking Meher Baba as her Master. Adding to it, the local papers were rife with anti-Meher Baba attacks. It was no wonder that indignation against him and his followers was the chief topic among the skeptical Zoroastrian wedding guests. Baba and his men had only just arrived, and already the compound was filled with tension. The climax came early in the morning on May 4th.

Gulmai's son Adi, the bridegroom's older brother, quietly informed the Master of the wedding guests' backbiting and criticism. Adi made clear that many in his family and especially Gulmai's brother were inciting other guests against him. Baba was annoyed at this and also upset she hadn't returned from Sakori on the previous day as he precisely instructed.

Without a word Baba abruptly stormed out of the compound. Some of his men were washing and shaving in bathrooms. Others were at breakfast. But the standing order was that wherever the Master went they followed, no matter what they were doing in that moment – even on the toilet. The men heard the cry that Baba was leaving.

They ran out from everywhere – bathrooms and bedrooms, hitching up pants, mouths full of toothpaste, stuffing dirty glasses and plates into their bags and hastily tying up bedding rolls – clueless to where he was going.

The First Glimpse of Meherabad

Baba strode rapidly out of Ahmednagar with a dark and aloof frown. When he suddenly stopped at the railway station, the men ran to catch up, thinking they might be taking a train and wondering about their belongings left behind. But Baba kept going across the Sina River Bridge and then turned south.

Without their knowing it, he was leading them 6 miles further south to the abandoned British military camp in a treeless, barren, snake-infested area outside town by the impoverished village of Arangaon. Here he'd soon establish his lifelong headquarters for serving humanity. It would also be the site of his final resting place.

They passed many huge banyan trees, seen today and known as "the tree of the Perfect Master." Finally they came upon a dusty, desolate, treeless area with dilapidated buildings on the outskirts of the small village of Arangaon. A watchman told them the structures had once been an old British military camp, a mail-drop-whistle-stop along the rail line, and were now owned by Khan Saheb Kaikhushru Irani – Gulmai's husband from whose home the Master had just stomped out in a mood of total displeasure! Ah, the divine comedy under it all.

Needless to say, the mandali were surprised. Yes, they'd heard the name "Arangaon" and Baba's vague intentions of staying there, but they had no idea where it was. Baba sat by the roadside under a neem tree beside an old water well. Scanning the neglected buildings, he pointed to the newly built roadside tomb of Gilori Shah who would die and be buried without ceremony as he had wished shortly after Baba's visit here today.

The saint had kept his coffin ready on which he inscribed: "He who has died before his death is alive. Gulmai's husband paid all the funeral expenses. After a year, a wooden canopy was built over the saint's marble tomb as is seen to this day – Gilori Shahs' superb piece of spiritual feng-shui. Meanwhile, the men were hungry and thirsty. 493–94

Though they were sitting by a well, there wasn't a bucket to draw water. Baba sent a couple of them to nearby Arangaon village to fetch something to eat. They approached a Catholic resident, Gangaram L. Pawar, saying, "We're pilgrims in need of food. We'll pay for whatever you can provide." He was willing, but could offer them only unleavened millet bread and chutney, and even that would take a while to prepare and bake.

Parwar sahib gave them a roped-bucket to refresh themselves with the well-water while he went to prepare their simple meal. Meanwhile, hot-tempered Rustom, upset hearing of Baba's sudden departure, raced on his motorcycle all through Ahmednagar, stopping people on the road, describing Baba and asking if they'd seen a group of men go by.

When some said they'd seen a group walking out toward Arangaon, Rustom wasted no time racing there. He found Baba and the mandali sitting by the well under the neem tree. With tears in his eyes, he ran to Baba. "Why the hell have you come out here? Baba replied sternly, "I no longer want to stay at Khushru Quarters." "But what about my wedding? You promised to attend!" "I've changed my mind!" was the curt reply.

"But it was only on your advice I even agreed to marry! If you don't attend, I'm not going through with it!" Baba lovingly calmed Rustom. Though he'd not be present, he'd later come to bless him and his new wife, Freiny. And yes, the marriage was his explicit wish.

CHRIST COME AGAIN

Baba then sent Rustom back to Ahmednagar to forward their luggage to this new Arangaon site. As it turned out, Baba attended the wedding, though he didn't stay at Khushru Quarters. Europeans, fellow Parsis and Iranis made up the wedding party.

Attention was given to the more distinguished guests' comfort, while Baba's men rendered whatever help was needed to the kitchen cooks – the servants' servants. This meant cutting and cleaning vegetables for the feast and helping out wherever needed. It felt humiliating in the glares of the wealthy guests. But in life with a Master, honor and insult are the same. 418

Meanwhile back at the abandoned army camp, as Rustom returned to Ahmednagar, Baba gestured to his companions, majestically sweeping his arm across the wide vista. "So what do you think of this place?" The men broke up, laughing – couldn't contain themselves. "Are you kidding? There's nothing here!" "What are you talking about?" Baba replied, "Where the Master stays, is everything! Nothing is lacking in his company."

The men went back to Gangaram's poor Arangaon hut and returned with delicious fresh-baked bread, chutney and a vegetable dish. They drank the cool bucket-drawn well-water by cupping it in the hollow of their palms. Gangaram also brought a kerosene lantern for them. The Master blessed him, "May there always be light in your house." 413–16

The old man would become Baba's main Arangaon disciple and his first Christian follower. Baba nicknamed him Ajoba, meaning "respected old man." Deeply devoted to the master, he'd bring the village headman and Arangaon people into Baba's orbit. Still relatively poor, the rooftops of this tiny country village today sport little satellite dishes.

The Avatar always associates with peacefully remote and barren places having arid landscapes. Baba revealed one day Meherabad would become a spiritual oasis and the largest center of spiritual pilgrimage in the entire world.

This property, given to Baba by Gulmai, was 6 miles outside Ahmednagar, the town where Gandhi and India's first Prime Minister, Jawaharlal Nehru, would later be imprisoned for civil disobedience by the British. Baba would have his attentive eye on both of them.

Gulmai's home, Khushru quarters, was taken over in later decades as Baba's in-town office, managed by her son and Baba's long-time secretary, Adi Irani "Sr.," to distinguish him from Baba's youngest brother Adi Irani "Jr." It remains today the office of the Avatar Meher Baba Perpetual Public Charitable Trust(AMBPPCT).

Long ago, the Hindu Perfect Master, Vithoba, stayed at Arangaon which means "Forest Village." It was a lush jungle forest, but mismanaged in the 18th and 19th centuries under British rule with increasing population and deforestation by the poor. It eventually became dry and barren – a windy, desolate slope overgrown with thorn bushes. 417

The still poor Arangaon villagers began growing nurseries for 35,000 trees in a re-forestation plan for Meherabad's lands. It began in late 1933 when Baba visited Valu Pawar's home. She was the Christian daughter of a wealthy Arangaon family with landed property and a widow who for years lovingly did all types of lowly jobs for Baba. MM 1: 167

As a wonderful example of selfless service, Valu wore elaborate gold ornaments around her neck and wrists in the beginning. When she later went to live with and help the women mandali on Meherabad Hill, she gave up all worldly riches to be near Baba and dedicate her life to serving him. Then one day he casually remarked to her: 1827 "You know, I come down the hill twice a day for the mandali and have to walk up twice more. Wouldn't it be great be if we had shade trees lining the path?" A very caring person, from that very day Valu began planting saplings on both sides of the narrow dirt road. A scarcity of water made it even more difficult to nourish them, so she would carry water from afar like a coolie in 2 buckets balanced on a bamboo pole across her shoulders.

Due to her labor of love, today we find shade trees on both sides of the path leading up Meherabad Hill. Although she had other chores, Valu still found time for this extra work, resulting in a boon for all pilgrims coming to Meherabad to this day. 1584

The transformation as of 2015 is stunning, with small lakes, ponds and shade trees, flowers and the return of abundant birds and wildlife. From once being a barren desert place, Meherabad is truly a growing natural oasis, and of course the world's primary spiritual oasis.

Snakes and Scorpions

After Rustom's wedding, Baba and the men returned for their first short stay at Arangaon, spending 2 weeks of backbreaking hard labor to begin reconditioning the old war camp. Then one evening as they made themselves comfortable moments after Gustadji had set down his bedroll, a small snake was found coiled under it.

How it got there was a mystery, as up till now no snake had been sighted on the property. Ramjoo's diary notes: "Baba ordered us all to immediately move into the post-office building, as if really scared of that snake." They found numerous dens of deadly cobras and adders hidden in the fields of Meherabad. Baba warned his men to be very careful of them.

So it was a strict order everyone had to carry a lantern when going out at night. On May 11th, 1924 Baba asked: "Do you carry a lantern going out at night?" Receiving a "no," he upbraided them: "What use are your devotional songs if you don't follow my instructions? What do you expect to gain by mere singing? Obeying my orders is the only real devotion. Only then will your devotional songs have any meaning!" With this, all promised to follow his behests.

But then he decided, "Maybe Arangaon's not such a good place after all; no good staying here now with all these snakes and scorpions." So once again, with this as a bald-face excuse, Baba uprooted his men. The diary continues, "We not only left Arangaon, but all of India for Persia. Just because of a snake! I wonder what meaning Baba gives to snakes?"

A Proposed First Trek to Persia

Before abandoning what they presumed was their final new home, Baba named the place MEHERABAD, meaning "full of mercy," painted on a large sign nailed between 2 poles by the railway tracks. And thus after so auspiciously naming it, they left it behind for yet another long trek throughout India and planned to eventually continue on to Persia. 422–23

Like divine dharma-bums, they trudged with the Master along dusty roads and river banks, carrying bedrolls on their heads and sleeping like gypsies under the trees or along railway lines. If lucky, a stationmaster might let them spend a night in an unused railway waiting room. One day on this journey they passed a large sculpture of Lord Buddha.

Here Baba revealed some amazing stories of his life and times wandering in India 2500 years ago, stating as Buddha he had a physically perfect body compared with all his other Avataric incarnations in this cycle, including his present one.

If they found a government rest house along the way, they might get permission after a lot of persuasion to bunk down there for the night – a bare, unsanitary room at most, or maybe just a porch, keeping night watch by turns to ward off intruders and wild animals. Proceeding in this way they reached Quetta at the present-day Pakistan/Afghan border.

CHRIST COME AGAIN

Staying there 3 weeks, Baba's unspoken reason for this layover was to contact a couple of special young ladies whom I'd get to know very well almost 60 years later – Goher and Katie Irani – young sisters whom Baba made laugh with his wonderful stories. They would live with him later on, and play important roles in his circle of women disciples. 428

Goher would become Baba's resident physician, even to signing his death certificate. Before leaving, Baba got 2 matchboxes and threaded a string through them. Keeping one end with him and giving the other to Gulmai who was also visiting there with him, he climbed stairs to the 2nd floor, telling her to stay where she was. Through this "telephone," Baba said, "As we communicate outwardly, so must we communicate inwardly as well."

Meher Baba at Urak Mt. in Quetta [Pakistan], 1923.

Then he talked to Katie through the matchbox phone, saying, "I'm leaving, but you must go on remembering me. Will you do that?" She replied, "How can I ever forget you, Baba?" The telephone had not yet arrived in India, but recalling this trick from his childhood, Baba was likely pre-figuring the telephonic age shortly to arrive in India. 433

Leaving Quetta, they arrived in Surat where the Master went to the bazaar near the railway station. On the way back, he spotted an 18-year-old Hindu boy in a pitiable condition shivering in the cold. At Baba' request, Ramjoo inquired and learned the boy had come from another city seeking work in Surat, but had suddenly fallen ill and was now penniless. Baba directed one of the mandali to take the boy to a nearby restaurant, where he was fed to his heart's content. A rail ticket was given to him with Baba instructing him to return home immediately. The Master's decision to pass through the bazaar that day was just a pretext to encounter and rescue the destitute lad. The mandali were deeply touched by Baba's omniscient love and spontaneous care for so young a stranger. 456

Later in a similar situation, Baba was travelling with Kaka, Gustadji and Baidul through northern India seeking God-intoxicated mad-men called masts [pronounced musts]. He made an unplanned stop in the town of Sitapur, south of the Nepal border. It was soon evident why Baba came here when they happened upon a helpless family of 3 children with their father and mother camping under a tree near the railway station.

The mother was so gravely ill she couldn't even move. One of their children had died the previous day. With no money plus the mother's illness and the death of a child, the father was in anguish. Baba instructed the mandali to feed them well and question the man about his condition, driven almost to despair by this tragic situation.

Baba had the family taken along with them on the train to Bareilly where the wife was admitted to a hospital. Baba gave the man money to feed his family. As Bareilly was a large city, he said he'd surely be able to find a job soon. Once again, the Compassionate One's timely help had saved a hopeless family on the point of starvation and despair. 2270–71

Back on the road, still heading for Persia, Baba's young brother Jal – always a joker – teased one of the mandali, Maruti Patel: "September is so-o-o cold up in the north people can't survive without drinking wine! So, we'll have to drink tons of it just to stay alive!"

Maruti took Jal seriously, and as a strict Hindu was worried he'd be made to drink alcohol. Hearing about it, Baba remarked, "It's true; the weather will be severely cold, but why worry about drinking wine? Don't we eat meat when we can't get vegetarian food? This kind of talk is rubbish." Explaining further to the men, he stated:

> "Wine is good as an intoxicant and tonic for both health and spiritual life. After drinking it, if thoughts are diverted to spiritual advancement, it's a great push toward the Goal; otherwise, it can lead to hell, either raise you to the highest pinnacle or push you into a ditch. The object of intoxicants in the ancient past was spiritual. Seekers then not only took wine but marijuana, hash and heroin – even Perfect Masters. Then ordinary people started taking these intoxicants for all the wrong reasons. Not understanding their proper use, the intoxication diverted their thoughts instead to totally carnal desires – to lust, the greatest obstacle on the spiritual path." 1095

Since his childhood, Baba passed through intense periods of illness and acute dysentery, as he was doing now during these exhausting, foot-blistering travels and trials. Severe restrictions on water and food with no decent place to rest were just further vexations.

After visiting Baghdad in Iraq, they returned to Bombay and boarded a ship bound for Persia. Baba was excited about visiting the land of his ancestors, but with a rough voyage he and a few of the mandali became quite seasick.

When they landed on Persia's southern coast at Bandar Abbas, typical with Baba's travel plans, the journey was halted as they abruptly reversed course and returned to India. One perspective of this first Persian journey and its apparently dizzying plan-changes had to do with the inner work Baba was doing regarding its people. 487–88

His brief presence there seeded a change in consciousness, as great improvements swept over the land, and for a time the country was greatly benefitted. And with the country's gradual modernization violent religious persecution of minorities lessened. 492

However, the later near-genocidal Iranian policies toward the Baha'i and the repression of other religious minorities including later followers of Meher Baba are a bleak and discouraging suppression of dissent with countless human rights violations.

But there was another boon in this short visit. Many may appreciate Meher Baba's favorite poet was the great God-Realized Master, Hafiz. Before leaving Persia, Baba learned Hafiz' tomb was in a very run-down condition. Returning to India, he sent one of his disciples to the Minister of Education in Shiraz and provided funds for a new structure over Hafiz's grave and for the full restoration of its gardens. 1125

CHRIST COME AGAIN

Meher Baba and mandali in Persia, 1923. Standing: Abdul Rehman, uncle Masaji, Baidul, Ramjoo, Asthma and Padri; Seated: Slamson, Babu Rao, Pendu and Nervous. On Floor: Brother Jal, Gustadji, Baba, Adi K. Irani and Beheramji.

CHRIST COME AGAIN

The Master Wanders Alone

Before returning to Meherabad, Baba assigned four of his men to go to specific different places and remain there until he contacted them. Though all boarded the same train, Baba got off alone at the Itarsi station stop, so exhausted that setting foot on the station platform he laid down and rested his head on his bedding roll. Observing from nearby, a ticket collector became suspicious and shouted, "Arrest that ticketless traveler!"

As he approached intimidatingly, Baba pulled out his ticket. "Here it is, sir!" Stunned by the radiance on Baba's face, the man bowed to him and backed off, leaving Baba alone to relax in peace. Over the next several days the Master roamed about Itarsi, contacting saints and likely some God-intoxicated souls called masts, many of whom we'll encounter later before and during WWII. Details of this unusual solitary wandering are unknown.

But it was evident that for his inner work he stayed behind there and wished his movements kept secret. This was a rare occasion, in fact the one and only time after setting out on his public life that Meher Baba ever travelled alone with no mandali with him. 491–92

Then returning to Meherabad for his work in the spring of 1924, Baba asked for a white horse, a white ox and a white dog. The dog would have been named Sadhu, but never materialized. However, a beautiful white horse and white ox were given. Baba named them "Sufi" and "Saint," but they hardly lived up to their names, as both were highly spirited and constantly getting loose, had to be chased all over Meherabad.

So he decided to send them with Padri and Nervous by freight train to be presented as "gifts" to Upasni Maharaj. With the animals biting and kicking the entire way on the train, they had to walk the final nine miles to Sakori. When they finally arrived exhausted, Maharaj was in a fiercely belligerent mood, sending word they must immediately return with the animals, shouting he was unable to accept "such gifts!"

They begged him to please accept this love offering from Baba, but Maharaj stood off at a distance, bursting with vituperation. "Call the police at once! They've stolen these animals and brought them here! You sons-of-bitches had better leave here immediately or you'll find yourselves locked up in jail!" Then Maharaj pointed an ominous curse at Padri.

Quite shaken, Padri and Nervous beat a hasty retreat, taking the unruly animals back the way they came. When they returned to Baba exhausted, he slyly questioned Padri if they'd "successfully" delivered Sufi and Saint to Maharaj. Padri just smiled and with choice swear words laid out the woeful tale in all its colorful details. Baba collapsed in laugher. Well, this was too much for Padri. He became livid. What was going on here?

What to make of these Masters' arcane shenanigans and the exhausting charade that he and Nervous were put through? Again, the old question began gnawing like acid in Padri's mind. "What the hell have I gotten myself into?" 531–32

Meanwhile, their journeys had taken them as far as Karachi [now in Pakistan]. Then on the night they were to return to Bombay, each of the men was given a bath. Baba had them lean over a fountain as he poured water over their heads, resembling Christian baptism. 538

Decades later, Baba's sister Mani would explain his way of grinding down his disciples' false minds with the analogy of washing clothes: "Have you ever watched an Indian washerwoman? After soaking the dirty clothes in soapy water for a while to loosen the dirt, she then holds a single piece by one end and raises it over her head. And with all her strength she bangs it down and smashes it on stone. She does this repeatedly.

"Finally, the clothes are spotless. Baba does this to his close lovers, clearing their accumulated sanskaric dirt. He appears merciless smashing his lovers' false egos by repeatedly humiliating those who agree to serve him." RT IV: 217

Baba's Enigmatic Monologue

But the strangest things over this recent period of wanderings were some of Baba's constant refrains, likely occasioned by some carelessness in the men's attitude. He'd repeat:

> "I want to touch the feet of 5000 sadhus, and I pray they'll abuse and insult me. May sadhus tear to shreds my divine ego and crush my Baba-hood! . . . . Never become a Baba! I want to shatter to smithereens my Baba-hood and my divine ego! What have you gained by being with me so long?
>
> I've journeyed this far to meet sadhus who will kick, insult, abuse and spit on me! It's my innermost wish – from the very bottom of my heart – that whenever and wherever I lay my head on the feet of a saint, he should violently kick me! Believe me; I'll bring about such situations.
>
> Oh God! I'll improve if I'm kicked. I'll be benefited if my ego is destroyed. And the mandali, too, will benefit. What have they gained being with me these last 2 years? At least, if my pride is crushed, they'll gain from that. It is [they] who have bestowed Baba-hood on me, and I now want to get rid of it, because I experience I myself have no stuff in me!
>
> In taking the darshan of sadhus and saints, if I come across a Perfect One who humiliates rebukes and abuses me, I'll follow him and never return. You men, too, should do the same so your life may become worthwhile; or else we're neither ascetics nor worldly men; neither here nor there!"

These baffling remarks bore on some of the men's ongoing arguments, especially Gustadji and Behramji. On the slightest pretext they'd quarrel like stubborn asses over the pettiest things. In such moments of anger they were disregarding Baba's order. Criticizing himself and them, the Master gave them a sharp lesson in humility and self-effacement. 540–43

But by now most of them were so fed up listening to his baffling refrain that they pleaded with him to just stop it. He replied, "I'm serious; I'm not a Baba. It is you who bestowed "Baba-hood" on me! Now sadhus and saints want to crush me! I've no stuff in me! And my Masters, Babajan and Maharaj have no stuff in them either! Maharaj isn't even a saint, let alone a God-Realized Master!"

When they asked why he'd utter such things about his own Masters, Baba explained, "Divine law compels me to say it, and that law applies to you also. You're obliged to act according to divine law [Baba's divine law!]" But these remarks were also directed at Padri.

His mind was totally unsettled from the recent disaster with Upasni and the animals. He kept thinking, "What the hell kind of spirituality is this when Masters behave toward one another in ways ordinary people would never dream? What have I fallen into?" 554–55

With the Avatar's inner work on a universal scale, it's impossible to understand any of his individual actions, especially the exhausting efforts and constant changes in his journeys. When he thinks of a place or a country with his universal mind, not only do all the people and things there feel the effect, but their thinking and consciousness changes as well.

Thus, his every action done with Christ-consciousness brings millions of unseen results. Baba might speak to someone, and the person listening would feel Baba's words weren't directed at him but to some distant person who actually felt the effect. The extent of the unseen force in the Avatar's actions can never be imagined.

Failing Monsoons – Farmers beg for Rain

When local rainfall was 85% below normal, millions of poor farmers trying to make their living off very small land plots faced immanent starvation – 60% of over a billion people. In many years the monsoon rains needed in early June were delayed in rural, arid farming areas typical of Meherabad. Electricity and irrigation systems were unknown then, and rainwater was key to crop survival and the lives of millions working the land.

Typical of these poor farmers around Meherabad is a mother, struggling to keep her toes from poking out through holes in her shoes as she pushes and pulls an ancient farm tool. She's bone thin, but has to be strong – a struggling widow feeding herself and 5 kids. With the soil hard as stone and desert-dry, this year the children will face hunger yet again.

A widowed farmer, struggling to feed herself and five children in the early years near Arangaon.

Still, she's trying to prepare the land for seeding. But if the rains fail, the fields will be empty and no one will call her for work. In the scorching mid-day sun she leaves the field and sits at home on a floor fashioned from dried cow dung. She's worried and troubled, knowing she'll not be the last in her family to rely on the whims of weather.

If something goes wrong with the meager crops, their entire economy goes topsy-turvy. Local village leaders hope beyond hope that there's still time for the monsoon to work its magic. But the poor farmers are beyond anxious, saying, "What we plant won't grow in dryness. Such is our poverty here. If the rains fail, people die of hunger."

They aren't educated and without money she can't even send her children to school. Though Baba is trying to change that with the free schools he's building for these poor local families. Still she worries, not just about her children's present, but what their future will bring. This was the typical of poor Meherabad farmers in 1925 and today in 2015.

The Rainmaker

With the failure of seasonal late-fall monsoon rains, villagers from neighboring areas in desperation approached Baba, begging him for rain. The fall crops would fail again in this prolonged drought. With the wells practically dry, there was little drinking water left. Baba advised them to have patience. After a day of exhausting activity, he was in the midst of a discussion with the mandali when suddenly the villagers reappeared.

They were back again beseeching him for rain. Upasni Maharaj's arti was sung and Baba ordered a small pit to be dug and a sacred Dhuni fire to be lit. The fire was started at 11 that night. Afterward, Baba informed the villagers, "God has heard your prayers. Now go home."

There wasn't a cloud in the sky prior to lighting the Dhuni. An hour later, heavy rains began falling, pummeling them for a blessed 15 hours. As the villagers' crops were saved, the mandali wrote poems to the Dhuni, while Baba penned his own stanzas to go down in history:

> "My pen has not the strength to sing your praise. At the first glow of your flame there was rain! How marvelous is your gift! To cool your radiant blaze, God Himself, in

CHRIST COME AGAIN

honor of you, showered rain for hours on end. May you come to the rescue of thousands!

May you receive the blessings of the poor! To those who pray to you, may you give protection. You have the attributes of a saint. Who loses himself in you becomes like you. Wonderful is your effect; wonderful your play! Wonderful your nature! Your gift nurtures or destroys.

You fructify seeds, while the tree you uproot – both are your blessings. One who uses you with care can cook 100s of dishes. But to the ignorant who treat you carelessly you are a calamity. You are like the saint, full of virtues as well as faults. You make one swim and another drowns – such is your nature! The whole region of Ahmednagar was without water.

But at the perfect time you rewarded the labor of the farmer. When you've surrendered to Baba, let your lips be sealed. Brave are those who serve at the feet of the Sadguru. In the form of fire you were hot. By becoming water you were cool. As those near you were warmed by your flame, so also was the world made happy by your light.

Surrendering to Baba let your lips be sealed. Brave are those who serve at the feet of the Sadguru. Limitless is your greatness, Oh Dhuni! Only rishis and silent ones can fathom you. You made Beheram sleep and the sky weep. Your warmth melted the heavens, wetting my sadra. You are the real servant of the Sadguru. Stay near him always! Difficult it was to live in the heat of the famine as it made you sweat. You are the true slave of the Master, a fiery rod in my cool hands!" 623–24

When farmers in the town of Toka asked Baba for rain, it fell heavily for 3 days, flooding the river. Now they had to beg him to save their town. Baba went to the river's edg,e and placing his feet in it, the river receded. To this day, many Baba followers light a Dhuni on the 12th of each month, throwing in a sacred fire stick on which they've "placed" an intention representing a particular attachment or desire they long to be freed from.

Meanwhile, with Meherabad's terrible water problem, Rustom had permission to dig another well near the railway line. He even brought in expert water diviners, and though they dug deeper than usual, still no water is found. Then one day, another very dejected farmer from a nearby village approached the Master.

He said, "I'm a very poor man with a small piece of land, but I can't farm it without water. I borrowed money to drill a well, but no water. Now I'm in desperate straits. You are someone great. I've come to beg water of you. I have full faith you'll grant me this boon."

Baba asked, "How deep did you go?" "40'." "Don't stop digging. Go 5' more. God is great; He will help you." The villager then left, satisfied with Baba's assurance. A week later, that farmer with a parade of other villagers showed up proclaiming joyfully, "Water was found in my well by your grace!" After the villagers garlanded Baba, he distributed sweets to them, and they turned back home singing his praises.

When the villagers left, the mandali glared at Baba. He shrugged, "Honestly, I did nothing! His faith brought him water. Outsiders get their desires filled by my blessings, but here at Meherabad our 3 wells are dry!" This was too much for Rustom, who complained bitterly, "What about us? We dig wells; we have faith in you, so why don't we find water?"

Baba replied, "I only know that villager found water due to his faith. I did nothing for him." This irritated Rustom all the more. "It's useless being with you. You really think we have no faith in you? We're with you day and night, but we don't have faith in you? But a villager who shows up one day has enough faith to strike water?" Baba then explained:

"You really don't get it, do you? That man came and his faith was connected with water. But here you are, and your faith isn't connected with anything. Whether finding water or not, whether your desires are fulfilled or not, your faith remains the same. Your faith is connected with me, not with anything else. So I can trust you. I can't trust that man who came only for water. How really fortunate you are I can trust you.

"But if you want to be like him, you'll find water. Decide if you want water or me. Even if I start dancing naked before you, your faith in me will remain unshaken, as you accept me as God. That villager's faith was based on an idol of hope; so feeling pity for him, God fulfilled his hope. God feels pity for you also, so He makes mincemeat out of you! I keep you with me not for an idol of hope, but to smash that idol to utter smithereens!" 724-25

Over the decades there were many such occasions when the autumn monsoon rains failed and local farmers came desperate for Baba's bounty. And without fail, rains soon came. Then in 1966 wasn't there yet another truly horrific water-crisis. The monsoon failure caused the Bombay government to announce the evacuation of that entire city's 5 million people. A longtime disciple, Minoo Desai, urgently cabled Baba on July 13th, 1966.

Echoing their grief, he said: "Baba, I'm praying on behalf of Bombay's 5 million people for your intervention for rain and blessings." Baba cabled back: "Bombay already starting receiving rains. – Love, Baba" As if on cue, the rains came and city's hopes were miraculously revived. The rains continued till the city's reservoirs were soon overflowing.

In addition, as letters and telegrams were read to Baba from other places, they too immediately received blessed rains on cue.

Just see how the Lord of the Universe has pity on his Beloved children needing precious rains to survive. 5239

On April 22nd 1924, a very strange-looking man appeared at the Meherabad well. Baba's brothers Jal and Adi were taken by the utter beauty of this strange man. After drinking, he said he was hungry. They brought him to Baba who was delighted at his arrival. The man was a mast – a God-intoxicated-soul traversing the inner spiritual planes.

He was served food and given sweets. But when questioned, his language was totally unintelligible. Baba put a new shirt and pants on him and then sent him on his way. Although his name is not recorded, he was the very first mast ever to enter Meherabad. 502

As said, masts would play an exceedingly important role in Baba's spiritual work in the future, especially before and during WWII, as we will soon see in extraordinary depth. Returning to Meherabad from travels in January 1925, Baba settled down for a longer stay, and would soon enter his startlingly unexpected lifelong Silence. Now, here's a Baba riddle: "What does a God-Realized one share with a materialist, an animal, an atheist, child and idiot?"

> Two do not care about religion –
> a materialist and a God-Realized person:
> Two who do not care about money –
> an animal and a God-Realized person.
> Two do not worship God –
> an atheist and a God-Realized person.
> Two are free from lust –
> a child and a God-Realized person.
> Two have no anger –
> an idiot and a God-Realized person. 716–17

Chapter Ten

The Avatar's Circle

We preface this chapter by considering the various roles of the Avatar's inner circle. Baba said: "Circle members are like sons of the Master, while others are like 'non-family members.' " And so, Baba's relationship with Mehera Irani, the closer of his 2 inner-circle female members, was the ultimate chaste divine Romance. 2079

When people asked, "What do you mean by your circle?" Baba answered: "The circle is composed of my deeply connected disciples who are unconsciously one with me now, and will be consciously one with me in the future when I have completed the work which I can do during the period of their apparent ignorance. It is like having a veil between us; they are one with me, but being behind the veil, they cannot see me yet." 1618

Decades later at the end of April 1955, Baba gave a fuller discourse responding to letters from the West asking for more clarification on the Avatar's circle. A word of warning: for the rest of this chapter you may find yourself spinning in circles with too much information. But it's included here for those fascinated by the never before revealed workings of the mystical body of Christ – his inner and outer circles. We begin:

> Although the Perfect Master remains in illusion as the center of the cosmic periphery and radiates his influence uniformly over the entire universe, in his lifetime he gathers around him 12 men who directly have their center of interest in his individuality. These men, through their constant and close association with him in the past, right from the evolutionary stages of consciousness, reap the greatest

benefit now, when their past close associate has become a Perfect Master.

Such a group of 12 men is called the "circle" of a Perfect Master. However, besides this group of 12 men, there is an appendage of two women to complete the circle of a Perfect Master in all its aspects. These two women also owe their position, in regard to the circle, to their past connection with the Perfect Master.

One or more of these 14 close ones associated with the Master realize the God-state during or immediately after his lifetime, and in a few instances after one or a few more incarnations. Still, the Perfect Master fulfills his obligations by establishing his circle during his lifetime; and the greatest good he bestows is God-Realization with all its Perfection to at least one from among his circle of 12 men. But the case of the Avatar is totally different, as He has 10 circles in all.

The first inner circle of the Avatar consists of 12 men with an extension of 2 women. Each of the following 9 outer circles has 12 persons, both men and women. In all, there are 120 in the 10 circles of the Avatar, plus the 2 women extensions of the inner circle – 122 in all. 3685

With his descent on earth, the Avatar brings along with him the position of roles or "job opening/descriptions" of his inner circle. The connection of the inner circle to the Avatar may be compared to a man who directly associates himself with the 14 parts of his own body – 2 eyes, 2 ears, 2 nostrils, 1 mouth, 2 hands, 2 legs, and the trunk of the body itself; plus the external genitals and anus that act as extensions to the body as a whole.

As soon as a man is born, he directly makes use of these 14 body parts, and they in turn will respond to his direct dictates, individually and collectively. Similarly, with the advent of the Avatar, his inner circle of 12 males and 2 females directly begin to function, individually and collectively as the same 14 types who always occupy their respective offices when the Avatar incarnates on earth.

After the Avatar's life span, they individually and collectively function exactly as their predecessors who had held and functioned in the same offices of the inner circle during all the Avatar's past advents. To put it another way, the Avatar's position regarding the inner circle and its function is like a man who is fast asleep. If he's made to wake up by some external agency, no sooner he's awake than he spontaneously finds all 14 parts of his body parts are already there in their individual roles, ready to function at the slightest wish and whim of the man.

Similarly, as soon as the Avatar is made to realize his Avatarhood through one or more of the 5 Perfect Masters of the time, he also realizes that the 14 personalities in their characteristic roles of the inner circle are ready at hand to discharge their precise duties.

So it's not wrong to say with Christ's coming, so does Peter, Judas, and all His apostles come again. Now this never means the very same Peter or self-same Judas reincarnates again. They never reincarnate, as all 12 of the individual personalities of the Avatar's inner circle attain God- Realization in every Avataric period, either during or very soon after the Avatar's life span. 3686

In all the Avatar's advents, each of the 12 men and 2 women of the inner circle hold exactly the same office and function in exactly the same manner; that's what is meant by saying that the Avatar "always brings with him his identical same circle."

As soon as the veil with which the Avatar descends on earth is rent by the then 5 living Perfect Masters, and the

Avatar realizes his Avatarhood, the 12 men and 2 women automatically gather around the Avatar like magnets to occupy their respective position in his inner circle, and to function as usual according to the dictates of the Avatar of that particular age.

To explain in detail why only these 14 particular personalities hold such positions in every advent of the Avatar, and who can become those 14 members, and how they become attached to the inner circle of the Avatar would require more volumes of explanations.

Suffice it to say each of these 14 particular personalities occupying the office and function of the inner circle not only must resemble the characteristic individuality of his or her predecessor in the previous advents of the Avatar, but must be exactly similar in all respects.

For example, one of the offices of the inner circle of Jesus was held by Peter. At the [next] advent of Christ, this particular office must be held by another Peter, who may be named "A," but must have the same qualities of mind and heart and other characteristics as Jesus' Peter.

The same applies to the offices held by Judas, John, James, etc., of the inner circle in Jesus' lifespan. All the 14 members of the Avatar's inner circle realize God by the Avatar's grace during the same Avataric period which lasts up to 100 years after the Avatar manifests on earth. 3687

Well, are we spinning in circles yet? As said, the total number of the Avatar's circle comes to 122. The theory of the 6 degrees of separation might be a fitting analogy for grasping an idea of the circle; that if a person is one "step," or "degree," away from each person he or she knows, then everyone is no more than 6 degrees away from all other persons on earth. And so we see how truly close the Avatar is to each individual human being.

CHRIST COME AGAIN

Over the years people would ask the mandali, "What have you gained being with Meher Baba for so long?" When this was asked of the close disciple Eruch Jessawala, he didn't know how to respond. So Baba responded for him:

> "The reason you can't answer is because it's a bad question. It's not what you've gained being with me so long. Rather they should ask, 'What have you lost in Baba's contact?' In coming to me one starts losing everything, including one's own false self. When you go, I come! Whoever forms a friendship with me loses all but his real Self." Much Love, T.K. Ramanujam, p. 332

The Avatar's Circle contains the following numbers of men and women:

>   1st Inner Circle – 12 men and 2 women
>   [followed by 9 Outer Circles]
>
>   1st Outer Circle – 8 men and 4 women
>   2nd Outer Circle – 4 men and 8 women
>   3rd Outer Circle – 8 men and 4 women
>   4th Outer Circle – 4 men and 8 women
>   5th Outer Circle – 8 men and 4 women
>   6th Outer Circle – 6 men and 6 women
>   7th Outer Circle – 8 men and 4 women
>   8th Outer Circle – 8 men and 4 women
>   9th Outer Circle – 10 men and 2 women

Next to the inner circle, members of the 1st outer circle of 12 are grouped round the Avatar according to their past connection with the members of the inner circle. Similarly, the 12 persons of the 2nd outer circle are also grouped round the Avatar in accord with their past connections with the members of the previous circle, and so on with all the remaining 7 circles. 3686–88

Regarding all souls in the creation, Meher Baba declared, "Your connection with me is settled and determined from 'roz-e-azal' [first day of creation] and no power on earth can alter or modify this connection." BG 65 The Avatar's 14 inner circle members each have one shadow, so the complete circle of 14 has 14 others members as their shadows making 28.

In that Avataric period, the original 14 reach 7th plane of Realization. Their 14 shadows reach the 6th inner plane, etc. Under strict obedience, circle members must carry out the Master's orders, even if puzzling or mind-numbing from a rational viewpoint; such tasks as travelling hundreds of miles seeking mad men to be cared for or lepers to be washed and fed.

They might arrange Baba's darshan for thousands of people, cook for them and lovingly manage crowd-control to avoid stampedes. They acted as night watchmen, attending him at any time during periods of seclusion and especially when he was working outside his body for the welfare of people over the globe or even in other worlds. They would rouse him at certain intervals and chat with him to help keep his gross consciousness link earth-bound.

They served as secretaries corresponding with his world-wide lovers and making travel arrangements for him and his party. Besides visits to Western countries, Meher Baba circled the globe 4 times during world tours. In short, as his 14 body parts, each member was required to do anything and everything the Master needed without question.

In his words: "Love is difficult, but obedience is far more difficult. My mandali try their utmost to obey me, but considering my nature and temperament, if I were in their place, I don't know if I'd have been able to obey me even for 5 minutes as they do." 3330

The Mandali

The specific role played by any inner-circle members was rarely revealed to them. Nor was it revealed who was an inner or outer-circle member, owing to the inevitable self-interest and competitiveness naturally arising, especially in the early days with mandali members still totally in ego and going around talking about "circles" all day long.

Baba found all this "circle-talk" amusing, and would pull their legs about it. But just imagine if the left hand knew what the right hand was doing what a headache it would be for the Avatar, for circle members are still living with false minds in illusion.

As stated, all 14 members of the Avatar's inner circle realize God by the grace of the Avatar during that same Avataric period, lasting for about 100 years after completing his work on earth and dropping his physical form. And if not in that very life, they are realized within 1 or 2 more lifetimes. Then the tsunami of Divine Love inundates the rest of the world as the spiritual treasure-house is opened and pours down abundantly upon us all.

When human beings are born, they instantly and automatically have as their primary life duty the spending of their karmic impressions or sanskaras – complex mental, emotional and physical imprints left on the body/mind as a result of the minutest action/impressions leftover from their past life or lives. How does one wipe off one's face? How does one strip false mind's mask from the face of Truth?

Karmic impressions collected in this life are never spent in this life, but only in the next life and body which they then necessarily precipitate. Without these impressions there would be no need to take birth in the present or future. A clear understanding of this is so important that it will be covered in considerable detail in 4 later Chapters, 34-37, dealing with the burdensome inevitability of sanskaric impressions even in the afterlife.

When he comes back down to the gross plane after God-Realization, the Avatar's greatest responsibility is toward his inner-circle members. This is his main work as he secretly arranges their affairs and undergoes tremendous sufferings and strivings so their different sanskaras can be spent. This enables their own God-Realization due to him.

This is the greatest of the Avatar's work and the most difficult. He explained, "Compared to this, all other matters in the creation, even giving a huge push to the whole universe towards Truth is effortless." In assuming this duty, he works very closely with his inner-circle members for the rest of their life or lives.

Even if he drops his body before them, his work continues intimately in them until their Realization. Before that, circle members remain "perfectly in the dark" about their divine advancements until the very end when suddenly the light is switched on. 865

700 Years

As to his next advent, Baba often stated, "I will come back again after 700 years; this much I can say now." As to this "700 years" projection, in the 20-volume online biography of Lord Meher [www.lordmeher.org] he speaks of "700 years" multiple times.

Of these, at least 8 times he says "in 700 years;" 24 times "after 700 years;" and once each for "about 700 years," or "in 700 odd years," and finally once for "between 700-1400 years." He once jokingly remarked, "Today I feel I should come again only after 1400 years, as even the thought of coming in just 700 years seems so tiresome." 5011

Making an educated guess from the ambiguity of these references, we might see the Avatar's next advent sometime between 2600-2700 AD. Baba indicated in 1927: "The seed of my present circle was laid 400 years ago at the time of Shivaji – India's 17th century Robin Hood-like hero . . . . 849 In the same way I've now laid the seeds of the new circle-to-be which will completely manifest in 400 to 500 years from now." ♣ 750

At that time he commented to his mandali, "You were all with me at the time of Shivaji." Shivaji's Guru, Swami Ramdas was one of the 5 Perfect Masters of the time, and laid the seed of Meher Baba's new 20th century spiritual circle-to-be at that time.

Baba also revealed, "Shivaji was the greatest warrior of them all, even greater than Napoleon who though brave and clever, was also proud, greedy and vicious. Shivaji was neither proud nor greedy and maybe not as clever as Napoleon, but he was brave"

Baba was also likely commenting on how and when the Avatar's circle will be brought forward to start manifesting well before his next advent. As this was said around 1927, it's still possible his next major Advent could take place earlier than 700 years or around 2326 AD. Jesus came just 670 years after his Advent as Buddha, and Mohammed 570 years after his previous advent as Jesus. Then there are minor advents.

> "The human forms which the Master and circle members take during their manifestation are similar and of the same sex as they had at the time when the seed was sown by a Perfect Master. For example, I now have a similar stature to Shivaji when I manifested as him and when the seed for this present circle was sown by Swami Ramdas. My present form is similar to Shivaji's in many ways . . . ."

> To restate what's gone before, "After a person becomes a member of the [Perfect Master's or Avatar's] circle, he or she attains Realization in 100-200 years. During this period, according to the fate of spending their remaining sanskaras after coming into the circle, a person may have to take on 1-3 more births. But when the time for Realization

comes, that person's form is similar and the same sex as when he or she first came into the circle." 750

One can deduce that suffering is a powerful burner of sanskaras – one's individual sufferings and especially those the Avatar takes upon himself during each advent. Baba said, "The process of spending old sanskaras and creating new ones applies to ordinary people."

Here he is referring to the masses of humanity. For those members of his inner circle the Perfect Master stops this creation of new sanskaras and gradually destroys their old ones. When all the old sanskaras are wiped away, Realization is always and immediately given:

> The Avatar's Universal Work has 7 levels of priority. 1) is to prepare his circle of 122 people for Realization, and then to bestow it on these 122 people, and also to his very closest lovers. 2) is to give Liberation (Mukti) to many people, freeing them forever from the rounds of births and deaths. 3) is to give a push to those on the inner subtle and mental planes; they are of a fixed number. 4) is to take many to the path of Truth to enter the planes. 5) is to awaken the whole of humanity toward the Truth of God's Existence. 6) is to give a universal push to all states of evolution in their progress toward higher evolutionary consciousness. 7) to allow new souls to enter creation. To achieve all this the Avatar must remove the binding impressions of each one, thereby taking upon himself those divine free impressions (yogayoga sanskaras) which remove bindings from others.   AA 14
>
> I rank my mandali 2nd to Mehera; then come my lovers and then the world. I daily invoke myself for Mehera, the mandali, my lovers and the world in that order . . . . Those

in the inner circle acquire no new sanskaras, even if they commit the worst actions. Their sanskaras automatically pass onto the Master whose suffering does away with them. 5370, 865

The working of the minds of the members of a Sadguru's circle is like a wheel turning in one direction only for the wiping off process; the working of the minds of other human beings is like a wheel turning in one direction and then in the other, spending old sanskaras, then creating brand new ones, like the balance wheel of a watch or clock, In short, only the total destruction of all sanskaras, old and new, good or bad, enables one to be ready for Realization. 780

Never before in any previous spiritual or religious tradition was this information known. We see now more clearly why circle-members' unblinking obedience to the Avatar is necessary so he may extricate them from the almost un-dissolvable Gordian knots of their false impressions. The few he leaves them are to fulfill their life and duty as circle members.

An illustration of the unthinking obedience required when following a Master is seen in a story I heard about the law of gravity, told with a great punch line by Baba's close mandali and my friend for over 20 years, the new "St. Peter," Eruch Jessawala:

> "There was once a man taking a stroll at the edge of a steep cliff. He slipped on some loose pebbles and fell over the edge. As he's falling, he grabs hold of a tree branch growing out of the cliff. Hanging on for dear life, the man screams for help at the top of his voice, 'Is there anyone up there – anyone who can help me?' As he's screaming, from the top of the cliff comes a thunderous voice: 'I am God and I can help if you have faith and obey me.'

"The desperate man replies, 'Yes, yes, I'll obey you, but help me quickly – I'm losing my grip.' The voice said to him, 'Then let go of the branch and I'll save your life.' There was complete silence. Then, after some moments, the man started shouting again, 'Is there anyone else up there?' The pilgrims in mandali hall broke out laughing. We're all like that.

All we have to do is trust him and let go our hold on Maya which we so strongly cling to. Just as the man finds it difficult to let go, we find it difficult to let go of all the Mayavic distractions we've been clinging to for endless lifetimes. RT III, 106–07
Describing how he uses Maya, Baba explained in 1940:

"I have activated Maya's 'machine' for a definite purpose. I permit humanity to have 1001 experiences by passing through various acts. The masses will come out of it all in the end. When they're capable of perceiving it, they'll find all this was a part of a great play which God in His unbounded cleverness had staged to extricate humanity from Maya, precisely through Maya." 2081

Although a code of ethics provides us necessary standards of conduct as a line between the opposites of good-bad, right and wrong, from a spiritual aspect, they are mere stepping stones toward the eventual unfoldment of our spiritual consciousness, and must ultimately be transcended.

With me, no one can live what the world calls a "moral life." Here we're only concerned with spirituality, not morals. A spiritual life isn't ruled or bound by any principles. Each individual's impressions are completely different, and so behavior and temperament are different.

In a virtuous life, evil is suppressed and good surfaces; but evil is still there underneath. The bad impressions still remain and have to be worked out, if not in this life then in the next or in the further next after that one. In spiritual life both get nullified. A spiritual life leads toward naturalness.

A virtuous life in the guise of humility inflates and perpetuates one's false ego! But a spiritual life is led only under guidance or orders of the Avatar or Perfect Master who knows the exact pulse of each, treating each for his own particular malady.

Personally, you may not like someone's behavior, but it may be naturally necessary for him. Thus, spiritual life is totally different and not judged on the basis of morality, ethics or any other principle. So how to understand it? Worldly people act on moral standards of acceptable behavior, but the Avatar or Perfect Masters deal with each as to his or her specific impressions. 3668–69

Preparing Circle Members

Spiritual life with the Master was jokes one moment and deadly serious business the next. Obedience meant living 1st class one day and sleeping in the cold under trees the next, and often inciting different circle members' conflicts to come out into the open. Normally, there were no specific devotions, meditations or yoga. His real work was grinding down their false ego minds to dust. Each had his own ways, personality and different duties.

Baba would bring these out and they'd fight like hell, not feeling, "Oh, we should respect each other." They'd argue and still remain true friends to the end. For example, the following exchange took place after the mandali had been with Baba for over 2 decades.

CHRIST COME AGAIN

Dr. Ghani one day said in jest, "Baba, no doubt, you are God; but what have we earned from being with you all these years? You've trapped us in such a way we're neither here nor there!" He went on teasing Baba, hoping with his usual baiting to elicit an interesting discourse. But this time Baba gave an order that made Ghani utterly dizzy.

Glancing around, Baba challenged Kaka Baria, "And why are you just sitting back there? Come up front here and answer this egg-headed idiot!" "I don't want any arguments," Kaka said. "What? You're afraid of Ghani?" Baba teased. "I'm not afraid of him or even his father!" Kaka countered. "Then come up and reply to him," Baba ordered. So, Kaka came forward for an argument that turned into a verbal free-for-all.

Kaka began, "You're a eunuch to beg from Baba! Only eunuchs beg!" Then he quoted Kabir: "What's given voluntarily is like milk; what's gotten by begging is like water; what's forcibly taken is like blood." At this Ghani snorted, "Who the hell are you teaching me Kabir?" "I'm a 100 times more conversant in his couplets than an ignoramus like you. I've liquefied and drunk them!" "Then why talk like a castrated eunuch?" Kaka demanded.

"You're speaking like the castrated one, m' friend. You're just a fool who can't even remotely understand," Ghani retorted. Kaka then stated a few choice opinions about Ghani's genealogical tree, as Baba just sat rocking his head back and forth, enjoying it immensely. At last, Kaka's tenacity prevailed and Ghani was reduced to silence. Amazed, Baba declared "Kaka has worked wonders here today! Ghani speechless? – now that's a miracle!"

Such arguments weren't rare, as we will later see. Baba worked with these heated situations to make his men unbiased, fearless, faithful and honest; to make them keep only one thought in mind – his pleasure in every situation. Oh, they knew it was all an improv charade, but they entered into it with all their hearts' zest simply for Baba's pleasure.   2856–57

Just see their love for him. If Baba criticized or chastised them, it was his divine blessing wiping off their minds' false binding impressions. "From time to time I scold the mandali so harshly. I don't do it unnecessarily, but to wipe out their binding impressions." In other words, he might sneer at the mandali one minute and cheer them on in the next.

He was often the quintessential "divine pain-in-the-ass" as he ground down their false minds over the slightest, most seemingly inconsequential things. And in this way he gradually prepared them to be vessels of his grace for so many others. GuG 356

"If I wished, I could give immediate Realization to my circle members. But how would this enable them to come back for duty; who then would do it? Suppose you give Realization to your hand, and mystified, it stops working. What would do its work? That's why Sadgurus always prepare their circle members in ways unknown to them – gradually taking them up for Realization." 683

So the first sufferings the Master must undergo upon coming down again through the inner spiritual planes to full gross consciousness is for each individual circle member who has sworn obedience and whose binding impressions he vows to take upon himself. These impressions foam up, becoming greatly exaggerated as they come to a head during his work with them. Everything boils to the surface so he can then skim it off.

Suffering for Individual Circle-Members

Meanwhile, he's burning their sanskaras by his own personal sufferings for them. Taking on their impressions during the early 1922 Manzil-e-Meem days, Baba would be in a good mood one moment, and then suddenly his body would react very strangely, though he wouldn't say why. But he'd undergo bizarre, acute illnesses, raging fevers and delirium, sometimes uttering strange, incoherent words and phrases.

At other times he'd suffer so-called "accidental injuries" or days on end of cramps and diarrhea for each of his individual circle members. He would actually weep, and then suddenly get extremely ill. As proof, he told the men to ask Gustadji, who had seen tears flowing from his eyes. Then Baba explained:

> "May my enemy never suffer like last night! This is the 3rd time in the last 8 years I've actually shed tears and gotten ill. The 1st 2 illnesses were a shoulder wound, then the dysentery at Ajmer. For various members of my circle, I will thus have to die 28 times, and every time I will have to cry! But the subsequent illnesses will be less severe. This fever is for Sadashiv, who always suffers from it.
>
> "The 1st 2 sicknesses concerned Gustadji and Behramji. The 2nd group, for whom I will have to suffer, includes Ghani. In the circle, Ghani's number is 7 – most significant, because even after Realization this number is always with the Perfect Master. The next 3 to 4 illnesses will be somewhat severe, but after that the suffering will lessen." 328–29

On June 25th 1929, there was a discussion about an editorial in the Times of India regarding the Prince of Wales, who later became England's King Edward VIII. Sharing the same 1894 birth year, Baba made some appreciative remarks about Edward, "He has a good character for a man of his position. He has a past connection with me and will join me." The mandali silently looked at each other wondering "But when?"

Then 7 years later in 1936 King Edward abdicated the throne to marry an American woman, Wallis Warfield Simpson. Baba commented: "Edward is free now to follow love and draw toward me.

To follow divine love, impersonal or personal, is to come to me." 1754

Remarking on the new King George and his wife, Queen Elizabeth, Baba stated, "At least it's some solace to the people that they both have good hearts." Then followed the Archbishop of Canterbury's address on which Baba commented, "They [church leaders] all speak of Christ our Lord, but do not follow him." 1839

During Baba's 1930 stay at Nasik, painful boils started appearing on his body. When Dr. Nilu gave him an injection, Baba candidly explained their mysterious significance:

Suffering Taken on for the Sake of the World

> These boils are different types – one irritating, one itching, one full of pus, one very small, one very large. Why are they so different and peculiar? Each one represents a particular country or continent. For instance, the one on my anus represents India, the other on my buttocks represents Persia and so on – different types according to sanskaras of the country it represents.
>
> In short, this means there are no physical defects on my body. Whatever physical ailments you see are due to the sanskaras taken on by me from my circle members and the world at large, for whose benefit and welfare I work. It's the same with other Sadgurus. Upasni Maharaj has piles; Sai Baba regularly had high fevers. I have stomach trouble, dysentery, blisters and boils." 1191

Shortly after this, Baba went to Rishikesh and seeing a group of sadhus said:

"Just look at them with their long hair, smearing ash all over their bodies and wearing robes to give spiritual discourses. It's all an outward show only; within they're merged in Maya. They're hypocrites; it's a sin to pretend one is free from Maya.

"These so-called sadhus are full of desires and have thoughts of eating, drinking and wearing such fine robes. Outwardly, they show themselves as sadhus, but inwardly they're quite the reverse. Only he who has annihilated himself is a real sadhu." 1024

Baba didn't seem happy in Rishikesh (1930) and soon left for Quetta, Pakistan. Suddenly, he got ill in the stifling mid-summer heat of the overcrowded railway car. He got off the train at midnight at Rohri. Standing motionless on the platform, he complained of heart pains.

He was ghastly pale and restless. One moment he'd want to sit and the next he'd get up and repeatedly pace back and forth. Plus the noise at the station was unbearable. The mandali spent an anxious night with him on the open railway platform. He looked just as ill the next day, but instead of seeking relief he told them all to go in town "sightseeing." Of course, no one wanted to leave him in this condition.

They were taken aback by his strange order, as they ached to ease his suffering. He called them on it: "Always remember, stay above your sentiments and wishes when they go against to my orders. I must shatter your minds and hearts to pieces! The greatest service is to obey me! Compared to my orders, your thoughts and emotions are nothing. You can't serve me if you fail to carry out my words; you only cause me greater pain." 1025

Though still feeling strange about it, they left Baba on the train platform and went "sightseeing." Here Baba was using his own vidyanic or super-conscious impressions to wipe out their sanskaric impressions. Vidnyani literally means "to the threshold." He then gives them what are known as superfluous, unbinding yoga-yoga sanskaras. These are automatic, divine-free impressions which work in a totally mechanical way to help free them.

Understanding this, one might begin to more deeply grasp Jesus' sufferings for his circle and the universe. Thus, as earlier stated, circle members take on no more new impressions in the future, regardless what they do – ever. And though they don't know or feel this, through these "divine-free impressions" they are enabled to do the Avatar's work of collecting later followers' impression whom they'll contact after he passes. 1890–91

When he enters his eternal state of Infinite Bliss, Knowledge and Power in the Beyond, he is still very much in contact with anyone who thinks of him and calls upon him deeply from their heart and not just from their minds. Baba illustrates this with an analogy:

> "A freight train has many carriages attached to it. Some carry good material, some bad – iron, copper, oil, waste products, etc. in different cars. But, whether it is good material or bad, if attached to the engine they go where the engine goes. The engine doesn't carry cars of only good things, leaving the bad behind. Similarly, I am like an engine, and those who remain attached to me reach their destination, whether they're virtuous or vicious." 3289

Although never revealed before, this is how the Avatar works through his circle members to mop up the impressions of his lovers with whom his circle will physically come in contact after the Avatar's initial work is done. This is why just before He physically left them after the crucifixion, Jesus gave a mandate to His Apostles to go out and witness to the lost tribes of Israel rather than to the Gentiles.

He urged them to go to those whose sanskaras he'd absorb through his Apostles' divine-free impressions [yoga-yoga sanskaras] given for their future work even though they didn't grasp it. It was their automatic duty, as He was still working with them in his physical body even fifty years after his crucifixion, as we will astonishingly see in Chapters 40 and 41.

Realization within 100 Years

Circle members may spend decades in the Master's company, feeling they're nothing but "broken-down furniture," as Baba referred to his men. They achieved nothing spiritually – not even a glimpse of truth or exalted experiences, nor even a saintly bearing in their personality; truly living like "pieces of broken-down furniture."

Still, they attain God-Realization within 100 years after the Avatar drops his body. Baba said in rare cases it may take longer, depending on their fate or how quickly they spend their remaining sanskaras. For remember, after coming into the circle they can never collect new sanskaras. Some attain Realization in that very life lived with him.

Others get it in the next or 2nd lifetime, but usually within 100 years. Not only for circle members was Baba to suffer, but later 2 serious auto accidents and a lifetime of inner crucifixion for the universe was his destiny as the Christ-Avatar of this age. About this inner crucifixion, Baba explained the burden of his "worries." His words give deeper insight into his most famous and most famously misunderstood expression, "Don't worry, be happy!"

"The Avatar incurs upon himself the infinite burdensome "worries" of the entire suffering world while working in it for the spiritual upliftment of humanity. This suffering of people steeped in the darkness of ignorance becomes the Avatar's suffering – his crucifixion. The Avatar is crucified every moment of his life on earth.

"But with this infinite suffering taken upon himself he also has the infinite bliss of the state of Perfection which he eternally experiences. Otherwise, it would be impossible. He would be literally crushed under the burden of such suffering from all sides. If an ordinary man, however great, were to feel even 1000th part of the Avatar's suffering, he'd go mad! The Avatar has to bear this burden to lighten the load of the world's suffering." 2020

Baba's last surviving inner-circle member, Bhau Kalchuri, was fond of referring to himself as a "potato-head." But what work he did as a "potato-head," no one knows. His 70s and 80s, the last 2 decades of his life, were spent in very precarious health.

Still, Bhau undertook grueling world tours each summer even after heart-bypass then cancer and colostomy surgeries. He could no longer freely walk, but travelled simply to contact and be with Baba's lovers in Europe, America and Australia.

He brought with him and shared his last 3 remaining possessions: undying love for Baba, unassailable conviction in Baba's divinity and heartfelt surrender to his Lord, borne of years of service during which his false mind was literally ground to dust by the Master.

We will witness this "grinding" in later chapters. Bhau filled the role of Baba's beloved "St. John." Returning to Meherabad at the end of July 2009, after one of his final trips to the West, Bhau went inside Baba's tomb to pray and tell Baba about his trip. While looking at the large photo of his Master, he saw tears in Baba's eyes. He emailed us later:

"This is the 1st time in my life this happened. I collected many things from Baba lovers in the West, and I am still feeling very heavy. So, on August 12th I'll attend the Dhuni [a sacred fire symbolizing the fire of divine love; the wood representing the lower self which is to be burned in that fire] to throw into it what I've collected and request Beloved Baba:

"Please burn to ash what I've brought from your lovers during my programs in the West." Then I'll feel I've completed my duty satisfactorily. But Beloved Baba's duty never ends. He'll remain active for all time. What work He is doing for His dear ones."

On his return to India, Bhau said, "This was my last trip to the West. I'll not be able to come again. "But still not giving up he did come again in 2010 as well as performing his weekly Sunday worldwide Internet chats with followers East and West. In the simple give and take of a chat room what inner work was done we have no idea.

During one of those chats from California on July 25th 2010, Bhau repeated, "I'll not be able to visit the West again. I have completed my 21st visit there and have passed through 21 surgeries." Though unable to walk in his last years, Bhau would quip, "I can't walk, but I sure can talk, talk, talk!" He said Baba's circle members remaining ignorant know nothing.

They may not know it, but they don't live for themselves but for the sake of Baba's other lovers; thus his fondness for referring to himself as an ignorant "potato." During his weekly internet chat on the auspicious date of 10/10/2010, Bhau suffered a mini-stroke. Regaining composure, he tried to go on with the chat, but his caregivers were adamant. By mid-week he was back to a full work schedule and emailed us:

> "Now my age is old, so such things may come. It happens, but please, don't worry for me. I'm all right. Thank you so much for your prayers to Beloved Baba. It's good you did it for me. These prayers touch my heart, as they come from your heart."

Bhau's poor health continued for exactly 2 more years, until after a final series of illnesses he passed to his Beloved Baba at age 86 on October 23, 2013.

Bhau Kalchuri (at the back) with his wife Rama, son Mehernath, daughter Sheela, and Meher Baba in Meherazad, 1968

CHRIST COME AGAIN

Baba Blames "Thinking"

While thinking belongs to the mind, the Realization of consciousness belongs to the soul. Baba explains how consciousness is separate from the mind and survives it:

> All the world's troubles are due to thinking. Soon, I will take this thinking upon myself and my health will be very seriously affected. This is essential for my future working, and will affect the entire world. It is the duty of Perfect Masters to give an onward push to the subtle universe as well as to the gross universe. This work entails them coming down from the state of Eternal Bliss.
>
> This is symbolized in the body as the top of the head [the crown chakra at the top of the skull] and positioned in the "Brahmand," symbolized between the eyebrows. This point – the junction between the state of Upper Bliss and the lower human form – is from where we can see the whole of the body's lower parts, and is equal to seeing the entire chain of all past lives and forms which one has to pass through before God-Realization.
>
> A few God-Realized ones are duty-bound to come down to that junction [to live in the world with full gross consciousness as Perfect Masters] to bring those in the world who are worthy to be taken up and God-Realized due to their preparedness and past spiritual connection.
>
> But such preparedness does not come easily, requiring ages upon ages of suffering, sacrifice and deep connection with a God-Realized One. Only then is one deemed worthy of being admitted into a Circle for God-Realization, meaning the destruction of all sanskaric mind-impressions – the "stopped" state of the mind, and the end of all false thinking forever.

This is very difficult; for if the mind tries to stop thinking, it tends towards the unconscious sound-sleep state. Even great yogis are unable to attain to this "stopped" state of mind for good. At most they can temporarily stop thinking in meditation, concentration or samadhi, but even this creates new indelible sanskaras. As soon as they come down from the samadhi state, their minds start working, and the store of past undestroyed sanskaras gets further endlessly added to. PM 70–71

Those who live near me must be very watchful. Knowing my love for you, Maya [the snake of false mind in the Garden of Eden] awaits an opportunity to use your weaknesses. The moment you neglect my instructions, Maya's purpose is served, and I have to put up a big fight with it – not to destroy it, but to make you aware of its nothingness. The moment you fail to obey me implicitly, it tightens its grip over you, and you fail to carry out the duties I've given – adding to my suffering.

In God there's no such thing as confusion – God is infinite Bliss and Honesty. Illusion is confusion, misery and chaos. As humanity's eternal Redeemer I am at the junction of Reality and Illusion, simultaneously experiencing the infinite bliss of Reality and the suffering of Illusion. With Reality on the one hand and Illusion on the other, I constantly experience a pull from either side.

This is my crucifixion. When you fall prey to Maya's persuasion, Illusion intensifies its pull and I must exert myself to stay stationed at the critical junction. I never let go my hold on Reality. If the pull becomes too great, my arm may be pulled from its socket, but I'll remain where I am. 4545

In short, the disciples had to surrender themselves 100% to the Master and then patiently wait however long for his acceptance of that surrender. Baba illustrates it in a story:

> A man had two priceless vessels encrusted with the tarnish from many decades of daily use. One he gave to a professional metal worker who said he'd have the work done in 40 days. The other vessel was given to a non-professional. He said, "No problem I'll have it finished over the weekend."
>
> The professional begins working, subjecting his vessel to slow, gentle, processes that restored a shining and remarkably durable vessel. It took him the full 40 days. But the shining vessel would now last a lifetime. The 2nd man adopted his drastic short-cut "no problem" method.
>
> He used caustic solvents and a very hot fire to quickly clean the vessel, but making its metal brittle and worthless. Losing its fine temper, the once treasured object would now quickly wear out. And so, a Perfect Master seldom gives quick realization to an aspirant, but leads him to it slowly, that he might become a robust, useful vessel for God's work. GS 262–64
>
> If Realization be imparted to one in a second, it is then for oneself with no benefit for others. The austerity and hardship one undergoes with a Master gives true power and the authority to use
>
> Realization for spiritually awakening others. GS 247 It takes a lot of time to clean out the vessel of a man's heart and grow love in him, so as well as being bright with God he can be useful to men. SG 24
>
> I am Infinite Knowledge, Power and Bliss. I can make anyone realize God if I choose to do so. You may ask why I don't make you realize God now. But why you? Why not

the one next to you or the beggar in the street, or that bird in the tree, or that stone – who are all one in different forms?

The more you love me the sooner you'll discard the falsehood you've chosen to hide under, hoodwinking you into believing you are what you are not. I am in all and love all equally. Your love for me will wear through your falseness and make you realize the Self you truly are. EN 50

During his physical life on earth, the Avatar is in the "collecting" phase of his work, gathering the impressions of his lovers and the entire universe. When he drops his body, he begins the "cleansing" phase of those impressions. That's the time for all the new people. The ones who never met or even heard of him start coming to him in droves.

Before dropping his body, Baba told his mandali quite explicitly, "Just wait and see. My children will come from all over the world." Needless to say, the mandali couldn't even imagine it. They thought when he passed on from them that was it; he left and it was time to close up shop. But they were totally overwhelmed in the months and years following his passing. People from all over the world, young and old, came to bow down at his Tomb.

Hearing from the mandali about the Ancient One's life and their years with him, they already believed and felt his divinity. Now they were hungry for his humanity, asking about his favorite soap and brand of toothpaste which by the way was an old India brand, Forhan's.

He'd either use a brush or his finger. Did he sleep or snore, and did he shave? Baba used Gillette blades for many years and liked a smooth shave. Then in 1958, American devotee Harry Kenmore gave him a rechargeable electric razor. He was happy not to have to fuss with soap and water especially in winter weather. TH 191, MM 1: 270 Sidenote; MM 3: 207

Baba works with his lovers anywhere in the world if they follow him closely with all their hearts. He is infinitely active as the Holy Spirit. You find people praying to the Holy Spirit in their various churches. Who is that Holy Spirit? It is none other than the Lord Himself, being active from the Beyond – from beyond time into the very fabric of our limited and illusory time and lives. Baba clearly indicated:

> "I may give you more, much more than you expect – or maybe nothing; but that nothing may prove to be the everything. So I say come with open hearts to receive much or nothing from your Divine Beloved. Come to receive not my words, but of my Silence." 4345

The Avatar is so ahead of his time in humanity's ignorance it takes about 100 years after he drops his form before mankind catches up to speed and realizes he had been here again. Lightning is seen 1st, and then comes the thunder. Baba explains and then warns:

> Before Realization, the veil must be torn away and mind must die. Due to this veil, every individual mind functions in gross and subtle bodies. Removing the veil separates the gross from the subtle. In the subtle state you see internal things with as much clarity as you see gross objects. While doing activities like eating, drinking, sitting, standing they are simultaneously happening in the subtle world. When the gross is separated from the subtle, it's like killing 2 birds with 1 stone.
> But the veil must be ripped off. Though thin, it's also very strong and not easily slit. Still it can be rent in an instant by a Perfect Master. Once torn, the soul instantly en-

ters the 1st plane. When a parrot escapes from its cage, it flies straight into the air without even looking back. 1082

But where are these planes and spheres? They are all within you. You're not conscious of them because different states of consciousness give rise to different levels of awareness. For example, take an ant as representing the 1st plane, a dog as the 3rd plane, an elephant the 5th plane and a man the 7th plane of consciousness. The ant, the dog, the elephant and the man move on the same earth, but there are worlds of difference in their levels of awareness. EN 31

Why run after gatekeepers or watchmen? Catch hold of the Emperor Himself! Never go after his servants; no minister or secretary will help. The Emperor is Perfect Knowledge. Forget everyone and everything in his company. One should stop all previous habits. No meditating, or repeating God's name or any other type of worship. What's the most that could happen with such practices?

You might enter a blissful samadhi which can never make you one with God. Instead, you should submit yourself to the Emperor's will, having only this thought: "O God, when will You meet me? When will I see You?" This longing must be present 24/7.

> Serve the Beloved – Intensely long to see him –
> and he'll come to you – elf

If the feeling is intense enough, God will surely fulfill it . . . false saints can give nothing, while those on the 1st and 2nd planes or Saints of the 5th and 6th planes, can raise you to a higher state with just a mere glance! Still, that's not the state of Perfection.

These advanced souls are themselves not yet perfect . . . . Except for the truly Perfect Ones, don't ever be beguiled by advanced souls of the 5th or even 6th planes. Stick to the Emperor himself and never leave for any reason! I am in everyone. If you catch hold of me you will have the root of the entire creation in your hands. Then you'll not need to go after mere branches and leaves . . . .

If you're after God, you have to give up everything – father, mother, and the whole world – each and every thing. So ponder well and *then* take your step. If not, leave this path and attend to your worldly duties. Once you fall for the path, be afraid of nothing. "Who will look after my parents? What about my job? What will the world think of me?" All these thoughts are useless.

If you died, who'd have looked after your near and dear ones? They'll care for themselves. God is the true sustainer, taking care of everyone. Once you've entered His path, abandon such thoughts . . . . All rivers flow into me, the Ocean. Stop looking elsewhere; look only at the Ocean. By concentrating on me and always carrying out my wishes you yourself will **become** the Ocean. 1084– 85

Concluding this long chapter on the Avatar's Circle, we now return to the earlier narrative when Baba visited his Poona home on Butler Mohalla [Lane] – renamed Meher Mohalla. He especially wanted to visit little sister, Mani. She was very special to him.

At age 5 in 1923 he gave her lots of attention as he and his men listened to her precocious inquiries. She was destined to be with him for life as the 2nd after Mehera of his female inner- circle members. A later chapter shows how this finally happened, but only after much agonizing push and pull with mother Shireen.

Baba and his men now return to Arangaon's windy, desolate slope, knowing that hidden in its fields are numerous dens of cobras. He kept warning the mandali to always carry a lantern at night. One day a 5 foot snake was seen with a sparrow in its mouth.

One of the men struck the snake on its back, releasing the sparrow which flew away. Baba gave the final killing blow, remarking:

> "If not killed by a human, a snake always remains a snake. Never leave one wounded. It will always stay near you to be killed outright.
>
> "A snake's evolution is like a knotted rope. If you try to unwind it, the knot becomes even tighter. But killed by a human, the knot blessedly untangles, and the soul is free to continue its path of evolution." 1905–06 Even if they're non-poisonous and you think they help by eating rodents, you'll help the snake far more by killing it.
>
> "In rare cases it could even incarnate as a human in its next birth. Snakes or other animals which may reincarnate as humans are temperamental in their 1st human form and will strike if teased or if one tries to harm them. GuG 92–

A new phase of hard labor now began as the men continued turning the ramshackle Arangaon military barracks into an ashram fitting for the Master's Avataric work. Baba was now devoting much time to Gulmai's family who gave the land for his Meherabad ashram. But her husband Khan Saheb [Kaikhushru] had a point of view that Baba didn't appreciate.

One day Baba argued with Rustom about his father's attitude and even threatened to leave Meherabad for good. He only remained because of Gulmai's tears. But he made conditions, including Meherabad lands were to be signed over to either her son Adi or in Gustadji' name. Khan Saheb grumbled over it, but in the end gave in. Later on his deathbed he would have a wonderful experience of Baba and die in his loving remembrance. 524–25

At this time, Arangaon's poor were suffering famine, compounded by perennial rainfall shortage. The one well at Meherabad nearly ran dry in the summer months. Meanwhile, Baba's presence near Arangaon caused a lot interest among local villagers. The poor farmers started thinking there was some sort of "holy man" living nearby.

The Wonderful Kind Stranger

The activity and sounds of leveling many of the old, dilapidated war-camp structures was sure to attract curious village children. One day, a couple of them sneaked onto Meherabad for a peek. Spotting them, Baba gestured them to approach. They got scared and started crying. He gently caressed them. "Don't be afraid. Where (do) you live?"

One lad silently pointed toward Arangaon. "And what do the children do all day?" Baba asked. By now they were gazing lovingly and dreamy-eyed at this beautiful stranger. They said many children were Untouchables who took goats and cows out grazing. "If I give them sweets will they come visit me?" One of the lads beamed, "For candy they'll all come!"

Baba smiled, "OK. Tomorrow, bring them all." They ran happily back to the village telling the other children of the kind stranger, the next day when more children came, Baba spoke gently to them, gave more sweets and began teaching them devotional songs. 511–12

During this Meherabad period, Baba's circle members had to work totally beneath their social standing – drawing water, doing laundry, cooking, as well as cleaning out latrines and remaking the old ruined British war-camp buildings. He had them re-convert some existing structures and then build some new ones which remain to this day.

CHRIST COME AGAIN

The old debris was carried and balanced on the mandali's' heads in large, round, wok-like pans called ghamelas. This period of "ghamela yoga" was a 6-hour grind every day of the week – backbreaking work with little comforts or food provided to the laborers. 492–93

By now most of them had well-calloused hands. Like some of the buildings, the men themselves felt like run-down ruins, given only bare necessities – lentils, rice, bitter spinach and weak, milkless lemongrass tea. Then there might be a feast day for occasional religious festivals circle-members traditionally observed to honor Baba's advents as their past Avatars.

One day when Padri showed his blistered palms, Baba remarked: "You people swear you're ready to give up your life for me, but you complain about a few blisters. This isn't even the beginning of giving up your life – yet you whimper and cry. It's a sin to complain on this path, where for years on end the body is cut up, bit by bit, remaining wounded till it gives up the ghost! Seal your lips and let me kill you slowly – inch by inch.

"Bravery doesn't lie in showing me your blistered palms!" But Padri's hands were badly burned and swollen from whitewashing the buildings barehanded with caustic lime. He was taken to Ahmednagar hospital for treatment.

Were outsiders to peek in, they'd see this hard labor as being like a concentration camp. But Baba took part in every phase of it himself, even to cleaning their latrines. And this is how Meherabad was restored. They were laying the groundwork for what was to be the Master's seat and base of operations for the rest of his life. 497

He often spent long periods in deep fasts and seclusion in a 6' deep ditch up on Meherabad Hill which decades later would become the crypt of his hilltop Tomb, built while he was still living. In future times it would become the world's foremost place of pilgrimage.

Besides this crypt, at other times his seclusion might be in a hut, a cave or a similar confined space. About such small spaces he once explained:

> "This physical confinement is only apparent. It's not in the least inconvenient. Certain kinds of work I must do in non-physical realms [outside the body], prompt me to shut myself up in a small area.
>
> "After becoming Perfect, Jesus stayed 40 days and nights on a mountain, not even allowing his apostles to approach him. It would be a great mistake to think that the Avatar's seclusions as simply periods of quiet deliberation for future planning." 1130

During these seclusions at Meherabad when Baba intensified his internal work on the inner planes, he would temporarily lay aside his gross body and work outside it. This required absolute stillness in the environment. During such out-of-body, work any sudden noise – even a crow or a barking dog – could break the delicate thread holding his body.

Liken it to a movie soundstage where absolute quiet reigns during "lockdown" as a scene is filmed. Not until the director yells, *"Cut!"* and the all-clear bell rings are behind-camera sounds permitted. So a watchman strictly guarded to prevent anyone approaching his form, especially disembodied spirits – *ghosts*. We will later encounter many of them. MM 3: 431

Among the new visiting Arangaon children was a clever lame boy, Wakadya. He'd lead 30 village children to Meherabad, marching them daily in parade fashion with music and singing, blowing his trumpet all the way with a loud *"toot-toot."* Baba gave the children 2 large fruit baskets that a devotee had brought for him and the mandali. 513

So now they began coming mornings and evenings to learn songs and poems under Arjun's leadership. Yes, an exciting new game was in town, and though they didn't yet know it yet, this was the grassroots of their new future free school. In fact, Baba gave these children the encouragement to learn to read and write.

He began looking after the village children's poor parents as well. Lower caste people in 1920s India were deeply discriminated against even more than blacks in the American South at that time. For centuries, caste determined everything in India. It dictated where you lived, your job, who you could marry, where you were buried – even where your shadow fell.

It was brutal lower-caste discrimination in a level of society deemed unworthy of even a caste, so reviled as to be labeled "*untouchables*." Baba said, "The real untouchables are those who can't enter the temple of their own hearts to see the Lord therein."

In modern times they are referred to as *dalits*, slowly but surely Indian's strict caste lines are dissolving, especially in major cities and undoubtedly due to Meher Baba's solemnly sworn oath to eradicate hateful discrimination forever. LB 44

Still, it was always difficult not only in the West but in the East to have to deal with ingrained personality types, tolerating and working with people's dizzying idiosyncrasies. It was a great feat of diplomacy for Baba not to offend religious prejudices.

CHRIST COME AGAIN

Meher Baba with a group of Arangaon village children in new clothes he gave them, circa early-mid 1920s

Meher Baba stated:

"That's why with a Hindu, I must act as a Hindu – Brahmin or even Untouchable; with a Muslim, as a Muslim; with a Parsi, as a Parsi; with a Christian, I act as a Christian, etc., for the sake of my duty and work to bring you all out of Maya's illusory bindings.

"And so I help you rise above religious and other prejudices to eventually realize the Self within which you fools have been seeking outwardly in your endless rounds of births and deaths. Vivekananda said, 'The real teacher comes to the level of his students.' " 1719

These are just the final 2 paragraphs of a masterful 9 page discourse on Maya as the principle of illusion and the necessity of the Avatar to at first handle people's false beliefs and religious prejudices with kid gloves. The full text is given at www.lordmeher.org pp. 1712–20.

Chapter Eleven

Meherabad Flourishing

Meanwhile, Arangaon's high caste people wouldn't even cross an untouchable's shadow. Baba asked the children, "Do you go to the temple?" "No! We can't even enter the temple! We belong to the lowest caste, so we can't even walk near high caste people."

"So, do you like God?" Baba asked. And they'd smile, bobbing their heads left/right, Indian fashion. "Oh, yes, we love and want God." Baba said, "Then come here and I will give you God." The children brightened, then answered wisely, "But only if you'll still give us sweets every day; then we'll come!" Baba laughed, "Ok, I'll give you sweets every day."

How could he not be enchanted by their simple candor? He then asked his women disciples to stitch clothes for the poor boys and girls. When the clothes were ready, he told the children, "Now tomorrow come at three P.M. and I'll bathe you and give you brand new clothes.

They frowned, "But that's when we have to take our animals out in the fields to graze. If we don't, our parents will beat us." Baba told them to ask their parents for special permission. They did, and the next afternoon about 75 came in a big procession, singing along the way songs Baba and Arjun had taught them. 565

The mandali helped Baba bath boys who didn't even know what soap or a towel was. Besides giving them the promised sweets, all received brand new clothes. Well, the children went home deliriously happy, and the next day their parents also came. So Baba went to Bombay to buy more clothes for them and the children.

Doing such types of work showed his mandali and humanity how to serve those in need as our very own nearest and dearest of kin. Bi-weekly bathing became part of the new routine for these Harijan children, while Baba would also help daily in washing their clothes.

When some high caste Brahmins came for Baba's darshan one day, he spoke plainly: "Look, I'm bathing boys from the untouchable's class. So it's no use having my darshan unless you're prepared to do the same work I do." They instantly shed their caste prejudices, rolled up their sleeves and pitched in for the 3½-hour bathing session. Baba vowed he would especially break down caste and other ingrained prejudices throughout the world.

One aged Brahmin devotee observing this bathing routine almost had apoplexy. Baba pointed at him. "Does this man want me to respect the prejudices and arrogance of the Brahmins?" Then, with fire in his eyes, he gave a sharp blow to his own body.

> "I've put on this body to destroy the entire fabric of the caste system, and destroy it I will, despite the opposition of bigoted Brahmins! The caste system is as absurd as it is tyrannous, and has nothing to do with religion in any sense of the word." MeM 1:12, 60–61

Baba would work 25 years later to break down black prejudice in America's south. To Brahmins who came for his darshan but refused to touch these "Untouchables," Baba would declare:

> "If you've come for God's darshan, these Harijan children are my God. "You're welcome here if you're willing to serve them; or else worship your own God in your house or temple. Here the only God you'll find are these children whom I worship!" Meanwhile, Baba's men and women lived very simply and poorly. HM 555; 572

CHRIST COME AGAIN

Since crockery might break, his teacup was the same aluminum cup he used for bathing and shaving. It was simply washed out and then he'd drink his tea from it – milk-less, weak, lemon-grass tea with a pinch of sugar. That was breakfast – no bread, butter or chapatti. Baba once commented about his innermost circle of friends and workers:

> "I don't need the rich, respectable and intelligent for my work; just simple, common people, despite their weaknesses. As Jesus I was surrounded by poor fishermen; as Krishna with lighthearted cow-herders. Wasn't the lame cowboy, Pendya, so dear to Krishna?
>
> "Now in this advent the crippled, fallen and deprived of means are my workers .... I prefer to make 100 people love God than to convert millions to "Baba-ism." Hold meetings only if it's work done for God; not just to make Baba known." 4227

He affectionately referred to his closest men as *jungli* – "world-class uncouth low-lifes," miraculously admitted to the Master class as raw recruits and spiritual apprentices. But make no mistake; each one had earned and inherited their enviable lot from dedicated past-life service and connection with the Master. He made that very clear to them.

We earlier saw that he also referred to them as "broken-down furniture," giving them funny nicknames; like calling his cousin Espandiar, "Pendu" because he rocked back and forth like a pendulum to stay awake meditating. Strangely, 35 years later in 1956, Pendu was with Baba in a serious auto accident, and just like Krishna's disciple Pendya, Pendu also became a lifelong cripple thereafter showing how roles repeat advent after advent. LA 470; 5342

CHRIST COME AGAIN

Baba was supremely affectionate and full of natural humor. He loved jokes and funny stories. He'd scope out the slightest irony in any situation. And dealing with his men it was always there. He loved nothing more than giving them a start by pulling the wool over their eyes before pulling the rug out from under their feet. Their false consciousness would be punctured then punctuated by humor, for to Baba the whole universe was a huge joke.

> Divinity includes all that is beautiful and gracious. How could you not expect a Perfect Being to have a terrific sense of humor? 1755 I know if I were in your place, I'd have loved a laughing and joking God; not a dry and dull one . . . One who'd even kill smilingly! Even were he to take your life, he'd do so laughingly! God's game is divine fun! HM 274, 2340
>
> Volumes can be written on the expression of God's sense of humor in His Great Ones. Everyone more or less has an ordinary sense of humor, and it doesn't undergo any change merely because of spiritual advancement; not only the sense of humor, but a person's ordinary individual nature as a whole remains unchanged, no matter how far advanced.
>
> The scope and range of God's sense of humor in Avatars, Prophets, Masters and saints differs with their respective duties and according to the prevailing times and circumstances. Whether I am the Avatar or Satan incarnate, one thing's for sure; I have a great sense of humor. 3157

The Arrival of Mehera

If humor is the very nature of the Universe, then God must indeed wear a terrific grin. Meanwhile on May 19th 1924, Mehera

CHRIST COME AGAIN

Irani, a shy Zoroastrian girl of 17, arrived at Meherabad's old Post Office with her mother, Daulatmai, to newly join Baba's ashram.

We remember Mehera caught a glimpse of him 3 years earlier when she and her mother were visiting Upasni Maharaj. The Post Office was special and significant to Mehera, for it was here on that day in May that she first bowed down to Baba. Here he also told Daulat not to force her to marry.© It was here Baba also revealed to Mehera her role as His beloved. Also her autobiography, *Mehera,* p.40-42 has the fascinating back story behind Baba's simple statement that Mehera should not to be forced to marry.

She was destined to become the Master's foremost woman disciple, chief among the two women and the most beloved in his inner circle. The other, his younger sister Mani, joined Baba later as the 2nd female inner-circle member for the rest of her 78 years. She was told by her God-Brother that she'd be a male in her next life and a Perfect Master. MM 1: 277

Did this mean being reborn immediately or perhaps in 700 years when he'd return to earth as the Avatar? I've often thought of the latter scenario, where Baba's sister Mani could possibly be the Perfect Master to unveil his next appearance as the Avatar. It's not farfetched considering how much he loved Mani and commented on their long past together.

As his primary female inner-circle member, Mehera assumed simple tasks – washing pots and dishes, bringing firewood and water, peeling onions and garlic, cleaning vegetables and grinding spices – whatever needed doing. In these early days, Baba rarely spoke directly to her but told his cousin Naja what he wanted to say to her. Mehera recalled:

> Then one evening while lighting the lantern, we were attracted hearing a drumbeat. In those days at sunset everything was so quiet you could hear the slightest sound. Suddenly we realized, "That's Baba. He's drumming in the

CHRIST COME AGAIN

Post Office!" Then aunt Dowla said, "Listen! He's singing too." This was the 1st time I'd heard Baba sing and accompany himself on the drum. We said, "Well, the men mandali are there, so why not us too? Let's go hear Baba sing!"

So we tidied up, crossed the field and went to the Post Office. When we arrived Baba was singing in such a lovely voice. Without disturbing him we quietly went inside and sat down. He was sitting with the mandali all on one side of him and reaching the high notes so beautifully.

When it came to the chorus, all of a sudden Baba stopped singing, pointed to me asking, "What are you thinking?" Well, that really startled me. I didn't know Baba asked about your thoughts, and it's very awkward to have to say out loud what you are thinking. Fortunately, I was thinking only of him and admiring his fingers – how lovely his hands looked playing the drum. His hands looked very beautiful in the light of the hurricane lamp.

So I said, "Baba, I'm looking at your hands, how beautiful they look playing the drum. You really have lovely hands." Okay, so I felt shy saying it, but I couldn't lie. I had to say what I was thinking. Baba looked at his hands as if he'd never seen them before, just nodded and continued to play the drum and sing. But he seemed pleased I was thinking only of him.

The men mandali were sitting around on one side of the room, but I never even glanced at them; I only looked at Baba. So perhaps that's one time I pleased him. It's very difficult to be with Baba; you can't think of anything without him knowing your thoughts. M 48–49

Those early days were so special to us. The only mandali with Baba then were Gustadji, Padri, and his uncle Masaji. Baba slept beside them on the open Post Office porch facing the road. It was the beginning of winter, and the porch was open to the chilly east breeze. Baba had no bed, just a thin mattress on a floor mat. It was so cold at night he couldn't sleep. With no mosquito net, a snake or scorpion might easily crawl into his bedding for warmth.

As he couldn't sleep, he'd be sitting up by 3:30, his blanket wrapped around him, and then about 5 he'd wake the deeply snoring mandali, throwing his sandal at one of them. He especially loved aiming for his uncle Masaji who would wake up, see Baba's sandal beside him and feel so happy! Masaji would get up, kiss Baba's sandal and hand it back to Him. M 64

One day sitting on the Post Office porch having a meal, Baba turned and addressed Mehera directly, "What school did you go to?" "We attended the Convent of Jesus and Mary," she answered. "Was it a good school?" "Yes, Baba, very nice."

"Didn't the nuns try to covert you to Catholicism?" "No, Baba, not at all. But out of respect non-Catholics would stand when a prayer was said in class. We weren't taught scriptures or catechism. If we went to church, it was on our own. I did go a couple of times."

On another day when Baba seemed in a talkative mood, Mehera asked him, "Have there been more Hindu God-Realized souls or Muslim ones?" Baba replied, "More Hindu ones and only a few Muslim ones." Mehera had another question:

"The nuns taught us Jesus was born to the Virgin Mary by an immaculate conception when the shadow of the Holy Ghost fell on her. Is it so?" "No, it's not," Baba stated. "Jesus was conceived and born in a natural way. How could it be otherwise? Every Avatar is born in a natural human way. Catholics in their veneration for Mary started this belief." MM 1: 150

On another day, Baba came inside the Post Office when no one else was there. As he asked Mehera to sit, she wondered what he'd

CHRIST COME AGAIN

say. "From today you are my orderly," She looked puzzled. "You don't know the meaning of orderly? Gustadji will give you my trunk and you'll have to look after all my things, keeping everything very carefully – my clothes, my plate and cup and so on; what Gustadji's been doing till now, you'll do." 558

As Baba was strict about who touched his things, Mehera felt happy and honored to wash his clothes, plate and drinking mug. His bath water was heated over a fire; 5 or 6 pails of warm water – not too hot – which he kept pouring over himself. "Oh, how he loved water!" she recalled. "On another day Baba gathered us on the Post Office porch he said, "Now sit in front of me; I'll teach you a song." MM 1: 199

Dread and dismay welled up in Mehera, who besides being shy felt she had no voice. He taught them a song about Krishna, his flute and happy cow-herd companions, and made them sing it back to him. Then each one had to sing their own favorite song.

Again Mehera went blank. Baba asked, "You went to an English school and you don't you know any English songs?" She bit her lower lip trying to remember, but couldn't. He persisted. "Now wasn't there a 'favorite song' the girls sang?" Then it came to her – Oh, yes! A Gershwin tune made famous by Al Jolson – "Swanee." The girls at St. Helen's sang it every day and she had also picked it up. Nervously, she sang it and he liked the lively tune.

"Now teach it to me – how does it go?" So line by line they sang it together as all the verses came back to her. "This is the first American song I've ever learned!" Baba was beaming in delight, "My first American song!"

Taking Baba's tea out to the porch the next day, Mehera heard him sing it: "Swanee, Swanee, how I love ya, how I love ya, my dear old Swanee. I'd give the world to be among the folks in D-I-X-I-E- even though my mammy's waiting for me, praying for me down by the Swanee . . . ." He was glowing and singing it to her like a love song. MM 1: 148 Decades later in 1952 they'd shed their blood in Dixie for the sake of Love in an Oklahoma car accident.

Shortly after this, pacing the Post Office porch and singing – always singing, couldn't do without singing – Baba stopped and looked at the girls. "You've no idea how fortunate you are to be with me now." How could they realize what he was referring to?

In a year they'd no longer hear him sing, laugh or speak; not his death, but the end of hearing his beautiful voice, and, well for them almost like a death. Then later during the years of his silence when he didn't speak or sing, the women might gather around him in the evenings with their wind-up record player and play a few songs.

Mani recalled in those days Baba listened to Western music. He liked Bing Crosby's "Lullaby and Goodnight," "The Isle of Capri," "La Cucaracha," "The Peanut Vendor" or Paul Robeson spirituals – truly an eclectic mix. By now they had Jolson's recording of "Swanee," knowing how Baba liked and sang it before entering silence. ♣ MM 1: 277

"In India we have classical music and singers which I don't like. They come and sing classical songs for me, but I don't appreciate it." 4385 But he liked Hungarian rhapsodies, Gounod's "Ave Maria," Spanish and Hawaiian guitar music or Indian quawaali – songs of love for God with the improv of jazz and the spirituality of gospel. MM 1: 438

Once he was introduced to a high-society European woman who had a passion for classical music. The lady's attention kept wandering off and the interview was going poorly. So Baba nudged one of his women, "Go get that record!" "That record?" the disciple gasped. "Yes!!" So, "La Cucaracha" was put on the phonograph. The appalled lady quickly excused herself and went away, leaving Baba with a mischievous twinkle in his eye. Aw vol.20, no. 2, p.16

In the early days, Baba's devotees referred to his headquarters as Arangaon, the name of the nearby village. They recall the day Baba told his men he wished to give it a more distinctive name. Several were suggested, but Baba himself settled on Meherabad. One day sitting on the porch, Baba said, "Guess what? I've given this place a new name."

Turning to Mehera, he added, "I've named it after you." Of course, Mehera was surprised and happy. Actually, it was chosen earlier as a combination of Meher + abad [Mercy + flourishing], but Baba wanted her to know her name was included. She comments: "Saying it fast, it sounds like Mehera-bad. He was so sweet and always so witty. He liked giving us happy little surprises, always something fun and startling." MM 1:14–44

Mehera's mother was Daulatmai. She gave Baba everything they owned – lands, gold jewelry, houses – laying all her assets at Baba's feet. Baba sent Rustom to Poona to dispose of their possessions. Then later, Daulatmai and Mehera were driven there with Baba.

They went to sign legal papers for Daulatmai's several properties. Mehera also had to sign papers relating to property earlier placed in her name. The safe's contents with gold jewelry and coins were brought in a box to Meherabad before being sold.

Among Daulatmai's jewelry was an exquisite heavy solid gold necklace that Mehera loved during childhood. Shortly after this, she came out to sweep the porch and saw Baba sitting there with the box in front of him. He was holding the coveted necklace in his hand, toying with it, tossing and jingling it up and down while slyly glancing at her. "I'll never forget that look with the necklace in his hand. It clicked. Baba must have known I loved it. I thought, 'Am I tempted to look and see how lovely it is and still want it?' Then I turned my face away and didn't even look, thinking, 'Let Baba do what he likes with it.' That was it," The amount was over 400,000 rupees – a fortune in those days. The prime reason Mehera's uncle, Colonel Irani, was so opposed Daulat and Mehera's joining Meher Baba's ashram was his feeling that he was only after their fortune!

Baba used all they gave to partly to finance a free hospital and the Hazrat Babajan School soon to be inaugurated at Meherabad. He also sent part of the fortune to Persia [Iran] with mandali member Raosaheb to open and oversee the construction of a poor children's school as well as paying teachers' salaries and providing its year to year running expenses.

Adi Sr.'s father and Gulmai's husband Khan Saheb saw no value in such "wasteful, frivolous projects." One day he asked Baba, "Why go around wasting so much money?" Baba replied, "In my charitable work I'm not wasting it, I'm investing it."

With their generous gift, countless of Daulat and Mehera's sanskaras were liquidated. Over the years, many wished to donate to the Master's work, but he'd accept it only from his closest and proven disciples. If new people offered money, he'd refuse it, due to the sanskaras of greed, lust and other forces that went to obtaining it. 1862

He explained: "Would you ever give shit to someone you really loved? No. You'd want to give something really nice. From a worldly point of view money is everything, but to me it's like shit. I accept it from those I love, but simply to cleanse them." MM 1:142

Meanwhile, Khan Saheb deeply resented his wife and 2 sons being so devoted to Baba, for whom he had very little understanding or appreciation. As mentioned, that would change dramatically on his deathbed 25 years later. Also, Freiny's marriage to his son Rustom turned out not a bed of roses but one full of thorns with their constant quarrelling.

As her older sister, Freiny was jealous of Mehera having so much of Baba's love. She'd even argue with Baba about it. "Why is Mehera so special?" He replied, "Because she does more for me than the others." At other times he said Mehera was "the purest soul in the universe," and her love for him was "unique."

Freiny asked, "Then why did you make me marry? I never wanted to marry." As with most, it is likely Rustom and Freiny married because they had to, due to past life impressions together going back lifetimes. But Freiny envied Mehera's status.

In a marriage discussion to a couple of Arangaon students some years later, Baba gave this enlightening discourse:

> "It's best if one has good moral conduct and leads a pure life not to marry, as marriage at times creates impediments in one's spiritual life.
>
> "But the marriage bond is preferable to leading an immoral, promiscuous lifestyle with its horrific consequences. Married partners should never involve themselves with any other man or woman." 610 An Indian woman once came to Baba and openly complained she wanted to stop sexual relations with her husband because of her desire to see God. But her husband was unwilling to go along with it. Consoling her, Baba tried to explain:
>
> "Isn't it better to treat your husband with love and affection, even disliking and not wanting to indulge in intercourse due to your spiritual aspiration and desire to love God? It's good to have no sexual desires, but when it comes to a question of duty, you must sacrifice a little of your interest to please your husband. Keep your mind focused on God and give your body to your husband. Recall Saint Mira's sacrifice. Try to be like her!" 1642

If difficult marriages are worked out in this lifetime, both parties gain enormously toward their real marriage to God, the Beloved behind all temporary beloveds; something to remember when working out a dizzyingly difficult marriage.

Meanwhile, with Mehera's help, Baba's cousin Naja cooked his meals. One day when Gustadji was relating an anecdote in the kitchen, Naja laughed loudly – something she was known for. Overhearing it, Baba angrily ordered her and Mehera to pack up and go.

Now, unknown to them, this action had to do with to some deep inner work Baba was doing at that moment. Shortly after, he ran after them to bring them back saying, "Never leave me. Even if I force you away, always hold fast to me." 560

Just after this, he told Chanji to take him and the ladies to a movie at the Madeline Cinema which Chanji owned. They were about to leave dressed in ordinary plain saris. Baba asked, "Have you all turned into nuns? Do clothes have any connection to spirituality? No! Change into nice clothes and let's go!" The ladies were happy to put on their finest saris, a bit of lipstick and go to the movies with Baba. 562

On another day, Baba again got upset with Naja for laughing uproariously in the presence of some dignified ladies visiting the ashram. Overhearing her raucous laughing, he slapped her face in front of everyone and then scolded her, "Aren't you ashamed of yourself, laughing hysterically like a mad woman with all these fine ladies?

"Don't you know where you are? This is Meherabad, a holy ashram – not some damned carnival!" Actually, it was the dignified women who were laughing far more loudly than Naja. They stood back silently witnessing the scene as Baba taught them a lesson they'd never forget, even though inflicting a humiliating punishment on his dear cousin. 583

Naja often wondered why she was given so many kitchen chores, while Mehera wasn't. Exhausted one day from all her kitchen duties, she thought, "Oh God, Baba makes me work so hard, while Mehera isn't given much work." She never complained. Then Baba told her the story of Mary and Martha of Bethany; how both loved Jesus so dearly. But Martha had little opportunity to be with Jesus being so busy cooking.

Jesus said, "Sitting by my side, Mary is serving me as much as you are cooking food for me and my Apostles." Baba said Mehera was like Mary and Naja like Martha. "Continue your duty with love, and don't even think what others are doing. 583–84; MM 1: 177–7

Nervous

Nervous, the out-of-work actor picked up on a Bombay street corner, had been a mandali member with Baba for 5 years now. One of his duties was to bring well-water in tin buckets. Beside Gustadji, he was the only man allowed near the women's quarters. One day pouring water into a tub, he spoke to Mehera, asking if she knew who Baba really was – of his great state as a Perfect Master and how fortunate she was to serve him.

He told her some wonderful incidents occurring around Baba. She didn't know they were being closely watched. The next day While Mehera was washing dishes the next day, she saw Baba approach and was transfixed by his beauty. "He came fast as if walking on air."

He began chatting and mentioned observing her talking with Nervous the day before. "Yes, she said, "he was telling me about your life and how lucky I am to be near you." Baba said, "Yes, he loves me and is very dear to me."

Another "Nervous story" occurred when Baba humiliated Padri by bowing down to him for not following instructions. Nervous was standing close by, and purely as a tease Baba also bowed to him. Nervous took it very badly, and with tears was prepared to leave Meherabad. Baba tried consoling him, saying, "I bowed to you on my own accord, not for any mistake on your part; there's nothing for you to object to." But Nervous was adamant.

And though willing to follow all the Master's other instructions, he was strangely obstinate about leaving and continued weeping. So, Baba permitted him to go, offering him train fare, which he refused. Baba asked, "How the hell will you travel without money?"

Mehera shortly after she joined Baba, Meherabad, 1923

Nervous pointed to the gold buttons on his shirt, implying he'd sell them. Baba instantly ripped them all off, saying "You can go on two conditions. One – you beg for your food, and the other is you don't borrow or steal." Nervous accepted the conditions and left. Baba called out after him, "Wherever you go, I will follow."

As Nervous set out to leave Meherabad, Baba followed him along the road. When Nervous began running, Baba also started running. After some distance, Nervous broke down and started laughing, turned around and came back smiling with Baba's arm around him. After he calmed down, Baba asked him, "Why so dramatic?" Nervous said, "I wasn't angry, nor speaking harshly with anyone, so why touch my feet?"

CHRIST COME AGAIN

Baba said, "For some other fault. "Had I not touched your feet, how could you know you still had shortcomings? Had there been no offense, you could've remained quiet, merely thinking, "Oh well, it's just his wish." Though you do have faults, you thought yourself faultless. I had to show you it's not so. Printed Lord Meher p.620

As seen earlier, Baba then left Meherabad to tour India with his men. They were in Quetta, Pakistan, when Nervous came down with typhoid. Baba went to him several times a day, but despite the best care under medical specialists, he died on July 16th 1924, becoming the 1st mandali to pass away in Baba's service. After his burial, Baba sent the mandali to a movie to honor Nervous' dream of becoming a great movie actor. 535–37

He indicated 30 years later that Nervous had rejoined him yet once again to serve amongst the mandali, reborn in January 1927 as Bhau Kalchuri. Baba would later claim Bhau the most beloved among all his men – his "St. John," and my good friend since 1981 for over 32 years. Then in a Sunday online chat Bhau revealed his time has come and he will come back for just one more lifetime before Realization in Baba forever. RD 349–50; MM 1:16–17

Mehera recalled a poignant moment in her earliest days with Baba:

> "I was standing in the kitchen near Baba one morning at upper Meherabad. I gave him something and turned to see what he was doing. He was sitting so quietly. In that moment he looked so dear and absolutely beautiful to me. After shaving, his cheeks looked smooth and silky.
>
> "I came near, but didn't know how to embrace him though feeling so much love. I put my cheek on his for a few seconds and looked into his eyes. It was so beautiful. Sometimes you feel like that; you just want to kiss and embrace him. I still remember it after all this time. Baba was

talking then, so lively and energetic – such a happy, cheerful nature. When I was 17 with Baba, I thought I was going to be 17 forever . . . ." MM 1: ix and 119

Meherabad's Free Schools and Clinics

While the first Bombay Manzil-e-Meem ashram was mostly off-limits to outsiders, Meherabad became a place of pilgrimage where hundreds flocked from neighboring villages and surrounding areas, out-stations and even distant cities to take the Master's darshan. Baba barely had time for a daily bath or to even move his bowels. Meherabad now became like a small country fair and quite cosmopolitan by Indian standards. PM 75

Besides starting his long silence here and writing his great Book, Baba gave his blessings both to individuals and larger crowds, while continuing without missing a beat to train his early disciples in his uniquely divine and one might say, "perilous ways.

Besides music and singing, Baba often rented movies from Bombay, projecting them for the villagers under the stars on the wall of the Post Office, anticipating American outdoor drive-in movies by at least a decade. On religious feast days, wrestling matches were also held in the afternoon with winners given brightly-colored turbans as prizes. 572–73

Providing such entertainment for the poor, Baba was drawing them toward himself and giving them the blessed opportunity of his intimate company. A free shelter for migrant poor was also opened, and Meher Charitable Dispensary and Hospital.

People were treated without charge, regardless of caste or creed. And if a patient soiled the bed, Baba himself took the lead in cleaning it. During its 2 years, over 7,500 out-patients and 5,000 in-patients from local villages benefited from the freely given care. 576

Meherabad's First School

One day he said, "You know, we really need to build a school for the children." And within 2 months it happened. The school for poor Harijan [Untouchable caste] children from Arangaon was started informally under a tree! But soon it hit a serious snag.

The village headman asked Baba to come and give darshan at Arangaon, to which he agreed. But when he arrived, most of his followers from the village were absent. He was so annoyed he sent everyone away without giving darshan even to the few who did show up.

The villagers again pleaded for his return the next day, but Baba said he'd not allow darshan unless they all promised to be present at every occasion when devotional music and singing programs were held so close by – barely a 2 minute walk from Meherabad.

Still, very few villagers attended even the next program. So Baba suddenly ordered the Harijan school children to go home and not come back. Frightened and not knowing what to do, they just stood there in tears. Their parents were called to take them home as Baba shouted sternly, "Take your children home if you can't spare time for an occasional singing program here!" He seemed really upset.

"Hurry up, take your children and get out of here! Never set foot in Meherabad again!" With lowered heads, some parents began returning toward the village with their disappointed children, while others stood their ground, solemnly promising to be present at all future programs. These few were forgiven and their children allowed to stay.

There was a good reason for Baba's reaction. Arangaon illiterates habitually passed their time drinking, gambling and visiting village prostitutes. To teach a lesson and compel their interest in spiritual matters, he had to resort to such extremes – trying to make them receptive to God, while regarding him as a God-Realized Being.

Despite Arangaon's illiteracy, poverty and vice, Baba became a more integral part of the villagers' lives, urging them to tread the righteous path toward God. He intervened in helping to resolve personal difficulties and quarrels, giving them employment and often financial aid. In other ways he established himself as the authority of Truth to whom they could turn and trust in every need, no matter what. Then a few free clinics were started. 579

There was a leper colony ashram, and among the hospitalized, many seemingly terminal diseases were miraculously cured. Complex surgery was performed with a special unit for cataract operations. Several who had lost their sight had it completely restored. Some of these clinics begun in 1925 continue operating today. In just the first week of 2014, the cataract surgery clinic treated 19 local patients.

Weekly grain rations were also given to the most helpless and needy villagers. When Baba briefly moved his ashram 45 miles away to Toka in 1928, the villagers walked all that distance on foot or in a bumpy bullock cart not to miss their weekly rations. That's how dependent they were on Baba, though they still had no idea he was the Avatar of their age.

Hazrat Babajan High School

That little school under a tree quickly expanded. When it became a high school and received state accreditation, it was moved from Arangaon to larger quarters at Meherabad, and formally christened by the Master in March, 1925 as the Hazrat Babajan High School. No longer a little village school, it now looked like a regular city high school.

Boarding over 200 children of mixed castes, creeds and including lower class untouchables, it was something radically new in

India. The children were well-fed, clothed, well-exercised and happy, with Baba supervising all aspects of their life.

Books and writing materials were freely provided, and with a passion for sports and games from his childhood, Baba happily gave out prizes to winners of athletic contests and awards to students excelling in exams. With expanded enrollment, the school soon formed a separate girls' division – The Hazrat Babajan Girls' High School in the village of Arangaon, overseen by a Christian lady. Arjun was assigned the school's director of education.[797]

Though illiterate and with others more qualified, all the teachers had to work under him. Baba expressed such great love for him, even putting his own food on Arjun's plate. Other mandali members became a bit jealous, for they all loved Baba, yet he seemed only to express his love for Arjun. One day during a school inspection, Baba got upset with one of the teachers, Vishnu, for a mistake he'd made.

Baba later said, "Vishnu, I got angry, and that's not good. Now take this stick and strike my hand 3 times." Baba extended his arm, but Vishnu just couldn't bring himself to strike Baba. Feeling it a sin to strike the Master, he'd rather commit suicide.

So Baba called on Rustom, the manager of Meherabad. But he felt like Vishnu and just couldn't do it, saying he'd prefer to leave Meherabad. Baba then called for Arjun who was working elsewhere on the property and hadn't heard about the fuss. When he arrived, Baba simply gave him the order to strike him hard on the hand 3 times.

Without even a thought, Arjun took the stick and struck Baba's hand soundly! Turning to the mandali, Baba beamed, "Now do you see why I love Arjun so much? Because he pleases me! Whatever I say, he does, while you people only think of your orthodox ideas.

"Now that doesn't mean you should go around beating me, but when I say such an action is my order, you must do it. This is obedience. It's not a question of sin or virtue but simply a matter of pleasing me. He who values my word loves me the most!"

Then pointing to Vishnu and Rustom, he said, "You love your own feelings and personal fancies more than my words. That's why I love Arjun more; and even he has only recently begun understanding the importance of carrying out my orders." 575

This was a veiled reference to Arjun's final wasting away. In December 1926 at age 31, Arjun died and was reborn as the son of Baba's mandali, Sidhu. He still had 14.5 years left on that previous life and died of an epileptic seizure in May 1941. 756; DD 20 He'd soon die as a result of that deeply disturbing ghost sighting back at Baba's Poona grass hut some years earlier when he disobeyed Baba's very explicit safety order to stay outside while on night watch.

Baba's first Christian Mandali

Lewis Henry Cox Nelmes was an Anglo-Indian religious seeker who met Baba at a darshan program in Poona the previous December, 1923. On seeing him, Nelmes, a Catholic, was stunned and felt he was seeing Jesus himself. He became speechless as tears welled up in his eyes simply gazing at the Master. He asked if he could come and stay in the ashram.

But his health soon weakened. For several days he suffered from a leg wound that became seriously infected, requiring treatment at the Meherabad hospital. During the next 3 days Baba kept him very close to his side. By July 26th he was running a very high fever. Seeing him, Baba remarked, "Nelmes will be free of all pain by tomorrow." Pendu and Padri nursed him all night, but Baba had other plans for him.

CHRIST COME AGAIN

Growing weaker, Nelmes died the next day. Catholic funeral rites were performed at a local church, while the men attended his burial 12 miles west of Ahmednagar at a Catholic cemetery near Bhingar. His unmarked grave was simply noted number H.H.6. It will be found in the cemetery record by future pilgrims close to the grave of another foreign Christian mandali, Christian Leik, whom we will also soon encounter. 605–06

Beginning in May 1925, Baba began something new – travelling incognito. Dressed in a felt hat, sunglasses, western clothes and boots, he told the men to keep his identity absolutely secret. Over decades Baba traveled thousands of miles in India and abroad on trains, boats, dugout canoes, bullock carts, by car, bus, airplanes, camels, elephants and donkeys. 586

A later close disciple, Eruch Jessawala, describes it: "On a train someone might nudge me, 'Is that Meher Baba?' Now what? We can't lie. But saying, 'Yes,' would also displease him as being recognized interfered with his work. So we'd just look at the person and say 'What?' as if hard of hearing. 'Is that Meher Baba?' 'Who?' 'Meher Baba.' 'What are you saying?' The person concluded we didn't know the name, so we could relax."   ITS 70

The Coming Silence

In an age of hellish digital noise, the world is not even remotely aware that on every July 10th hundreds of thousands worldwide observe 24 hours of silence, going about their jobs and lives communicating by gestures and notes to honor the Silence of Meher Baba's Eternal Presence. A human being's goal is the Real Silence existing only in Nirvikalp Samadhi – God's infinite conscious state beyond false mind's magnificent illusion of the entire creation.

Baba's apparent silence, about to be taken up for the rest of his earthly life, was the medium he would work through to make us tired and fed up with illusion and our attachment to the deafening noise of gross materialism. As the world becomes increasingly disgusted with its dissonant turmoil, and as mankind's materialistic desires weaken, consciousness will be prepared to hear the real sound of the Avatar's Infinite Silence – his true voice.

Now how did this silence come about? We saw Baba take his companions on a grueling, year-long, zigzag, wandering road-trip up and down the expanse of India. During that and the following year, he observed silence on 4 occasions, but rarely for more than a few days at a time. Early morning at Meherabad he'd go to the small Post Office building.

There he would sing, dance and play the drum with such strength and feeling it seemed as if the very ocean's waves were moving. Mehera recalls Baba's singing voice as a medium baritone in pitch. He sang with all his heart, taking low and high notes beautifully, looking up as he sang the highs. Each note was so perfect.

His voice was beautiful. He was always so talkative, singing and joking, but then he'd say, "I talk too much, no? I talk all day long." So then occasionally, he'd observe these short silences. Though speaking 6 languages, Meher Baba was about to undertake lifelong silence out of infinite love and compassion for humanity MM1: 118, 145

Chapter Twelve

In the Kingdom of Silence

Drown all sound in my silence to hear my Word of Words. 4636

Behold the Silence. Allow the Lord to speak One Word within us – that He IS.

For ages and ages, God has been working in silence, unobserved and unnoticed, except by those who experience His Infinite Silence. 3195

June 26th 1925, two weeks before Baba's silence began. He summoned his disciples to carefully explain the meaning of his coming silence due to very heavy spiritual work when his primary Master Babajan will drop her body in the near future.

> "Disturbances, wars and disasters are looming on humanity's horizon. There will be religious hostilities, riots, wars, and natural disasters causing millions throughout the world to shed their blood; but thereafter, peace and brotherhood will come back into the world."

He added that he'd not speak until his Universal work was done. "Well, how long will that take?" the women wondered. On July 9th, the day before entering his great silence, Baba repeated his ominous prediction about many long disasters. 595

> "There will be another world war far more destructive and extensive than the one before. Rivers of blood will flow in which I will dip my kerchief and tie it around my

head. Not till the world cries out for God will I give up my silence."

He gave detailed instructions on how they were to proceed and their individual work duties during his silence, explaining the necessity of living and using one's body for the sake of others. "Don't be sad over it. Be happy, do your duties and stick to all my orders. Cook for our school children with love and care. Don't think they're just poor villagers and it doesn't matter. Do it with all your heart like they're your own children. That will please me." 599

Well, the men especially didn't believe he'd pull it off. They took it lightly, joking among themselves. It was another of his typical bluffs and wouldn't last long. But then later, when they realized he was serious, they became alarmed. "How will we get our instructions and training; how will the world receive your teachings?"

His shocking response was: "I haven't come to teach but to awaken." These last spoken words to his disciples expressed the deepest meaning of his divine mission in coming to earth for the sake of the humanity. As language resides in un-Truth, it is impossible for it to conform or reside in Truth while sporting with untruth. Meher Baba was taking upon himself a Silence to true the world as it had never been trued before.

The night before entering silence, Baba retired to his stone Jhopdi hut after reminding the mandali to always to carry a lantern when going out at night. He said he'd protect them from anything except snake bites! A few minutes later, Padri went out to relieve himself.

Finding a cobra, he shouted, "Snake!" The other men came running with staffs. Baba came out of his hut to see what the ruckus was. He was pleased Padri had obeyed his order to carry a lantern. Padri handed Baba a staff, and he crushed the head of the cobra.

CHRIST COME AGAIN

Then he went to the Post Office where the women were staying and told them how fortunate the incident with the snake was, as it gave them one more chance to hear him speak. How could they know they would never again hear Baba speak?

The next morning it came – July 10th 1925, a singular day to be celebrated by all humanity for ages to come. At 5 AM Meher Baba emerged from his stone hut in stone silence. After taking a bath, he made the rounds with his usual inquires about sleep, health, teachers and children – writing notes on a small chalk slate.

Baba's "jhopdi," a 12-foot square stone hut which Baba helped built and from which he emerged in lifelong Silence on the morning of July 10th 1925

Garbo Talks – Baba Doesn't

Ironically, as Baba was entering life-long silence, the "telephone talking-age" arrived in India, and on the other side of the globe Hollywood was forever abandoning silence to make "talking pictures." When MGM's Leo the lion suddenly began to roar, audiences stood up with goose bumps and cheered. As they whistled and clapped in wild anticipation, "Garbo Talks!" was being plastered all over theatre marquees.

CHRIST COME AGAIN

With such fanfare the new era was heralded in. Garbo would be proclaimed 7 years later by Meher Baba as "the greatest actress in portraying spirituality." As to his wish, she would have several chances to meet him – each one missed by some strange quirk of fate. Meanwhile, Mehera recalls Baba beginning his Silence:

Never Again to Sing or Laugh

> We thought Baba might be silent for a week. Then after a week we thought, well . . . maybe a month. But how can one keep silence so long? A month passed, then another. Well, 7 is a good number; ok, we reasoned, he might keep silence for 7 months.
>
> Once or twice we asked, but it didn't help. We were too shy to ask directly, so we'd write a note, "Baba, we must hear your lovely voice. How beautifully you used to sing. When will we hear you sing again?" Baba gestured, "Later on when my work is finished – in my own time."   .MM 1: 172

The first few days were difficult. The times Baba wanted to laugh, he'd quickly cover his mouth with a handkerchief. He held his lips tight, so he couldn't really enjoy a good laugh. Not a sound was allowed to escape. He kept guard on himself at all times. Just imagine the total awareness this required – enjoying laughing and singing – that too he denied himself. Every second, every minute, every day, month and year, Baba couldn't say what he wanted to express. M 85

He kept giving them confidence so they wouldn't feel hopeless. Imagine their shock on hearing his silence would last a year. Like his young sister Mani, a self-described "chatterbox," being so talkative how on earth could he observe silence for a whole year?

And the way he loved joking and teasing people? He'd wink at someone and go on seriously talking to another; so you knew he was joking with that one. Mehera poignantly recalls his silence increased his utter helplessness:

> "Baba's nature was so happy and cheerful. He loved to talk, laugh and sing, but in silence he could do none of these things. He had such a keen sense of humor, but if he wanted to be funny or to tease someone he'd have to point to letters on an alphabet board!
>
> "So by the time he'd finished saying it, half the fun was lost. He so loved to laugh, but even that sound he denied himself. So from July 10th we heard a new sound – Baba's loud clap to get the mandali's attention." M 23

I once heard a tape recording of Baba's "clap" made in the barn at his Myrtle Beach center in South Carolina. It was startling like a loud gunshot. In Zen, the clapping of hands signifies "It." A Japanese Zen haiku may explain "It:"

> When we clap our hands –
> birds fly up, pond fish gather
> and the maid serves tea

Years later, Baba noted wistfully, "He who is so fond of singing devotional songs and who'd enjoy doing so 24 hours a day has not gotten to enjoy them for years!" But if in a very good mood, he might be heard "merrily humming to himself." Mehera continues: 1710

> "It wasn't long before we noticed Baba had a new habit of rubbing his left thumb and forefinger together, forming a thick callus. Well, maybe he was restless. He was so outgo-

ing; maybe he needed some outlet to distract himself." A band-aid was put on his thumb so he'd remember not to do this and to help prevent infection. MM 1: 173

One might say before keeping silence Baba was often "full of piss and vinegar." His fiery moods now gave way to a far milder disposition. Words are generally spoken to keep the mind happy. When Baba's silence began, it strangely didn't seem like he was silent at all, because suddenly he became so much more dynamic. His companions were quickly learning that real communication is unspoken.

Baba's silence kept them laser-focused on him. They had difficulty interpreting his gestures, so he began writing everything swiftly and emphatically on a small chalk slate – his thoughts, wishes and orders in minutest details. He'd dictate the most profound and extraordinary discourses, and also give them simple daily instructions, pointing out and correcting their mistakes, big and small.

They figured he'd eventually make a slip up and a few words would escape from his lips. But it never happened – even decades later and after 2 serious car accidents with multiple broken bones. Vocal communication was transmuted to a higher vibration – intuition. His silence drew their attention to a place where his inner voice is heard.

> "I'm never silent. I speak eternally. The voice heard deep within the soul is my voice, the voice of inspiration, intuition and guidance. Through those receptive to this voice, I speak." 1795 "I don't speak with my tongue but continuously with my heart. But when I open my lips to speak the Word, all sorts of things will happen. All will be topsy-turvy. But the hearts of those in the world will get the Word. That time is very near." 4849

"Listen not to mind's voice but to the voice of the heart. Mind wavers. Heart falters not. Mind fears. Heart is undaunted. Mind houses doubts and reasoning full of theories, while the purified heart becomes the dwelling of Beloved God. So rid your heart of low desires, temptations and selfishness, and God will manifest as your own True Self." 3457

Baba recalled the fearlessness of both Saint Francises:

"Francis of Assisi and Francis Xavier loved Christ with all their might. None of you can guess how they suffered; but they had no fear. So don't fear, love me. Don't be bothered; think of Baba and be happy." 3587

The cotton Sadra becomes the Master's standard dress

Sometime before this, Gulmai presented Baba with a sadra – a long, thin white ankle-length cotton robe. From that day on, this was his normal attire. Then, one morning a month into his silence, Baba appeared unexpectedly at the women's quarters.

They hadn't seen him so often as when he was speaking, but he had warned them about that. So imagine their delight to suddenly find him on their doorstep. Mehera had been living there a year now. She was inside and hadn't heard his approach:

"A couple of the kitchen girls rushed in. 'Quick, Mehera, Baba wants you.' As I went out to the porch I thought, "Oh, Baba wants to tell me something. I hope I didn't make a mistake." Baba had just bathed and was wearing a fresh new white sadra open at the neck with the little 'v' on his chest, pink from being in the sun. I couldn't believe my eyes. He was so beautiful, young and slim, his skin so fair, and there was also a pink flush on his face.

CHRIST COME AGAIN

"His brown hair was loose, shining in the sun with golden tips like a halo around him. He asked, 'What were you doing?' 'Just my work, Baba,' 'Are you happy?' 'Oh, yes, very happy.' He was making small talk with me. Then he sat on a packing case, took his slate and wrote,' From the first time I saw you, I recognized you as my Radha.' " [Radha was the pure female consort and Beloved of Lord Krishna, the Avatar previous to Buddha.]

In this way Baba proclaimed to Mehera and the world her unique role – the one special soul chosen to play that role in each Avataric advent. As years passed Mehera assumed her position as the Master's chief woman disciple. Later when she wasn't present, Baba addressed the other ashram women: "I love you all. But Mehera is my Beloved – like my Radha, my very breath. I cannot live without her."

Shortly after this, Baba again called Mehera, writing on his slate, "I love you." She was surprised but unsure how to respond. Thus he continued the work begun years before in their strict basic training of how to work as close disciples and circle members. M 109

On Christmas Eve 1925, Baba asked the mandali to stay awake till midnight.

The last speaker was the Arangaon Christian, "Ajoba" [Gangaram Pawar], who entered dressed in a long white robe and carrying an 8' wooden cross while delivering a stirring speech about Jesus' crucifixion to the mandali, teachers, students, hospital patients and pilgrims.

The school boys then sang Christian hymns and carols, while Baba gave out tea, sweets and other treats. Games were also played Christmas morning and afternoon, and at 10 that evening a singer performed. 630

Sometimes the mandali would just sit before Baba in perfect, heart-filled silence for 2 hours at a stretch. His silence had no resemblance to people in religious life who undertake silence for the

PAGE 337

sake of meditation or contemplation. But it helped in his monumental task of taking on his lovers' and the world's binding impressions.

He later poetically wrote on his slate: "It's most difficult to keep my mind, not to talk through the tongue. I want to speak, speak, speak! And yet I remain dumb." He was also fed-up. We take speech for granted, but lest we think it a lark to be silent or a way to avoid hassle, even after 3 decades Baba had a long litany of complaints about it: 603

> You're all no doubt tired of all these things, but have no idea how sick I am about things like my silence – billions of times more disgusted than you all are – fed up and miserable. Why should I be when I'm free? Because as Buddha said, "I'm eternally free and eternally bound." I'm bound because of people's bondage, fed up and miserable due to their fed-upness and misery. NL 565; EN 89
>
> Honest to God, I'm absolutely, infinitely fed up and looking forward to breaking my silence, then this feeling will disappear. Although it's no bother for me, I feel so disgusted I occasionally wonder when I'll be free of this silence, and when the world too will be free 2984
>
> But even feeling fed up is a delusion, as when I say I'm waiting to break my silence. But this is high grade delusion to make others undeluded. The Master Juggler does his tricks to sustain the Truth so the children shouldn't go wrong. But he gets fed up, wondering when the children will be able to understand him and come to know the Truth and be able to say all else is a fake. 3345
>
> I'm silent and don't speak. Have you any idea how disgusted I am with this silence? I'm fed up with it; so is everyone else; and the disgust of everyone devolves on me. The disgust the world feels also falls to my lot, added to the

disgust I already feel about my silence. But this will all be gone when I finally break my silence. 3386

I'm infinitely bored, so much so I'm waiting for the moment when I can break my silence – when at last the heart of the world can be touched. I'm eager for the Word to come out! But I have infinite patience. I know just that Word can solve everything; for the Word is the Source of all words. Yet, I am so infinitely patient I go on day after day repeating the same old truths. 4847

Yes, he was fed up as were all his men, and venting his feelings included theirs also. Everyone was exhausted but said nothing; so Baba said it for them. Meanwhile, the Master would have his "imitators," men who would foolishly try to emulate his silence as a way of putting on spiritual airs to draw attention to themselves.

In 1953 to such a one named Krishnaji, Baba explained the difference between that man's "affected silence" and his:

"Your keeping silence has no meaning. My observing silence is not for any ulterior purpose, but for my Manifestation. I say this because God knows it as gospel truth. My silence is for the world. When I speak, God will speak; otherwise, silence as a spiritual exercise has no great value. Mind must be silent. Don't even think of observing silence to imitate me." 3304

The Beautiful Dumb Man

Taken upon himself with divine seriousness, Meher Baba's silence also had its comic moments, as at the end of September 1947 while returning from a long trip. Dressed in dirty clothes, hot, exhausted, unshaven and using hand signs, Baba began giving instructions on a train platform to a couple of his mandali about some upcoming work.

Observing Baba's gestures, a bystander walked up asking, "Has he been dumb since birth?"

Eruch, also exhausted, replied in exasperation, "Please, don't bother us just now."

The man replied, "But I've come to help, not trouble you! There's a shrine here in town. Just take him there and perhaps he'll be able to speak. Countless disabled have benefited by pilgrimage there."

Eruch replied, "We're not seeking a cure. Now for God's sake, please leave us in peace."

By now a crowd had gathered talking among themselves: "Oh, such a beautiful face! What radiance! Poor man, speechless from childhood – why doesn't he go to the tomb? Surely he'll be helped!"

Another man stepped forward and told Eruch, "Just listen to us, will you! Take him to the shrine. You won't regret it. I assure you it'll be to his benefit."

Eruch protested, "We have to catch a train and –"

"You still have plenty of time," the man assured them. "The shrine is so close; you'll be back in no time."

Finally, Baba gestured to Eruch, "For God's sakes, we better we go to the shrine to get rid of them once and for all."

Eruch asked, "Okay, where's the shrine?"

"Oh, we'll come and show you."

"No, please, just point out the direction; we don't want you to come with us," Eruch pleaded. Given the address, Baba proceeded toward the Muslim shrine with Eruch and Pendu, leaving Baidul on the platform to guard their luggage. Only then was the crowd gratified. He who speaks innumerable tongues was paying homage to a shrine to regain his lost speech. Such was the divine comedy!
2595–96

The Book

Besides not speaking from 1925, Baba also stopped touching money, except when giving it to the poor. Meanwhile, just 3 days after entering silence, Baba began a year-long project of writing the only book of his remaining unpublished and unseen, predicting after his Manifestation it would become like a new bible for humanity.

The book was begun in the Jhopdi stone hut where he began his silence. We know of no previous Avatar who transmitted anything of length in writing directly with his own hand. Thus, we assume Meher Baba's handwritten book is of utmost importance for the world, especially when on completion of his secret book, he completely gave up writing.

Much of it was done sitting confined inside a low, cramped cabin 4'x 4' x 7', with enough room for one person to sit. It was like a big doghouse, built as was the Jhopdi by Ajoba, the Christian carpenter who befriended Baba and his men the 1st day they hiked out to Meherabad. He was now helping the mandali to build and repair things around the ashram. Baba would also have him read aloud scriptures from the New Testament. 619, 557

That entire year, Baba spent early mornings and nights in this tiny cabin, writing by hand in various languages. After finishing his book and when travelling, he'd bring the manuscript with him, locked in a metal case with one of the mandali in charge of it.

CHRIST COME AGAIN

The table cabin near Meher Baba's jhopdi and the small desk kept in the museum atop Meherabad Hill on which Baba wrote his "Book" while cramped in the tiny cabin in his first year of Silence.

Below: Meher Baba wearing sandals given him by Babajan. Photo from 1926, the year he wrote the Book.

The case went wherever Baba went, with the key kept on a string around his neck. No one at that time had read any of what Baba had written in the book. He warned his men not to read it as their minds were not yet prepared for the material. 746

Mahatma Gandhi was destined to read several pages in 1931. Then it went with Baba to America where a secret custodian – perhaps Malcolm Schloss – kept it in a safe-deposit box. In the mid-1950s, it was returned to Baba. Before Baba's passing, Eruch asked about the book's whereabouts. He was told it was safe and will come out at the right time.

Whenever Baba gave discourses or explanations to the mandali, and later on to the school boys, Chanji took it all down in shorthand and later wrote it out in longhand, often staying up late nights compiling notes. The next day he'd hand them to Baba for corrections.

Baba would look at them, and after nine days he would return them with his remarks. Chanji then typed Baba's explanations in their final form. He also kept a separate diary of daily events at Meherabad. Thus, due to Chanji's prodigious secretarial efforts, the record of Meher Baba's activities is bountiful beyond any previous Avatar in human history. Blessed Chanji.

Observing him typing up his discourses, Baba remarked, "You find these very interesting, but they're nothing compared to what I've written at Meherabad in my book. Its 300 pages cover only short points, but when they're fully rewritten and amplified, the points will comprise several large volumes. It is full of spiritual and scientific secrets which no previous saint, Prophet or Avatar has ever divulged to humanity." 746

Infinite Intelligence

Each time he comes, the Avatar always opens a new window, a fresh revelation of Truth which itself never changes, but is adapted to the understanding and mentality of the age. While basing his teaching on love, we will see Baba giving deeply satisfying answers to ancient and perennially troubling questions about God, man and the cosmos.

His narrative of the "Divine Theme," the soul's journey from Unconscious-God to Conscious-God, was never before given to humanity. An outline of it with diagrams is given in this book's end Supplement, titled The Soul's Amazing Journey from A-Z.

While continuing silence and writing in seclusion, in the evenings Baba greatly increased his spiritual discourses to the mandali with Chanji taking it all down. He was preparing humanity for a whole new understanding of the spiritual cosmos in both his public discourses and secret writings. The following is a diary entry from one of the mandali:

> "Baba occasionally gave lectures and explanations, but since observing silence he's been very regular in explaining deep, divine subjects, so much so in the last 4 months his silent lectures were so frequent if put together they'd make a huge volume in itself. Chanji took the lectures down in many notebooks." These deeper explanations were not simply hasty notes on Baba's chalk slate, nor conveyed by simple gestures.
>
> The men enjoyed the explanations with Baba's constant repetitions, many side explanations and examples. And so a page of Chanji's diary is the result of many of Baba's fully written chalk-slates and a long process of his gesturing."

The above description may well refer to the Infinite Intelligence manuscripts. The handwriting of these so called "Intelligence Notebooks" is neither Baba's nor Chanji's, and so the scribe remains unknown. But it's most likely a carefully transcribed copy of the original notes Chanji took down hastily on odd pieces of paper.

Though the location of those original notes is unknown, a copy of the manuscript surfaced in 1969 after Baba's passing. The mandali came across it sorting through a pile of collected items stored in a shed at Baba's final home at Meherazad.

Baba had reformulated some of these same themes into material intended for a major motion picture, "How It All Happened," presented to executives of the film industry during his 3rd visit to America and 2nd visit to Hollywood during 1934-35, as we will later see.

The Alphabet Board – A Precursor of Laptop Cyber Language

Eighteen months after entering silence and completing his major Book, on January 1st 1927, Meher Baba stopped writing, reading, and for some decades not even signing his name. On that New Year's Eve, he gave his last handwritten discourse on love:

> Love is all pervading in the universe, but the types of love differ. The love pulsating in inanimate creation is mere magnetic attraction. Then there's love in the animal kingdom among animals and birds, but it is passionate – full of carnal desires. Carnality signifies bodily wants – eating, drinking, procreation and fear. Suppose a tiger pounces on a deer, kills and eats it.
>
> This is also love, but of the lowest type. Consider to what mean level love descends in an animal that's hungry and wants to satisfy its hunger by killing another innocent animal. And consider also to what length the lover (tiger) hunts his beloved (the victim, the deer) by following it stealthily.

In human beings love is also sometimes passionate. If a person is hungry, he thinks of a favorite dish, his mouth waters and he longs to eat it. If there are sweets, the person wants to fill his stomach. This is "candy" love. Once satisfied and his stomach is bloated, he's finished. A good belch, and no hunger; no more candy love. Some desire name and fame or money surpassing their reason, so much so they lack hunger and sleep. Thus greed means a type of love – money-love, name-and-fame-love, greatness-love. This is not the case with animals.

But a true hero longs intensely for the true nectar of divine love, and he's an exception. Such pure love isn't found in the ordinary run of mankind. This love is not inborn, but given and imparted by a [spiritual] Master. Love is therefore one, but it is of several kinds. The lowest is attraction.

It develops with progress in evolution and transforms into real love, which is like a stream flowing silent, serene, passionless, eternal, perfect and pure. Divine love is the highest of all, but it is not silent or peaceful. It has terrible longing. The winds of evolution, reincarnation and involution blow the stream of attraction through the inanimate world, turning it into a wild river in animal and human kingdoms, finally transforming itself into an ocean of divine love upon Realization. 757–58

By now Baba was also conveying his thoughts and feelings through hand gestures, or simply pointing to alphabet letters in the newspaper. With his animated nature, the mandali had all but forgotten he was silent. But now as Baba stopped writing, they became keenly aware of it once again. Later, while explaining about creation, he quoted some couplets and then explained in more detail what happened at the beginning of creation:

CHRIST COME AGAIN

I am That which began, out of me, world and man! It is I who began it all; from me God, man and the whole world sprung forth . . . . Life on my sources first drifted and swam. Out of me all the forces that save it or damn! Out of me, birds and beasts, men and women. Before God was I. Beside and above me, nowhere is there to go. Love or unlove me, unknow me or know. That which unloves me and loves me. I am that which is stricken, and I am the blow! 760

When Energy [Pran] clashed with Matter [Akash] 4 things appeared in quick succession – fire, water, air and earth. Stones, metals and vegetation have connection with earth; worms with earth and water; fish with water; birds with air; animals with fire; and human beings with all the elements.

By fire is meant lightning. Lightning is everywhere, but it is covered by a layer of ether and directly connected with animals; so their digestive powers and sexual forces are strong. They eat frequently and have sex often; so it seems as if they're born only for eating and sex.

The first worm form after the vegetable kingdom is totally green in color. The last worm form is the crab. It is found in moist earth; that is, it goes in water, too. It has to become a fish and therefore seeks water. In birds, you will mark some species have an affinity with water.

These are the 1st forms after fish. The next most advanced forms of birds have affinity with air, and the very last bird forms with the earth – such as roosters. After that is the kangaroo form – the 1st form of animal life. And the last animal forms, as you can guess, is the monkey or ape. 876 [This exposition is fully delineated in 'How it all Happened' in this book's end Supplement.]

Vishnu now ingeniously devised a thin plywood laptop alphabet board pasted with English letters and numbers – a simple visual aid which has gone down in history. A digital space-age version of it is on my lap now as I type and tell you of it. Through this board, Baba began silently speaking once again. Moving speedily with no breaks in conversation, using his finger he spelled out, "The world is dancing every moment to the signs of my fingers.

Thus in 1927 the age of "texting" was quietly ushered in. The world only caught on with its own texting devices 65 years later in December, 1992. Today, the number of daily text messages is well beyond the total world-population, and it all began with Meher Baba.

Meanwhile, what made it difficult was Baba dictating in Gujarati, Marathi, English, and switching between all 3. I actually see this as Meher Baba's pre-figuring and ushering in the biggest jumps in the history of communications the world has ever seen, by simply inaugurating a crude laptop alphabet board to text all his messages. This is how God works.

Tim Berners-Lee invented the world-wide web/internet in 1989 and gave it away free, typing out "This is for everyone." In 2004, Berners-Lee was knighted by Queen Elizabeth II for his pioneering work. It's certainly no coincidence or even stretching the imagination that countless millions of people are daily using Meher Baba's little alphabet board to instantly communicate with each other anywhere in the world.

One must remember when the Avatar does some action on what appears to be a small, individual scale – like using a simple alphabet board to point to letters – he is actually working universally, and the results are eventually felt and manifest on a worldwide, planetary scale. Baba himself in 1930 openly pointed to this:

CHRIST COME AGAIN

A drawing of Meher Baba inaugurating the keyboard (Drawing courtesy of Susan Roth)

"Notice how nations were brought into instant communication with each other during this modern epoch. Railways, steamships, telephone, telegraph, radio, newspapers [film, TV and the internet] have caused the whole world to become a closely woven unit.

"There's a special reason why these developments are taking place. A time is coming to give mankind a universal spiritual belief which will serve people in every country. A way is being made to enable me to deliver a worldwide message to humanity." 1207–08

In his novel, Fierce Invalids Home from Hot Climates, author Tom Robbins has his main character, CIA operative Switters, rant about the future of the word in cyber culture:

"From the alphabet's invention, if not before, all technologies have originated in language. In cyberspace we don't see or hear information as much as neurologically feel it on surrounding surfaces. Then there's the binary digital system, Brother One and Sister Zero, that light/dark relationship making computers possible.

Then, factor in the electron rather than the word as the primary information link between the brain and external world .... language wasn't utterly doomed, but to be transformed as it had been by the invention of the Phoenician alphabet, and liberated by the Greek alphabet." [Fierce Invalids Home from Hot Climates, by Tom Robbins, p. 180]

Although it's my own theory, history may interpret Baba's alphabet board in exactly the same way. It is significant that the world's first multiple-site computer network in 1969, uttered its 1st word: "lo," as in "lo and behold." This was the year Meher Baba finished his work on earth and dropped his physical form. When I compared Baba's alphabet board to computer texting and mentioned it Bhau Kalchuri in 2005, he thought for a moment and said, "You're right; there's surely something to that."

Besides an alphabet board, Baba sometimes simply gestured his meanings with both hands, like a double high-five, or pinching his Adam's apple for "I swear." Mehera humorously recalls, "How many sworn promises Baba kept, I truly don't know." MM 1: 181

In 1928, Baba temporarily moved his ashram 45 miles from Ahmednagar to the nearby village of Toka. It appeared deserted, but the pleasant scenery of hills, trees and rivers with its peaceful atmosphere appealed to Baba.

Here he began a long fast, continuing his silence as in the previous three years at Meherabad. This deeply disturbed mother Shireen who knew what a superb voice he had. Why on earth was he doing this? Why imprison his beautiful voice; why fast and wear out his beautiful body? Baba's sister Mani relates:

> "So, one day mother said, 'Merog, why are you fasting for months on end thin as a rail? And why observe silence locking up your beautiful voice? You say there's nothing for you to gain and that you're doing it for all these young characters around you. So make them do it; make them observe silence; make them fast! Why should you do it?' "

That's when Baba gave us a glimpse of the difference when we do something and he does it for us – his silence, his fasting or whatever he does in his love for mankind. He said, "Mother, were the whole world to fast and observe silence for the rest of their lives, it wouldn't equal one day of my fasting or equal one hour of my silence." Tavern Talk, 7/24/2008

At another time he said: "Speaking with the tongue is mere speech. Sealing the lips is external silence. But the mind also has a tongue of its own and talks continually. The creation of a thought is like speaking internally. Hence, the "mind's lips" must be totally sealed." 2341

The Beginning of Many Broken Promises

Meher Baba always challenged his disciples to connect with his silence, while using it to grind down their expectations and wear out their minds with promises so often given to "break" his silence, and then his apparent failure to do so. Silence-breaking themes were a constant, never-ending saga from the very earliest days; sometimes charming, sometimes frustratingly incomprehensible and mysterious, and at other times hilariously grandiose.

For example, in the early years Baba arranged to break his silence in the presence of his inner-circle men. With great anticipation they hiked strenuously for several days to reach a remote location where Baba arranged them sitting in a large circle with him in the middle, their backs toward him. When he clapped, they were to turn and he would speak.

His clap was like a pistol shot. In breathless anticipation they turned. Nobody heard him utter a sound. Questioned, he simply gestured with a question of his own, "Don't you know I'm always speaking?" Baba's sister Mani relates another humorous story about a promise Baba had made to her when she was a young school girl. GM 413

CHRIST COME AGAIN

Every now and then we'd hear a mention about Baba planning to break his Silence. So I went and extracted a special promise from him. I said, "Baba, when you break your Silence, I want to be with you." He said, "Of course you'll be with me." I said, "Promise, promise!" So He did. He promised solemnly with his hand in mine. After I had him do that again and again, I felt for sure the matter was now sealed. This happened about 5 years after Baba began his Silence.

Summer vacation was over, so I went back to school. But somewhere in the middle of the term I heard Baba had sent out a circular saying he was going to break his Silence soon. I was shocked. I couldn't believe it. Baba knew my next school break wouldn't be till after November. He had forbidden me to go to him while I was at school, but had promised me most solemnly to have me with him when he broke his Silence. And here he was deciding to break Silence during school term!

I immediately sat down and wrote a letter to my dear brother, saying, "You solemnly promised me I'll be with you when you break your Silence. I'm most surprised to hear you're going to break it soon while I'm still in school. So, either you allow me to come and be with you when you break your Silence or you just have to postpone it. P.S. I can come right now."

This must have scared Baba, as a quick reply came back. "No, don't come," he wrote. "I've decided to postpone breaking my Silence." So it seemed quite natural Baba postponed his Silence breaking till the time when his kid sister could be with him during her school vacation! GB 126–27

CHRIST COME AGAIN

Then a few years later there was his much-ballyhooed announcement of silence-breaking in the Hollywood Bowl during his 1st visit to the film capital in 1932. That flamboyance delighted some and totally disarmed others, as we'll see in Chapter 21, "Christ in Hollywood." Meanwhile, for 27 years the alphabet board would be the Master's medium.

Jumping forward in time — He gathered his men before discarding the board on October 7th 1954, after which he would "speak" only by gestures. He brought 3 boards with him – a plywood one given away to disciple, Kumar, a plastic one given to Dhake, and a cardboard one on which he pointed out,

> "The zero of this board is partially torn off, but a portion of it is still hanging on. I've been using this board quite roughly; still the zero is suspended to it. Due to a broken piece, 3/4ths of the zero on the board is wiped out; 1/4th is saved. If that dangling piece separates from the board, it will be best for the world."

He then flung the board across the room to one of his disciples, and of course the dangling piece fell off. He gave the board to Eruch with instructions to preserve and take utmost care of it, adding, "Only God knows the value of this zero and what it signifies."

Then giving just the detached zero to his disciple Savak Kotwal, the one who caught the board, he said, "Keep this most carefully till your last breath." Turning to Savak later, Baba asked, "Where did you put that piece of the zero?"

"I put it in my trunk," he said.

"Had I been in your place," Baba told him, "I'd have cut a slit in my flesh and kept the zero-piece there! Do you really want it?"

"I didn't realize its importance," Savak replied.

"That zero will create great havoc," Baba warned. "Then it's useless for me to keep it,"

Savak said, "I'll return it."

Baba added, "Actually, I wanted the piece, and Savak gave it back voluntarily without my asking." As Savak gave it back to Baba, he remarked, "You're such a fool to return it!"

Then smiling, Baba invoked the following prayer:

"O Sai Baba, Upasni Maharaj, Babajan, Tajuddin Baba and Narayan Maharaj! To You, the Five in One and the One in Five Divine Beings representing the Absolute One, I bow in homage. Due to you Five Men-God I am what I am – the Ancient Everlasting One!

May the Beloved God, with Whom you Five are One and for Whom you are working universally, give me in your names, the strength, power and wisdom to fulfill all I have taken this form for, and see that all I have declared at the last Meherabad meeting comes to pass. I now give up using the board, it being my gesture before God for breaking my silence soon."

There was a divine glow on Baba's face and a luster in his eyes. He stood with folded hands before Gustadji, and asked the prayer be read again, twice by Eruch and once by Bhau. Then at exactly 7 PM, he instructed Eruch to give the cardboard alphabet board with the torn zero to Padri for safe keeping, along with the white sheet on which he stood during the ceremony. For a few minutes after that, Baba sat quietly in serenity.

Suddenly, he gestured, "I am happy! Everything went well. All will be well." From that moment, Baba depended only on intuition, simple hand gestures and facial expressions to communicate. Without realizing it, humanity was jumping into the age of intuition. 3647–49

That day also pre-figured a future occurrence when he added that besides the alphabet board he would also put his body aside.

His followers over the world were shaken at the thought of his leaving. This was after he had dictated his final message on the board:

There's no reason at all for any of you to worry. Baba was, is and will also be eternally existent. Severing external relations does not mean the termination of internal connections. It was only for establishing the internal connections the external contacts were maintained till now.

The time has now come for being bound in the chain of internal connections. Hence, external contact is no longer necessary . . . . I am with you always and never away from you. I was, am and will remain eternally with you, and to promote this realization I've severed external contact. This will enable all persons to realize Truth by being bound to each other with internal links.

Oh, my lovers, I love you all! Only because of my love for my creation have I descended on Earth. Let not your hearts be torn asunder by my declarations about the dropping of my body. On the contrary, accept my Divine Will cheerfully. You can never escape from me. Even if you try to escape from me, it is impossible to get rid of me. So have courage and be brave . . . .

CHRIST COME AGAIN

A New Sign Language

Though Baba says, "Remember, I'm always with you," he added, "But you must always keep me with you" – that we never leave him alone. At the start without his alphabet board, some new difficulties arose for Baba conveying what he wanted. Starting out, one of the men repeated the English alphabet, and Baba would stop him at the right letter.

Or he'd form English letters with his fingers, using his ear for "E," and pointing to his eye for "I." Later, Baba began writing in the air with his fingers or sometimes on the floor. But this was tedious and difficult to follow or decipher. 3651–52

So he'd began making finger signs, gradually creating a whole new language of gestures. He was fast in this new language which evolved into an alphabet-less language of pure gestures and facial expressions communicated more deeply and absorbed with greater feeling. This is seen in films from late 1954 on. Of the men, Eruch was the quickest to recognize Baba's signs which he then spoke out, and Mani was best interpreter among the women. MM 3: 463

The Breaking of His Silence – Releasing the Word of Words

Baba observed the world's consciousness was reverberating loudly, and sounds of darkness were totally out of proportion, causing imbalance in the world. Consciousness was already too deeply involved in the language of darkness, with ordinary minds incapable of understanding the language of Light. AA 62

> "I must break my silence, and when I do, all who've come in my contact will have a glimpse of me; some small, some big, some little, some a little more. When an electric power station main switch is turned on, wherever there's a connection, there the light comes on.

"If the bulb is small, you get low wattage. If it is high, good light; and if shorted out, no light! That's why I say I have performed no miracle; but when I break my silence, the first and the last of the greatest of all miracles will be performed. Love me with all your hearts; that is the only thing. Love me, love me, love and you will find me." 3510

The time for the Power House to be switched on is so near the only thing which will count now is Love. Though all Avatars maintain periods of silence during their advent, the 44 years of silence Meher Baba undertook on July 10th 1925 is a special, particular characteristic of the 7th and final Avatar at the end of a 5,000 year cycle.

Like the silence before dawn, its breaking will open up a secret to eventually result in a major jump in planetary consciousness. The tectonic plates of the inner spiritual world will shift – the real paradigm shift foretold for the Age of Aquarius – but far beyond what any Nostradamus or Edgar Cayce astrologers could have ever predicted.

Becoming silent, Baba increased not only his discourses, but his daily activities and physical labors at Meherabad – grinding corn, bathing the children, washing their clothes, finishing his book, rendering service to the poor and afflicted, hearing complaints of the poor Arangaon Village people and aiding them in their difficulties.

He oversaw everything at Meherabad, especially the mandali. Not only did he express anger and forgiveness, displeasure and happiness, seriousness and humor, but he gave darshan to thousands and attended daily correspondence. He fully participated in games, and even in the height of excitement never uttered a sound. 690

With the soaring emphasis Baba placed on both his silence and its breaking, one instantly recognizes silence was the prime aspect

CHRIST COME AGAIN

of his divine ministry in this advent. The Avatar is the source of everything, and his silence is the source of all words in all worlds.

Many believe the breaking of his silence may happen at the time of or after a major cataclysmic global event, likely by or before 2069. If this is so or only pure fancy only time will tell. Before his passing, Mehera pressed Baba about when he would break his silence.

He smiled, putting her off. "Later – not now." Then he gestured a 'J' – for what, they didn't know; maybe January, June or July? My guess is some July 10th in the next few decades – that month and day being the anniversary of undertaking his lifelong silence in 1925. Such an event will quickly be recognized by the world as beyond coincidence. Baba now revealed how he would guide the world holocaust soon to appear on the horizon:

The Coming Upheaval of a New War

Great upheavals are coming soon throughout the world, particularly in India. There will be great tension between the British and the Indian people on one hand, and between Hindus and the Muslims on the other, resulting in terrible bloodshed and massacres. Hindus and Muslims will kill each other, and the British will kill both! Rivers of blood will flow with corpses everywhere!

Civil war will break out in India and all the parties will clash against one another. Nothing but chaos and confusion will reign everywhere. Out of this cry and clamor for independence, quite a new situation will arise with others intervening and abruptly appearing.

But before this violence, a greater war will break out and rage between the Western nations – Russia, America, England, Italy, Germany and others. There will be such chaos and confusion throughout the world not even one leader will understand what to do. And out of this confusion and chaos, the Avatar will appear to guide misguided humanity onto the path of peace, prosperity and toward eternal bliss. But that will take time and require great upheavals throughout the world.

These disorders, disturbances and unrest are necessary to make the world turn its face toward spirituality and ensure its future salvation. That's why I am sitting and staying secluded for a few days and why I've been continually saying, "Good times are coming for all," particularly for those with me and those with other great God-realized Masters.

All this intense political activity and widespread agitation for independence throughout India, turning the country upside down, is to me like a game of gilli-danda. I'm more interested in the thrill and excitement of the game we were just playing, because at that time my spiritual work is at its zenith, and great internal workings are effected. During such uproar and disorder, the British leave their country to come to India, and Indians leave here to go to England.

It is all the effect of my work. Every country has my agents, and according to my wish they work internally toward the Goal. These games – flying kites, marbles, etc, are my ways of working; every action of mine is an inner working, signifying messages sent here, there and everywhere. Whether taking a stroll or merry-making, I am working and nobody knows what I really do. 1180–81

At breakfast one morning, illustrating to the women the complete transformation to take place in the world on the breaking of his silence, Baba cupped his left hand over his right, as though holding a big ball, and then with a deft movement brought his right hand over his left in an absolute turnover of the imaginary ball's position. "Upside down," one of the women called out. With a half-smile Baba gestured, "No, right side up!" 5250

As a result of his silence breaking and releasing the Word of Words, concomitant and additional changes will occur in everyday consciousness, as human beings interface and interact with each other in a totally new ways. As big as the jump when consciousness went from sensation in animals to reason in humans, when mind went from finite to infinite, we now expect to enter an age when reason will jump to intuition.

Heart and mind [feelings and thought] will be connected in such balance that speaking words will no longer be so necessary as the primary means of communication. People will be more connected heart-to-heart in this new language of intuition. Intuition's heart-knowing will be our main and most trusted source of knowing; feeling with the mind, thinking with the heart, while giving reason the backseat when need be.

Heart-knowing will change everything from medical techniques to politics and government. Lies will absolutely be known to be lies, and motivation will be transparent. We are getting there now. Our one common destiny will be obvious and our actions based on that. Even before his Manifestation and the breaking of his silence, people worldwide are already sensing the beginning of this major paradigm shift in feeling and communication.

It's no small wonder besides loving the great comedy "talkers," Laurel and Hardy, Baba especially loved Charlie Chaplin's silent films where frame by frame true genius unfolded as the little tramp conveyed delicate feelings of humor and pathos in masterful, wordless pantomime. This also includes the other great comedic jewels of silent expression –Buster Keaton, Harold Lloyd and the Zen-like silent comic, Harpo Marx.

Harpo instantly saw through anyone's ego expectations and reduced them by simple comedic absurdity. Dressed like a bum, he moves about pompous high-society types as an equal or better, his sides splitting in silent glee at others' misfortunes. As they got more and more bent out of shape, he'd slap his face and silently guffaw, making it worse. Then he'd do it again with a wide smirking cross-eyed gaggle, shaking his head side to side, tongue stuck out in mindless idiocy. Then he would play his harp with such heart-feeling you just knew here was a true Zen comic/master.

I'm also often struck by the endearing intimacy so evident when mute people are together signing to each other unobtrusively. With just a mere look or a facial expression, pure heart to heart communication effortlessly transpires. It's fascinating and beautiful to watch hearts tuned to each other like this without the noise and distant formality of words.

Baba beautifully illustrated this when questioned about his silence. He asked why people shout at one another when they're angry? Even if someone is sitting beside them they'll shout at that person. Couldn't they just speak softly? When one is angry with another, that person is far removed from his heart, and distance is created between them. That's why the physical reaction is to shout; the greater the heart distance, the louder the shouting.

Love disappears as each one goes on shouting. "Now take the case of 2 people in love. They instinctively speak softly; and the greater the love between them, the softer their tone. And when still further in love, no words at all are needed; just a look at each other. Eventually, there's no need at all even to look." Baba finished by saying, "I am closer to you than your breath." His silence reaches into peoples' hearts. AO 101

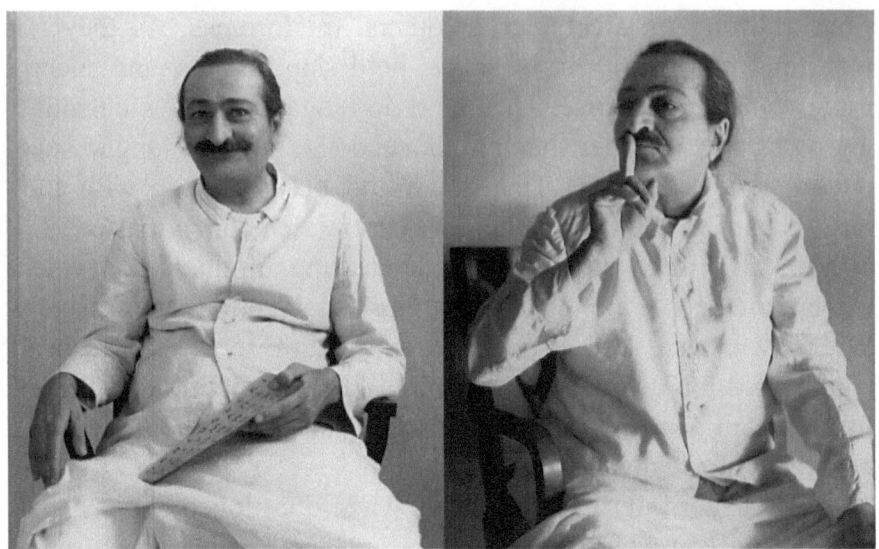

The Word took flesh and dwelt among us in Silence

In this present age when the accumulation of words has become meaningless, and all my previous words in the form of Precepts are neglected and distorted, I maintain Silence. When I break my silence I will speak the Primal Oceanic "Om-m-m" through my human mouth.

And because all forms and words are from this Primal Sound or Original Word, and are continuously connected with It and have their life from It, when It is uttered by me It will reverberate in all people and creatures, and all will know I have broken my silence and have uttered that Sound or Word. The effective force of this Word in individuals and their reaction to it will be in accordance with the magnitude and receptivity of each individual mind.

And the reaction will be as instantaneous and various as people's reaction in a room through which a cobra suddenly and swiftly passes, when some would nervously laugh, some lose control of their bowels and some feel great courage or reasonless hope and joy . . . . The breaking of my silence will shatter the seeker's hard crust of ignorance and reveal to him true meaning. SG 66

No sound is ever lost in the universe. Every thought we think – good or bad – every sound we make stays as a sound byte impression in the universe. But sound resulting in feeling has unbelievable force behind it to help or hurt others. Eruch Jessawala tells a story:

"When I was young I took pride in always telling the truth. I hurt a lot of people telling them what I took to be the truth. But here's what Baba told me: 'The Truth when told uplifts another. Anything which crushes another person cannot be true.' " TH 180

Baba explains sound bytes this way: "All this war noise of guns, bombs, planes, etc., will be utilized for the spiritual life of the world in the future. Yes, it all stays. Where can it go? Water evaporates to form clouds and comes pouring down upon us again as rain." 2158

In a flight of fancy, I once imagined some great cosmic event dropped onto earth's doorstep unexpectedly, like a mega-sonic boom maybe from a huge asteroid entering earth's atmosphere, so intense as to shatter and permanently destroy the delicate ear membrane and sense of hearing in all living beings. We would suddenly be plunged into a silent world.

But then I realized this would merely be an external silence; the mind's deafening roar with its own interminable chatter and noise would still be there! In March 1954, the editor of Velugu, an Indian weekly magazine, asked, "Baba, will the South India Andhra lovers be informed of the time and place of the breaking of your silence?"

Baba looked highly amused and with a twinkle he said: "Velugu my dear, if this is what's meant by breaking of my silence, it would be better if I didn't break it!" At another time Baba expounded on the power of sound and the human voice: GG V: 254

> Now what is the voice? Where does it originate? When one hears sound coming out of his mouth, it must exist somewhere. In truth, sound pervades the universe. God is sound, light – everything. There is a point from where sound issues forth, and from that Creation point, or Om point, evolution starts. Sound has been given a door – our mouth – to manifest from. When a sound comes out of the mouth it is lost in the Universal Sound which is everywhere.
> So what wonder if the tune produced by singing the mega rag reaches the clouds 2 miles above the earth and produces rain, when it is a recognized fact sound waves are sent through telegraphy [radio frequencies] 1000s of miles away. There's nothing supernatural here.
> For this reason, because sound travels and creates various vibrations, a person should read the holy books whether he understands their meaning or not. The words in Zoroaster's Zend Avesta, the Hindus' Gita, or the Muslims' Koran, and other scriptures, are arranged so that when pronounced the sound created comes nearly in unison with the Universal Voice, or the Universal Sound, and is a great help in spiritually influencing a person. 360

On the mystical aspects of sound and music in the universe, as an example of God's Song or Voice, in 1940, Baba explained there are 132 tunes in music. The singing of an expert musician or maestro is wonderful, but so very rare. He continues:

A blind singer in Delhi, who's now passed, used to perform quite superbly, "God is Infinite Voice" [Naad]. 89 of these tunes exist in the gross world and are all nothing but the seventh shadow of the Infinite Voice. There are 7 tunes in each of the 6 subtle and mental planes.

Thus 42 tunes in the subtle and mental worlds and 1 of God's Tune. That means 89 gross + 42 subtle and mental +1 (God's Tune) = 132. The Perfect Master and poet, Kabir, calls it Anhad Naad or Infinite Voice. Even the best and most exquisite true voice of the gross plane is only the 7th shadow of God's voice, and which Jesus, Zarathustra [Zoroaster] and Kabir call the "Word of God."

The voice of the best singer that can make rain fall, lights play and people weep, is only the seventh shadow of God's voice. This happens on the first subtle plane. If the pilgrim keeps listening to that note which is continuous on the first plane, he cannot continue on [i.e. he can get stuck in the heaven of that plane]. On the second plane, when the pilgrim hears the fifth shadow of that Eternal Voice, he neither eats nor sleeps. The second plane is far more powerful than the first.

It is simply called naad, meaning "tune" [voice or word]. Don't take these examples literally. For how can it really be explained? The Hindus call the Word of God "Om." With a closed mouth you can't say anything, but you can utter, "Ommm ...mmm ... Mmm" – that sound of Om is only the seventh shadow of the Voice of God. God is Infinite Voice, Infinite Light and Infinite Love.

On the first plane, one hears with the subtle ear; on the fifth and sixth planes, with the mental ear; on the seventh plane, one becomes the Voice itself. How to grasp it? It's impossible. How to understand God as Voice, and you becoming that Voice?

Then Baba laughed and sadly shook his head. He went on to say God's Voice isn't "voice" in the sense of when we speak words; they just call it voice to merely try to explain it. Sufis sometimes explain it not as a shadow but as a "veil."

Perhaps we can visualize it this way. Imagine you're looking between 2 mirrors facing each other. What you'll see is a series of repeated mirrored images in layers, each one behind the other – what I call the "infinity mirror." Baba continues:

> "Say you are God looking into a mirror. What's first seen in the mirror is on the sixth plane (the first reflection). Then, you see the reflection behind a veil in the mirror and that's on the fifth plane (the second reflection). There are subsequent reflections behind each other.
>
> "They are like further veils and planes, veil after veil until the seventh. The reflection behind another veil, behind the first veil, is on the fourth plane (the third reflection), and so on until the seventh. Those in the gross world live in the seventh veil." These are the "Seven veils." 2148–49

In every advent the Avatar charges certain symbols with his infinite power, knowledge and bliss. Jesus' symbol was his sacrificial Cross; Buddha's was his meditative Wheel of Law. Meher Baba's symbol may well be his human and divine Silence, resonating with the mystery of his profound identity. Only in profound internal Silence is Baba found.

> "Although I appear silent, I speak through you all. I am ever silent and everlastingly speaking; but the time is coming when I will break this apparent silence."

When Bhau Kalchuri's children complained keeping silence each July 10th was hard, Baba replied: 3438

But just think by keeping silence for one day how many less sanskaras you have . . . . When angry, if you're silent you have to keep it in check. It comes to your mind, but you can't express it. Those sanskaras lessen. That's why I tell people to keep silence at least once a year.

You don't realize how many things you say in a day – good, bad, lies, truth – still, you get sanskaras even if what you say is good. The day you're silent you prevent countless sanskaras [good or bad] from coming and are freed from that. So, it's very important to keep silence that day. As soon as I break my silence, that first Word will make your hearts vibrate. GuG 597

In my previous advents, I gave so many words. In this advent also, while observing silence, I have given more words than in any previous ones. At the same time I warn my lovers to be careful not to treat these words as rituals and ceremonies, but put them into direct action. That means to silence the mind. My silence is active; you will see how it awakens the world, makes the mind less and less active, and the heart more and more active. AW 13

As the end of the 19th century ushered in the birth of the Silent One, 2 great poets of that era prophetically sensed it in the air. The great Danish philosopher and religious poet Søren Kierkegaard vividly diagnosed both the malady and cure for modern society:

"The present state of the world and all life is diseased. If I were a doctor and asked for my advice, I would reply: Create silence! The Word of God cannot be heard in today's noisy world. Even if it were blazoned forth with noise so it could be heard in the midst of all the other noise, it would no longer be the Word of God. Therefore create Silence."

CHRIST COME AGAIN

The great French poet, Charles Péguy [1873-1914], in his poem, "Night," puts it this way:

> O Silence of darkness, such silence as reigned before the creation of unrest, before the beginning of the reign of unrest. Such a silence will reign, but it will be a silence of light, when all that unrest is brought to an end and exhausted, when they have drawn all the water from the well . . . .
>
> O beautiful night of the great mantle, daughter of the starry mantle. You remind me, even me, of that great silence that was before I had opened up the floodgates of ingratitude; and you announce to me, even to me, you announce the great silence to be when I will have closed them.

Meanwhile, Baba's sister, Mani, vividly recalls her early childhood visits to Meherabad: "The silence of Meherabad's long nights and isolated wildness would boom with calls of 'ALL WELL' echoing in the darkness outside. "Baba had 3 watchmen keeping night duty stationed at different points on the property. They'd call out to each other at intervals in the night "All is well." Their calls rolled and echoed across the vast grounds as if a 3-cornered game were being played in space.

"The first watchman would call out in long, drawn-out sing-song: "NUMBER ONE, A-L-L WELL." From far away the second would respond in same way, "NUMBER TWO, A-L-L WELL." The third then echoed, "NUMBER THREE, A-L-L WELL . . . ." This went on all night. Waking up in the dark and hearing these calls, I'd snuggle in and fall back to sleep, feeling totally safe and cared for with Baba's love telling the entire world, 'Don't worry. All is well . . . .' " GB 29–30

CHRIST COME AGAIN

50,000 Attend Baba's 32nd Birthday

The earliest mega-event at Meherabad occurred in February 1926. Baba's parents Sheriar and Shireen, together with brothers Beheram, Adi Jr., Jamshed and little sister, Mani, arrived there for his 32nd birthday celebration. All structures in lower Meherabad and up on the Hill were decorated with potted palms and flower garlands.

Anticipating the huge party, throngs from near and far were already gathered from early morning the day before. The next day thousands more travelling by bus, truck, car, horse carriage and bullock carts began descending to form a sea of humanity at Meherabad.

Baba insisted the mandali take care of the guests' food and lodging. At 8 o'clock on his birthday morning, the women mandali gave him a ceremonial bath. It was repeated afterwards by the men as they all poured a small pot of warm water over Baba's chest.

And thus, countless liters of water were showered upon him as thousands touched his delicate flower-like body, while the Arangaon village band played spirited rural music. By this time, the gathering had grown so large the mandali had problems with crowd control, having to surround Baba on all sides to keep the pushing throngs in check and prevent a crushing stampede. There was a short speech on Baba's life and mission.

Ceremonial red powder was then thrown in the air, and Baba was covered in heaps of flower garlands piled one on top of the other over his body and seat making him invisible with all the flowers! Devotional songs were sung, while thousands were served a great feast with plenty of food left over, like Jesus feeding the multitudes with just a few loaves and fishes.

This often happened around Baba. After the meal 50,000 people bowed to him as he gave darshan for hours on end. At night, fireworks lit up the sky. Yes, *Christ had come again*. The echoes seemed to reflect the bursting of each lover's heart. For those of us who missed the show, it may be hard to imagine. But when God takes human form such things happen.

When Baba appeared early next morning, the crowd rushed to him. So again for 6 hours Baba continued giving darshan without taking even a short break. His father and brothers left when the celebration was over. We recall as boys Jamshed and Merwan quarreled a lot, but by now Jamshed had grown to love his God-Brother so deeply he had trouble sleeping just thinking of Baba.

Brother Jamshed Goes to Baba

Knowing what was about to happen, after the celebration Baba sent Jamshed and his wife Khorshed to stay "for a few days" with his maternal aunt Dowla and husband Faredoon who had raised him till age 5 in the country village of Lonavla outside of Poona. Jamshed went to bed that night with a splitting headache and a heavy feeling in his heart.

He must have sensed something, as he urged Khorshed, "Never leave Baba; never under any circumstances." Then, suddenly feeling blissful, he shouted out Baba's name and fell into a coma for 3 hours. Only his lips moved repeating Baba's name.

Then before dawn on February 27th, beloved Jamshed age 33 had a heart attack and with his last breath called out loudly, "Baba! Baba! Baba!" Baba later recalled his brother's love to his Western disciples: 637–39

> My brother Jamshed was mad with love for me. He was so full of love for me he couldn't contain himself. The vein on his head snapped and he dropped his body, but just before dying he shouted out loudly Baba! He has come to me and is now with me eternally – liberated forever. 4000

CHRIST COME AGAIN

Mani was there and saw Jamshed in this state when he died and came to me. All my relatives and old school friends love and accept me as the Avatar. You have no idea how hard it was for them to accept me as the Avatar after quarreling, flying kites and playing marbles with me. To come to me means liberation – experiencing me as I am. Then, no more bondage of births and deaths.

But that doesn't mean the state of a Perfect Master – Perfection. That's attained only alive in the gross body. So, if you're not blessed with this state of Perfection in the body, at least you can have liberation. Just by taking my name at the moment of dropping your body, you will come to me. Yes, anyone. It's not easy to take my name at the very moment of leaving the body.

But if you do, you experience infinite bliss. On attaining liberation, you continue experiencing infinite bliss eternally. Why? Because you experience what has belonged to you eternally. Even spiritual ecstasy cannot be compared with divine bliss. Now remember this. 4407

Not just at the time of death, but anytime one is threatened by any impending disaster, Baba said, "Remember to always take my name wholeheartedly if anything untoward is about to happen, and I will save you – even from tigers!" An Indian Baba-lover once told me the story of his father's tiger experience in the 1940s. In his father's words: 3732

I was doing contract work in a forest full of tigers. One day, some of my men were confronted by one and ran for their lives. Luckily, no one was hurt, but they were very scared. Several hundred workmen were employed by me in that forest. The tiger appeared continuously for a few days.

By now, the workers protested they'd no longer work and started leaving the job site.

I tried my best to allay their fears, but nothing convinced them. I was in a really tight spot. Then, in the spur of a moment I hit upon an idea. I took pieces of cloth and made Meher Baba's 7-colored flag, hoisting it at the site where everyone was living. I gathered all the workmen, saying I had prayed to Meher Baba to see that tigers don't come there henceforth. "If you see any tiger despite of the flag, then I promise I'll stop all work at whatever cost it might be to me."

The workmen agreed to my proposal, and to everyone's surprise from that day no tiger ever came into that area. Then one day weeks later, a worker came running into the camp, petrified and panicking to everyone's horror. It was presumed he had seen the tiger. A doctor was called.

He recovered after several days of delirium. We were all anxious to know what happened that fateful day. The worker then revealed on reaching the spot where the flag was hoisted, he saw the giant form of Meher Baba near the flag. Meher Baba's hands and legs were very huge.

He had taken on gigantic proportions! Seeing Baba's huge form, the worker almost fainted. This explained his fear and anxiety. We then realized we had directly experienced the Master's protection. Such stories inspire many to place their faith in him without another thought.

Striking the Set

We understand all Meherabad activities were undertaken in connection with Baba's Universal work and not simply for the humanitarian good they provided. For as soon as the hidden work was finished, some of these medical and social projects might suddenly be torn down and abandoned. And so in October 1926, Baba decided to close all schools and institutions at Meherabad, disposing of them lock, stock and barrel – finished.

It was also a sign that funds had simply run out. The paid staff was given notice and the schoolboys' parents were told to arrange to bring their children home, unless they were willing to let their children remain in his hands unconditionally. He also didn't just turn away the destitute, helpless or homeless, but made special arrangements for each of the residents according to their circumstances. Baba explained the closing of Meherabad:

> "When you erect a big building, temporary scaffolding is raised, and when finished, the scaffolding is removed. The school, hospital, hermitage, cataract clinic etc. were such scaffoldings for my real work. What have I to do with works done by public municipalities? When my real work is finished, I see no further need for these scaffoldings."
> 730

Within 2 weeks, all buildings except the Post Office, mess quarters and Baba's stone jhopdi hut were brought down. After the building materials were auctioned off, Baba and the mandali left in trucks to stay for a month just outside Poona in the town of Lonavla. With the school closed, they then moved up to Bombay for 3 weeks.

On December 22nd 1926, early mandali member Arjun died. He had been director of the school for the untouchable village children and was the second circle-member after Nervous foretold by Baba to pass. Then 3 days later when funds came in unexpectedly, Baba announced they'd resettle back in Meherabad as his permanent headquarters.

And thus began his second Long Stay at Meherabad. The children were especially happy as they had missed Baba, but now were assured of his entertaining company and special treats they'd come to expect from him. On New Year's Eve, December 31st 1926, the village school was reopened, while none of the other early institutions were revived. RD 408

Meherabad means "Meher [Compassion] flourishing." But the thing that flourished most in these early years was the continual grinding down the men's minds like flour for a new kind of bread – the Master's loaf whose ingredients were their pulverized false minds.

His chief weapons in crushing and eliminating his disciples' falseness were obedience, humiliation and exhaustion, while deeply instilling brotherly feelings amongst their wildly different personalities. But something else was going on here as well . . . .

From January 25, 1925 to November 25, 1926 Baba worked his mandali like chess-pieces on a world game-board. Without realizing it, they were like improv actors having to play out different roles which might switch from one moment to the next. Through them the Master's work affected individuals, nations or world situations that might need immediate attention.

He typically picked on this one or that, or pitted one against the other – always to arouse feelings, for in this realm of emotions he did his Universal work. And so to bring this about, he'd try to stir up the emotional nature of one or more of his disciples.

Exasperated, the men would ask why he put them through such seemingly senseless ordeals. He explained for his Universal work at times he needed the energy of strongly felt emotions, saying if he couldn't stir up the feelings of his intimate disciples, the work was far more difficult. "Whom else should I use for my work, if not my own?" It didn't look like pretending, but it was often the "divine pretence" of the world's greatest actor.

His divine energy worked on such wavelengths for the sake of humanity and the universe. Usually when the situation changed after these "pinches," Baba would suddenly become loving with them again, teaching them to quickly brush off their bruises and not let their minds take any negative effect. In this way he'd restore tranquility and joviality to life at Meherabad or wherever they were. For sure, he was the universal Master actor. Av 200

> "I do my work in my own way. Why worry over things if you haven't done anything wrong? I may create a scene or a storm, anything for my work involving anyone I choose, even if they're not at fault. So that person should never worry or feel sad . . . ." 2279–80

We end this chapter with a humorous lizard story that occurred while Baba was travelling in northern India with his men and women mandali. He spent some time each day with the women in one of the rooms. One day as they sat talking, the largest lizard Naja had ever seen ran along high on the wall. It stopped over Baba's head and voided on him!

Without losing a beat, he continued his conversation with the women, took out a hanky, wiped his head clean and discarded the hanky. Naja saw this, but could do nothing to stop the lizard. Next day, the same thing happened with Baba again quietly wiped his head without any sign of irritation or impatience. The following day Naja brought a long broom, resolved to deal with the lizard if it came to do its business again.

Sure enough it appeared, but as she leapt to her feet to strike it, Baba stopped her in surprise, "What's with the broom?" "Baba, I want to stop the lizard from reaching you." "Why? What have you against the lizard? He circled the room with his hand and said, "All of you are much more a burden around my neck than that poor lizard!" DH vol. 2. pp.161–162

Chapter Thirteen

The Second Long Stay at Meherabad

For a few days after resettling at Meherabad, ill-feeling for one another was strong among some of the men. So one morning Baba called them to his hut and rebuked them for their frequent quarrels. He was especially harsh on his uncle Masaji and Adi Irani, concluding, "Each of you is my father!" – meaning Baba had to listen and obey them.

Then, getting down on his hands and knees, he bowed to each man, humiliating them deeply. With this he observed, "By the oath of my Master, had he told me I was his father and saluted me as I've just done to you, I wouldn't have stayed with him a moment longer, thinking I was totally unfit for his company. But you lack even the courage to leave." Well, it didn't end until after several more biting criticisms.

Chowdhari was particularly disturbed by the Master's cutting remarks, and after lunch decided that was it; he was leaving. Some of the men did their best to prevent him, but he was too upset to listen. When Gustadji ran to tell Baba, he again called all the men to his hut and confronted Chowdhari sternly:

"Whatever possessed you to agree to stay with me under every and all circumstances? Now you want to leave because of a few harsh words!

"What's the meaning of 'holding onto me under any circumstance?' With me you have to learn how to live and remain like dust!" Chowdhari stubbornly refused to listen. He packed his things and immediately left for Poona. After his sad departure, Baba asked the other men, "Okay, who else wants to leave me? Anyone wants to go, he can leave right now!"

When no one moved, Baba warned them not to heed the mind:

"With your own spiritual welfare at heart, stick to me through it all. As Truth personified, I can never make a mistake! From Truth flows Truth! So don't try to gauge the depth of my words or actions with your limited minds." Carefully rethinking his position, Chowdhari happily returned and begged the Master's forgiveness. 517

Over 60 years after this early period, a long-time American resident worker at Meherabad, Eric Nadel, visited the Kedgaon ashram of Baba's Master, Narayan Maharaj. He came back with a wonderful story of how Narayan's close disciples heard of Meher Baba as the Avatar of this age. Narayan's old disciple Krishna Jogelekar related this story.

A Train Stops in the Middle of Nowhere

He was travelling on a train in a special private rail car with his Master Narayan Maharaj and other disciples in the early 1920s. Suddenly, the train halted. As if he knew nothing, Narayan asked, "What happened? Why did the train stop? Are we at a station?" "No Master, the station's some distance away. We're in the countryside."

"Well, did someone pull the emergency cord? Go see." The disciples queried passengers in the other cars. "No, Master, no one's pulled the cord." "Well, there must be some reason. Maybe the engine broke down? Go ask the engineer." After inquiries, "No, Master, the engine's fine."

"Well, could a wheel have fallen off? Check with the guard."

Yet again the disciples inquired. "No, Master, all wheels are intact." "Well, maybe a signal went down? Go ask the conductor what's going on here." Again there was no apparent cause. Continuing in the same bluffing manner, Narayan finally said:

"Okay. Now open our carriage door and see if there's a longhaired young man with a slight beard wearing a long white sadra with his sandals off, hands folded, gazing reverently in my direction." "Lord, it's exactly as you said!" "Then tell me, are there 2 rows of young men behind him?" "Yes, Lord, again it's just as you describe."

"He's Meher Baba, the Avatar of this age. Now bow down and take his darshan."

So the disciples rushed out to do so, while Baba's disciples in turn approached Narayan's carriage. He came to the door and stood with his feet sticking out just over the edge so Baba's mandali could easily place their heads beneath his feet.

After a few minutes, looking at Baba, Narayan silently gestured, "Should I go?" Baba smiled, waving back gracefully 3 times for him to leave. Krishna recognized Baba's gesture as a bestowal of his blessings. And once again the train began to move. 703–04

Krishna Jogelekar went on to say the love flowing between these Masters and the whole experience itself was so astonishing that no one could ever forget its wonder. They were constantly reminded of it, because on every later rail journey on that line whenever the train passed through Meherabad, it would unexplainably stop for a few moments.

CHRIST COME AGAIN

It was such a feature of rail journeys with Narayan, that if the train stopped abruptly on a remote stretch of track anywhere in India – north or south – Narayan would sit up and ask, "Look out the window; see if we've come to Arangaon." This is where the railway line separates upper and lower Meherabad by the poor village of Arangaon, and where Baba's pilgrims today cross daily to walk up and bow down to his Tomb. Gl Int Fall, 2009 p.31-32

Perfect Master Narayan Maharaj, 1930s

More Frustrated Disciples Leave

The Hill, or "upper" Meherabad where Baba's Tomb is, and "lower" Meherabad is separated by these railway tracks. Below are many of the old buildings as well as the cemetery for Baba's deceased men mandali.

CHRIST COME AGAIN

Despite his daily interactions keeping them very busy, none had any of the spiritual experiences they'd expected and hoped for. In fact, they felt deeply pained by what seemed to be their totally aimless lives. As always, Baba urged them to become as dust at his feet.

Their egos were being ground to divine powder by his persistent little harassments: "Your arrogance, conceit and pride are to be turned into dust; and then alone will your dust be seen in its full brilliance." Still, at times they wondered what in hell they'd gotten into. 790

Even during so-called sleep Baba was restless, and quiet only at specific moments of silence or when receiving visitors. When awake, he seldom allowed his companions to remain still; activity and disturbance seemed to characterize the atmosphere around him. He could turn on a dime, change plans or cancel projects he seemed to have his heart set on, even after much time, work and tremendous expense were invested in them. PM 266

A joke made the rounds: "How to make Baba laugh? Just tell him your plans." To allow nothing to be settled, to create movement or apparent chaos were the daily living conditions of those wishing to accompany him without expectations, fulfilling the Beatitude, "Blessed are the flexible, for they shall not be bent out of shape."

During travels no one knew from day to day what his requirements might be, what he'd do or how long he might stay in a particular place they were visiting. He'd often make arduous journeys to remote places in India, and then once there where the disciples expected some much needed rest, he might suddenly decide to return home or go elsewhere.

No explanations – changes had to be accepted without hesitation simply as his modus operandi. His comfort seemed to be in discomfort, and when travelling he'd try to ensure everyone was as uncomfortable as possible! Eruch Jessawala tells of one of these occasions.

"We were in our as usual overcrowded railway car, and Baba asked: 'Which is more beautiful – sunrise or sunset?' 'Sunset.' 'Correct,' replied Baba. 'And which are people more aware of – sunrise or noon?' 'Sunrise. 'Correct,' said Baba. 'It's just like my Advent.

"With its dawning, people are aware something great is to happen. Yet when I'm in your midst [at noon], so few are aware of me. But after I drop the body, then will come the Glorification – so beautifully stupendous that many will notice it and come flocking."

Well, a few more got so fed up they really did go home with the understanding that Baba would allow them back to visit him, if they desired; for in the secret of their hearts they really did love him. Their pessimistic tone wasn't a lack of respect or faith in Baba's Perfection. They were just being put through the painful wringer which a Master as a rule puts one through to be ground to dust before the crown of gold.

Most who left eventually returned to stay. Baba liked to say, "There are 2 types of people in the world: one type bothers me, and the other type [his lovers] I bother." Adi Irani Sr. said, "Baba didn't come to give peace of mind, but to break your mind to pieces." MM 1: 491

So a military camp was a fitting metaphor for what he was forming inside them – a spiritual army to fight a war against Maya's illusion – one day to overcome that principle of cosmic ignorance by being warriors against their false selves and lovers of God.

No one in our recorded history ever took upon themselves such a task on such a global scale with such gargantuan Mayavic forces working against them. Baba then gave a discourse to the mandali on the illusion of false Maya. Here's what he expounded:

CHRIST COME AGAIN

The God-Man uses Maya to conduct the affairs of the universe. Paramatma [Beyond-Beyond God or the "Father"] never uses Maya to free others from Maya. Take Arjun as Paramatma and his cane as the God-Man. Then if you wrap a 7-colored string around his cane, that string is Maya.

How different is Arjun and the string which has only touched the God-Man – and not Paramatma, Who is totally aloof. Suppose you come along and mistake the string for a snake. This creates Maya. But, if we see the string is only a string and nothing else, then where is Maya?

It's only your false supposition that all this really is; this is Maya. In the end, when found to be only a string, you laugh at your false idea, because now your fears are gone and the illusion removed. In the same way, attaining Realization, one laughs at these false notions of Maya – the world and all its [comedic] connections – totally false and not real . . . are now understood as such.

So the very moment Maya – lust, anger or greed – enters your head, thrust it out. Don't even let it in. If a rabid dog goes after you, you shout to drive it away. But if you feed it, it will follow you and never go away. Similarly, Maya is a mad dog. Don't allow it to enter your mind.

Drive it away with all your strength as you would a mad dog, for once it sticks to you, it will be quite impossible for you to free yourself from it . . . . Who renounces Maya finds everything! Don't be a slave to it. Subjugate it and you'll see God in all His perfection.

But it's next to impossible to realize God, as one must really "die" to gain this state; not by drowning or committing suicide, but by renouncing Maya and freeing oneself from it. But Maya is so powerfully tyrannical even the best succumb to its lures. The real heroes who eat her up are very rare. So, hold tightly to my feet to ease your way or else you'll not get even a whiff of Reality, and your strenuous efforts to reach the Goal age after age will bring you no closer to it. 684–86

Everything is Like the Coiled Rope-Snake – a Total Fake!

He who comes down from the 7th plane – from the state of the Father – and acquires gross consciousness is like a great magician. When he does his tricks, the whole of humanity is like children to him, and his children consider his activities as totally real. But there's a heaven-and-earth difference between a magician of the 7th plane and a fake juggler of the gross earth plane.

The duty of the Divine Magician [the Christ/Avatar] is to sustain the universe. This means while doing his work, he must teach his children what they see and hear isn't true. To do this he has to raise the children's powers of perception. Many books have been written on this; but everything is like a coil of rope which deluded ones are apt to take for a serpent. Everything is like a coil of rope – totally fake! Even feeling fed up is a delusion.

And also when I say, "I'm waiting to break my silence," is a high-grade delusion to make others undeluded. The Master Juggler does his tricks to sustain the Truth so that the children shouldn't go wrong. Doing it, he gets fed up, wondering when the children will finally understand him, know the Truth and be able to say in their hearts that the rest is all a fake.

There's really nothing to know. Everything is about forgetting. Whatever can be understood is illusion. The highest understanding and the lowest are both illusion. What cannot be understood is

Reality. All that has to be understood is illusion, but if you understand what cannot be understood, then you'll know that we were, we are and we always shall be. You have to gain that as real consciousness. In short, there's been no change in us, nor will there ever be.

The only difference lies in knowing we're unaware of what we are – Infinite God and One. We began to understand ourselves differently as separate entities, and this thinking of separateness is pure illusion. The wonder is we were One with Infinite God, and yet take ourselves as separate from Him. We began to think in terms of individuality – I am sick, I am happy, and so forth.

Such understanding must be forsaken. Whether you bother or don't bother, your children, wife and even the body itself serve as a binding for you. In reality, there's nothing but continuous bliss, but now you can't even have an inkling about it. We are infinitely powerful.

Once you get that consciousness, you can make or break the whole universe; make the whole universe happy or miserable as you choose. It is said in Sufism the highest bliss of human beings is but the 7th shadow of that Original Bliss. This understanding has to come gradually.

Everything we know is an illusion. Whatever we're now talking is also an illusion. When the real understanding comes, it comes in the twinkling of an eye, because we are that Ocean of Divinity, in which all drops exist. When the drops seemingly form into us, they experience a different state. Waves cannot burst them; but once they are burst, then they instantly become the Ocean!

If it's explained to these bubbles they're really not bubbles at all, but the Ocean, they'll not grasp it without bursting. The more the effort to explain to the bubbles, the more illusion increases. So why explain it? The bubble [false mind] must burst itself to make it Self-aware. 3345–46

It was around this time that Baba asked his disciples a deep theological question:

Who Is Greater – God the Father or God the Son?

If someone were to ask me who is greater: Personal or Impersonal God . . . Zoroaster or Ahuramazda, Jesus or God the Father, I would definitely answer . . . Zoroaster and Jesus are greater. In fact, the Greatest of the Great, for they are both Sadguru and the Avatar.

They render infinite service to the universe and suffer infinitely by taking on the burden of the world's infinite amount of sanskaras [false impressions]. Undoubtedly, a conscious divine person such as Zoroaster, compared to the unconscious Ahuramazda [formless God], is definitely greater! 662

Not God, but the God-Man is more than God, the absolute [Father]. One who manifests the absolute is the God-Man [Son]. A God-man is greater than God Almighty [Paramatma – Impersonal God], God's Beyond-Beyond state outside creation . . . . The Father isn't meant to do Universal work; but the Son's state is one of universal duty. The Father state is contained in the Son state; so from a standpoint of universal work, the Son state is higher than the Father state. MM 2: 143, 3344–4

So while we may accept Jesus, Meher Baba or any other Avatar as God in human form, we unconsciously think they are "lesser" than God the Father in the Beyond-Beyond state. It's the exact opposite; something most people have never considered or understood.

We saw that 1925-26 were extremely dynamic years in Meher Baba's life as Meherabad now became a small model town with 500 people working under his silent, watchful gaze. It cost 1000 rupees a day just to run it – a lot of money in those days.

Even tea, flower and knick-knack shops sprang up. Many early historic and still-standing Meherabad structures were also built then. Most importantly, it set the stage for something entirely new – the Prem Love Ashram for spiritually inclined boys that extended over a major 2 year period of Baba's early life at Meherabad.

In 1926, Baba distinguished between his disciples and his devotees. "The number of my devotees is great, but the number of my true disciples is far less. A devotee seeks the pleasure of his own devotion, while the disciple's only duty is to obey the Master's commands – far more difficult. Devotees select a Master to surrender to. A Master selects his own disciples. So while many may become devotees, very few can become disciples."   671

Jesus put it simply: "Many are called, but few are chosen. [Matthew 22:16]   After a year writing his secret book in that tiny cramped cabin no more than a large doghouse, Baba began preparing his men for advanced states of spiritual bliss they would soon observe – not in themselves, but in those whom they would soon be serving in the schools opened at Meherabad. On May 14th 1926, he revealed to his men:

Real Darkness – Real Light

> Before the veil was torn asunder and I became God conscious, I experienced the greatest electric-like shock creating indescribably severe vibrations. This was followed by intense darkness, and finally The Light. The greatest imagination fails to conceive the idea of such Effulgence.

The light of the worldly sun in comparison is but a shadow of a drop in the infinite ocean of dazzling Light. Similarly, the darkness [Nirvan] which I experienced [the moment before] my Realization can never be described. The world experiences darkness and light, but what I'm explaining bears no similarity. Very few persons can see the Real Darkness and then the Real Light.

And very few experience the real pain and misery which begins with the longing to experience God, and the intense suffering at separation from Him. Worldly pain and happiness are nothing but the outcome of mental weakness. No one in the world suffers as much as the person who thirsts for sight of the Divine Beloved. He feels like a fish flopping about out of water. 652

> 4.
>
> natural Light
> natural darkness
> unnatural darkness
>
> unnatural light i.e.
> The whole universe
> i.e. The whole
> maya.
>
> i.e. Light   i.e. natural darkness
> where only self is   only nothingness is
> From this natural darkness (i.e. nothingness)
> unnatural darkness (i.e. mind working,
> the false I, egoism) is produced.
>   i.e. egoism
> From unnatural darkness unnatural
> light (i.e. universe is produced) is produced.

At another time, Baba spoke of 7 kinds of bliss in the universe; the 1st is Vishvananda, experienced by all forms from fish to human beings. The 2nd type, Chitananda, is experienced by human beings alone. The remaining 5 states of bliss are experienced by those on the higher inner spiritual planes. Baba says in reality, we are bliss itself – but what a comedy Maya's Illusion stages to make us finally aware of it!

You cannot invite Bliss. It is ever present – everywhere

If you were to experience even for a moment an infinitesimal part of that Knowledge, you would derive infinite bliss. You would then experience only bliss from every external thing. Every particle would tell you its story in Knowledge. This whole world, which now seems full of misery, would shine forth as heaven! 514

This endless and fathomless Ocean of Bliss is within everyone. There is no individual entirely devoid of happiness in some form, since there is no individual who is entirely cut off from God as the Ocean of Bliss. Every type of pleasure which he ever had is ultimately a partial and illusory reflection of God as Ananda (Bliss). 3208 God alone exists as Existence Eternal, and all else is illusion – a creation of Maya. And what is Maya? Maya is the principle of cosmic ignorance.

Maya makes you feel what in fact does not exist. In Reality, neither man nor woman, neither so-called animate beings nor inanimate things exist. It is Maya which causes the unreal to appear as real and existing. Mind, issuing from Maya, imagines infinite divisions and creates innumerable worries. As long as mind exists, ignorance persists. And what a joke!

CHRIST COME AGAIN

Mind trying to gain bliss by furious thinking and worrying is nothing but empty dreaming! For bliss to come into being, mind must be quiet. You cannot invite bliss. It is ever present – everywhere. Really speaking, everywhere in the entire universe is bliss. 4747

It is all bliss, bliss and nothing but bliss! But poor, ignorant mankind can't enjoy it – doesn't know how. The whole universe is full of infinite bliss, but disregarding it, man hankers after the transient happiness of affluence, influence, possessions, lust, name and fame. Due to his ignorance of what is real man runs only after this false illusion. For real happiness, one must spit out the false.

I am bliss personified! This 5-foot, 6-inch physical form you see is not real. If you could see my Real Form, you'd not be yourself. The limited human mind hasn't the least conception of this – Infinite Power-Knowledge-Bliss. This state is beyond the realm of the mind.

It is called the Nirvikalp state – the "I am God" state. Nirvikalp is the Infinite Bliss state of Paramatma, or God's Infinite Consciousness [which belongs to you by your Divine Origin]. Everyone is destined to attain this state and it is their duty to make efforts toward that end. Some may acquire Realization today; if not today, then tomorrow. Some get it after years and some after many births. But at some time or other, one and all have to experience this elevated state. 1039

It is all bliss everywhere, but people are miserable because ignorance forces them to fulfill desires . . . . It is really all happiness, infinite unfathomable bliss when you desire nothing. Everything beyond needs is wants, and wanting inevitably leads to suffering. So try your very best to want less and less of that which is beyond your needs . . . Don't want, be happy! 1818

This state of desirelessness, wanting nothing, is a faculty latent in all. It's within you, but you have to discover it. I've found and continually experience it. The difference between us is although we both have this faculty, I actually experience and feel it, while you have yet to do so. I see myself in you all, as you see all material things with your eyes. It is a fact for me. 2071

According to the Law governing the universe, all suffering is your labor of love to unveil your Real Self. Compared to the Infinite Bliss on attaining the I-am-God state, all the suffering and agony you go through amounts to nothing. As Infinite Bliss, I draw you to me and to make you realize you are Bliss Itself, I come amidst you [as the Eternal Christ] and suffer infinite agony. EN 48

But while suffering agony himself, Baba had a soft spot for animals, and never liked seeing them suffer or being abused. One day, he saw a gypsy leading a donkey limping with a wounded hind leg along the road passing Meherabad. Baba stopped what he was doing and went out to meet the gypsy. After petting the animal lovingly, he persuaded the man to let him take it to the Meherabad hospital where Baba cleaned the wound, applied antiseptic and bandaged the blessed donkey's leg. 688

A Feared Criminal's Darshan and Repentance

July 10th 1926 was approaching, and the mandali were excitedly looking forward to Baba giving up his year long silence, only be to slyly informed he'd continue it for "at least" another 7 months. It was around this time that Satya Mang, a notorious Ahmednagar bandit, happened to stop by Meherabad with his gang to take Baba's darshan.

He hoped with the Master's blessing "his chosen profession" would continue to be lucrative; meaning he'd not get caught. He was on Ahmednagar's most wanted list and deeply feared by local people. Baba was talking with about 50 of his men when informed of a group's arrival. No one had any idea who they were. After prostrating themselves at Baba's feet, Satya Mang and his accomplices sat on the ground before him.

The Master became very serious and remained quiet for some moments. Then he asked, "Where do you come from and where are you going?" When Satya Mang answered, Baba looked directly at him and spelled out, shaking his wrist, "How come you're not wearing bangles!" Not getting Baba's meaning, he asked, "Why? What have I done?"

"You're a coward!" exclaimed Baba. "What are you talking about?" Satya Mang shouted. Baba said, "A hefty man like you can extract water from stone" – meaning he could work hard to earn an honest living. "Instead, you rob people. Your very name strikes terror in the hearts of women and children who are unable to sleep at night just thinking of you."

Till that moment the mandali had no idea who he was, but on hearing this exchange they felt sure it was the infamously dreaded Satya Mang whom the district police had been unable to catch despite their best concerted efforts. Baba continued: "You support yourself on illegal gains. Aren't you ashamed to grow a moustache? You're not a man!"

Satya Mang defended himself. "I inherited my profession. If I don't pursue it, how am I to maintain myself and my family?" "Oh, you mean everyone in the world lives on stolen property? Can't you find job like the rest of the world instead of robbing people?"

Making such bold statements to a dangerous a criminal was unheard of – foolhardy, as even police were terrified of this gang. But the wolf became a lamb before Baba, whom he addressed as Maharaj – humbly asking, "Maharaj, show me what I'm to do. I'm ready to give up this way of life if I can only find a job to maintain my family."

Baba said, "Oh, that's easy for me to arrange. But how can you stop stealing? Every cell in your body is infected with this virus!" "No, Maharaj, I swear I'll turn my face from such a life if provision is made for my children. Once that's done, I'll never rob again."

Baba then seriously asked, "Do you know before whom you're swearing? Do you have any idea to whom you're giving your promise? If you break your promise to God, your life will be ruined. God knows everything. You understand?" "Yes, Maharaj, I do. I'll never repeat my past actions. I'll never break my promise!" Baba stretched out his hand. "Okay, give me your promise!" Immediately Satya Mang came forward and they exchanged high-fives.

Baba warned, "Remember, if you go back on your word to me, you'll become completely paralyzed." Baba then arranged for the maintenance of his family, telling him to come to Meherabad once a week. And from that day the threat of robbery disappeared, while Ahmednagar people were stunned at the "miracle" of Baba's intervention.

Successfully eluding police for years, for a robber like Satya Mang to submit to a spiritual Master and surrender to him on the spot was unheard of – bizarre beyond bizarre. And he kept his promise to be faithful; well, for a good while.

But eventually his hands again began itching, and one night he stealthily entered a house to rob it. He was about to take a cache of loot when his body shuddered in fright as he saw Baba standing before him. In that moment, Baba's words reverberated in him:

"God is ever present. He sees everything. Nothing is hidden from Him!" Suddenly all became dark, as if he had gone blind. He grew pale and closed his eyes. On opening them, Baba's form had disappeared. Gratefully leaving the stolen goods behind, he hastened to Meherabad and with tears streaming down his cheeks confessed to Baba:

"Maharaj, please forgive me this once. I went back on my word." Feigning ignorance, Baba asked, "What are you talking about?" Satya Mang cried out falling at Baba's feet weeping, "Oh, God, you know all. Forgive me!" Baba pardoned him for his sincere repentance while warning him, "Never do it again. Paramatma knows and sees all."

After this Satya Mang never committed a crime or theft again, and the police even availed themselves of his help in tracking down other criminals. He made it a practice to be at Meherabad every Thursday to take part in the gatherings there. Faith in Baba's divinity was born in him, and at a mere word from the Master he was ready to sacrifice his very life.

He even begged for the chance to serve him. Baba replied, "Don't worry; when the time's right, I'll give you an opportunity to serve me." And in later years he did serve as chief of security during many large gatherings at Meherabad. 674–77

Now just how truthful was Satya Mang to Baba? Well, 7 years later in December 1933, some galvanized tin sheets from Baba's cabin over his underground crypt – his future tomb on Meherabad Hill – were stolen. Baba immediately sent for Satya Mang and asked him about it. He denied the theft. Baba countered, "If you didn't steal them then surely one of your associates did. Find out who and bring him to me."

So Satya Mang called a meeting of his former gang members. But when no one admitted to the crime, Satya Mang said, "Meher Baba says the thief is among us, and his words are always true." Then one of the men named Fakira cried out, "Is that's so? Then you yourself must be the thief!" Satya Mang replied, "All right, let's both go to Meher Baba. Then we'll go to the Dhuni and taking its ash in our mouths, we'll repeat these words:

" 'May he who is the thief die within 8 days!' " Fakira agreed, and both acted accordingly. Fakira was dead within the week. Satya Mang came to Baba and narrated the story of the man's dying for not admitting his theft from Meherabad Hill.

Baba arranged for Satya Mang be given a monthly stipend. When the rest of former gang learned Fakira was indeed the thief, they were greatly impressed and to everyone's relief they also completely stopped all their left over criminal tendencies. 1579

In 1929 when Baba left with the mandali for a trip to Persia [Iran], he had just one family to look after at Meherabad. They were poor and barely subsisting. Satya Mang was living close by and went begging village to village to bring food to this family. 3608

25 years later in 1955, Baba held a large gathering at Meherabad to wash the feet of the poor. Stretching out his arm, he pointed to a man way back in the crowd and introduced him. It was Satya Mang. Though he'd now fallen on hard times and was poverty stricken, he remained honest to his promise and never committed another robbery. How blessed to turn one's old accustomed life of selfishness upside down and end it so honestly for the Lord. 3757

A Catholic Priest is the Avatar's First American Contact

On Saturday January 1st 1927, Baba received many New Year's cards, including one from Father Joseph Nathan Oldenburg, 52, an Irish/German pastor of a Catholic church in Telluride, Colorado. Born in Galena, Illinois, Fr. Oldenburg had heard about Meher Baba in the late 1920s and began writing him deeply devotional letters.

As the very first American to contact Baba, we presume he heard of the Avatar from Rustom ("Rusi") Driver (Naorooz N. Rustom, 1897-1989), a friend of Baba's at Deccan College in 1911 and the older brother of Baba's mandali, my dear friend Padri (Faredoon Driver).

He was a cinema operator and was advised by Babajan to go to America. He had aspirations to break into the Hollywood film business and never returned to India. He wrote his family for a number of years, and his mother would write back Baba news and send him Baba photo buttons. But then letters stopped and they finally lost trace of him. MM 1: 59-60

Fr. Oldenburg's final heart-filled letter to Baba was posted in April, 1931 from Holly, Colorado. Although he then made a trip to India in 1935, there's strangely no record of him meeting Baba. But the Master surely had his eye in him. 758

The Meher Ashram School

Approaching his 33rd birthday in February 1927, Baba was invited and warmly received with several of the mandali at Ahmednagar's National School. Its director made a formal announcement about the opening of the new Meher Ashram School.

"In the very near future, a boarding school will be opened in the holy place of Meherabad where children will be provided free education, food and clothing. The school will be called Meher Ashram, and the children there will be given the best education.

"But the highest benefit will be having the sacred company of Shri Sadguru Meher Baba – a significance beyond our comprehension." Baba would now daily concentrate his full efforts in raising even simple school children to advanced states of spiritual bliss. 786

The Prem Ashram – Gustadji's Silence

It began in a small way on May 1st 1927 when a new kind of boys' free-school modestly opened with 10 Hindu students and a

Christian boy named John. Then 14 more arrived from Persia – 12 Zoroastrians and 2 Muslims.

I would be blessed to know two of them in their later lives, Muslim, Ali Akbar [Aloba] in India, and Zoroastrian, Espandiar Vesali in California. Espandiar and I would also attend the 2002 50th anniversary of Baba's 1952 auto accident in Prague, Oklahoma.

Prem Ashram student Ali Akbar Shapurzaman in 1927, decades later to become Baba's mandali Aloba.

CHRIST COME AGAIN

The Meher Ashram started as a sort-of live-in prep school for boys who had a more spiritual leaning than the earlier Arangaon village "readin,' writin' and 'rithmetic" students. Many more Muslims would soon come. It would later be called the Prem Ashram.

Another significant event also occurred then. Baba's oldest mandali, Gustadji, was a garrulous raconteur with a wealth of stories from his early days with 3 Perfect Masters – Sai Baba, Upasni Maharaj and Hazrat Babajan. He was so talkative that the men sometimes wished he'd just "shut the hell up." So, Baba instructed him to live alone.

He was so strict with Gustadji that while keeping aloof from all the other men he forbade him to leave the veranda except to answer calls of nature. Then one day Behramji teased him about something. Gustadji became so upset he went on abusing him for 2 hours! After this harangue, Baba reached another level of fed-upness with Gustadji and ordered, "From now you on you're to remain silent."

But Master that he was, Baba had carefully created this row through Behramji to provide an excuse to put Gustadji on silence from that day forward; a silence leading ultimately to something truly beyond great. Baba explained to him:

"Observing silence will be such a tremendous help to me in my work. So, be silent now for my sake!" Although loquacious by nature, Gustadji s began observing silence for 31 years until his 1958 death, ending in God-Realization. He was Baba's delightful silent companion communicating by hand gestures and great animation. It was their own intimate little club. Meanwhile, Baba's love for his new school children knew no bounds: 807; RD 310

"With children, I'm a child; with the old, I'm old. With women, I'm a woman; with men, a man. With the rich, I am rich; with the poor, I am poor. But I so love children most, as they are desireless. I so much enjoy playing with them, and this makes them drink wine (feel love) of which they drink more while playing and feeling great happiness." 1170

One of the mandali who witnessed these days said: "You really had to see him among his ashram boys to grasp the deep closeness between Baba and his pupils. It's truly touching to see these little urchins crowd around him when he enters the room. They rush to embrace him, placing their tiny arms about his waist, while Baba plays with them, teasing them gently and filling their hearts with extraordinary happiness." Av 113

Baba now announced he wanted teachers who'd be willing to work just for food and clothing. One of the men expressed his reservations. "As this charitable school would create a big public impression with Baba's name spreading far and wide. How can we create faith in them Meher Baba is a Perfect Master – God in human form? It'll be difficult to find good teachers without paying them."

But Baba's intention was to keep both boys and teachers for their spiritual benefit and not for a paid salary. So after a couple of hours he assembled the mandali. Echoing what he had told them just a few years earlier, he made these cryptic remarks:

Neither God nor Perfect, I Am an Ordinary Man

This discussion has really opened my eyes. You ask how the world is to know I am God in human form, a Perfect Master or a great spiritual authority, and how to convince people of this. Hearing this, I now find neither am I God, nor a Perfect Master, which up to now I've claimed. I was doing it only with the view to make people believe in me. I'm an ordinary man!

Those harboring hopes of spiritual advancement or expecting blessings have now absolutely nothing of the sort to gain from me. When I myself haven't experienced God, how could I make others have His darshan? So, those who want to stay with me may stay, but only on your own accord, with the conviction and clear understanding you'll gain absolutely nothing from my hands.

And so I hereby withdraw all agreements, oral promises and sacred oaths I've taken from you, and make you free of all the restraint I imposed on you. Still . . . . If any of you wish to remain with me, it should be with the clear knowledge I am not God, but merely a friend; and you shouldn't have the slightest expectation of any spiritual or material benefit from me.

If you're lucky you might barely get food and clothing, but nothing else. You'll have to act in strict accord with my orders like before. I impress upon you everything in this world is absolutely nothing. It is all unreal – only a dream, a total illusion. I've known and experienced this much, and there is nothing beyond. I wish to say nothing about God. So, I'll only keep a few suitable ones around me away from worldly attachments – lust, anger and greed. 773–74

From now on, you'd best be like a football. Wherever it's kicked it goes and never cries out or complains. Its fortune is to get kicked. The force and height of its kicks are its beauty which finally makes it reach the goal. In the same way, whatever difficulties are put in your way, whatever amount of opposition you have to face, bear it silently. It will one day bring you across the Goal line . . . .

So, try to reach that level to accept and remain humble and unaffected by my critical kicks. They'll raise you up so high, higher and infinitely higher and beyond! The greater the kick-force to the football, the higher it flies. And so you will rise high above the world.

Baba told Padri, "Continue your medicines to sufferers, and I'll go on blessing you." From then Padri's homeopathy carried Baba's grace to cure seemingly incurables. He helped my own illness 55 years later in the spring of 1982 a week before he passed to Baba. 590

Only the Avatar Controls the Sun

Then one day after working tirelessly overseeing all Meherabad matters, it seemed Baba needed some rest and relaxation. But the weather was totally uncooperative over several days of cloudiness and gloom. The bad weather affected him deeply. He said he wanted to stop his spiritual work completely and needed some "RandR." This occasioned a fascinating revelation from him regarding the Avatar's control of the sun:

> "After many years, I want a bit of rest. But nature which I've created won't allow it. When I stop my work, my universal mind wants to disconnect itself from illusion and simply rest in my Divinity. So, I need to climb a mountain, run or play games or bask in the sun. But now I can't do any of those things. I have 2 possibilities: not to rest, or break my own law.
>
> "If I want in 5 seconds I can make the sun shine by breaching the law governing creation. No one's to blame, no one can help. Even great yogis or Perfect Masters who control all elements and raise the dead are helpless to make the sun shine, because as the Avatar, I am personally involved with the sun.
>
> "Sadgurus normally do anything except break the law. Law makers won't be law breakers!" So if the sun doesn't shine on your parade, don't blame God, for he has an estab-

lished order which even for his own needed benefit Baba would not go against. 820

Meanwhile, with newspapers everywhere were full of Mahatma Gandhi's work, everyone was talking about him. The mandali were excited, thinking how greatly he'd benefit by Baba's contact. Baba then mentioned he and Gandhi would soon travel together.
They'd be on the same ship to the West. Gandhi's picketing years earlier had closed Baba's toddy shops in Poona, restricting the Avatar's work both in his limited and Universal venue. Baba continued, "The sanskaras of those who follow him now and who suffer in doing so, will cause Gandhi such great suffering in his next birth. Still, Gandhi is doing all this with best intentions, and so he will realize God in his 3rd lifetime after this one." 836

Baba with some of the ashram students on a river outing in Toka, 1928

CHRIST COME AGAIN

One day, someone donated several crates of books which the Master kept beside his seat on Meherabad Hill, not letting anyone even touch them. That night while the others slept, he carefully arranged and stacked all the books in specific piles, soaking them in the wine of his love, pouring into each book the required measure for each individual child.

The next day, he handed books out to each boy, not just for their minds, but pushing their hearts toward loving God. As Baba also liked being read to, the mandali took turns evenings reading aloud from his favorite British mystery writer, Sexton Blake. As he distributed the books, the boys asked him about his favorite authors – especially poets:

Shakespeare Reincarnated in India

In Persian Hafiz; in English, Shakespeare, John Milton and Percy Bysshe Shelley. Shakespeare is presently reincarnated in India, a Brahmin taking a leading part in politics, but one of the most sincere, selfless workers for the country. His thought force of the past is now transformed into action. He was a genius, and controversies on the original author of his works are meaningless.

He wrote all the plays – no one else. It was entirely the result of his giant intellect. Still, there's not even a breeze of the spiritual in all his dramas and poetry; and yet he was a genius. Milton was spiritually advanced, but not beyond the 2nd subtle plane. He saw heaven and hell; that's how he was able to write Paradise Lost and Paradise Regained. His books depict the result of his personally seeing them. Shelley wasn't spiritually advanced, but was a thorough gentleman.

He was a lover of God and nature. But Hafiz was something else; not only excelling in spiritual writings and in poetic meters/style, he was a God-Realized Perfect Master. Shams-e-Tabriz and Jalal al-Din Rumi were also God-Realized. Omar Khayyam was advanced but not Realized. 849

After hearing a lot about "Meher Baba," a Mr. Bharucha arrived one afternoon at Meherabad to meet the so-called "Great Master." Barely veiling his cynicism, Barucha began with abrupt, direct questions and received similarly sharp replies:

"Is there a great war coming?"

"Yes, A war much greater than the last and with terrible bloodshed."

Bharucha asked, "Why on earth would you allow such a war to begin and go on?"

"For pleasure."

"You'll allow such an outright massacre of mankind?"

"It's my will and wish – my craze!"

"You don't speak. Why are you so quiet?"

"My choice."

Baba's curt replies so upset the man he abruptly rose to leave. Baba was having a bit of fun with him to reduce his inflated ego. Then the man was asked if he had time, things would be carefully explained. Bharucha agreed, saying he could leave by a later train. Baba took him aside and explained many things to him. This totally pacified the man. 854

During this spring of 1927, Baba had a cabin of bamboo mats and tin sheets built on Meherabad Hill, with a door, window and a pit dug in the floor of this small cabin, 6' x 6' x 6.' He did not disclose its purpose – the place where his body would finally be laid to rest.

That would occur 42 years later, when he would become the planet's magnet for souls loving him without measure and the means of their eternal release. The floor of the pit was stone masonry with small steps leading down to it – utter simplicity.

Its east window overlooked the playground. In front was a platform for Prem Ashram students and visitors to sit as Baba gave discourses through the window on his alphabet board. By now he had entered his 2nd year of strict silence, quickly pointing to letters read out by a disciple, skilled at reading Baba's rapid "texting." 837

It was around this time Baba first revealed, "Gandhi will become a Perfect Master in 3 more lifetimes, and those very close to him [India's Prime Minister, the great Jawaharlal Nehru, Sadav Patel and other of Nehru's cabinet ministers] will become his inner-circle members."

Meanwhile, students found a great difference between the teachers' lectures and Baba's discourses, and so they began paying less attention to regular lessons finding them tedious and boring. They only wanted to be near the Master to concentrate on his revelations.

On November 10th Baba quit eating solid food and lived on tea for nearly 5½ half months while working with these boys. After just a week on this regime, he began conveying the importance of love to the boys. Through stray hints and in more lengthy explanations on concentration and meditation, he directly began to inspire them toward divine yearnings.

The Rag Doll Discourses

Within days, Meherabad's atmosphere was totally transformed with spiritual wine overflowing the children's hearts from the Master's silent discourses. Illustrating his points, he'd bring out a rag doll to explain evolution. Bending the doll's head down and folding its limbs inside: "This is the state of inanimate objects – stones, rocks, minerals."

Then bringing the arms and legs down, Baba put the doll on all fours to show it in animal form. When he walked it, the children giggled in delight. Finally, he made the doll stand on its 2 legs: "The soul has now reached human state – the final and highest form."

Baba's rag-doll discourse with eloquent and comic silent gestures entranced the children. Then taking out a small mirror for a final illustration, he slowly moved it to his closer and closer, drawing the following points on the chalk board: 857

> Let's say this mirror represents the mind's false impressions, while Consciousness is still unconscious-Consciousness. Now the moment Consciousness is created in the unconscious mind, it arouses a "whim" in the sound sleep state of God to know its Self. One of the 1st movements of consciousness takes the mirror to stone-state form, where only a slight corner of the mirror barely falls within the line of one's vision. Going to vegetable form brings more of the mirror in sight.
>
> The next, to the worm, fish, bird and animal kingdoms, brings still greater areas into view. A final movement – toward the human form – brings the entire mirror before the eyes. Then one sees his own full reflection in it, believing this reflection. One believes this reflection – the false shadow of the Self – is the Real Self or Real I, which is just not true. So the mirror, slanted with the evolution of forms, is slowly brought upright with more and more consciousness until it reaches human form.
>
> But the soul, instead of seeing itself inside, sees only its own body and the false universe in the mirror's reflection. And what it sees is total illusion! So what should it do now to see the Real Self? It must remove the mirror – not only remove, but smash and destroy it! . . . .

> They [body and universe] remain as they are, presenting themselves again and again each time you die and take a new birth. For example, the [false] mirror mind is there, even when you've left bodies after bodies and taken countless other births.
> So you must remove this mirror mind of impressions to see your own Real Self. Remember, you are not this body; you are soul – spirit. Stop thinking you're the body; stop thinking you are energy; try to stop thinking you are mind. Think: I am soul; I am spirit. 858

And in this silent way Baba beautifully described the creation and other themes in terms the children could easily grasp, enjoy and remember. One boy was later found shouting out to his body, "You're not real!" On another occasion, when asked, "What's higher than the clouds?" The children were puzzled and looked at each other for clues. So Baba answered, "Isn't a mother's love much higher? My love is infinitely higher!"

And with such discourses the Master's wine began flowing. The children drew closer to him and less attentive to studies, writing his name over and over in their notebooks or on their chalk slates. Even their appetites declined. With each discourse, Baba urged them:

> Love me and you'll realize me. I'm ready to make you like the Saints. The only price asked is love. Spirituality is being plundered here, but only real love can unlock the treasure house. I'm auctioning off Godliness here. Be ready to bid everything you own to acquire it! God is within you, but you have to search within for Him. How to search? By creating love for Him in your heart . . . .
> Once there's appetite and you're starving, thoughts of eating are incessant. So when love of God comes, one be-

gins thinking of Him continuously. Then real striving begins. A hungry boy seeks food; the seeker searches for Beloved God. Eventually, both achieve their goals. How to create this love? Not by crying for it, but shedding your very blood for the Beloved. This is the highest state of love! Is there one among you like that? No, but don't worry. Still try to love.

My initial intention was to advance you gradually, but considering the spiritual outburst in the world during certain ages, I've changed my mind for the few ready to be consumed in the light of love. So make your hearts restless to taste this wine of love. During spare time create love by remembering me. Ask yourself: "Oh, when will the Master put me in the line? When will I see and be united with God? What lies there on the path?" 857–63

Entering the threshold of the 1st subtle spiritual plane produces 3 definite experiences: 1) A faintly audible but unimaginably rich musical sound is heard. 2) A suppressed, indescribably sweet scent is smelt. 3) Unsteady but clear flashes of very dazzling light are seen.

Experiences of hearing, smelling and seeing have nothing to do with gross body organs. One may have no physical sense of smell and be totally deaf, dumb and blind, yet when about to start on the inner life, one is bound to hear, smell and see. It is simply the path's beginning. Aw V.2, no.2, p.26

The ideal period of life to take an interest in spirituality is childhood. Impressions received at a young age are deeply ingrained. Divine beauty, grandeur and bliss are deeply impressed upon children. This highly fires their imaginations about God and His greatness. The Prem Ashram is more to create divine mad ones rather than academic degrees, and I much prefer the former to the latter. 860

CHRIST COME AGAIN

Then a simple prayer – the 7 names of God – Hari, Paramatma, Allah, Ahuramazd, God, Yezdan, Hu – was composed by Baba for the boys to recite each day. In the morning, one recited the 7 names alone, and then all the boys joined together, chanting the prayer for 15-30 minutes. The prayer was also recited 5 minutes before and after classes, as the boys stood with folded hands facing the sun. Baba told his women years later:

> "Saying the 7 Names of God from the heart, you must feel you're taking the true names of God. Then you must have the fixed idea all these names are One. I've selected and arranged them so they vibrate and help if done with true feeling." 2140

At first, the chosen boys were kept down below Meherabad Hill with the regular boys who were more inclined to studies than meditation. But soon the Prem Ashram boys were moved up the Hill closer to Baba. He was absorbed every second in the affairs of these little ones. How could they suspect they were soon to touch the threshold of the Infinite? 871

While praying the 7 Names of God, some began feeling love-stricken while Baba gave them extra attention. And so began the Prem Ashram – The Abode of Divine Love – boys awakened to the Master's Infinite love beyond lust, with hearts now on the verge of dancing permanently to the divine . . . .

Chapter Fourteen

The Prem Love Ashram Blooms

.. will continue in the next book, Christ Come Again, Volume Two.

End Notes

[1] ♣.Page references as noted in the above line by page number in bold at the end of a paragraph are from the 2014 revised online edition of Lord Meher which can be found and checked with that page number typed into the search box on the left of the homepage at: www.lordmeher.org This English version of Bhau Kalchuri's Hindi biography, Meher Prabhu [Lord Meher], which Bhau translated into English with Feram Workingboxwala and David Fenster, was edited by Lawrence Reiter who published 20 hardbound English volumes from 1979-2000.

Other page numbers not in bold and preceded by letter code abbreviations refer to books and source materials other than Lord Meher. These letter codes are alphabetically listed in the Appendix and Reference Key final 2 pages at the very end of this book. The 3rd paragraph of that Reference Key shows how to freely find many books online. References noted by a page number not in bold and followed by "Printed Lord Meher" Are from the original 1st American hardbound 20 volumes still found online at: www.lordmeher.org/v1/index.jsp

Meher Baba's words after July 10th 1925 were not verbally "uttered," as from that day on he remained silent. They were taken down by disciples, translated into English and later edited for publication. Baba's words after this date are without the exactness of a recording, however they are very close. We recall Baba advising:

"My explanations may be recomposed in forceful and stylish language, but the spirit and meaning must remain unchanged" [www.lordmeher.org p.834]. Author Ed Flanagan's comments and interpolations are [in brackets]. Though Meher Baba's "words" are intact, I have simplified and clarified some awkward sentence structures from parts of Lord Meher. My initials "elf" denote my own couplets, verses and original haiku poems.

As Meher Baba kept silence from 1925 till his passing in 1969, he used shortcuts when "speaking or texting" with the alphabet board and in using numbers.

[2] Noah, named Ziusudra in 6,000 years old ancient Sumerian tablets, was a Perfect Master in an earlier 5,000 year cycle 11–13,000 years ago at the last mini-pralaya [collapse], known as "the great flood." Buddha named 6 ancient Avatars in the Pali language – Kashyapa, Krakuchanda, Matuposaka, Subedha, Vipashyin and Vishvaban, and 2 future Avatars, Dipamkara and Maitreya – the All-Compassionate One, Meher Baba.   LBE 3

Meanwhile, with confusion about the advents of Zoroaster and Abraham, Meher Baba's chief disciple, Eruch Jessawala, states: "Baba told us, 'I came to arouse and awaken humanity as Abraham, Zoroaster, Rama, Krishna, Buddha, Jesus, and Mohammed and now I have come as Meher Baba.'" AO 212

[3] See: www.huffingtonpost.com/brent-landau/on-revelation-of-the-magi_b_788238.html4

[4] For a full exposition of this point see: Real Birth and Real Death www.lordmeher.org pp.4388–89

See also: www.reincarnation.ws/ and Kevin Williams www.near-death.com/religion/christianity.html This is an excellent treatise on Reincarnation and the Early Christians

[5] In the Hadith, Muhammad states, "Man ra'ani faqad ra'al-Haqa." "Seeing Me you have seen God" [al Haq = Truth = God]. This Hadith saying is in the canons of al-Bukhari vol. 4 p. 135, Muslim vol. 7, p. 54, etc., and is equal to Jesus' words, "Anyone who sees me has seen the Father" (John 14:9). Likewise the Parsis falsely believed Ahuramazda was greater than Zarathustra, just as

Mohammed's followers got the wrong impression that Allah was greater than the Prophet, who Himself was very God incarnate.

[6] www.rots.com/video/7448/fifth-graders-from-1995-perfectly-predicted-what-the-internet-would-be-like

[7] https://groups.google.com/d/topic/atheism-vs-christianity/3voiR1YdZCI

[8] This wonderful story is given in full in The Nothing and the Everything by Bhau Kalchuri:
www.ambppct.org/Book_Files/NandE.pdf   pp. 9-25

[9] Hafiz [1325-1389] was a God-Realized Perfect Master and the world's most beloved Persian/Muslim Sufi poet.

[10] See pp. 84-104 at: www.lordmeher.org detailing the extraordinary adventures of Sheriar's early life.

[11] A "wali" (waliullah, 'friend of God') – a 5th mental plane saint can read, control and direct anyone's thoughts, while a mast is usually stuck in bliss.

[12] I visited this school in 1982 to observe the students and share with them facts of their illustrious earlier schoolmate. I also reviewed Merwan's impressive studies and sports records. But both grammar and high school records are off a year on his birth date, listed as 1895 instead of 1894.

[13] Parvardigar – "to continually and repeatedly sustain." In the opening line of Meher Baba's The Master's Prayer, the 1st as-

pect of God is invoked as "O Parvardigar, preserver and protector of all.

[14] Upas" = "fast;" "Maharaj" = "a great king" who fasted before being God-Realized by Sai Baba. M 43

[15] Taken from Bill Wilson's obituary notice: www.morerevealed.com/library/coc/chapter3.htm

CHRIST COME AGAIN

Multivolume Table of Contents

Avatar: The Life and Teachings of Meher Baba 1894 – 1969
and the Avatar's revelations on his hidden life as Jesus

VOLUME ONE

Preface, Synopsis–Overview: i – viii….
Chapter Contents
Introduction
1 The Avatar's Last 7 Major Advents
2 Christ's Return to Earth in the 20th century
3 Beyond Religion
4 The Birth of Merwan – All Merciful Light
5 Merwan's Friends and Early Life
6 The Kiss of Infinite Radiant Light
7 A Mother's Agony
8 First Disciples – First Ashram
9 Meherabad and Persia
10 The Avatar's Circle
11 Meherabad Flourishing.
12 In the Kingdom of Silence
13 The 2nd Long Stay at Meherabad.

VOLUME TWO and onward

14 The Prem Love Ashram Blooms
15 Lust and Love
16 Secret Visits – Persia and the West.
17 The Avatar Reaches America's Shores
18 Gandhi's Final Destiny.
19 Publicity in America
20 Baba in Italy – Lighting the Fuse for Rome's Demise

21 Christ in Hollywood
22 Greta Garbo – More Missed Connections
23 Hollywood – Take 2
24 The Ten Commandments
25 The Intrepid Mother Shireen – Doing It Her Way
26 War Clouds – Spiritual Agents and the God-Mad
27 The Wayfarers
28 A Remote-Controlled War
29 From the Holocaust to D-Day
30 The Universe as the Mind's Dream – The Secret of Sleep
31 Angels and Life on Other Planets.
32 Meher Baba's Final Declaration on Global Devastation
33 The New Heaven on Earth
34 The 3 Sanskaric Veils Obstructing Divine Consciousness
35 Natural and Un-Natural Impression
36 Non-Natural Impression
37 The Afterlife.
38 Miracles Attributed to Meher Baba
39 The Avatar's Spiritual Consort
40 Jesus' 50 year Exile in India after His Crucifixion
41 Meher Baba's Seclusion at Jesus' Tomb in Kashmir.
42 The Curtain Rises on The New Life
43 Gypsy Beggars
44 A Terrorist's Mistake
45 Manonash – Annihilating False Mind
46 Manonash Seclusion Postscript – The *Hijras*
47 The Trail of Tears
48 Oklahoma – "Oh, What a Beautiful Morning
49 The Fiery Free Life
50 Grinding Down His Disciples' Minds
51 Revisiting Hamirpur and Andhra
52 The Avatar's First TV Appearance .
53 Another Tragedy for the Sake of the World

CHRIST COME AGAIN

54 Real Life – Real Obedience
55 A Last Visit to the West..
56 Investing in Loss and Dealing with Ghosts
57 The East-West Gathering .
58 More of Baba's Favorite Things
59 The Beginning of the End
60 Selfish and Selfless Service
61 The Final Decade – Fighting a *Drug-net* of Illusion
62 Lost in Rajasthan
63 The Last Deep Seclusion
64 Baba is Filmed for a Documentary
65 My Time Has Come
66 "Remember This"
67 The Eternal Moment
68 Inconsolable Grief
69 Mehera's Visions and Dialogues with Baba

CODA
St. Peter's Gate: Rome –
The 3rd Fatima Secret and 2 Suspicious Papal Deaths

Supplement

April 24, 1932 N.Y. Times article by James Forman
On Fate and Destiny
For the Sake of Love
Food for the Lion of Love
A Letter to Children.
How to Love God
The Universe – An Illusory Holograph
The Dream of Creation
Existence is Substance and Life is Shadow
12 Ways of Realizing Me

CHRIST COME AGAIN

Creation of the Universe and Consciousness
Be Like a Stone
Life Eternal
The Soul's Amazing A–Z Journey.
Manonash Discourse.
The Travail of the New World Order
On Love Divine and Profane
Dream State and Divine Knowledge – *Swayambhu*
Meher Baba's Manifestation
The Aura and Halo
Demystifying Death and the Afterlife
Evolution and Human Consciousness.
A Love Poem by Meher Baba
Baba's Favorite Things and Pets
Poem to the Blue Bus
Praising His Disciples
Real Light/False Darkness
Repeating God's Name
Mohammed and Meher Baba's Lineage
GOD SPEAKS Amazon's favorite Book
You Alone Exist
101 Names of God

Reference Codes and Copyrights.

See note below for * symbols

Permission for the use of the quoted material in this work has been obtained both orally and in writing, except where unnecessary due to the brevity of quoted passages. Words of Meher Baba reprinted by permission, © 1956, 1967 and all subsequent years, by the Avatar Meher Baba Perpetual Public Charitable Trust, India, cited as AMBPPCT, including source material from Lord Meher, by Bhau Kalchuri and ABBPCCT. This includes photographs with additional permission given by Lawrence Reiter and photos from the MSI [Mani S. Irani] collection, Meherabad, India. Permission has also been given by the following copyright holders as well as permissions quoted at the start of this work.

Please note: Free online works cited in this book, Christ Come Again, are on this site: http://ambppct.org/library.php This site First lists alphabetically all books written "by" Meher Baba, noted in the Appendix below by a single *asterisk. Double ** denotes online books written "about" Meher Baba and are found at the same site from which you can select the book and then click on "Read Me." Lord Meher and The Awakener Magazine have their own online address given below under their reference. Also see these websites:

    https://sites.google.com/site/babawebsites/

A - Answer / Conversations with Meher Baba, edited by Naosherwan Anzar from The Silent Teachings of Meher Baba 2001 © Beloved Archives.
**AA - Avatar of the Age Meher Baba Manifesting, by Bhau Kalchuri © Lawrence Reiter 1985

AO - The Ancient One, by Eruch Jessawala, ed. Naosherwan Anzar 1985 © AMBPPCT
ASL - The Advancing Stream of Life, by Meher Baba ed. Adi Irani © 1969 AMBPPCT
**Av - Avatar, © 1947 by author Jean Adriel
AW- -Awakenings, © 2011 by Bhau Kalchuri
Aw - The Awakener Magazine www.theawakenermagazine.org ©Universal Spiritual League In America, Inc. All quotes used by permission of AMBPPCT
*Be - Beams from Meher Baba on the Spiritual Panorama, ed. by Ivy Duce 1958 © Sufism Reoriented, Walnut Creek, CA
BG - Best of the Glow, 1984 edited and © by Naosherwan Anzar, Beloved Archives
CD - The Combined Diary {of 5 early Baba disciples] © AMBPPCT
Dar - Darshan Hours, ed. Eruch Jessawala and Rick Chapman © 1971 Meher Baba Information
DC - The Die is Cast, compiled by a disciple © 1955 The Meher Center, Myrtle Beach, SC
DD - Donkin's Diary © 2011 AMBPPCT
DH - The Divine Humanity of Meher Baba, Edited by Bill LePage © 1999 AMBPPCT
*Di - Discourses, by Meher Baba 7th Edition 1987 © AMBPPCT
DL - Dance of Love, by Margaret Craske © 1980 Sheriar Press, Inc
elf - The author's initials, Edward Louis Flanagan for couplets, poems and haiku in the text
*EN - The Everything and the Nothing, by Meher Baba 1989 © AMBPPCT
FL - 82 Family Letters, written by Mani Irani 1956-69 © AMBPPCT
GB - God-Brother, by Mani Irani © 1993 AMBPPCT

*GD - Gems from the Discourses of Meher Baba © 1945 Circle Productions, Inc
**GG - Glimpses of the Godman, by Bal Natu, 6 volumes (Vols. 2, 5 and 6 cited) 1979 © AMBPPCT
Gi - Gift of God, by Arnavaz Dadachanji © 1996 AMBPPCT
Gl/Gl - The Glow and The Glow International, edited and © by Naosherwan Anzar, Beloved Archives; Meher Baba quotes © AMBPPCT
**GM - The God Man, by Charles Purdom 1971 © AMBPPCT
*GMMG - God to Man and Man to God, ed. Charles Purdom © 1975 AMBPPCT
*GS - God Speaks by Meher Baba 1955, 1973 (2NDEdition) © Sufism Reoriented, Walnut Creek, CA
    online at: www.ambppct.org/Book_Files/godspeaks_r.pdf
GuG - Growing Up with God, by Sheela Fenster © 2009 David and Sheela Fenster
HGO - He Gives the Ocean, by Meherwan Kotwal, © 2006 ©AMBPPCT
HM - How a Master Works, by Ivy Duce 1975 © Sufism Reoriented, Walnut Creek, CA
HT - Heart Talks ©AMBPPCT
*INF - Infinite Intelligence, by Meher Baba © 2005 AMBPPCT – listed as Intelligence Notebooks
IS - It So Happened, ed. Bill LePage 1998 © AMBPPCT
ITC - In the Company of Avatar Meher Baba, by M.R. Dhakephalkar © 1992
ITS - Is That So, ed. Bill LePage 1985 ©
JLH - Just To Love Him by Adi K. Irani ©1985 AMBPPCT
JOG - Jesus among Other Gods, by Ravi Zacharias, Nashville: Word, ©2000
LA - Love Alone Prevails, by Kitty Davy, 1981 © Meher Spiritual Center, Myrtle Beach, SC

*LB - Life at Its Best, by Meher Baba, © 1957 Sufism Reoriented, Walnut Creek, CA

LBE - Lord Buddha's Explanation of the Universe, English transl/edited Lawrence Reiter ©2004

LFM - Letters from the Mandali, Edited by Jim Mistry © 1983 AMBPPCT

LGM - Let's Go to Meherabad! © 1985 AMBPPCT

*LH - Listen Humanity, by Meher Baba, ed. Don Stevens 1982 © AMBPPCT

LJ - Life is a Jest, Published by R. P. Pankhraj © AMBPPCT

LL - Lives of Love, by Judith Garbett, © 1998 AMBPPCT

LM - Lord Meher, by Bhau Kalchuri, © 1979 L. Reiter and AMBPPCT online www.lordmeher.org

LOL - Letters of Love, by Jane Barry Haynes ©1997 EliNor Publications

M - Mehera, compiled from tape recordings; Published by Naosherwan Anzar ©1989 AMBPPCT

MC - The Mystic Christ, by Ethan Walker, 2003 © by author

MBC. - Meher Baba Calling © 1964 AMBPPCT

MeM - Meher Message Magazine 1929 © AMBPPCT

MM - Mehera-Meher, by David Fenster, First English printed edition © 2003 by author

MS - Much Silence, by Tom and Dorothy Hopkins, 1974 © Meher Baba Association, London

MW - Meher Baba on War, ed. K.K. Ramakrishnan 1972 © AMBPPCT

MZ - Memoirs of a Zetetic by Amira Kuman Hazra 1987 © by author

**NE - The Nothing and The Everything, by Bhau Kalchuri © Lawrence Reiter 1981 and AMBPPCT

NL - Meher Baba's New Life, by Bhau Kalchuri 2008, co-publisher Ed Flanagan © AMBPCCT

NW - Nowhere To Now Here, by Michael Da Costa, © 1999 by author
OL - Ocean of Love, © 1991 Meher Baba Association
OY - Over the Years with Meher Baba, by Bill Le Page 1999 © AMBPPCT
PA - Poems to Avatar Meher Baba, ed. Ben Leet and Steve Klein © 1985 Manifestation, Inc.
*PL - The Path of Love, ed. Filis Frederick, 1986 © AMBPPCT
PM - The Perfect Master, by Charles Purdom 1971 © Meher Spiritual Center Inc.
PS - Practical Spirituality, by John Grant © 1985 AMBPPCT
QA - Shri Meher Baba, The Perfect Master, Questions and Answers ©AMBPPCT
RD - Ramjoo's Diaries, by Ramjoo Abdulla, © 1979 AMBPCCT
RT - The Real Treasure, Volumes I-IV, by Rustom Falahati, © 2008 by author
S - The Samadhi, by Bal Natu © 1997 Sheriar Foundation
Sa - The Sayings of Shri Meher Baba, 1933 ©AMBPPCT
**SG - Stay With God, by Francis Brabazon, 1977 © by author, held by Bill LePage, Australia
SH - Surrendering to Him, by Rhoda Adi Dubash © 2002 AMBPPCT
SL - Seekers of Love, by Amiya Hazra and Keith Gunn, © 2008 Meher Mownawani Publications
SOF - Souls on Fire, by William M. Stephens © 1998 Oceanic Press
SS - The Secret of Sleep, by Meher Baba © 1983 AMBPPCT
*ST - Sparks of the Truth, ed. C.D. Deshmukh 1967 ©AMBPPCT
STP - The Spiritual Training Program, by Bhau Kalchuri © 2005 AMBPPCT
TNL - Tales from the New Life with Meher Baba, ed. Don E. Stevens © 1973 AMBPPCT

T - Treasures from the Meher Baba Journals, compiled and edited by Elizabeth Patterson and Jayne Barry Haynes, © 1980 Meher Spiritual Center and AMBPPCT.
TGS - The God-Seeker, The Diaries of Minoo Kharas © 2013 Beloved Archives, Inc.
TH - That's How It Was, by Eruch Jessawala © 1995 AMBPPCT
TK - Turning the Key, by Bill Le Page 1999 © by author
TIW - Three Incredible Weeks, ed. Malcolm Schloss and Charles Purdom ©1979 AMBPPCT
TY - Twenty Years with Meher Baba, © 1975 Avatar Meher Baba Poona Centre
**W - The Wayfarers, by William Donkin, 1948 ©AMBPPCT
WK - Words of Kabir and Other Stories, by Sam Kerawalla © 2006

CHRIST COME AGAIN

CHRIST COME AGAIN

www.ingramcontent.com/pod-product-compliance
Lightning Source LLC
Chambersburg PA
CBHW021350290426
44108CB00010B/179